THE OXFORD

General Editor: Fra

THOMAS HARDY was born in H
Dorchester, in 1840. He was trained as an architect, and
practised that profession for several years in his early manhood,
but even then he had begun to write—first poems, which were
not published until much later, and then novels. His first novel,
Desperate Remedies, appeared in 1871, and for the next twenty-
five years he wrote virtually nothing but fiction: fourteen novels
and four collections of tales in all.

Hardy's novel-writing came to an end with *Jude the Obscure* in
1896, and from that time until his death more than thirty years
later he wrote only verse and verse-drama: eight volumes of
poems, the vast epic-drama *The Dynasts* (1902–8), and *The
Famous Tragedy of the Queen of Cornwall* (1923). He died on 11
January 1928, in his eighty-eighth year.

SAMUEL HYNES is the editor of the five-volume Oxford
English Texts edition of *The Complete Poetical Works of Thomas
Hardy*, from which the texts of this selection have been taken.
His other works include *The Pattern of Hardy's Poetry*, *The
Edwardian Turn of Mind*, and *The Auden Generation*. He is
Woodrow Wilson Professor of Literature at Princeton Uni-
versity.

THE OXFORD AUTHORS

THOMAS HARDY

EDITED BY
SAMUEL HYNES

OXFORD UNIVERSITY PRESS
1984

Oxford University Press, Walton Street, Oxford OX2 6DP

London Glasgow New York Toronto
Delhi Bombay Calcutta Madras Karachi
Kuala Lumpur Singapore Hong Kong Tokyo
Nairobi Dar es Salaam Cape Town
Melbourne Auckland

and associated companies in
Beirut Berlin Ibadan Mexico City Nicosia

Oxford is a trade mark of Oxford University Press

British Library Cataloguing in Publication Data

Hardy, Thomas, 1840–1928
[Poems. Selections]. Thomas Hardy
I. Title   II. Thomas Hardy
III. Hynes, Samuel
821'.8   PR4742
ISBN 0–19–254177–3
ISBN 0–19–281338–2 Pbk

Library of Congress Cataloging in Publication Data

Hardy, Thomas, 1840–1928.
Thomas Hardy.
(The Oxford Authors)
Bibliography: p.
Includes index.
I. Hynes, Samuel Lynn.   II. Title.
PR4741.H9 1984   821'.8   83-13330
ISBN 0–19–254177–3
ISBN 0–19–281338–2 (pbk.)

Set by Rowland Phototypesetting Ltd.
Printed in Great Britain by
Cox & Wyman Ltd.,
Reading, Berks.

CONTENTS

from MOMENTS OF VISION

from HUMAN SHOWS

UNCOLLECTED POEMS

PROSE

INTRODUCTION

ENGLISH writers who endeavour to appraise poets, and discriminate the sheep from the goats, are apt to consider that all true poets must be of one pattern in their lives and developments . . . They must all be impractical in the conduct of their affairs; nay, they must almost, like Shelley or Marlowe, be drowned or done to death, or like Keats, die of consumption. They forget that in the ancient world no such necessity was recognized; that Homer sang as a blind old man, that Aeschylus wrote his best up to his death at nearly seventy, that the best of Sophocles appeared between his fifty-fifth and ninetieth years, that Euripides wrote up to seventy.

Among those who accomplished late, the poetic spark must always have been latent; but its outspringing may have been frozen and delayed for half a lifetime.[1]

This is Hardy, writing in his journal in his seventy-eighth year, and placing himself as a poet, not among the Romantic young, but with the ancients, the old poets of the old, tragic world. And rightly so; for Hardy's life as a poet did not really begin until he was well past fifty. *Wessex Poems*, his first book of verse, appeared in 1898, when he was fifty-eight, and his last book, *Winter Words*, was published after his death in his eighty-eighth year. No other English poet wrote his major poems so late in his life.

It is true that Hardy began to write verse when he was young: his earliest known poem, 'Domicilium', was begun when he was seventeen, and nearly forty dated poems survive from the decade of his twenties (the years between 1860 and 1870) when he was working as an architect in London. But once he began his career as a novelist the flow of poems virtually stopped, to begin again only when his novel-writing years were coming to an end.

If one reads through all the poems that Hardy dated before 1895 (the year of *Jude the Obscure*, his last novel), it becomes clear not only that there are not many of them, as compared to the 900-odd that he was still to write, but that they are not very good poems, and that they are not, on the whole, characteristically Hardyesque, either in style or in subject. An honest critic would have to admit that if the whole lot were lost he would regret at most two or three—'Neutral Tones', 'Hap', the comic 'Ruined

---

[1] *Later Years*, p. 184 (*Life*, p. 384). Full references to abbreviated items will be found in 'Further Reading', pp. 521–2 below. References to Florence Hardy's biography of her husband include both the first edition (*Later Years*) and the later one-volume edition (*Life*).

Maid', but surely no others. The rest do not speak with Hardy's unique poetic voice: they are merely the conventional verses of a young man who would in time become the poet Hardy.

And then, in the 1890s, the novel-writing ended, and the great flood of poems began, and continued for more than thirty years. What had happened, to cause such a fundamental change? Hardy's own explanation is set down in the biography written by his second wife (but largely dictated by Hardy); it says, in effect, that Hardy was reacting to hostile reviews of *Jude* and *The Well-Beloved* (a novel written earlier, but first published in book form in 1897):

The misrepresentations of the last two or three years affected but little, if at all, the informed appreciation of Hardy's writings, being heeded almost entirely by those who had not read him; and turned out ultimately to be the best thing that could have happened; for they well-nigh compelled him, in his own judgement at any rate, if he wished to retain any shadow of self-respect, to abandon at once a form of literary art he had long intended to abandon at some indefinite time, and resume openly that form of it which had always been more instinctive with him, and which he had just been able to keep alive from his early years, half in secrecy, under the pressure of magazine writing.[2]

This is a tidy explanation, but not a convincing one; for the change that occurred in Hardy's career in the mid nineties was far more than simply a change of literary form: it was a radical change in his entire way of life.

Consider Hardy as he appeared to the world at the beginning and at the end of the nineties. In 1890 he was a successful, famous, admired English man-of-letters, wealthy enough to have built a country house, to take a flat in London for the season, to travel in Europe, and to move among fashionable and titled London society; a man who had dined with Matthew Arnold and with Browning, and who was regarded by critics as a novelist in the class of George Eliot and Meredith. Yet by the end of the decade he had withdrawn from that life, to lead a reclusive existence on the outskirts of a country town, and to write only verse for the rest of his life.

The change is evident not only in the shift from prose to verse, but in the tone of the poems that he began to write. No one would ever have called Hardy a cheerful poet, but the poems of the nineties are noticeably darker than those of his early years. 'In Tenebris', for example, which is dated 1895–6, expresses a personal pain and a sense of alienation from human society so intense that the speaker sees death as a welcome

---

[2] *Later Years*, p. 65 (*Life*, p. 291).

release; and there are others similar in tone—'The Division', 'The Dead Man Walking', 'Wessex Heights'. Can one possibly read such despairing poems as Hardy's reaction to unfavourable reviews? Obviously not. Nor can one argue, I think, that such poems are simply the latest term in an increasingly pessimistic view of the universe that Hardy had previously recorded in his novels: the sense of bereavement and lost hope is too personal in the poems for that.

Recent biographies, less reticent than Mrs Hardy's account, suggest some of the sources of Hardy's personal crisis during those years when he became himself as a poet. Certainly his feelings about the reception of his later fiction were a part of it: not simply that reviewers had stupidly abused him (a few had, but only a few), but that he had been more widely condemned by his society for expressing the thoughts that many of his contemporaries shared, but would not utter. And there had been other, more intimate failures: the failure of his marriage, after more than twenty years; and a sudden, deep love for another woman, which had come to nothing. The details of the failed marriage and of the unrequited love are lost in Hardy's reticence, and in the bonfires in which he destroyed personal papers before his death. And perhaps that is just as well; the details are not our business.

It is important, though, to recognize that at the time Hardy turned from prose to poetry he was silently suffering deep feelings of personal loss, alienation, loneliness, and emotional and intellectual failure. For Hardy was essentially a lyric poet, and the sources of lyric poetry are personal. I would argue that the sources of Hardy's philosophy were personal too, and that the poems in which he argues with God and Nature rise from the same deeply personal sources. I do not mean to suggest that a single unhappiness, or even a particular period of suffering, made Hardy a poet. The process of preparation was no doubt a gradual one, the imagination filling slowly with the losses and regrets and memories that are the accumulations of time, and that form the substance of Hardy's poetry. But by the mid nineties he had lived long enough, and had failed and suffered enough: his imagination was full. In a letter of 1895 concerning *Jude*, Hardy wrote: 'As for the story itself, it is really sent out to those into whose souls the iron has entered, and has entered deeply, at some time of their lives.'[3] The iron had entered Hardy's soul; and he turned his thoughts inward, to brood over feelings too urgent to ignore, and too personal for prose.

It may well be that Hardy could not have moved successfully into verse

[3] Letter to Edmund Gosse, 10 November 1895 (*Letters*, ii. 93).

if the novels had not existed. Ezra Pound thought so: he described the *Collected Poems* as 'the harvest of having written 20 novels first', taking Hardy's twenty-five years of novel-writing as merely a long apprentice-ship in the use of language.[4] And I think it is true that the mature poetic voice does come out of the later novels. One might also argue that the novels had to precede the poems because it is in the novels that Hardy's world of Wessex is created, and that until Wessex was fully and completely imagined Hardy could not write the poems, which are local events in that imagined world.

But neither the apprenticeship theory, nor any theory of the necessity of Wessex, will explain why, when Hardy turned to poetry, he had to turn away from prose. One must conclude that he saw the change as a radical disjunction in his imaginative life. In this he was different from other poet-novelists like Meredith, Kipling, and Lawrence: they could write prose and poetry alternately, but for Hardy the two forms seemed to express fundamentally different relationships between mind and reality, which could not be simultaneously sustained. It seems that he could only become a great poet by ceasing to be a great novelist.

It also seems clear that to be a great poet he had to be an *old* poet. He needed time, for time would be his central subject; and he needed the retrospective vision of age. By 1900, when he was sixty, he was thinking of himself as an old man: 'We go about very little now,' he explains, declining an invitation; and the phrase 'as I grow older' creeps more and more into his letters. It is this state of mind—the poet in his age—that the poems embody.

This is not to say that the poems are primarily *about* old age, or that they are addressed primarily to old readers. They are about the whole flow of human time, in its most common and fundamental terms: birth, childhood, love, marriage, age, and death are all here; life begins and life ends, sometimes in a single poem (as in 'Life and Death at Sunrise'); generation succeeds generation (as in 'Night in the Old Home' and 'Heredity'). To read such poems one need only be old enough to be aware of time, change, and common human feelings: they are surely 'universal', if any poems are. But to write them, Hardy apparently had to live sixty years first, in order that he could look back on his themes, as though down a long corridor of time.

Being in his old age, Hardy was also, in another sense, *out* of his age: he was an essentially nineteenth-century poet who had waited so long to find his voice that he found himself adrift in the next century. He had

---

[4] D. D. Paige (ed.), *Letters of Ezra Pound* (New York, 1950), p. 294. The letter is dated April 1937.

been born only three years after Queen Victoria ascended the throne, and had lived more than sixty years under her reign, and his mind had been shaped by the intellectual and spiritual crises of the Victorian period. More than any other writer of his generation, Hardy grasped what the ideas of the great Victorian scientists implied for the human imagination: that Lyell, Darwin, and Huxley had stretched Time and Space, and by so doing had diminished Man, and made God an unnecessary hypothesis. Like many other Victorians, he accepted the new thought; but he felt it as a heavy human loss, for his sensibility remained essentially a religious one. He had been raised in the English church, and he remained, as he said, 'churchy; not in an intellectual sense, but in so far as instincts and emotions ruled',[5] and though he had lost his faith he went on haunting churches and churchyards, and smuggling hymn metres and Biblical quotations into his poems. And more than that, he filled his poems with metaphysical presences, sometimes in the forms of ghosts and phantoms, sometimes as abstract figures with names like The Immanent Will, King Doom, The Sleep-Worker, and even God. To the mind of science (and Hardy conceded that science embodied rational truth) such figures are mere fictions; but to the imagination they may have a felt reality. Hardy's mind contained *both* realities, and his 'philosophical' poems enact the struggle in his mind between the two.

It is in philosophical poems like 'The Mother Mourns' and 'God-Forgotten' that Hardy speaks in his most Victorian voice—the voice of a troubled Victorian myth-maker trying to mythologize the Post-Darwinian world. Such myth-making was an important part of the role that Hardy saw himself playing in poetry, as he turned away from fiction. The following notebook entry, dated 17 October 1896, makes this point very clearly:

Poetry. Perhaps I can express more fully in verse ideas and emotions which run counter to the inert crystallized opinion—hard as a rock—which the vast body of men have vested interests in supporting. To cry out in a passionate poem that (for instance) the Supreme Mover or Movers, the Prime Force or Forces, must be either limited in power, unknowing, or cruel—which is obvious enough, and has been for centuries—will cause them merely a shake of the head; but to put it in argumentative prose will make them sneer, or foam, and set all the literary contortionists jumping upon me, a harmless agnostic, as if I were a clamorous atheist, which in their crass illiteracy they seem to think is the same thing. . . . If Galileo had said in verse that the world moved, the Inquisition might have let him alone.[6]

[5] *Later Years*, p. 176 (*Life*, p. 376).   [6] *Later Years*, pp. 57–8 (*Life*, pp. 285–5).

These poems in which Hardy quarrels with a God who does not exist are important for a proper understanding of his mind and career: they connect him with a Victorian tradition of speculative poetry, and they also show that his alienation from his time had philosophical as well as personal bases.

The best of Hardy's poems, however, the ones that embody the essential qualities of his genius, are not the philosophical ones. Nor are they his occasional poems, nor (surprisingly, in view of his achievements as a novelist) his narratives. All of these are essentially public kinds, addressed to some definable audience; but Hardy's greatest gift was a private one. It is expressed most purely in his short lyrics—poems written, as it seems, for himself alone, to give a private order to his feelings, so that he might live with them. These are poems of an ordinary and everyday reality, small in scale and not usually very eventful: they record a local world in which time passes, the eye observes, and age remembers. You might call this poetic world of remembering and watching an old man's reality, but only if that phrase is understood to be a defining, and not a limiting term; for clearly Hardy's reality is a world that we all share.

Time passes in the poems. Time is the medium in which the present becomes the irrecoverable past, and in which observation becomes memory; in this poetic world of Hardy's, its passage is a primary subject, and even a philosophical principle. It is also, in a way, a *formal* principle; for the poems are often organized in ways that set the present against the past, and observation against memory in a two-term, ironic pattern that reveals how expectations are defeated, losses suffered, and hope and happiness destroyed, simply because time *does* pass.

A good example of this pattern is 'During Wind and Rain', in which, stanza by stanza, Hardy contrasts the remembered past with the observed present. In the past, as memory preserves it, human beings gather, act, and are happy; in the present, the only reality is in natural processes, which go on destructively and relentlessly (the poem occurs *during* wind and rain—the weather survives the poem, as the remembered human actors do not). The point of the refrain—'Ah, no; the years, the years'—is not, I take it, a denial of the reality of the past, but only of what is implied in the present-tense verbs that describe it—that the past survives into the present. And the agent of that denial is simply 'the years, the years'—time itself, passing.

Poems like 'During Wind and Rain' suggest that old age may be seen as a kind of habitual structure that the mind acquires in time, and through which it perceives reality—an observed present framing and confining the remembered past. Certain patterns of action in the poems support this structure—for example, the Return—in which a person (often the old Hardy) revisits a scene of his past, and finds there change and loss; and that other kind of Return, in which a figure from the past enters the present as a ghost or phantom (there are examples of both kinds in the 'Poems of 1912–13'). The point is essentially the same in either version: that memory validates the past—what happened *did* happen, and its reality survives in memory—but that the past remains irretrievably past.

In personal terms this sense of the pastness of the past finds its ultimate expression in the theme of Death. It is a subject to which Hardy returned again and again as he grieved for the loss of parents, friends, lovers, even family pets; and one isn't surprised that he did so, for death must become an ordinary, everyday presence for the old. There was one death, though, that was overwhelmingly, shatteringly important to him (though one would have to say that to the world it, too, was ordinary and everyday enough); in 1912 his first wife, Emma, died. Hardy responded to her death with a series of elegies that are his finest poems. All of the central themes of his poetry are in them—the persistence of memory, the denying power of the present, the passage of time, the finality of loss. Other great elegies idealize the dead one, and the speaker's relation to that person, and commonly end on a consoling note—that the dead one is still alive, that death can be transcended. But Hardy's elegies are not like that. They deal honestly with his complex feelings: his guilt for his unkindnesses, his regret that his marriage had failed, his need to believe that his wife somehow still lived, and his bleak knowledge that she did not. These elegies are an extraordinary achievement. They are an old man's love poems to a dead woman—the love poems that he could not write while she lived—full of love and desire, but honest, and therefore also full of loss. In them, one hears the essential voice of Hardy:

> Well, well! All's past amend,
> Unchangeable. It must go.
> I seem but a dead man held on end
> To sink down soon. . . . O you could not know
> That such swift fleeing
> No soul foreseeing—
> Not even I—would undo me so![7]

In this world of loss and death, loneliness is an inevitable condition. This is no doubt partly a fact of Hardy's age; but it is also the condition of

[7] 'The Going'.

man in Hardy's universe. One notices, in reading the poems, how uninhabited they are, how often they reveal a solitary figure, alone in reality (see for example 'The Darkling Thrush', one of Hardy's best-known poems). In such poems a self observes the world, but is not quite a part of it; and that is perhaps another condition of age—the sense of separation from the business of life, the existence of the self as a *watcher* of the living. The figure in the poems is rarely engaged in an action, or involved with other persons; sometimes he is even rendered as already removed from the world—as a ghost (in 'I Travel as a Phantom Now'), or as a dead man (in 'The Dead Man Walking')—or he moves forward in time to imagine a time when he *will* be dead (as in the fine 'Afterwards'). Every one of Hardy's eight volumes of verse has some kind of farewell, or acknowledgement of separating age, at the end—as though Hardy expected each book to be posthumous. But this sense of retrospection, of a voice speaking from the far side of life, is not confined to such formal farewells; it is a part of the dominant tone of the poetry.

Hardy's lyrics render an ordinary world—a present such as any old man might observe, and a past such as any old man might remember. Often they seem to be written almost from habit, or from some private need to record reality, but as if not intended for publication, and with no thought of an audience. Some resist interpretation simply because they do not provide the information that would explain them. This is not a matter of allusiveness, or of Modernist obscurity; it seems, rather, that Hardy understood the circumstances that had prompted the poems and that, since he was his own audience, this was enough. Consider, for example, the little poem entitled 'That Moment':

> The tragedy of that moment
>   Was deeper than the sea,
> When I came in that moment
>   And heard you speak to me!
>
> What I could not help seeing
>   Covered life as a blot;
> Yes, that which I was seeing,
>   And knew that you were not.

I can see no way in which a reader can penetrate this inscrutable utterance. Yet for Hardy it was clearly a complete piece of his reality, and adequate to his poetic needs.

This sense of the poem as a habitual, private act of ordering may explain the presence among Hardy's poems of a great many that record what must seem to the reader quite trivial incidents. In 'Autumn in King's Hintock Park', for example, an old woman sweeps up leaves in the grounds of a grand country house, and thinks about nature and the passage of time—that's all. Yet to Hardy 'the scene as I witnessed it was a poem'.[8] The fact that he had *witnessed* it was clearly significant: that which really happened—observed reality itself—was for him a primary source of poetry, however uneventful it might seem to someone else.

I said at the beginning of this Introduction that Hardy had placed himself among the old poets of the old, tragic world. That placement was partly a matter of age; but it was more than that. The old poets and dramatists with whom he claimed alliance were *tragic* writers, and Hardy felt that he belonged to their world. This may seem paradoxical in a poet whom I have been describing as a recorder of the ordinary and everyday, but in fact it is not. For Hardy, tragedy was simply a true perception of reality; it was evident in all conditions of life, however humble, if one saw them truly.[9]

This tragic sense of life is most obviously evident in those ballad-like narratives of humble life that he labelled tragic: poems like 'A Tramp-woman's Tragedy' and 'A Sunday Morning Tragedy'. But it is also present in the lyrics, however ordinary their subjects may be: they express Hardy's sense of the tragic nature of *all* human existence: the failure of hopes, the inevitability of loss, the destructiveness of time, all those themes that are so central to his poetry and to his world.

This sense of everyday tragedy one finds in modest little poems like 'The Farm-Woman's Winter' and 'Bereft'; and even so brief and enigmatic a poem as 'That Moment' begins: 'The tragedy of that moment . . .' Hardy would not have said that *all* of his lyric poems were tragic; in fact he did a calculation on the proofs of *Human Shows*, and concluded that of the 152 poems in that volume, only about two-fifths were 'poems of tragedy, sorrow or grimness'.[10] But the point is that he saw tragedy as a constituent of ordinary existence, and not as a quality only of noble and dramatic lives.

Hardy's poems belong to an English tradition that goes back to Romantic poets like Wordsworth and John Clare, and beyond them to the anonymous beginnings of the English lyric in the Middle Ages. It is a poetry, essentially, of normative experience: plain, low-pitched, physical, and abiding. It says that life goes on, and that human beings think and feel in much the same way from one generation to another, and from one

---

[8] Letter to Gosse, 11 November 1906 (*Letters*, iii. 235).
[9] See Hardy's notebook entry for October 1888, p. 486 below.
[10] The proofs are in the Dorset County Museum.

century to another, and that because they think and feel, they are capable of tragedy, and of poetry. It is the principal tradition in English verse.

To the twentieth century, Hardy has been a principal example of the continuity and vitality of this tradition, and this, no doubt, is why he has been so important to poets who came after him. One can think at once of younger poets whose work resembles Hardy's in one way or another, and who have expressed their indebtedness to him: Edward Thomas, Robert Graves, Edmund Blunden, Philip Larkin. But other modern poets who seem radically unlike Hardy in their work have also praised him as a model. Who could be less like Hardy than Ezra Pound? Yet Pound wrote in 1934: 'Nobody has taught me anything about writing since Thomas Hardy died.' What Hardy taught Pound we may infer from another letter of the same year:

I do not believe there are more than two roads:

1. The old man's road (vide Tom. Hardy)—CONTENT, the INSIDES, the subject matter.
2. Music.[11]

Pound's antithetical roads seem clear enough: one may approach poetry via its subject-matter, or via its lyric forms, and Hardy's way was the former. The poetry in Hardy's poems, Pound seems to be saying, lies in what they are *about*—their *insides*. But Pound calls it 'the *old man's* road', as though Hardy had chosen it, and old age was part of its path.

W. H. Auden, another poet whose work seems remote from Hardy's sort, has also praised him as a master and model, but in terms quite opposite to Pound's. Auden's most important debt to Hardy, he wrote, was a debt of technical instruction:

In the first place Hardy's faults as a craftsman, his rhythmical clumsiness, his outlandish vocabulary were obvious even to a schoolboy, and the young can learn best from those of whom, because they can criticize them, they are not afraid. Shakespeare or Pope would have dazzled and therefore disheartened. And in the second place no English poet, not even Donne or Browning, employed so many and so complicated stanza forms. Anyone who imitates his style will learn at least one thing, how to make words fit into a complicated structure . . .[12]

What Auden sees as clumsiness and outlandishness, others will see as the elements of Hardy's unique voice, the qualities that made him poetically himself. But by seeming to be clumsy, he made poetry seem possible, just as, by constructing endless variations on traditional stanza-

---

[11] *Letters*, pp. 264 and 248–9; 30 Dec. and 30 Oct. 1934.
[12] 'A Literary Transference', *Southern Review*, vi (Summer 1940), 85.

patterns, he made it seem a craft that could be learned and practised.

Content and technique: there are, then, *two* old man's roads by which
younger poets have found their way through Hardy to their own poetry.
And even when Hardy was not in the end a visible model, he remained an
example, an old poet faithful to his world, and to his personal vision
of it.

Hardy's poems are a record of how an honest old man came to terms
with reality: with the actual, ordinary, rather humdrum dailiness of life;
with the inevitable losses that time brings, and the irrecoverable nature of
those losses; with the grief and regret that are the inevitable conse-
quences of living in time, with a memory; and with his own approach-
ing death. These poems are not, I think, written for us, or for any imagin-
able audience; we *overhear* Hardy when we read them. What we overhear
is the unmediated voice of an old man, communing with himself: more
than a kind of poetry, it is a way of enduring. That old man's road involves
both honesty and craft: reality seen as it is, without consolations; but
mastered, and made endurable, through a fine and private art.

CHRONOLOGY

1840	Hardy born 2 June, at Higher Bockhampton, near Dorchester.
1850–6	Attends school in Dorchester.
1856–61	Articled to John Hicks, Dorchester architect. Continues to study Greek and Latin, and begins to write poems ('Domicilium' is dated 'between 1857 and 1860'). Becomes friendly with Horace Moule, poet-critic and son of vicar of Fordington, Dorchester, who introduces him to current books and ideas.
1862–7	In London as assistant to Arthur Blomfield, architect. Goes to theatres and art galleries; continues to write poems.
1867	Returns to family home at Higher Bockhampton, where he lives until 1874, writing and taking occasional architectural work.
1868–9	Writes first novel, *The Poor Man and the Lady*; it is never published, and the manuscript is later destroyed.
1869–70	Encouraged by George Meredith to write a novel with a stronger plot, he writes *Desperate Remedies*.
1870	Travels to St Juliot, Cornwall, on an architectural commission; meets Emma Lavinia Gifford.
1871	*Desperate Remedies* published.
1872	*Under the Greenwood Tree* published.
1873	*A Pair of Blue Eyes* published. Moule commits suicide.
1874	Marries Emma Gifford, 17 September. *Far from the Madding Crowd* published.
1874–5	Living in London.
1875	The Hardys return to south-west England, living briefly in Bournemouth, Swanage, and Yeovil.
1876	*The Hand of Ethelberta* published. Hardys take holiday in northern Europe.
1876–8	Living in Sturminster Newton, Dorset: 'our happiest time', Hardy wrote.
1878	*The Return of the Native* published.
1878–81	In London. *The Trumpet-Major* published 1880. Hardy seriously ill 1880–1, but continues writing *A Laodicean* (published 1881). Marital troubles begin.
1881	Hardys return to Dorset, thereafter their home.
1882	*Two on a Tower* published.
1883	Construction of Max Gate, new house designed by Hardy, begins near Dorchester.
1885	Hardys move into Max Gate.

1886   *The Mayor of Casterbridge* published.

1887   *The Woodlanders* published. Hardys journey to Italy.

1888   *Wessex Tales* published.

1891   *Tess of the d'Urbervilles* and *A Group of Noble Dames* published.

1891–4   Marriage deteriorates.

1892   Death of Thomas Hardy Senior, 20 July.

1893   Hardy meets Florence Henniker (The Hon. Mrs Arthur Henniker); a deep but unrequited attachment follows.

1894   *Life's Little Ironies* (stories) published.

1895   *Jude the Obscure* published.

1897   *The Well-Beloved* published in book form (it had appeared as a serial in 1892). Hardys travel to Switzerland.

1898   *Wessex Poems* published.

1899–1902 Boer War. Hardy writes 'War Poems'.

1901   Death of Queen Victoria, 27 January. *Poems of the Past and the Present* published.

1902–8   Hardy at work on *The Dynasts*. Published: Part I, 1904; Part II, 1906; Part III, 1908.

1904   Hardy's mother, Jemima Hardy, dies 3 April.

1905   Hardy meets Florence Dugdale (later the second Mrs Hardy).

1909   Deaths of Swinburne (10 April) and Meredith (18 May). *Time's Laughingstocks* published.

1910   Death of Edward VII, 6 May. Hardy awarded Order of Merit.

1912   First volumes of Wessex Edition published. Emma Hardy dies, 27 November. Hardy begins elegiac 'Poems of 1912–13'.

1913   *A Changed Man and Other Tales* published.

1914   Hardy marries Florence Dugdale, 10 February. *Satires of Circumstance* published.

1914–18   First World War. Hardy writes 'Poems of War and Patriotism'.

1915   Hardy's favourite sister, Mary, dies, 24 November.

1916   *Selected Poems* published.

1917   *Moments of Vision* published.

1919   *Collected Poems* published.

1922   *Late Lyrics and Earlier* published.

1923   *The Famous Tragedy of the Queen of Cornwall* published.

1925   *Human Shows* published.

1928   Hardy dies at Max Gate, 11 January. His ashes are buried in Westminster Abbey, his heart in the churchyard at Stinsford, Dorset. *Winter Words* published posthumously.

NOTE ON THE TEXT

THE poetic texts in this volume are based on my edition of *The Complete Poetical Works of Thomas Hardy* (Oxford: 1982–). Sources of prose selections are given at the end of each extract.

The principal problem for the editor of Hardy's poems stems from the fact that Hardy was a life-long reviser of his work. He revised on the manuscripts that he prepared as printer's copy; he revised in proofs; and he sent lists of corrections to his publisher as soon as a volume was published. He made further substantial revisions at several subsequent stages: in 1910–12 for the Wessex Edition; in 1916 for *Selected Poems*; in 1919 for *Collected Poems*; and in 1927, in the last months of his long life (he was 87), in the printer's copy for *Chosen Poems*.

The changes that he made in his poems were rarely extensive, and they do not often change the sense of a poem. Hardy did not 'remake' himself, as Yeats did; rather, he seemed continually to strive, through small adjustments of language and cadence, to make his poems speak more exactly in his own voice.

These many small revisions were never brought together in one correct text during Hardy's lifetime; nor indeed did this happen for more than fifty years after his death. That is what the *Complete Poetical Works* is intended to accomplish, and the texts printed here reflect that same intention.

I have also drawn upon my edition for materials included in the Notes, though I have restricted my selection to such matter as seems necessary to a full understanding of the poems, and have omitted such supplementary data as textual variants and passages from Hardy's journals and letters.

The degree sign (°) indicates a note at the end of the book. More general notes and headnotes are not cued.

from WESSEX POEMS

PREFACE

OF the miscellaneous collection of verse that follows, only four pieces have been published, though many were written long ago, and others partly written. In some few cases the verses were turned into prose and printed as such in a novel, it not having been anticipated at that time that they might see the light in their original shape.

Here and there, when an ancient and legitimate word still current in the district, for which there was no close equivalent in received English, suggested itself, it has been made use of, on what seemed good grounds.

The pieces are in a large degree dramatic or personative in conception; and the dates attached to some of the poems do not apply to the rough sketches given in illustration,[1] which have been recently made, and, as may be surmised, are inserted for personal and local reasons rather than for their intrinsic qualities.

September 1898.

[1] The early editions were illustrated by the writer.

Hap

If but some vengeful god would call to me
From up the sky, and laugh: 'Thou suffering thing,
Know that thy sorrow is my ecstasy,
That thy love's loss is my hate's profiting!'

Then would I bear it, clench myself, and die,
Steeled by the sense of ire unmerited;
Half-eased in that a Powerfuller than I
Had willed and meted me the tears I shed.

But not so. How arrives it joy lies slain,
And why unblooms the best hope ever sown?

10

—Crass Casualty obstructs the sun and rain,
And dicing Time for gladness casts a moan. . . .
These purblind Doomsters had as readily strown
Blisses about my pilgrimage as pain.

1866.
16 Westbourne Park Villas.

Neutral Tones

We stood by a pond that winter day,
And the sun was white, as though chidden of God,
And a few leaves lay on the starving sod;
　　—They had fallen from an ash, and were gray.

Your eyes on me were as eyes that rove
Over tedious riddles of years ago;
And some words played between us to and fro
　　On which lost the more by our love.

The smile on your mouth was the deadest thing
Alive enough to have strength to die;　　　　　　　　10
And a grin of bitterness swept thereby
　　Like an ominous bird a-wing. . . .

Since then, keen lessons that love deceives,
And wrings with wrong, have shaped to me
Your face, and the God-curst sun, and a tree,
　　And a pond edged with grayish leaves.

1867.

Valenciennes

(1793)

By Corp'l Tullidge: in *The Trumpet-Major*

(Wessex Dialect)

IN MEMORY OF S. C. (PENSIONER). DIED 184–

We trenched, we trumpeted and drummed,
And from our mortars tons of iron hummed
   Ath'art the ditch, the month we bombed
     The Town o' Valencieën.

'Twas in the June o' Ninety-dree
(The Duke o' Yark our then Commander beën)
   The German Legion, Guards, and we
     Laid siege to Valencieën.

This was the first time in the war
That French and English spilled each other's gore;   10
   —Few dreamt how far would roll the roar
     Begun at Valencieën!

'Twas said that we'd no business there
A-topperèn the French for disagreën;
   However, that's not my affair—
     We were at Valencieën.

Such snocks and slats, since war began
Never knew raw recruit or veteràn:
   Stone-deaf therence went many a man
     Who served at Valencieën.   20

Into the streets, ath'art the sky,
A hundred thousand balls and bombs were fleën;
   And harmless townsfolk fell to die
     Each hour at Valencieën!

And, sweatèn wi' the bombardiers,
A shell was slent to shards anighst my ears:
   —'Twas nigh the end of hopes and fears
      For me at Valencieën!

They bore my wownded frame to camp,
And shut my gapèn skull, and washed en cleän,   30
   And jined en wi' a zilver clamp
      Thik night at Valencieën.

'We've fetched en back to quick from dead;
But never more on earth while rose is red
   Will drum rouse Corpel!' Doctor said
      O' me at Valencieën.

'Twer true. No voice o' friend or foe
Can reach me now, or any livèn beën;
   And little have I power to know
      Since then at Valencieën!   40

I never hear the zummer hums
O' bees; and don' know when the cuckoo comes;
   But night and day I hear the bombs
      We threw at Valencieën. . . .

As for the Duke o' Yark in war,
There may be volk whose judgment o' en is meän;
   But this I say—he was not far
      From great at Valencieën.

O' wild wet nights, when all seems sad,
My wownds come back, as though new wownds I'd had; 50
   But yet—at times I'm sort o' glad
      I fout at Valencieën.

Well: Heaven wi' its jasper halls
Is now the on'y Town I care to be in. . . .
   Good Lord, if Nick should bomb the walls
      As we did Valencieën!

                   1878–1897.

San Sebastian

(*August* 1813)

WITH THOUGHTS OF SERGEANT M—— (PENSIONER), WHO DIED 185–

'Why, Sergeant, stray on the Ivel Way,
As though at home there were spectres rife?
From first to last 'twas a proud career!
And your sunny years with a gracious wife
  Have brought you a daughter dear.

'I watched her to-day; a more comely maid,
As she danced in her muslin bowed with blue,
Round a Hintock maypole never gayed.'
—'Aye, aye; I watched her this day, too,
  As it happens,' the Sergeant said.   10

'My daughter is now', he again began,
'Of just such an age as one I knew
When we of the Line, the Forlorn-hope van,
On an August morning—a chosen few—
  Stormed San Sebastian.

'She's a score less three; so about was *she*—
The maiden I wronged in Peninsular days. . . .
You may prate of your prowess in lusty times,
But as years gnaw inward you blink your bays,
  And see too well your crimes!   20

'We'd stormed it at night, by the flapping light
Of burning towers, and the mortar's boom:
We'd topped the breach; but had failed to stay,
For our files were misled by the baffling gloom;
  And we said we'd storm by day.

'So, out of the trenches, with features set,
On that hot, still morning, in measured pace,
Our column climbed; climbed higher yet,
Past the fauss'bray, scarp, up the curtain-face,
  And along the parapet.   30

'From the battered hornwork the cannoneers
Hove crashing balls of iron fire;
On the shaking gap mount the volunteers
In files, and as they mount expire
          Amid curses, groans, and cheers.

'Five hours did we storm, five hours re-form,
As Death cooled those hot blood pricked on;
Till our cause was helped by a woe within:
They were blown from the summit we'd leapt upon,
          And madly we entered in.   40

'On end for plunder, 'mid rain and thunder
That burst with the lull of our cannonade,
We vamped the streets in the stifling air—
Our hunger unsoothed, our thirst unstayed—
          And ransacked the buildings there.

'From the shady vaults of their walls of white
We rolled rich puncheons of Spanish grape,
Till at length, with the fire of the wine alight,
I saw at a doorway a fair fresh shape—
          A woman, a sylph, or sprite.   50

'Afeard she fled, and with heated head
I pursued to the chamber she called her own;
—When might is right no qualms deter,
And having her helpless and alone
          I wreaked my will on her.

'She raised her beseeching eyes to me,
And I heard the words of prayer she sent
In her own soft language. . . . Fatefully
I copied those eyes for my punishment
          In begetting the girl you see!   60

'So, to-day I stand with a God-set brand
Like Cain's, when he wandered from kindred's ken. . . .
I served through the war that made Europe free;
I wived me in peace-year. But, hid from men,
          I bear that mark on me.

'Maybe we shape our offspring's guise
From fancy, or we know not what,
And that no deep impression dies,—
For the mother of my child is not
    The mother of her eyes.   70

'And I nightly stray on the Ivel Way
As though at home there were spectres rife;
I delight me not in my proud career;
And 'tis coals of fire that a gracious wife
    Should have brought me a daughter dear!'

The Stranger's Song

(As sung by MR CHARLES CHARRINGTON in the play of
The Three Wayfarers)

O my trade it is the rarest one,
    Simple shepherds all—
  My trade is a sight to see;
For my customers I tie, and take 'em up on high,
  And waft 'em to a far countree!

My tools are but common ones,
    Simple shepherds all—
  My tools are no sight to see:
A little hempen string, and a post whereon to swing,
  Are implements enough for me!   10

To-morrow is my working day,
    Simple shepherds all—
  To-morrow is a working day for me:
For the farmer's sheep is slain, and the lad who did it ta'en,
  And on his soul may God ha' mer-cy!

The Dance at The Phœnix

To Jenny came a gentle youth
    From inland leazes lone,
His love was fresh as apple-blooth
    By Parrett, Yeo, or Tone.
And duly he entreated her
To be his tender minister,
    And take him for her own.

Now Jenny's life had hardly been
    A life of modesty;
And few in Casterbridge had seen   10
    More loves of sorts than she
From scarcely sixteen years above;
Among them sundry troopers of
    The King's-Own Cavalry.

But each with charger, sword, and gun,
    Had bluffed the Biscay wave;
And Jenny prized her rural one
    For all the love he gave.
She vowed to be, if they were wed,
His honest wife in heart and head   20
    From bride-ale hour to grave.

Wedded they were. Her husband's trust
    In Jenny knew no bound,
And Jenny kept her pure and just,
    Till even malice found
No sin or sign of ill to be
In one who walked so decently
    The duteous helpmate's round.

Two sons were born, and bloomed to men,
    And roamed, and were as not: 30
Alone was Jenny left again
    As ere her mind had sought
A solace in domestic joys,
And ere the vanished pair of boys
    Were sent to sun her cot.

She numbered near to sixty years,
 And passed as elderly,
When, on a day, with flushing fears,
 She learnt from shouts of glee,
And shine of swords and thump of drum,   40
Her early loves from war had come,
  The King's-Own Cavalry.

She turned aside, and bowed her head
 Anigh Saint Peter's door;
'Alas for chastened thoughts!' she said;
 'I'm faded now, and hoar,
And yet those notes—they thrill me through,
And those gay forms move me anew
  As they moved me of yore!' . . .

'Twas Christmas, and the Phœnix Inn   50
 Was lit with tapers tall,
For thirty of the trooper men
 Had vowed to give a ball
As 'Theirs' had done ('twas handed down)
When lying in the self-same town
  Ere Buonaparté's fall.

That night the throbbing 'Soldier's Joy',
 The measured tread and sway
Of 'Fancy-Lad' and 'Maiden Coy',
 Reached Jenny as she lay   60
Beside her spouse; till springtide blood
Seemed scouring through her like a flood
  That whisked the years away.

She rose, arrayed, and decked her head
 Where the bleached hairs grew thin;
Upon her cap two bows of red
 She fixed with hasty pin;
Unheard descending to the street
She trod the flags with tune-led feet,
  And stood before the Inn.   70

Save for the dancers', not a sound
    Disturbed the icy air;
No watchman on his midnight round
    Or traveller was there;
But over All-Saints', high and bright,
Pulsed to the music Sirius white,
    The Wain towards Bullstake Square.

She knocked, but found her further stride
    Checked by a sergeant's call:
'Gay Granny, whence come you?' he cried;   80
    'This is a private ball.'
—'No one has more right here than me!
Ere you were born, man,' answered she,
    'I knew the regiment all!'

'Take not the lady's visit ill!'
    The steward said; 'for, see,
We lack sufficient partners still,
    So, prithee let her be!'
They seized and whirled her 'mid the maze,
And Jenny felt as in the days   90
    Of her immodesty.

Hour chased each hour, and night advanced;
    She sped as shod with wings;
Each time and every time she danced—
    Reels, jigs, poussettes, and flings:
They cheered her as she soared and swooped,
(She had learnt ere art in dancing drooped
    From hops to slothful swings).

The favourite Quick-step 'Speed the Plough'—
    (Cross hands, cast off, and wheel)—   100
'The Triumph', 'Sylph', 'The Row-dow-dow',
    Famed 'Major Malley's Reel',
'The Duke of York's', 'The Fairy Dance',
'The Bridge of Lodi' (brought from France),
    She beat out, toe and heel.

The 'Fall of Paris' clanged its close,
 And Peter's chimed to four,
When Jenny, bosom-beating, rose
 To seek her silent door.
They tiptoed in escorting her,   110
Lest stroke of heel or clink of spur
 Should break her goodman's snore.

The fire that lately burnt fell slack
 When lone at last was she;
Her nine-and-fifty years came back;
 She sank upon her knee
Beside the durn, and like a dart
A something arrowed through her heart
 In shoots of agony.

Their footsteps died as she leant there, 120
 Lit by the morning star
Hanging above the moorland, where
 The aged elm-rows are;
As overnight, from Pummery Ridge
To Maembury Ring and Standfast Bridge
 No life stirred, near or far.

Though inner mischief worked amain,
 She reached her husband's side;
Where, toil-weary, as he had lain
 Beneath the patchwork pied   130
When with lax longings she had crept
Therefrom at midnight, still he slept
 Who did in her confide.

A tear sprang as she turned and viewed
 His features free from guile;
She kissed him long, as when, just wooed,
 She chose his domicile.
She felt she would give more than life
To be the single-hearted wife
 That she had been erstwhile. . . . 140

Time wore to six. Her husband rose
    And struck the steel and stone;
He glanced at Jenny, whose repose
    Seemed deeper than his own.
With dumb dismay, on closer sight,
He gathered sense that in the night,
    Or morn, her soul had flown.

When told that some too mighty strain
    For one so many-yeared
Had burst her bosom's master-vein,   150
    His doubts remained unstirred.
His Jenny had not left his side
Betwixt the eve and morning-tide:
    —The King's said not a word.

Well! times are not as times were then,
    Nor fair ones half so free;
And truly they were martial men,
    The King's-Own Cavalry.
And when they went from Casterbridge
And vanished over Mellstock Ridge,
    'Twas saddest morn to see.   160

A Sign-Seeker

I mark the months in liveries dank and dry,
    The noontides many-shaped and hued;
    I see the nightfall shades subtrude,
And hear the monotonous hours clang negligently by.

I view the evening bonfires of the sun
    On hills where morning rains have hissed;
    The eyeless countenance of the mist
Pallidly rising when the summer droughts are done.

I have seen the lightning-blade, the leaping star,
   The cauldrons of the sea in storm,   10
   Have felt the earthquake's lifting arm,
And trodden where abysmal fires and snow-cones are.

I learn to prophesy the hid eclipse,
   The coming of eccentric orbs;
   To mete the dust the sky absorbs,
To weigh the sun, and fix the hour each planet dips.

I witness fellow earth-men surge and strive;
   Assemblies meet, and throb, and part;
   Death's sudden finger, sorrow's smart;
—All the vast various moils that mean a world alive.   20

But that I fain would wot of shuns my sense—
   Those sights of which old prophets tell,
   Those signs the general word so well,
As vouchsafed their unheed, denied my long suspense.

In graveyard green, where his pale dust lies pent
   To glimpse a phantom parent, friend,
   Wearing his smile, and 'Not the end!'
Outbreathing softly: that were blest enlightenment;

Or, if a dead Love's lips, whom dreams reveal
   When midnight imps of King Decay   30
   Delve sly to solve me back to clay,
Should leave some print to prove her spirit-kisses real;

Or, when Earth's Frail lie bleeding of her Strong,
   If some Recorder, as in Writ,
   Near to the weary scene should flit
And drop one plume as pledge that Heaven inscrolls the wrong.

—There are who, rapt to heights of trancelike trust,
   These tokens claim to feel and see,
   Read radiant hints of times to be—
Of heart to heart returning after dust to dust.   40

Such scope is granted not to lives like mine . . .
  I have lain in dead men's beds, have walked
   The tombs of those with whom I had talked,
Called many a gone and goodly one to shape a sign,

And panted for response. But none replies;
  No warnings loom, nor whisperings
   To open out my limitings,
And Nescience mutely muses: When a man falls he lies.

Her Immortality

  Upon a noon I pilgrimed through
    A pasture, mile by mile,
  Unto the place where last I saw
    My dead Love's living smile.

  And sorrowing I lay me down
    Upon the heated sod:
  It seemed as if my body pressed
    The very ground she trod.

  I lay, and thought; and in a trance
    She came and stood thereby—   10
  The same, even to the marvellous ray
    That used to light her eye.

  'You draw me, and I come to you,
    My faithful one,' she said,
  In voice that had the moving tone
    It bore ere she was wed.

  'Seven years have circled since I died:
    Few now remember me;
  My husband clasps another bride;
    My children's love has she.   20

'My brethren, sisters, and my friends
    Care not to meet my sprite:
Who prized me most I did not know
    Till I passed down from sight.'

I said: 'My days are lonely here;
    I need thy smile alway:
I'll use this night my ball or blade,
    And join thee ere the day.'

A tremor stirred her tender lips,
    Which parted to dissuade: 30
'That cannot be, O friend,' she cried;
    'Think, I am but a Shade!

'A Shade but in its mindful ones
    IIas immortality;
By living, me you keep alive,
    By dying you slay me.

'In you resides my single power
    Of sweet continuance here;
On your fidelity I count
    Through many a coming year.'   40

—I started through me at her plight,
    So suddenly confessed:
Dismissing late distaste for life,
    I craved its bleak unrest.

'I will not die, my One of all!—
    To lengthen out thy days
I'll guard me from minutest harms
    That may invest my ways!'

She smiled and went. Since then she comes
    Oft when her birth-moon climbs,   50
Or at the seasons' ingresses,
    Or anniversary times;

But grows my grief. When I surcease,
    Through whom alone lives she,
Her spirit ends its living lease,
    Never again to be!

The Ivy-Wife

I longed to love a full-boughed beech
    And be as high as he:
I stretched an arm within his reach,
    And signalled unity.
But with his drip he forced a breach,
    And tried to poison me.

I gave the grasp of partnership
    To one of other race—
A plane: he barked him strip by strip
    From upper bough to base;   10
And me therewith; for gone my grip,
    My arms could not enlace.

In new affection next I strove
    To coll an ash I saw,
And he in trust received my love;
    Till with my soft green claw
I cramped and bound him as I wove . . .
    Such was my love: ha-ha!

By this I gained his strength and height
    Without his rivalry.   20
But in my triumph I lost sight
    Of afterhaps. Soon he,
Being bark-bound, flagged, snapped, fell outright,
    And in his fall felled me!

A Meeting with Despair

As evening shaped I found me on a moor
    Sight shunned to entertain:
The black lean land, of featureless contour,
    Was like a tract in pain.

'This scene, like my own life,' I said, 'is one
    Where many glooms abide;
Toned by its fortune to a deadly dun—
    Lightless on every side.'

I glanced aloft and halted, pleasure-caught
    To see the contrast there:
The ray-lit clouds gleamed glory; and I thought,
    'There's solace everywhere!'

Then bitter self-reproaches as I stood
    I dealt me silently
As one perverse—misrepresenting Good
    In graceless mutiny.

Against the horizon's dim-discernèd wheel
    A form rose, strange of mould:
That he was hideous, hopeless, I could feel
    Rather than could behold.

'\'Tis a dead spot, where even the light lies spent
    To darkness!' croaked the Thing.
'Not if you look aloft!' said I, intent
    On my new reasoning.

'Yea—but await awhile!' he cried. 'Ho-ho!—
    Now look aloft and see!'
I looked. There, too, sat night: Heaven's radiant show
    Had gone that heartened me.

10

20

Unknowing

When, soul in soul reflected,
We breathed an æthered air,
    When we neglected
    All things elsewhere,
And left the friendly friendless
To keep our love aglow,
    We deemed it endless. . .
    —We did not know!

When panting passion-goaded,
We planned to hie away,   10
    But, unforeboded,
    All the long day
The storm so pierced and pattered
That none could up and go,
    Our lives seemed shattered . . .
    —We did not know!

When I found you helpless lying,
And you waived my long misprise,
    And swore me, dying,
    In phantom-guise   20
To wing to me when grieving,
And touch away my woe,
    We kissed, believing . . .
    —We did not know!

But though, your powers outreckoning,
You tarry dead and dumb,
    Or scorn my beckoning,
    And will not come:
And I say, 'Why thus inanely
Brood on her memory so!'   30
    I say it vainly—
    I feel and know!

Friends Beyond

William Dewy, Tranter Reuben, Farmer Ledlow late at
plough,
Robert's kin, and John's, and Ned's,
And the Squire, and Lady Susan, lie in Mellstock churchyard now!

'Gone,' I call them, gone for good, that group of local
hearts and heads;
Yet at mothy curfew-tide,
And at midnight when the noon-heat breathes it back from
walls and leads,

They've a way of whispering to me—fellow-wight who yet
abide—
In the muted, measured note
Of a ripple under archways, or a lone cave's stillicide:

'We have triumphed: this achievement turns the bane to
antidote,   10
Unsuccesses to success,
Many thought-worn eves and morrows to a morrow free of
thought.

'No more need we corn and clothing, feel of old terrestrial
stress;
Chill detraction stirs no sigh;
Fear of death has even bygone us: death gave all that we
possess.'

W. D.—'Ye mid burn the old bass-viol that I set such value by.'
Squire.—'You may hold the manse in fee,
You may wed my spouse, may let my children's memory of
me die.'

Lady S.—'You may have my rich brocades, my laces; take each
household key;
Ransack coffer, desk, bureau;   20
Quiz the few poor treasures hid there, con the letters kept by
me.'

Far.—'Ye mid zell my favourite heifer, ye mid let the charlock
           grow,
                Foul the grinterns, give up thrift.'
Far. Wife.—'If ye break my best blue china, children, I shan't
           care or ho.'

All.—'We've no wish to hear the tidings, how the people's for-
           tunes shift;
                What your daily doings are;
Who are wedded, born, divided; if your lives beat slow or
           swift.

'Curious not the least are we if our intents you make or mar,
           If you quire to our old tune,
If the City stage still passes, if the weirs still roar afar.'   30

—Thus, with very gods' composure, freed those crosses
           late and soon
                Which, in life, the Trine allow
(Why, none witteth), and ignoring all that haps beneath the
           moon,

William Dewy, Tranter Reuben, Farmer Ledlow late at
           plough,
                Robert's kin, and John's, and Ned's,
And the Squire, and Lady Susan, murmur mildly to me now.

Thoughts of Phena

At News of Her Death

Not a line of her writing have I,
           Not a thread of her hair,
No mark of her late time as dame in her dwelling, whereby
           I may picture her there;
And in vain do I urge my unsight
           To conceive my lost prize
At her close, whom I knew when her dreams were upbrimming
           with light,
                And with laughter her eyes.

What scenes spread around her last days,
    Sad, shining, or dim?   10
Did her gifts and compassions enray and enarch her sweet ways
    With an aureate nimb?
    Or did life-light decline from her years,
      And mischances control
Her full day-star; unease, or regret, or forebodings, or fears
    Disennoble her soul?

    Thus I do but the phantom retain
      Of the maiden of yore
As my relic; yet haply the best of her—fined in my brain
    It may be the more   20
    That no line of her writing have I,
      Nor a thread of her hair,
No mark of her late time as dame in her dwelling, whereby
    I may picture her there.

                March 1890.

Middle-Age Enthusiasms

To M. H.

    We passed where flag and flower
    Signalled a jocund throng;
    We said: 'Go to, the hour
    Is apt!'—and joined the song,
And, kindling, laughed at life and care,
Although we knew no laugh lay there.

    We walked where shy birds stood
    Watching us, wonder-dumb;
    Their friendship met our mood;
    We cried: 'We'll often come: 10
We'll come morn, noon, eve, everywhen!'
—We doubted we should come again.

    We joyed to see strange sheens
    Leap from quaint leaves in shade;

A secret light of greens
They'd for their pleasure made.
We said: 'We'll set such sorts as these!'
—We knew with night the wish would cease.

'So sweet the place,' we said,
'Its tacit tales so dear,   20
Our thoughts, when breath has sped,
Will meet and mingle here!' . . .
'Words!' mused we. 'Passed the mortal door,
Our thoughts will reach this nook no more.'

In a Wood

From *The Woodlanders*

Pale beech and pine so blue,
        Set in one clay,
Bough to bough cannot you
        Live out your day?
When the rains skim and skip,
Why mar sweet comradeship,
Blighting with poison-drip
        Neighbourly spray?

Heart-halt and spirit-lame,
        City-opprest,   10
Unto this wood I came
        As to a nest;
Dreaming that sylvan peace
Offered the harrowed ease—
Nature a soft release
        From men's unrest.

But, having entered in,
        Great growths and small
Show them to men akin—
        Combatants all!   20

Sycamore shoulders oak,
Bines the slim sapling yoke,
Ivy-spun halters choke
        Elms stout and tall.

Touches from ash, O wych,
        Sting you like scorn!
You, too, brave hollies, twitch
        Sidelong from thorn.
Even the rank poplars bear
Lothly a rival's air,   30
Cankering in blank despair
        If overborne.

Since, then, no grace I find
        Taught me of trees,
Turn I back to my kind,
        Worthy as these.
There at least smiles abound,
There discourse trills around,
There, now and then, are found
        Life-loyalties.   40
                        1887: 1896.

Nature's Questioning

When I look forth at dawning, pool,
        Field, flock, and lonely tree,
        All seem to gaze at me
Like chastened children sitting silent in a school;

        Their faces dulled, constrained, and worn,
                As though the master's way
                Through the long teaching day
        Had cowed them till their early zest was overborne.

        Upon them stirs in lippings mere
                (As if once clear in call,   10
                But now scarce breathed at all)—
        'We wonder, ever wonder, why we find us here!

'Has some Vast Imbecility,
    Mighty to build and blend,
    But impotent to tend,
Framed us in jest, and left us now to hazardry?

'Or come we of an Automaton
    Unconscious of our pains? . . .
    Or are we live remains
Of Godhead dying downwards, brain and eye now gone?   20

'Or is it that some high Plan betides,
    As yet not understood,
    Of Evil stormed by Good,
We the Forlorn Hope over which Achievement strides?'

Thus things around. No answerer I. . . .
    Meanwhile the winds, and rains,
    And Earth's old glooms and pains
Are still the same, and Life and Death are neighbours nigh.

The Impercipient

(At a Cathedral Service)

That with this bright believing band
    I have no claim to be,
That faiths by which my comrades stand
    Seem fantasies to me,
And mirage-mists their Shining Land,
    Is a strange destiny.

Why thus my soul should be consigned
    To infelicity,
Why always I must feel as blind
    To sights my brethren see,   10
Why joys they have found I cannot find,
    Abides a mystery.

Since heart of mine knows not that ease
      Which they know; since it be
That He who breathes All's Well to these
      Breathes no All's-Well to me,
My lack might move their sympathies
      And Christian charity!

I am like a gazer who should mark
      An inland company   20
Standing upfingered, with, 'Hark! hark!
      The glorious distant sea!'
And feel, 'Alas, 'tis but yon dark
      And wind-swept pine to me!'

Yet I would bear my shortcomings
      With meet tranquillity,
But for the charge that blessed things
      I'd liefer not have be.
O, doth a bird beshorn of wings
      Go earth-bound wilfully!   30

            .   .   .   .   .

Enough. As yet disquiet clings
      About us. Rest shall we.

At an Inn

When we as strangers sought
      Their catering care,
Veiled smiles bespoke their thought
      Of what we were.
They warmed as they opined
      Us more than friends—
That we had all resigned
      For love's dear ends.

And that swift sympathy
    With living love
Which quicks the world—maybe   10
    The spheres above,
Made them our ministers,
    Moved them to say,
'Ah, God, that bliss like theirs
    Would flush our day!'

And we were left alone
    As Love's own pair;
Yet never the love-light shone
    Between us there!   20
But that which chilled the breath
    Of afternoon,
And palsied unto death
    The pane-fly's tune.

The kiss their zeal foretold,
    And now deemed come,
Came not: within his hold
    Love lingered numb.
Why cast he on our port
    A bloom not ours?   30
Why shaped us for his sport
    In after-hours?

As we seemed we were not
    That day afar,
And now we seem not what
    We aching are.
O severing sea and land,
    O laws of men,
Ere death, once let us stand
    As we stood then!   40

In a Eweleaze near Weatherbury

The years have gathered grayly
  Since I danced upon this leaze
With one who kindled gaily
  Love's fitful ecstasies!
But despite the term as teacher,
  I remain what I was then
In each essential feature
  Of the fantasies of men.

Yet I note the little chisel
  Of never-napping Time   10
Defacing wan and grizzel
  The blazon of my prime.
When at night he thinks me sleeping
  I feel him boring sly
Within my bones, and heaping
  Quaintest pains for by-and-by.

Still, I'd go the world with Beauty,
  I would laugh with her and sing,
I would shun divinest duty
  To resume her worshipping.   20
But she'd scorn my brave endeavour,
  She would not balm the breeze
By murmuring 'Thine for ever!'
  As she did upon this leaze.

                1890.

The Bride-Night Fire

Or, The Fire at Tranter Sweatley's

(Wessex Dialect)

They had long met o' Zundays—her true love and she—
  And at junketings, maypoles, and flings;
But she bode wi' a thirtover uncle, and he
Swore by noon and by night that her goodman should be

Naibour Sweatley—a wight often weak at the knee
From taking o' sommat more cheerful than tea—
 Who tranted, and moved people's things.

She cried, 'O pray pity me!' Nought would he hear;
 Then with wild rainy eyes she obeyed.
She chid when her Love was for vanishing wi' her: 10
The pa'son was told, as the season drew near
To throw over pu'pit the names of the pair
 As fitting one flesh to be made.

The wedding-day dawned and the morning drew on;
 The couple stood bridegroom and bride;
The evening was passed, and when midnight had gone
The feasters horned, 'God save the King', and anon
 The twain took their home-along ride.

The lover Tim Tankens mourned heart-sick and lear
 To be thus of his darling deprived: 20
He roamed in the dark ath'art field, mound, and mere,
And, a'most without knowing it, found himself near
The house of the tranter, and now of his Dear,
 Where the lantern-light showed 'em arrived.

The bride sought her chamber so calm and so pale
 That a Northern had thought her resigned;
But to eyes that had seen her in tide-times of weal,
Like the white cloud o' smoke, the red battlefield's vail,
 That look spak' of havoc behind.

The bridegroom yet loitered a beaker to drain,   30
 Then reeled to the linhay for more,
When the candle-snoff kindled some chaff from his grain—
Flames spread, and red vlankers, wi' might and wi' main,
 And round beams, thatch, and chimley-tun roar.

Young Tim away yond, rafted up by the light,
 Through brimbles and underwood tears,
Till he comes to the orchet, when crooping from sight
In the lewth of a codlin-tree, bivering wi' fright,
Wi' on'y her night-rail to cover her plight,
 His lonesome young Barbree appears.   40

Her cold little figure half-naked he views
  Played about by the frolicsome breeze,
Her light-tripping totties, her ten little tooes,
All bare and besprinkled wi' Fall's chilly dews,
While her great gallied eyes through her hair hanging loose
  Shone as stars through a tardle o' trees.

She eyed him; and, as when a weir-hatch is drawn,
  Her tears, penned by terror afore,
With a rushing of sobs in a shower were strawn,
Till her power to pour 'em seemed wasted and gone   50
  From the heft o' misfortune she bore.

'O Tim, my *own* Tim I must call 'ee—I will!
  All the world has turned round on me so!
Can you help her who loved 'ee, though acting so ill?
Can you pity her misery—feel for her still?
When worse than her body so quivering and chill
  Is her heart in its winter o' woe!

'I think I mid almost ha' borne it,' she said,
  'Had my griefs one by one come to hand;
But O, to be slave to thik husbird for bread,   60
And then, upon top o' that, driven to wed,
And then, upon top o' that, burnt out o' bed,
  Is more than my nater can stand!'

Like a lion within him Tim's spirit outsprung—
(Tim had a great soul when his feelings were wrung)—
  'Feel for 'ee, dear Barbree?' he cried;
And his warm working-jacket then straightway he flung
Round about her, and bending his back, there she clung
Like a chiel on a gipsy, her figure uphung
  By the sleeves that he tightly had tied.   70

Over piggeries, and mixens, and apples, and hay,
  They lumpered straight into the night;
And finding erelong where a bridle-path lay,
Lit on Tim's house at dawn, only seen on their way
By a naibour or two who were up wi' the day;
  But who gathered no clue to the sight.

Then tender Tim Tankens he searched here and there
   For some garment to clothe her fair skin;
But though he had breeches and waistcoats to spare,
He had nothing quite seemly for Barbree to wear,   80
Who, half shrammed to death, stood and cried on a chair
   At the caddle she found herself in.

There was one thing to do, and that one thing he did,
   He lent her some clothes of his own,
And she took 'em perforce; and while swiftly she slid
Them upon her Tim turned to the winder, as bid,
Thinking, 'O that the picter my duty keeps hid
   To the sight o' my eyes mid be shown!'

In the tallet he stowed her; there huddied she lay,
   Shortening sleeves, legs, and tails to her limbs;   90
But most o' the time in a mortal bad way,
Well knowing that there'd be the divel to pay
If 'twere found that, instead o' the elements' prey,
   She was living in lodgings at Tim's.

'Where's the tranter?' said men and boys; 'where can he be?'
   'Where's the tranter?' said Barbree alone.
'Where on e'th is the tranter?' said everybod-y:
They sifted the dust of his perished roof-tree,
   And all they could find was a bone.

Then the uncle cried, 'Lord, pray have mercy on me!'   100
   And in terror began to repent.
But before 'twas complete, and till sure she was free,
Barbree drew up her loft-ladder, tight turned her key—
Tim bringing up breakfast and dinner and tea—
   Till the news of her hiding got vent.

Then followed the custom-kept rout, shout, and flare
Of a skimmity-ride through the naibourhood, ere
   Folk had proof of old Sweatley's decay.
Whereupon decent people all stood in a stare,
Saying Tim and his lodger should risk it, and pair: 110
So he took her to church. An' some laughing lads there
Cried to Tim, 'After Sweatley!' She said, 'I declare
   I stand as a maiden to-day!'

Written 1866; *printed* 1875.

'I look into my glass'

I look into my glass,
And view my wasting skin,
And say, 'Would God it came to pass
My heart had shrunk as thin!'

For then, I, undistrest
By hearts grown cold to me,
Could lonely wait my endless rest
With equanimity.

But Time, to make me grieve,
Part steals, lets part abide;
And shakes this fragile frame at eve
With throbbings of noontide.

10

from POEMS OF THE PAST AND THE PRESENT

PREFACE

HEREWITH I tender my thanks to the editors and proprietors of the *Times*, the *Morning Post*, the *Daily Chronicle*, the *Westminster Gazette*, *Literature*, the *Graphic*, *Cornhill*, *Sphere*, and other papers, for permission to reprint from their pages such of the following pieces of verse as have already been published.

As was said of *Wessex Poems*, of the subject-matter of this volume much is dramatic or impersonative even where not explicitly so. And that portion which may be regarded as individual comprises a series of feelings and fancies written down in widely differing moods and circumstances, and at various dates; it will probably be found, therefore, to possess little cohesion of thought or harmony of colouring. I do not greatly regret this. Unadjusted impressions have their value, and the road to a true philosophy of life seems to lie in humbly recording diverse readings of its phenomena as they are forced upon us by chance and change.

T. H.
August 1901.

WAR POEMS

The Going of the Battery

Wives' Lament

(*Casterbridge: November* 2, 1899)

I

O it was sad enough, weak enough, mad enough—
Light in their loving as soldiers can be—
First to risk choosing them, leave alone losing them
Now, in far battle, beyond the South Sea! . . .

II

—Rain came down drenchingly; but we unblenchingly
Trudged on beside them through mirk and through mire,
They stepping steadily—only too readily!—
Scarce as if stepping brought parting-time nigher.

III

Great guns were gleaming there, living things seeming there,
Cloaked in their tar-cloths, upmouthed to the night;
Wheels wet and yellow from axle to felloe,
Throats blank of sound, but prophetic to sight.

IV

Gas-glimmers drearily, blearily, eerily
Lit our pale faces outstretched for one kiss,
While we stood prest to them, with a last quest to them
Not to court perils that honour could miss.

V

Sharp were those sighs of ours, blinded these eyes of ours,
When at last moved away under the arch
All we loved. Aid for them each woman prayed for them,
Treading back slowly the track of their march.

VI

Someone said: 'Nevermore will they come: evermore
Are they now lost to us.' O it was wrong!
Though may be hard their ways, some Hand will guard their
    ways,
Bear them through safely, in brief time or long.

VII

—Yet, voices haunting us, daunting us, taunting us,
Hint in the night-time when life beats are low
Other and graver things . . . hold we to braver things,
Wait we, in trust, what Time's fulness shall show.

A Christmas Ghost-Story

South of the Line, inland from far Durban,
A mouldering soldier lies—your countryman.
Awry and doubled up are his gray bones,
And on the breeze his puzzled phantom moans
Nightly to clear Canopus: 'I would know
By whom and when the All-Earth-gladdening Law
Of Peace, brought in by that Man Crucified,
Was ruled to be inept, and set aside?
And what of logic or of truth appears
In tacking "Anno Domini" to the years?   10
Near twenty-hundred liveried thus have hied,
But tarries yet the Cause for which He died.'

Christmas-eve, 1899.

Drummer Hodge

I

They throw in Drummer Hodge, to rest
    Uncoffined—just as found:
His landmark is a kopje-crest
    That breaks the veldt around;
And foreign constellations west
    Each night above his mound.

II

Young Hodge the Drummer never knew—
    Fresh from his Wessex home—
The meaning of the broad Karoo,
    The Bush, the dusty loam,   10
And why uprose to nightly view
    Strange stars amid the gloam.

III

Yet portion of that unknown plain
    Will Hodge for ever be;
His homely Northern breast and brain
    Grow to some Southern tree,
And strange-eyed constellations reign
    His stars eternally.

A Wife in London

(*December*, 1899)

I

She sits in the tawny vapour
    That the Thames-side lanes have uprolled,
    Behind whose webby fold on fold
Like a waning taper
    The street-lamp glimmers cold.

A messenger's knock cracks smartly,
    Flashed news is in her hand
    Of meaning it dazes to understand
Though shaped so shortly:
    He—has fallen—in the far South Land. . . .   10

II

'Tis the morrow; the fog hangs thicker,
    The postman nears and goes:
    A letter is brought whose lines disclose
By the firelight flicker
    His hand, whom the worm now knows:

Fresh—firm—penned in highest feather—
    Page-full of his hoped return,
    And of home-planned jaunts by brake and burn
In the summer weather,
    And of new love that they would learn.   20

The Souls of the Slain

I

The thick lids of Night closed upon me
    Alone at the Bill
    Of the Isle by the Race—
Many-caverned, bald, wrinkled of face—
And with darkness and silence the spirit was on me
    To brood and be still.

II

No wind fanned the flats of the ocean,
    Or promontory sides,
    Or the ooze by the strand,
Or the bent-bearded slope of the land,   10
Whose base took its rest amid everlong motion
    Of criss-crossing tides.

III

Soon from out of the Southward seemed nearing
    A whirr, as of wings
    Waved by mighty-vanned flies,
Or by night-moths of measureless size,
And in softness and smoothness well-nigh beyond hearing
    Of corporal things.

IV

And they bore to the bluff, and alighted—
    A dim-discerned train   20
    Of sprites without mould,
Frameless souls none might touch or might hold—
On the ledge by the turreted lantern, far-sighted
    By men of the main.

V

And I heard them say 'Home!' and I knew them
    For souls of the felled
    On the earth's nether bord

Under Capricorn, whither they'd warred,
And I neared in my awe, and gave heedfulness to them
    With breathings inheld.   30

VI

Then, it seemed, there approached from the northward
    A senior soul-flame
    Of the like filmy hue:
And he met them and spake: 'Is it you,
O my men?' Said they, 'Aye! We bear homeward and hearthward
    To feast on our fame!'

VII

'I've flown there before you,' he said then:
    'Your households are well;
    But—your kin linger less
On your glory and war-mightiness   40
Than on dearer things.'—'Dearer?' cried these from the dead then,
    'Of what do they tell?'

VIII

'Some mothers muse sadly, and murmur
    Your doings as boys—
    Recall the quaint ways
Of your babyhood's innocent days.
Some pray that, ere dying, your faith had grown firmer,
    And higher your joys.

IX

'A father broods: "Would I had set him
    To some humble trade,   50
    And so slacked his high fire,
And his passionate martial desire;
And told him no stories to woo him and whet him
    To this dire crusade!"'

X

'And, General, how hold out our sweethearts,
    Sworn loyal as doves?'
     —'Many mourn; many think
It is not unattractive to prink
Them in sables for heroes. Some fickle and fleet hearts
    Have found them new loves.'   60

XI

'And our wives?' quoth another resignedly,
    'Dwell they on our deeds?'
     —'Deeds of home; that live yet
Fresh as dew—deeds of fondness or fret;
Ancient words that were kindly expressed or unkindly,
    These, these have their heeds.'

XII

—'Alas! then it seems that our glory
    Weighs less in their thought
    Than our old homely acts,
And the long-ago commonplace facts   70
Of our lives—held by us as scarce part of our story,
    And rated as nought!'

XIII

Then bitterly some: 'Was it wise now
    To raise the tomb-door
    For such knowledge? Away!'
But the rest: 'Fame we prized till to-day;
Yet that hearts keep us green for old kindness we prize now
    A thousand times more!'

XIV

Thus speaking, the trooped apparitions
    Began to disband   80
    And resolve them in two:
Those whose record was lovely and true
Bore to northward for home: those of bitter traditions
    Again left the land,

XV

And, towering to seaward in legions,
    They paused at a spot
    Overbending the Race—
That engulphing, ghast, sinister place—
Whither headlong they plunged, to the fathomless regions
    Of myriads forgot.   90

XVI

And the spirits of those who were homing
    Passed on, rushingly,
    Like the Pentecost Wind;
And the whirr of their wayfaring thinned
And surceased on the sky, and but left in the gloaming
    Sea-mutterings and me.

December 1899.

POEMS OF PILGRIMAGE

Shelley's Skylark

(The neighbourhood of Leghorn: March, 1887)

Somewhere afield here something lies
In Earth's oblivious eyeless trust
That moved a poet to prophecies—
A pinch of unseen, unguarded dust:

The dust of the lark that Shelley heard,
And made immortal through times to be;—
Though it only lived like another bird,
And knew not its immortality.

Lived its meek life; then, one day, fell—
A little ball of feather and bone;   10
And how it perished, when piped farewell,
And where it wastes, are alike unknown.

Maybe it rests in the loam I view,
Maybe it throbs in a myrtle's green,
Maybe it sleeps in the coming hue
Of a grape on the slopes of yon inland scene.

Go find it, faeries, go and find
That tiny pinch of priceless dust,
And bring a casket silver-lined,
And framed of gold that gems encrust;   20

And we will lay it safe therein,
And consecrate it to endless time;
For it inspired a bard to win
Ecstatic heights in thought and rhyme.

In the Old Theatre, Fiesole

(April, 1887)

I traced the Circus whose gray stones incline
Where Rome and dim Etruria interjoin,
Till came a child who showed an ancient coin
That bore the image of a Constantine.

She lightly passed; nor did she once opine
How, better than all books, she had raised for me
In swift perspective Europe's history
Through the vast years of Cæsar's sceptred line.

For in my distant plot of English loam
'Twas but to delve, and straightway there to find   10
Coins of like impress. As with one half blind
Whom common simples cure, her act flashed home
In that mute moment to my opened mind
The power, the pride, the reach of perished Rome.

Rome

THE VATICAN: SALA DELLE MUSE

(1887)

I sat in the Muses' Hall at the mid of the day,
And it seemed to grow still, and the people to pass away,
And the chiselled shapes to combine in a haze of sun,
Till beside a Carrara column there gleamed forth One.

She looked not this nor that of those beings divine,
But each and the whole—an essence of all the Nine;
With tentative foot she neared to my halting-place,
A pensive smile on her sweet, small, marvellous face.

'Regarded so long, we render thee sad?' said she.
'Not you,' sighed I, 'but my own inconstancy!   10
I worship each and each, in the morning one,
And then, alas! another at sink of sun.

'To-day my soul clasps Form; but where is my troth
Of yesternight with Tune: can one cleave to both?'
—'Be not perturbed,' said she. 'Though apart in fame,
As I and my sisters are one, those, too, are the same.'

—'But my love goes further—to Story, and Dance, and Hymn,
The lover of all in a sun-sweep is fool to whim—
Is swayed like a river-weed as the ripples run!'
—'Nay, wooer, thou sway'st not. These are but phases of one;   20

'And that one is I; and I am projected from thee,
One that out of thy brain and heart thou causest to be—
Extern to thee nothing. Grieve not, nor thyself becall,
Woo where thou wilt; and rejoice thou canst love at all!'

Rome

AT THE PYRAMID OF CESTIUS
NEAR THE GRAVES OF SHELLEY AND KEATS

(1887)

Who, then, was Cestius,
    And what is he to me?—
Amid thick thoughts and memories multitudinous
    One thought alone brings he.

I can recall no word
    Of anything he did;
For me he is a man who died and was interred
    To leave a pyramid

Whose purpose was exprest
    Not with its first design,   10
Nor till, far down in Time, beside it found their rest
    Two countrymen of mine.

Cestius in life, maybe,
    Slew, breathed out threatening;
I know not. This I know: in death all silently
    He does a finer thing,

In beckoning pilgrim feet
    With marble finger high
To where, by shadowy wall and history-haunted street,
    Those matchless singers lie. . . .   20

—Say, then, he lived and died
    That stones which bear his name
Should mark, through Time, where two immortal Shades abide;
    It is an ample fame.

Lausanne

IN GIBBON'S OLD GARDEN: 11–12 P.M.

June 27, 1897

(The 110th anniversary of the completion of the *Decline and Fall* at the same hour and place)

A spirit seems to pass,
Formal in pose, but grave withal and grand:
He contemplates a volume in his hand,
And far lamps fleck him through the thin acacias.

Anon the book is closed,
With 'It is finished!' And at the alley's end
He turns, and when on me his glances bend
As from the Past comes speech—small, muted, yet composed.

'How fares the Truth now?—Ill?
—Do pens but slily further her advance?   10
May one not speed her but in phrase askance?
Do scribes aver the Comic to be Reverend still?

'Still rule those minds on earth
At whom sage Milton's wormwood words were hurled:
"Truth like a bastard comes into the world
Never without ill-fame to him who gives her birth"?'

Zermatt

TO THE MATTERHORN

(*June–July*, 1897)

Thirty-two years since, up against the sun,
Seven shapes, thin atomies to lower sight,
Labouringly leapt and gained thy gabled height,
And four lives paid for what the seven had won.

They were the first by whom the deed was done,
And when I look at thee, my mind takes flight
To that day's tragic feat of manly might,
As though, till then, of history thou hadst none.

Yet ages ere men topped thee, late and soon
Thou didst behold the planets lift and lower;   10
Saw'st, maybe, Joshua's pausing sun and moon,
And the betokening sky when Cæsar's power
Approached its bloody end: yea, even that Noon
When darkness filled the earth till the ninth hour.

*   *   *

The Mother Mourns

When mid-autumn's moan shook the night-time,
    And sedges were horny,
And summer's green wonderwork faltered
    On leaze and in lane,

I fared Yell'ham-Firs way, where dimly
    Came wheeling around me
Those phantoms obscure and insistent
    That shadows unchain.

Till airs from the needle-thicks brought me
    A low lamentation,   10
As though from a tree-god disheartened,
    Perplexed, or in pain.

And, heeding, it awed me to gather
    That Nature herself there
Was breathing in aërie accents,
    With dirgelike refrain,

Weary plaint that Mankind, in these late days,
    Had grieved her by holding
Her ancient high fame of perfection
    In doubt and disdain. . . .   20

—'I had not proposed me a Creature
    (She soughed) so excelling
All else of my kingdom in compass
    And brightness of brain

'As to read my defects with a god-glance,
    Uncover each vestige
Of old inadvertence, annunciate
    Each flaw and each stain!

'My purpose went not to develop
    Such insight in Earthland;
Such potent appraisements affront me,
    And sadden my reign!

'Why loosened I olden control here
    To mechanize skywards,
Undeeming great scope could outshape in
    A globe of such grain?

'Man's mountings of mind-sight I checked not,
    Till range of his vision
Now tops my intent, and finds blemish
    Throughout my domain.

'He holds as inept his own soul-shell—
    My deftest achievement—
Contemns me for fitful inventions
    Ill-timed and inane:

'No more sees my sun as a Sanct-shape,
    My moon as the Night-queen,
My stars as august and sublime ones
    That influences rain:

'Reckons gross and ignoble my teaching,
    Immoral my story,
My love-lights a lure, that my species
    May gather and gain.

30

40

50

'"Give me", he has said, "but the matter
      And means the gods lot her,
My brain could evolve a creation
      More seemly, more sane."

—'If ever a naughtiness seized me
      To woo adulation
From creatures more keen than those crude ones
      That first formed my train—   60

'If inly a moment I murmured,
      "The simple praise sweetly,
But sweetlier the sage"—and did rashly
      Man's vision unrein,

'I rue it! . . . His guileless forerunners,
      Whose brains I could blandish,
To measure the deeps of my mysteries
      Applied them in vain.

'From them my waste aimings and futile
      I subtly could cover;   70
"Every best thing", said they, "to best purpose
      Her powers preordain."—

'No more such! . . . My species are dwindling,
      My forests grow barren,
My popinjays fail from their tappings,
      My larks from their strain.

'My leopardine beauties are rarer,
      My tusky ones vanish,
My children have aped mine own slaughters
      To quicken my wane.   80

'Let me grow, then, but mildews and mandrakes,
      And slimy distortions,
Let nevermore things good and lovely
      To me appertain;

'For Reason is rank in my temples,
    And Vision unruly,
And chivalrous laud of my cunning
    Is heard not again!'

'I said to Love'

I said to Love,
'It is not now as in old days
When men adored thee and thy ways
        All else above;
Named thee the Boy, the Bright, the One
Who spread a heaven beneath the sun,'
        I said to Love.

I said to him,
'We now know more of thee than then;
We were but weak in judgment when,   10
        With hearts abrim,
We clamoured thee that thou would'st please
Inflict on us thine agonies,'
        I said to him.

I said to Love,
'Thou art not young, thou are not fair,
No elfin darts, no cherub air,
        Nor swan, nor dove
Are thine; but features pitiless,
And iron daggers of distress,'   20
        I said to Love.

'Depart then, Love! . . .
—Man's race shall perish, threatenest thou,
Without thy kindling coupling-vow?
The age to come the man of now
        Know nothing of?—
We fear not such a threat from thee;
We are too old in apathy!
Mankind shall cease.—So let it be,'
        I said to Love.

A Commonplace Day

The day is turning ghost,
And scuttles from the kalendar in fits and furtively,
To join the anonymous host
Of those that throng oblivion; ceding his place, maybe,
To one of like degree.

I part the fire-gnawed logs,
Rake forth the embers, spoil the busy flames, and lay the ends
Upon the shining dogs;
Further and further from the nooks the twilight's stride extends,
And beamless black impends.   10

Nothing of tiniest worth
Have I wrought, pondered, planned; no one thing asking blame
or praise,
Since the pale corpse-like birth
Of this diurnal unit, bearing blanks in all its rays—
Dullest of dull-hued Days!

Wanly upon the panes
The rain slides as have slid since morn my colourless thoughts;
and yet
Here, while Day's presence wanes,
And over him the sepulchre-lid is slowly lowered and set,
He wakens my regret.   20

Regret—though nothing dear
That I wot of, was toward in the wide world at his prime,
Or bloomed elsewhere than here,
To die with his decease, and leave a memory sweet, sublime,
Or mark him out in Time. . . .

—Yet, maybe, in some soul,
In some spot undiscerned on sea or land, some impulse rose,
Or some intent upstole
Of that enkindling ardency from whose maturer glows
The world's amendment flows;   30

But which, benumbed at birth
By momentary chance or wile, has missed its hope to be
Embodied on the earth;
And undervoicings of this loss to man's futurity
May wake regret in me.

The Lacking Sense

SCENE.—*A sad-coloured landscape, Waddon Vale*

I

'O Time, whence comes the Mother's moody look amid her
    labours,
  As of one who all unwittingly has wounded where she loves?
Why weaves she not her world-webs to according lutes and
    tabors,
  With nevermore this too remorseful air upon her face,
      As of angel fallen from grace?'

II

—'Her look is but her story: construe not its symbols keenly:
  In her wonderworks yea surely has she wounded where she
    loves.
The sense of ills misdealt for blisses blanks the mien most
    queenly,
  Self-smitings kill self-joys; and everywhere beneath the sun
      Such deeds her hands have done.'   10

III

—'And how explains thy Ancient Mind her crimes upon her
    creatures,
  These fallings from her fair beginnings, woundings where she
    loves,
Into her would-be perfect motions, modes, effects, and features
  Admitting cramps, black humours, wan decay, and baleful
    blights,
      Distress into delights?'

IV

—'Ah! knowest thou not her secret yet, her vainly veiled
    deficience,
  Whence it comes that all unwittingly she wounds the lives she
    loves?
That sightless are those orbs of hers?—which bar to her
    omniscience
  Brings those fearful unfulfilments, that red ravage through her
    zones
        Whereat all creation groans.   20

V

'She whispers it in each pathetic strenuous slow endeavour,
  When in mothering she unwittingly sets wounds on what she
    loves;
Yet her primal doom pursues her, faultful, fatal is she ever;
  Though so deft and nigh to vision is her facile finger-touch
      That the seers marvel much.

VI

'Deal, then, her groping skill no scorn, no note of malediction;
  Not long on thee will press the hand that hurts the lives it
    loves;
And while she plods dead-reckoning on, in darkness of affliction,
  Assist her where thy creaturely dependence can or may,
      For thou art of her clay.'   30

Doom and She

I

There dwells a mighty pair—
Slow, statuesque, intense—
Amid the vague Immense:
None can their chronicle declare,
Nor why they be, nor whence.

II

Mother of all things made,
Matchless in artistry,
Unlit with sight is she.—
And though her ever well-obeyed
Vacant of feeling he.   10

III

The Matron mildly asks—
A throb in every word—
'Our clay-made creatures, lord,
How fare they in their mortal tasks
Upon Earth's bounded bord?

IV

'The fate of those I bear,
Dear lord, pray turn and view,
And notify me true;
Shapings that eyelessly I dare
Maybe I would undo.   20

V

'Sometimes from lairs of life
Methinks I catch a groan,
Or multitudinous moan,
As though I had schemed a world of strife,
Working by touch alone.'

VI

'World-weaver!' he replies,
'I scan all thy domain;
But since nor joy nor pain
It lies in me to recognize,
Thy questionings are vain.   30

VII

'World-weaver! what *is* Grief?
And what are Right, and Wrong,
And Feeling, that belong
To creatures all who owe thee fief?
Why is Weak worse than Strong?' . . .

VIII

—Unanswered, curious, meek,
   She broods in sad surmise. . . .
—Some say they have heard her sighs
On Alpine height or Polar peak
   When the night tempests rise.   40

The Subalterns

I

'Poor wanderer,' said the leaden sky,
   'I fain would lighten thee,
But there are laws in force on high
   Which say it must not be.'

II

—'I would not freeze thee, shorn one,' cried
   The North, 'knew I but how
To warm my breath, to slack my stride;
   But I am ruled as thou.'

III

—'To-morrow I attack thee, wight,'
   Said Sickness. 'Yet I swear   10
I bear thy little ark no spite,
   But am bid enter there.'

IV

—'Come hither, Son,' I heard Death say;
   'I did not will a grave
Should end thy pilgrimage to-day,
   But I, too, am a slave!'

V

We smiled upon each other then,
   And life to me had less
Of that fell look it wore ere when
   They owned their passiveness.   20

The Sleep-Worker

When wilt thou wake, O Mother, wake and see—
As one who, held in trance, has laboured long
By vacant rote and prepossession strong—
The coils that thou hast wrought unwittingly;

Wherein have place, unrealized by thee,
Fair growths, foul cankers, right enmeshed with wrong,
Strange orchestras of victim-shriek and song,
And curious blends of ache and ecstasy?—

Should that morn come, and show thy opened eyes
All that Life's palpitating tissues feel,   10
How wilt thou bear thyself in thy surprise?—

Wilt thou destroy, in one wild shock of shame,
Thy whole high heaving firmamental frame,
Or patiently adjust, amend, and heal?

God-Forgotten

I towered far, and lo! I stood within
     The presence of the Lord Most High,
Sent thither by the sons of earth, to win
     Some answer to their cry.

     —'The Earth, sayest thou? The Human race?
     By Me created? Sad its lot?
Nay: I have no remembrance of such place:
     Such world I fashioned not.'—

     —'O Lord, forgive me when I say
     Thou spakest the word that made it all.'—   10
'The Earth of men—let me bethink me.... Yea!
     I dimly do recall

'Some tiny sphere I built long back
(Mid millions of such shapes of mine)
So named . . . It perished, surely—not a wrack
            Remaining, or a sign?

'It lost my interest from the first,
My aims therefor succeeding ill;
Haply it died of doing as it durst?'—
            'Lord, it existeth still.'—   20

'Dark, then, its life! For not a cry
Of aught it bears do I now hear;
Of its own act the threads were snapt whereby
            Its plaints had reached mine ear.

'It used to ask for gifts of good,
Till came its severance self-entailed,
When sudden silence on that side ensued,
            And has till now prevailed.

'All other orbs have kept in touch;
Their voicings reach me speedily: 30
Thy people took upon them overmuch
            In sundering them from me!

'And it is strange—though sad enough—
Earth's race should think that one whose call
Frames, daily, shining spheres of flawless stuff
            Must heed their tainted ball! . . .

'But sayest it is by pangs distraught,
And strife, and silent suffering?—
Sore grieved am I that injury should be wrought
            Even on so poor a thing!   40

'Thou shouldst have learnt that *Not to Mend*
For Me could mean but *Not to Know*:
Hence, Messengers! and straightway put an end
            To what men undergo.' . . .

Homing at dawn, I thought to see
One of the Messengers standing by.
—O childish thought! . . . Yet still it comes to me
When trouble hovers nigh.

By the Earth's Corpse

I

'O Lord, why grievest Thou?—
Since Life has ceased to be
Upon this globe, now cold
As lunar land and sea,
And humankind, and fowl, and fur
Are gone eternally,
All is the same to Thee as ere
They knew mortality.'

II

'O Time,' replied the Lord,
'Thou readest me ill, I ween;   10
Were all *the same*, I should not grieve
At that late earthly scene,
Now blestly past—though planned by me
With interest close and keen!—
Nay, nay: things now are *not* the same
As they have earlier been.

III

'Written indelibly
On my eternal mind
Are all the wrongs endured
By Earth's poor patient kind,   20
Which my too oft unconscious hand
Let enter undesigned.
No god can cancel deeds foredone,
Or thy old coils unwind!

IV

'As when, in Noë's days,
I whelmed the plains with sea,
So at this last, when flesh
And herb but fossils be,
And, all extinct, their piteous dust
Revolves obliviously,
That I made Earth, and life, and man,   30
It still repenteth me!'

To an Unborn Pauper Child

I

Breathe not, hid Heart: cease silently,
And though thy birth-hour beckons thee,
Sleep the long sleep:
The Doomsters heap
Travails and teens around us here,
And Time-wraiths turn our songsingings to fear.

II

Hark, how the peoples surge and sigh,
And laughters fail, and greetings die:
Hopes dwindle; yea,
Faiths waste away,   10
Affections and enthusiasms numb;
Thou canst not mend these things if thou dost come.

III

Had I the ear of wombèd souls
Ere their terrestrial chart unrolls,
And thou wert free
To cease, or be,
Then would I tell thee all I know,
And put it to thee: Wilt thou take Life so?

IV

Vain vow! No hint of mine may hence
To theeward fly: to thy locked sense   20
    Explain none can
    Life's pending plan:
Thou wilt thy ignorant entry make
Though skies spout fire and blood and nations quake.

V

Fain would I, dear, find some shut plot
Of earth's wide wold for thee, where not
    One tear, one qualm,
    Should break the calm.
But I am weak as thou and bare;
No man can change the common lot to rare.   30

VI

Must come and bide. And such are we—
Unreasoning, sanguine, visionary—
    That I can hope
    Health, love, friends, scope
In full for thee; can dream thou wilt find
Joys seldom yet attained by humankind!

To Lizbie Browne

I

Dear Lizbie Browne,
Where are you now?
In sun, in rain?—
Or is your brow
Past joy, past pain,
Dear Lizbie Browne?

II

Sweet Lizbie Browne
How you could smile,
How you could sing!—
How archly wile   10
In glance-giving,
Sweet Lizbie Browne!

III

And Lizbie Browne,
Who else had hair
Bay-red as yours,
Or flesh so fair
Bred out of doors,
Sweet Lizbie Browne?

IV

When, Lizbie Browne,
You had just begun   20
To be endeared
By stealth to one,
You disappeared,
My Lizbie Browne!

V

Ay, Lizbie Browne,
So swift your life,
And mine so slow,
You were a wife
Ere I could show
Love, Lizbie Browne.   30

VI

Still, Lizbie Browne,
You won, they said,
The best of men
When you were wed. . . .
Where went you then,
O Lizbie Browne?

VII

Dear Lizbie Browne,
I should have thought,
'Girls ripen fast,'
And coaxed and caught   40
You ere you passed,
Dear Lizbie Browne!

VIII

But, Lizbie Browne,
I let you slip;
Shaped not a sign;
Touched never your lip
With lip of mine,
Lost Lizbie Browne!

IX

So, Lizbie Browne,
When on a day   50
Men speak of me
As not, you'll say,
'And who was he?'—
Yes, Lizbie Browne!

The Well-Beloved

I went by star and planet shine
    Towards my Dear's abode
At Jordon, there to make her mine
    When the next noon-tide glowed.

I edged the ancient hill and wood
    Beside the Ikling Way,
Near where the Pagan temple stood
    In the world's earlier day.

And as I quick and quicker walked
    On gravel and on green,   10
I sang to sky, and tree, or talked
    Of her I called my queen.

—'O faultless is her dainty form,
    And luminous her mind;
She is the God-created norm
    Of perfect womankind!'

A shape whereon one star-blink gleamed
    Slid softly to my side,
A woman's; and her motion seemed
    The motion of my bride.   20

And yet methought she'd drawn the while
    Adown the ancient leaze,
Where once were pile and peristyle
    For men's idolatries.

—'O maiden lithe and lone, what may
    Thy name and lineage be,
Who so resemblest by this ray
    My darling?—Art thou she?'

The Shape: 'Thy bride remains within
    Her father's grange and grove.'   30
—'Thou speakest rightly,' I broke in,
    'Thou art not she I love.'

—'Nay: though thy bride remains inside
    Her father's walls,' said she,
'The one most dear is with thee here,
    For thou dost love but me.'

Then I: 'But she, my only choice,
    Is now at Jordon Grove?'
Again her soft mysterious voice:
    'I am thy only Love.'   40

Thus still she vouched, and still I said,
    'O sprite, that cannot be!' . . .
It was as if my bosom bled,
    So much she troubled me.

The sprite resumed: 'Thou has transferred
    To her dull form awhile
My beauty, fame, and deed, and word,
    My gestures and my smile.

'O fatuous man, this truth infer,
    Brides are not what they seem;   50
Thou lovest what thou dreamest her;
    I am thy very dream!'

—'O then,' I answered miserably,
    Speaking as scarce I knew,
'My loved one, I must wed with thee
    If what thou say'st be true!'

She, proudly, thinning in the gloom:
    'Though, since troth-plight began,
I've ever stood as bride to groom,
    I wed no mortal man!'   60

Thereat she vanished by the lane
    Adjoining Budmouth town,
Near where, men say, once stood the Fane
    To Venus, on the Down.

—When I arrived and met my bride
    Her look was pinched and thin,
As if her soul had shrunk and died,
    And left a waste within.

A Broken Appointment

    You did not come,
And marching Time drew on, and wore me numb.—
Yet less for loss of your dear presence there
Than that I thus found lacking in your make
That high compassion which can overbear
Reluctance for pure lovingkindness' sake
Grieved I, when, as the hope-hour stroked its sum,
    You did not come.

      You love not me,
And love alone can lend you loyalty;   10
—I know and knew it. But, unto the store
Of human deeds divine in all but name,
Was it not worth a little hour or more
To add yet this: Once you, a woman, came
To soothe a time-torn man; even though it be
      You love not me?

'Between us now'

Between us now and here—
      Two thrown together
Who are not wont to wear
      Life's flushest feather—
Who see the scenes slide past,
The daytimes dimming fast,
Let there be truth at last,
      Even if despair.

So thoroughly and long
      Have you now known me,   10
So real in faith and strong
      Have I now shown me,
That nothing needs disguise
Further in any wise,
Or asks or justifies
      A guarded tongue.

Face unto face, then, say,
      Eyes my own meeting,
Is your heart far away,
      Or with mine beating?   20
When false things are brought low,
And swift things have grown slow,
Feigning like froth shall go,
      Faith be for aye.

A Spot

In years defaced and lost,
Two sat here, transport-tossed,
Lit by a living love
The wilted world knew nothing of:
    Scared momently
    By gaingivings,
    Then hoping things
    That could not be.

Of love and us no trace
Abides upon the place;   10
The sun and shadows wheel,
Season and season sereward steal;
    Foul days and fair
    Here, too, prevail,
    And gust and gale
    As everywhere.

But lonely shepherd souls
Who bask amid these knolls
May catch a faery sound
On sleepy noontides from the ground: 20
    'O not again
    Till Earth outwears
    Shall love like theirs
    Suffuse this glen!'

The To-Be-Forgotten

I

I heard a small sad sound,
And stood awhile among the tombs around:
'Wherefore, old friends,' said I, 'are you distrest,
    Now, screened from life's unrest?'

II

—'O not at being here;
But that our future second death is near;
When, with the living, memory of us numbs,
    And blank oblivion comes!

III

'These, our sped ancestry,
Lie here embraced by deeper death than we;   10
Nor shape nor thought of theirs can you descry
    With keenest backward eye.

IV

'They count as quite forgot;
They are as men who have existed not;
Theirs is a loss past loss of fitful breath;
    It is the second death.

V

'We here, as yet, each day
Are blest with dear recall; as yet, can say
We hold in some soul loved continuance
    Of shape and voice and glance.   20

VI

'But what has been will be—
First memory, then oblivion's swallowing sea;
Like men foregone, shall we merge into those
    Whose story no one knows.

VII

'For which of us could hope
To show in life that world-awakening scope
Granted the few whose memory none lets die,
    But all men magnify?

VIII

'We were but Fortune's sport;
Things true, things lovely, things of good report   30
We neither shunned nor sought ... We see our bourne,
    And seeing it we mourn.'

Wives in the Sere

I

Never a careworn wife but shows,
    If a joy suffuse her,
Something beautiful to those
    Patient to peruse her,
Some one charm the world unknows
    Precious to a muser,
Haply what, ere years were foes,
    Moved her mate to choose her.

II

But, be it a hint of rose
    That an instant hues her,   10
Or some early light or pose
    Wherewith thought renews her—
Seen by him at full, ere woes
    Practised to abuse her—
Sparely comes it, swiftly goes,
    Time again subdues her.

An August Midnight

I

A shaded lamp and a waving blind,
And the beat of a clock from a distant floor:
On this scene enter—winged, horned, and spined—
A longlegs, a moth, and a dumbledore;
While 'mid my page there idly stands
A sleepy fly, that rubs its hands . . .

II

Thus meet we five, in this still place,
At this point of time, at this point in space.
—My guests besmear my new-penned line,
Or bang at the lamp and fall supine.   10
'God's humblest, they!' I muse. Yet why?
They know Earth-secrets that know not I.

Max Gate. 1899.

Birds at Winter Nightfall

(Triolet)

Around the house the flakes fly faster,
And all the berries now are gone
From holly and cotoneaster
Around the house. The flakes fly!—faster
Shutting indoors that crumb-outcaster
We used to see upon the lawn
Around the house. The flakes fly faster,
And all the berries now are gone!

Max Gate. 1900.

The Puzzled Game-Birds

(Triolet)

They are not those who used to feed us
When we were young—they cannot be—
These shapes that now bereave and bleed us?
They are not those who used to feed us,
For did we then cry, they would heed us.
—If hearts can house such treachery
They are not those who used to feed us
When we were young—they cannot be!

Winter in Durnover Field

SCENE.—*A wide stretch of fallow ground recently sown with wheat, and frozen to iron hardness. Three large birds walking about thereon, and wistfully eyeing the surface. Wind keen from north-east: sky a dull grey.*

(Triolet)

Rook.—Throughout the field I find no grain;
        The cruel frost encrusts the cornland!
Starling.—Aye: patient pecking now is vain
        Throughout the field, I find . . .

Rook.— No grain!
Pigeon.—Nor will be, comrade, till it rain,
      Or genial thawings loose the lorn land
      Throughout the field.
Rook.— I find no grain:
      The cruel frost encrusts the cornland!

The Last Chrysanthemum

Why should this flower delay so long
    To show its tremulous plumes?
Now is the time of plaintive robin-song,
    When flowers are in their tombs.

Through the slow summer, when the sun
    Called to each frond and whorl
That all he could for flowers was being done,
    Why did it not uncurl?

It must have felt that fervid call
    Although it took no heed,   10
Waking but now, when leaves like corpses fall,
    And saps all retrocede.

Too late its beauty, lonely thing,
    The season's shine is spent,
Nothing remains for it but shivering
    In tempests turbulent.

Had it a reason for delay,
    Dreaming in witlessness
That for a bloom so delicately gay
    Winter would stay its stress?   20

—I talk as if the thing were born
    With sense to work its mind;
Yet it is but one mask of many worn
    By the Great Face behind.

The Darkling Thrush

I leant upon a coppice gate
    When Frost was spectre-gray,
And Winter's dregs made desolate
    The weakening eye of day.
The tangled bine-stems scored the sky
    Like strings of broken lyres,
And all mankind that haunted nigh
    Had sought their household fires.

The land's sharp features seemed to be
    The Century's corpse outleant,   10
His crypt the cloudy canopy,
    The wind his death-lament.
The ancient pulse of germ and birth
    Was shrunken hard and dry,
And every spirit upon earth
    Seemed fervourless as I.

At once a voice arose among
    The bleak twigs overhead
In a full-hearted evensong
    Of joy illimited;   20
An aged thrush, frail, gaunt, and small,
    In blast-beruffled plume,
Had chosen thus to fling his soul
    Upon the growing gloom.

So little cause for carolings
    Of such ecstatic sound
Was written on terrestrial things
    Afar or nigh around,
That I could think there trembled through
    His happy good-night air   30
Some blessed Hope, whereof he knew
    And I was unaware.

                31 *December* 1900.

The Milkmaid

Under a daisied bank
There stands a rich red ruminating cow,
     And hard against her flank
A cotton-hooded milkmaid bends her brow.

The flowery river-ooze
Uplifts and falls; the milk purrs in the pail;
     Few pilgrims but would choose
The peace of such a life in such a vale.

The maid breathes words—to vent,
It seems, her sense of Nature's scenery,   10
     Of whose life, sentiment,
And essence, very part itself is she.

She throws a glance of pain,
And, at a moment, lets escape a tear;
     Is it that passing train,
Whose alien whirr offends her country ear?—

Nay! Phyllis does not dwell
On visual and familiar things like these;
     What moves her is the spell
Of inner themes and inner poetries: 20

Could but by Sunday morn
Her gay new gown come, meads might dry to dun,
     Trains shriek till ears were torn,
If Fred would not prefer that Other One.

The Levelled Churchyard

'O passenger, pray list and catch
     Our sighs and piteous groans,
Half stifled in this jumbled patch
     Of wrenched memorial stones!

'We late-lamented, resting here,
    Are mixed to human jam,
And each to each exclaims in fear,
    "I know not which I am!"

'The wicked people have annexed
    The verses on the good;   10
A roaring drunkard sports the text
    Teetotal Tommy should!

'Where we are huddled none can trace,
    And if our names remain,
They pave some path or porch or place
    Where we have never lain!

'Here's not a modest maiden elf
    But dreads the final Trumpet,
Lest half of her should rise herself,
    And half some sturdy strumpet!   20

'From restorations of Thy fane,
    From smoothings of Thy sward,
From zealous Churchmen's pick and plane,
    Deliver us O Lord! Amen!'

                                    1882.

The Ruined Maid

'O 'Melia, my dear, this does everything crown!
Who could have supposed I should meet you in Town?
And whence such fair garments, such prosperi-ty?'—
'O didn't you know I'd been ruined?' said she.

—'You left us in tatters, without shoes or socks,
Tired of digging potatoes, and spudding up docks;
And now you've gay bracelets and bright feathers three!'—
'Yes: that's how we dress when we're ruined,' said she.

—'At home in the barton you said "thee" and "thou",
And "thik oon", and "theäs oon", and "t'other"; but now　10
Your talking quite fits 'ee for high compa-ny!'—
'A polish is gained with one's ruin,' said she.

—'Your hands were like paws then, your face blue and bleak,
But now I'm bewitched by your delicate cheek,
And your little gloves fit as on any la-dy!'—
'We never do work when we're ruined,' said she.

—'You used to call home-life a hag-ridden dream,
And you'd sigh, and you'd sock; but at present you seem
To know not of megrims or melancho-ly!'—
'True. One's pretty lively when ruined,' said she.　20

—'I wish I had feathers, a fine sweeping gown,
And a delicate face, and could strut about Town!'—
'My dear—a raw country girl, such as you be,
Cannot quite expect that. You ain't ruined,' said she.

Westbourne Park Villas, 1866.

The Respectable Burgher on 'The Higher Criticism'

Since Reverend Doctors now declare
That clerks and people must prepare
To doubt if Adam ever were;
To hold the flood a local scare;
To argue, though the stolid stare,
That everything had happened ere
The prophets to its happening sware;
That David was no giant-slayer,
Nor one to call a God-obeyer
In certain details we could spare,　10
But rather was a debonair
Shrewd bandit, skilled as banjo-player:
That Solomon sang the fleshly Fair,

And gave the Church no thought whate'er;
That Esther with her royal wear,
And Mordecai, the son of Jair,
And Joshua's triumphs, Job's despair,
And Balaam's ass's bitter blare;
Nebuchadnezzar's furnace-flare,
And Daniel and the den affair,   20
And other stories rich and rare,
Were writ to make old doctrine wear
Something of a romantic air:
That the Nain widow's only heir,
And Lazarus with cadaverous glare
(As done in oils by Piombo's care)
Did not return from Sheol's lair:
That Jael set a fiendish snare,
That Pontius Pilate acted square,
That never a sword cut Malchus' ear;   30
And (but for shame I must forbear)
That — — did not reappear! . . .
—Since thus they hint, nor turn a hair,
All churchgoing will I forswear,
And sit on Sundays in my chair,
And read that moderate man Voltaire.

The Self-Unseeing

Here is the ancient floor,
Footworn and hollowed and thin,
Here was the former door
Where the dead feet walked in.

She sat here in her chair,
Smiling into the fire;
He who played stood there,
Bowing it higher and higher.

Childlike, I danced in a dream;
Blessings emblazoned that day;   10
Everything glowed with a gleam;
Yet we were looking away!

In Tenebris

I

'Percussus sum sicut foenum, et aruit cor meum.'—Ps. ci.

Wintertime nighs;
But my bereavement-pain
It cannot bring again:
    Twice no one dies.

Flower-petals flee;
But, since it once hath been,
No more that severing scene
    Can harrow me.

Birds faint in dread:
I shall not lose old strength   10
In the lone frost's black length:
    Strength long since fled!

Leaves freeze to dun;
But friends can not turn cold
This season as of old
    For him with none.

Tempests may scath;
But love can not make smart
Again this year his heart
    Who no heart hath.   20

Black is night's cope;
But death will not appal
One who, past doubtings all,
    Waits in unhope.

In Tenebris

II

'Considerabam ad dexteram, et videbam; et non erat qui cognosceret me. . . .
Non est qui requirat animam meam.'—Ps. cxli.

When the clouds' swoln bosoms echo back the shouts of the
    many and strong
That things are all as they best may be, save a few to be right
    ere long,
And my eyes have not the vision in them to discern what to
    these is so clear,
The blot seems straightway in me alone; one better he were not
    here.

The stout upstanders say, All's well with us: ruers have nought
    to rue!
And what the potent say so oft, can it fail to be somewhat true?
Breezily go they, breezily come; their dust smokes around their
    career,
Till I think I am one born out of due time, who has no calling
    here.°

Their dawns bring lusty joys, it seems; their evenings all that is
    sweet;
Our times are blessed times, they cry: Life shapes it as is most
    meet,   10
And nothing is much the matter; there are many smiles to a tear;
Then what is the matter is I, I say. Why should such an one be
    here? . . .

Let him in whose ears the low-voiced Best is killed by the clash
    of the First,
Who holds that if way to the Better there be, it exacts a full look
    at the Worst,
Who feels that delight is a delicate growth cramped by crooked-
    ness, custom, and fear,
Get him up and be gone as one shaped awry; he disturbs the
    order here.

                                                    1895–96.

In Tenebris

III

'Heu mihi, quia incolatus meus prolongatus est! Habitavi cum habitantibus
Cedar; multum incola fuit anima mea.'—Ps. cxix.

There have been times when I well might have passed and the
    ending have come—
Points in my path when the dark might have stolen on me,
    artless, unrueing—
Ere I had learnt that the world was a welter of futile doing:
Such had been times when I well might have passed, and the
    ending have come!

Say, on the noon when the half-sunny hours told that April was
    nigh,
And I upgathered and cast forth the snow from the crocus-
    border,
Fashioned and furbished the soil into a summer-seeming order,
Glowing in gladsome faith that I quickened the year thereby.

Or on that loneliest of eves when afar and benighted we stood,
She who upheld me and I, in the midmost of Egdon together,   10
Confident I in her watching and ward through the blackening
    heather,
Deeming her matchless in might and with measureless scope
    endued.

Or on that winter-wild night when, reclined by the chimney-
    nook quoin,
Slowly a drowse overgat me, the smallest and feeblest of folk
    there,
Weak from my baptism of pain; when at times and anon I awoke
    there—
Heard of a world wheeling on, with no listing or longing to join.

Even then! while unweeting that vision could vex or that know-
    ledge could numb,
That sweets to the mouth in the belly are bitter, and tart, and
    untoward,

Then, on some dim-coloured scene should my briefly raised
    curtain have lowered,
Then might the Voice that is law have said 'Cease!' and the
    ending have come.   20

                    1896.

Tess's Lament

I

I would that folk forgot me quite,
        Forgot me quite!
I would that I could shrink from sight,
        And no more see the sun.
Would it were time to say farewell,
To claim my nook, to need my knell,
Time for them all to stand and tell
        O' my day's work as done.

II

Ah! dairy where I lived so long,
        I lived so long;   10
Where I would rise up stanch and strong,
        And lie down hopefully.
'Twas there within the chimney-seat
He watched me to the clock's slow beat—
Loved me, and learnt to call me Sweet,
        And whispered words to me.

III

And now he's gone; and now he's gone; . . .
        And now he's gone!
The flowers we potted p'rhaps are thrown
        To rot upon the farm.
And where we had our supper-fire   20
May now grow nettle, dock, and briar,
And all the place be mould and mire
        So cozy once and warm.

IV

And it was I who did it all,
    Who did it all;
'Twas I who made the blow to fall
    On him who thought no guile.
Well, it is finished—past, and he
Has left me to my misery,   30
And I must take my Cross on me
    For wronging him awhile.

V

How gay we looked that day we wed,
    That day we wed!
'May joy be with ye!' all o'm said
    A-standing by the durn.
I wonder what they say o's now,
And if they know my lot; and how
She feels who milks my favourite cow,
    And takes my place at churn!   40

VI

It wears me out to think of it,
    To think of it;
I cannot bear my fate as writ,
    I'd have my life unbe;
Would turn my memory to a blot,
Make every relic of me rot,
My doings be as they were not,
    And leave no trace of me!

Ἀγνώστῳ Θεῷ

Long have I framed weak phantasies of Thee,
    O Willer masked and dumb!
    Who makest Life become,—
As though by labouring all-unknowingly,
    Like one whom reveries numb.

How much of consciousness informs Thy will,
    Thy biddings, as if blind,
    Of death-inducing kind,
Nought shows to us ephemeral ones who fill
    But moments in Thy mind.   10

Perhaps Thy ancient rote-restricted ways
    Thy ripening rule transcends;
    That listless effort tends
To grow percipient with advance of days,
    And with percipience mends.

For, in unwonted purlieus, far and nigh,
    At whiles or short or long,
    May be discerned a wrong
Dying as of self-slaughter; whereat I
    Would raise my voice in song.   20

from TIME'S LAUGHINGSTOCKS

PREFACE

IN collecting the following poems I have to thank the editors and proprietors of the periodicals in which certain of them have appeared for permission to reclaim them.

Now that the miscellany is brought together, some lack of concord in pieces written at widely severed dates, and in contrasting moods and circumstances, will be obvious enough. This I cannot help, but the sense of disconnection, particularly in respect of those lyrics penned in the first person, will be immaterial when it is borne in mind that they are to be regarded, in the main, as dramatic monologues by different characters.

As a whole they will, I hope, take the reader forward, even if not far, rather than backward. I should add that some lines in the early-dated poems have been rewritten, though they have been left substantially unchanged.

T. H.
September 1909.

A Trampwoman's Tragedy

(182–)

I

From Wynyard's Gap the livelong day,
  The livelong day,
We beat afoot the northward way
  We had travelled times before.
The sun-blaze burning on our backs,
Our shoulders sticking to our packs,
By fosseway, fields, and turnpike tracks
  We skirted sad Sedge-Moor.

II

Full twenty miles we jaunted on,
    We jaunted on,—   10
My fancy-man, and jeering John,
    And Mother Lee, and I.
And, as the sun drew down to west,
We climbed the toilsome Poldon crest,
And saw, of landskip sights the best,
    The inn that beamed thereby.

III

For months we had padded side by side,
    Ay, side by side
Through the Great Forest, Blackmoor wide,
    And where the Parret ran.   20
We'd faced the gusts on Mendip ridge,
Had crossed the Yeo unhelped by bridge,
Been stung by every Marshwood midge,
    I and my fancy-man.

IV

Lone inns we loved, my man and I,
    My man and I;
'King's Stag', 'Windwhistle' high and dry,°
    'The Horse' on Hintock Green,
The cozy house at Wynyard's Gap,
'The Hut' for quaffs on Bredy Knap,   30
And many another wayside tap
    Where folk might sit unseen.

V

Now as we trudged—O deadly day,
    O deadly day!—
I teased my fancy-man in play
    And wanton idleness.
I walked alongside jeering John,
I laid his hand my waist upon;
I would not bend my glances on
    My lover's dark distress.   40

VI

Thus Poldon top at last we won,
  At last we won,
And gained the inn at sink of sun
  Far-famed as 'Marshal's Elm'.°
Beneath us figured tor and lea,
From Mendip to the western sea—
I doubt if finer sight there be
  Within this royal realm.

VII

Inside the settle all a-row—
  All four a-row   50
We sat, I next to John, to show
  That he had wooed and won.
And then he took me on his knee,
And swore it was his turn to be
My favoured mate, and Mother Lee
  Passed to my former one.

VIII

Then in a voice I had never heard,
  I had never heard,
My only Love to me: 'One word,
  My lady, if you please!   60
Whose is the child you are like to bear?—
His? After all my months o' care?'
God knows 'twas not! But, O despair!
  I nodded—still to tease.

IX

Then up he sprung, and with his knife—
  And with his knife
He let out jeering Johnny's life,
  Yes; there, at set of sun.
The slant ray through the window nigh
Gilded John's blood and glazing eye, 70
Ere scarcely Mother Lee and I
  Knew that the deed was done.

X

The taverns tell the gloomy tale,
        The gloomy tale,
How that at Ivel-chester jail
        My Love, my sweetheart swung;
Though stained till now by no misdeed
Save one horse ta'en in time o' need;
(Blue Jimmy stole right many a steed°
        Ere his last fling he flung.)   80

XI

Thereaft I walked the world alone,
        Alone, alone!
On his death-day I gave my groan
        And dropt his dead-born child.
'Twas nigh the jail, beneath a tree,
None tending me; for Mother Lee
Had died at Glaston, leaving me
        Unfriended on the wild.

XII

And in the night as I lay weak,
        As I lay weak,   90
The leaves a-falling on my cheek,
        The red moon low declined—
The ghost of him I'd die to kiss
Rose up and said: 'Ah, tell me this!
Was the child mine, or was it his?
        Speak, that I rest may find!'

XIII

O doubt not but I told him then,
        I told him then,
That I had kept me from all men
        Since we joined lips and swore.   100
Whereat he smiled, and thinned away
As the wind stirred to call up day . . .
—'Tis past! And here alone I stray
        Haunting the Western Moor.

                                        April 1902.

A Sunday Morning Tragedy

(*circa* 186–)

I bore a daughter flower-fair,
In Pydel Vale, alas for me;
I joyed to mother one so rare,
But dead and gone I now would be.

Men looked and loved her as she grew,
And she was won, alas for me;
She told me nothing, but I knew,
And saw that sorrow was to be.

I knew that one had made her thrall,
A thrall to him, alas for me;   10
And then, at last, she told me all,
And wondered what her end would be.

She owned that she had loved too well,
Had loved too well, unhappy she,
And bore a secret time would tell,
Though in her shroud she'd sooner be.

I plodded to her sweetheart's door
In Pydel Vale, alas for me:
I pleaded with him, pleaded sore,
To save her from her misery.   20

He frowned, and swore he could not wed,
Seven times he swore it could not be;
'Poverty's worse than shame,' he said,
Till all my hope went out of me.

'I've packed my traps to sail the main'—
Roughly he spake, alas did he—
'Wessex beholds me not again,
'Tis worse than any jail would be!'

—There was a shepherd whom I knew,
A subtle man, alas for me:
I sought him all the pastures through,
Though better I had ceased to be.

30

I traced him by his lantern light,
And gave him hint, alas for me,
Of how she found her in the plight
That is so scorned in Christendie.

'Is there an herb. . . . ?' I asked. 'Or none?'
Yes, thus I asked him desperately.
'—There is', he said; 'a certain one. . . .'
Would he had sworn that none knew he!

40

'To-morrow I will walk your way,'
He hinted low, alas for me.—
Fieldwards I gazed throughout next day;
Now fields I never more would see!

The sunset-shine, as curfew strook,
As curfew strook beyond the lea,
Lit his white smock and gleaming crook,
While slowly he drew near to me.

He pulled from underneath his smock
The herb I sought, my curse to be—
'At times I use it in my flock,'
He said, and hope waxed strong in me.

50

''Tis meant to balk ill-motherings'—
(Ill-motherings! Why should they be?)—
'If not, would God have sent such things?'
So spoke the shepherd unto me.

That night I watched the poppling brew,
With bended back and hand on knee:
I stirred it till the dawnlight grew,
And the wind whiffled wailfully.

60

'This scandal shall be slain', said I,
'That lours upon her innocency:
I'll give all whispering tongues the lie;'—
But worse than whispers was to be.

'Here's physic for untimely fruit,'
I said to her, alas for me,
Early that morn in fond salute;
And in my grave I now would be.

—Next Sunday came, with sweet church chimes,
Next Sunday came, alas for me: 70
I went into her room betimes;
No more may such a Sunday be!

'Mother, instead of rescue nigh,'
She faintly breathed, alas for me,
'I feel as I were like to die,
And underground soon, soon should be.'

From church that noon the people walked
In twos and threes, alas for me,
Showed their new raiment—smiled and talked,
Though sackcloth-clad I longed to be.   80

Came to my door her lover's friends,
And cheerly cried, alas for me,
'Right glad are we he makes amends,
For never a sweeter bride can be.'

My mouth dried, as 'twere scorched within,
Dried at their words, alas for me:
More and more neighbours crowded in,
(O why should mothers ever be!)

'Ha-ha! Such well-kept news!' laughed they,
Yes—so they laughed, alas for me.   90
'Whose banns were called in church to-day?'—
Christ, how I wished my soul could flee!

'Where is she? O the stealthy miss,'
Still bantered they, alas for me,
'To keep a wedding close as this. . . .'
Ay, Fortune worked thus wantonly!

'But you are pale—you did not know?'
They archly asked, alas for me.
I stammered, 'Yes—some days—ago,'
While coffined clay I wished to be.   100

''Twas done to please her, we surmise?'
(They spoke quite lightly in their glee)
'Done by him as a fond surprise?'
I thought their words would madden me.

Her lover entered. 'Where's my bird?—
My bird—my flower—my picotee?
First time of asking, soon the third!'
Ah, in my grave I well may be.

To me he whispered: 'Since your call—'
So spoke he then, alas for me—   110
'I've felt for her, and righted all.'
—I think of it to agony.

'She's faint to-day—tired—nothing more—'
Thus did I lie, alas for me. . . .
I called her at her chamber door
As one who scarce had strength to be.

No voice replied. I went within—
O women! scourged the worst are we. . . .
I shrieked. The others hastened in
And saw the stroke there dealt on me.   120

There she lay—silent, breathless, dead,
Stone-dead she lay—wronged, sinless she!—
Ghost-white the cheeks once rosy-red:
Death had took her. Death took not me.

I kissed her colding face and hair,
I kissed her corpse—the bride to be!—
My punishment I cannot bear,
But pray God *not* to pity me.

January 1904.

The House of Hospitalities

Here we broached the Christmas barrel,
    Pushed up the charred log-ends;
Here we sang the Christmas carol,
    And called in friends.

Time has tired me since we met here
    When the folk now dead were young,
Since the viands were outset here
    And quaint songs sung.

And the worm has bored the viol
    That used to lead the tune,   10
Rust eaten out the dial
    That struck night's noon.

Now no Christmas brings in neighbours,
    And the New Year comes unlit;
Where we sang the mole now labours,
    And spiders knit.

Yet at midnight if here walking,
    When the moon sheets wall and tree,
I see forms of old time talking,
    Who smile on me.   20

The Curate's Kindness

A Workhouse Irony

I

I thought they'd be strangers aroun' me,
    But she's to be there!
Let me jump out o' waggon and go back and drown me
    At Pummery or Ten-Hatches Weir.

II

I thought: 'Well, I've come to the Union—
    The workhouse at last—
After honest hard work all the week, and Communion
    O'Zundays, these fifty years past.

III

''Tis hard; but', I thought, 'never mind it:
    There's gain in the end: 10
And when I get used to the place I shall find it
    A home, and may find there a friend.

IV

'Life there will be better than t'other,
    For peace is assured.
The men in one wing and their wives in another
    Is strictly the rule of the Board.'

V

Just then our young Pa'son arriving
    Steps up out of breath
To the side o' the waggon wherein we were driving
    To Union; and calls out and saith: 20

VI

'Old folks, that harsh order is altered,
    Be not sick of heart!
The Guardians they poohed and they pished and they paltered
    When urged not to keep you apart.

VII

'"It is wrong", I maintained, "to divide them,
    Near forty years wed."
"Very well, sir. We promise, then, they shall abide them
    In one wing together," they said.'

VIII

Then I sank—knew 'twas quite a foredone thing
    That misery should be   30
To the end! ... To get freed of her there was the one thing
    Had made the change welcome to me.

IX

To go there was ending but badly;
    'Twas shame and 'twas pain;
'But anyhow,' thought I, 'thereby I shall gladly
    Get free of this forty years' chain.'

X

I thought they'd be strangers aroun' me,
    But she's to be there!
Let me jump out o' waggon and go back and drown me
    At Pummery or Ten-Hatches Weir.   40

The Farm-Woman's Winter

I

If seasons all were summers,
    And leaves would never fall,
And hopping casement-comers
    Were foodless not at all,
And fragile folk might be here
    That white winds bid depart;
Then one I used to see here
    Would warm my wasted heart!

II

One frail, who, bravely tilling
   Long hours in gripping gusts,   10
Was mastered by their chilling,
   And now his ploughshare rusts.
So savage winter catches
   The breath of limber things,
And what I love he snatches,
   And what I love not, brings.

Bereft

   In the black winter morning
No light will be struck near my eyes
While the clock in the stairway is warning
For five, when he used to rise.
      Leave the door unbarred,
      The clock unwound,
      Make my lone bed hard—
      Would 'twere underground!

   When the summer dawns clearly,
And the appletree-tops seem alight,   10
Who will undraw the curtain and cheerly
Call out that the morning is bright?

   When I tarry at market
No form will cross Durnover Lea
In the gathering darkness, to hark at
Grey's Bridge for the pit-pat o' me.

   When the supper crock's steaming,
And the time is the time of his tread,
I shall sit by the fire and wait dreaming
In a silence as of the dead.   20
      Leave the door unbarred,
      The clock unwound,
      Make my lone bed hard—
      Would 'twere underground!

1901.

She Hears the Storm

There was a time in former years—
      While my roof-tree was his—
When I should have been distressed by fears
      At such a night as this.

I should have murmured anxiously,
      'The pricking rain strikes cold;
His road is bare of hedge or tree,
      And he is getting old.'

But now the fitful chimney-roar,
      The drone of Thorncombe trees,   10
The Froom in flood upon the moor,
      The mud of Mellstock Leaze,

The candle slanting sooty wick'd,
      The thuds upon the thatch,
The eaves-drops on the window flicked,
      The clacking garden-hatch,

And what they mean to wayfarers,
      I scarcely heed or mind;
He has won that storm-tight roof of hers
      Which Earth grants all her kind.   20

Autumn in King's Hintock Park

         Here by the baring bough
            Raking up leaves,
         Often I ponder how
            Springtime deceives,—
         I, an old woman now,
            Raking up leaves.

         Here in the avenue
            Raking up leaves,

Lords' ladies pass in view,
    Until one heaves   10
Sighs at life's russet hue,
    Raking up leaves!

Just as my shape you see
    Raking up leaves,
I saw, when fresh and free,
    Those memory weaves
Into grey ghosts by me,
    Raking up leaves.

Yet, Dear, though one may sigh,
    Raking up leaves,   20
New leaves will dance on high—
    Earth never grieves!—
Will not, when missed am I
    Raking up leaves.

                                            1901.

Shut Out That Moon

Close up the casement, draw the blind,
    Shut out that stealing moon,
She bears too much the guise she wore
    Before our lutes were strewn
With years-deep dust, and names we read
    On a white stone were hewn.

Step not forth on the dew-dashed lawn
    To view the Lady's Chair,°
Immense Orion's glittering form,
    The Less and Greater Bear: 10
Stay in; to such sights we were drawn
    When faded ones were fair.

Brush not the bough for midnight scents
    That come forth lingeringly,

And wake the same sweet sentiments
   They breathed to you and me
When living seemed a laugh, and love
   All it was said to be.

Within the common lamp-lit room
   Prison my eyes and thought;   20
Let dingy details crudely loom,
   Mechanic speech be wrought:
Too fragrant was Life's early bloom,
   Too tart the fruit it brought!

             1904.

Reminiscences of a Dancing Man

I

Who now remembers Almack's balls—
   Willis's sometime named—
In those two smooth-floored upper halls
   For faded ones so famed?
Where as we trod to trilling sound
The fancied phantoms stood around,
   Or joined us in the maze,
Of the powdered Dears from Georgian years,
Whose dust lay in sightless sealed-up biers,
   The fairest of former days.   10

II

Who now remembers gay Cremorne,
   And all its jaunty jills,
And those wild whirling figures born
   Of Jullien's grand quadrilles?°
With hats on head and morning coats
There footed to his prancing notes
   Our partner-girls and we;
And the gas-jets winked, and the lustres clinked,
And the platform throbbed as with arms enlinked
   We moved to the minstrelsy.   20

III

Who now recalls those crowded rooms
    Of old yclept 'The Argyll',
Where to the deep Drum-polka's booms
    We hopped in standard style?
Whither have danced those damsels now!
Is Death the partner who doth moue
    Their wormy chaps and bare?
Do their spectres spin like sparks within
The smoky halls of the Prince of Sin
    To a thunderous Jullien air?   30

The Dead Man Walking

They hail me as one living,
    But don't they know
That I have died of late years,
    Untombed although?

I am but a shape that stands here,
    A pulseless mould,
A pale past picture, screening
    Ashes gone cold.

Not at a minute's warning,
    Not in a loud hour,   10
For me ceased Time's enchantments
    In hall and bower.

There was no tragic transit,
    No catch of breath,
When silent seasons inched me
    On to this death. . . .

—A Troubadour-youth I rambled
    With Life for lyre,
The beats of being raging
    In me like fire.   20

But when I practised eyeing
    The goal of men,
It iced me, and I perished
    A little then.

When passed my friend, my kinsfolk,
    Through the Last Door,
And left me standing bleakly,
    I died yet more;

And when my Love's heart kindled
    In hate of me,   30
Wherefore I knew not, died I
    One more degree.

And if when I died fully
    I cannot say,
And changed into the corpse-thing
    I am to-day;

Yet is it that, though whiling
    The time somehow
In walking, talking, smiling,
    I live not now.   40

The Division

Rain on the windows, creaking doors,
    With blasts that besom the green,
And I am here, and you are there,
    And a hundred miles between!

O were it but the weather, Dear,
    O were it but the miles
That summed up all our severance,
    There might be room for smiles.

But that thwart thing betwixt us twain,
    Which nothing cleaves or clears,   10
Is more than distance, Dear, or rain,
    And longer than the years!

                1893.

On the Departure Platform

We kissed at the barrier; and passing through
She left me, and moment by moment got
Smaller and smaller, until to my view
    She was but a spot;

A wee white spot of muslin fluff
That down the diminishing platform bore
Through hustling crowds of gentle and rough
    To the carriage door.

Under the lamplight's fitful glowers,
Behind dark groups from far and near,   10
Whose interests were apart from ours,
    She would disappear,

Then show again, till I ceased to see
That flexible form, that nebulous white;
And she who was more than my life to me
    Had vanished quite. . . .

We have penned new plans since that fair fond day,
And in season she will appear again—
Perhaps in the same soft white array—
    But never as then!   20

—'And why, young man, must eternally fly
A joy you'll repeat, if you love her well?'
—O friend, nought happens twice thus; why,
    I cannot tell!

In a Cathedral City

These people have not heard your name;
No loungers in this placid place
Have helped to bruit your beauty's fame.

The grey Cathedral, towards whose face
Bend eyes untold, has met not yours;
Your shade has never swept its base,

Your form has never darked its doors,
Nor have your faultless feet once thrown
A pensive pit-pat on its floors.

Along the street to maids well known   10
Blithe lovers hum their tender airs,
But in your praise voice not a tone. . . .

—Since nought bespeaks you here, or bears,
As I, your imprint through and through,
Here might I rest, till my heart shares
The spot's unconsciousness of you!

Salisbury.

'I say I'll seek her'

I say, 'I'll seek her side
    Ere hindrance interposes';
    But eve in midnight closes,
And here I still abide.

When darkness wears I see
    Her sad eyes in a vision;
    They ask, 'What indecision
Detains you, Love, from me?—

'The creaking hinge is oiled,
    I have unbarred the backway,   10
      But you tread not the trackway;
And shall the thing be spoiled?

'Far cockcrows echo shrill,
    The shadows are abating,
      And I am waiting, waiting;
But O, you tarry still!'

The End of the Episode

Indulge no more may we
In this sweet-bitter pastime:
The love-light shines the last time
    Between you, Dear, and me.

There shall remain no trace
Of what so closely tied us,
And blank as ere love eyed us
    Will be our meeting-place.

The flowers and thymy air,
Will they now miss our coming?   10
The dumbles thin their humming
    To find we haunt not there?

Though fervent was our vow,
Though ruddily ran our pleasure,
Bliss has fulfilled its measure,
    And sees its sentence now.

Ache deep; but make no moans:
Smile out; but stilly suffer:
The paths of love are rougher
    Than thoroughfares of stones.   20

The Sun on the Letter

I drew the letter out, while gleamed
The sloping sun from under a roof
Of cloud whose verge rose visibly.

The burning ball flung rays that seemed
Stretched like a warp without a woof
Across the levels of the lea

To where I stood, and where they beamed
As brightly on the page of proof
That she had shown her false to me

As if it had shown her true—had teemed   10
With passionate thought for my behoof
Expressed with their own ardency!

The Night of the Dance

The cold moon hangs to the sky by its horn,
    And centres its gaze on me;
The stars, like eyes in reverie,
Their westering as for a while forborne,
    Quiz downward curiously.

Old Robert draws the backbrand in,
    The green logs steam and spit;
The half-awakened sparrows flit
From the riddled thatch; and owls begin
    To whoo from the gable-slit.   10

Yes; far and nigh things seem to know
    Sweet scenes are impending here;
That all is prepared; that the hour is near
For welcomes, fellowships, and flow
    Of sally, song, and cheer;

That spigots are pulled and viols strung;
   That soon will arise the sound
Of measures trod to tunes renowned;
That She will return in Love's low tongue
   My vows as we wheel around.   20

The Voice of the Thorn

I

When the thorn on the down
  Quivers naked and cold,
  And the mid-aged and old
Pace the path there to town,
  In these words dry and drear
    It seems to them sighing:
    'O winter is trying
  To sojourners here!'

II

When it stands fully tressed
  On a hot summer day,   10
  And the ewes there astray
Find its shade a sweet rest,
  By the breath of the breeze
    It inquires of each farer:
    'Who would not be sharer
  Of shadow with these?'

III

But by day or by night,
  And in winter or summer,
  Should I be the comer
Along that lone height,   20
  In its voicing to me
    Only one speech is spoken:
    'Here once was nigh broken
  A heart, and by thee.'

He Abjures Love

At last I put off love,
  For twice ten years
The daysman of my thought,
  And hope, and doing;
Being ashamed thereof,
  And faint of fears
And desolations, wrought
  In his pursuing,

Since first in youthtime those
  Disquietings   10
That heart-enslavement brings
  To hale and hoary,
Became my housefellows,
  And, fool and blind,
I turned from kith and kind
  To give him glory.

I was as children be
  Who have no care;
I did not shrink or sigh,
  I did not sicken;   20
But lo, Love beckoned me,
  And I was bare,
And poor, and starved, and dry,
  And fever-stricken.

Too many times ablaze
  With fatuous fires,
Enkindled by his wiles
  To new embraces,
Did I, by wilful ways
  And baseless ires,   30
Return the anxious smiles
  Of friendly faces.

No more will now rate I
  The common rare,
The midnight drizzle dew,
  The gray hour golden,

The wind a yearning cry,
    The faulty fair,
Things dreamt, of comelier hue
    Than things beholden! . . .   40

—I speak as one who plumbs
    Life's dim profound,
One who at length can sound
    Clear views and certain.
But—after love what comes?
    A scene that lours,
A few sad vacant hours,
    And then, the Curtain.

                                    1883.

Let Me Enjoy

(*Minor Key*)

I

Let me enjoy the earth no less
Because the all-enacting Might
That fashioned forth its loveliness
Had other aims than my delight.

II

About my path there flits a Fair,
Who throws me not a word or sign;
I'll charm me with her ignoring air,
And laud the lips not meant for mine.

III

From manuscripts of moving song
Inspired by scenes and dreams unknown   10
I'll pour out raptures that belong
To others, as they were my own.

IV

And some day hence, toward Paradise
And all its blest—if such should be—
I will lift glad, afar-off eyes,
Though it contain no place for me.

At Casterbridge Fair

I

THE BALLAD-SINGER

Sing, Ballad-singer, raise a hearty tune;
Make me forget that there was ever a one
I walked with in the meek light of the moon
    When the day's work was done.

Rhyme, Ballad-rhymer, start a country song;
Make me forget that she whom I loved well
Swore she would love me dearly, love me long,
    Then—what I cannot tell!

Sing, Ballad-singer, from your little book;
Make me forget those heart-breaks, achings, fears;   10
Make me forget her name, her sweet sweet look—
    Make me forget her tears.

II

FORMER BEAUTIES

These market-dames, mid-aged, with lips thin-drawn,
    And tissues sere,
Are they the ones we loved in years agone,
    And courted here?

Are these the muslined pink young things to whom
    We vowed and swore
In nooks on summer Sundays by the Froom,
    Or Budmouth shore?

Do they remember those gay tunes we trod
    Clasped on the green;   10
Aye; trod till moonlight set on the beaten sod
    A satin sheen?

They must forget, forget! They cannot know
    What once they were,
Or memory would transfigure them, and show
    Them always fair.

III

AFTER THE CLUB-DANCE

Black'on frowns east on Maidon,
    And westward to the sea,
But on neither is his frown laden
    With scorn, as his frown on me!

At dawn my heart grew heavy,
    I could not sip the wine,
I left the jocund bevy
    And that young man o' mine.

The roadside elms pass by me,—
    Why do I sink with shame   10
When the birds a-perch there eye me?
    They, too, have done the same!

IV

THE MARKET-GIRL

Nobody took any notice of her as she stood on the causey kerb,
All eager to sell her honey and apples and bunches of garden
    herb;
And if she had offered to give her wares and herself with them
    too that day,
I doubt if a soul would have cared to take a bargain so choice
    away.

But chancing to trace her sunburnt grace that morning as I
    passed nigh,
I went and I said, 'Poor maidy dear!—and will none of the people
    buy?'
And so it began; and soon we knew what the end of it all must be,
And I found that though no others had bid, a prize had been
    won by me.

V

THE INQUIRY

And are ye one of Hermitage—
Of Hermitage, by Ivel Road,
And do ye know, in Hermitage,
A thatch-roofed house where sengreens grow?
And does John Waywood live there still—
He of the name that there abode
When father hurdled on the hill
    Some fifteen years ago?

Does he now speak o' Patty Beech,
The Patty Beech he used to—see,   10
Or ask at all if Patty Beech
Is known or heard of out this way?
—Ask ever if she's living yet,
And where her present home may be,
And how she bears life's fag and fret
    After so long a day?

In years agone at Hermitage
This faded face was counted fair,
None fairer; and at Hermitage
We swore to wed when he should thrive.   20
But never a chance had he or I,
And waiting made his wish outwear,
And Time, that dooms man's love to die,
    Preserves a maid's alive.

VI

A WIFE WAITS

Will's at the dance in the Club-room below,
  Where the tall liquor-cups foam;
I on the pavement up here by the Bow,°
  Wait, wait, to steady him home.

Will and his partner are treading a tune,
  Loving companions they be;
Willy before we were married in June,
  Said he loved no one but me;

Said he would let his old pleasures all go
  Ever to live with his Dear.   10
Will's at the dance in the Club-room below,
  Shivering I wait for him here.

VII

AFTER THE FAIR

The singers are gone from the Cornmarket-place
  With their broadsheets of rhymes,
The street rings no longer in treble and bass
  With their skits on the times,
And the Cross, lately thronged, is a dim naked space
  That but echoes the stammering chimes.°

From Clock-corner steps, as each quarter ding-dongs,
  Away the folk roam
By the 'Hart' and Grey's Bridge into byways and 'drongs',
  Or across the ridged loam;   10
The younger ones shrilling the lately heard songs,
  The old saying, 'Would we were home.'

The shy-seeming maiden so mute in the fair
  Now rattles and talks,
And that one who looked the most swaggering there
  Grows sad as she walks,
And she who seemed eaten by cankering care
  In statuesque sturdiness stalks.

And midnight clears High Street of all but the ghosts
    Of its buried burghees,   20
From the latest far back to those old Roman hosts
    Whose remains one yet sees,
Who loved, laughed, and fought, hailed their friends, drank
    their toasts
  At their meeting-times here, just as these!

                            1902.

The Dark-Eyed Gentleman

I

I pitched my day's leazings in Crimmercrock Lane,°
To tie up my garter and jog on again,
When a dear dark-eyed gentleman passed there and said,
In a way that made all o' me colour rose-red,
      'What do I see—
      O pretty knee!'
And he came and he tied up my garter for me.

II

'Twixt sunset and moonrise it was, I can mind:
Ah, 'tis easy to lose what we nevermore find!—
Of the dear stranger's home, of his name, I knew nought,   10
But I soon knew his nature and all that it brought.
      Then bitterly
      Sobbed I that he
Should ever have tied up my garter for me!

III

Yet now I've beside me a fine lissom lad,
And my slip's nigh forgot, and my days are not sad;
My own dearest joy is he, comrade, and friend,
He it is who safe-guards me, on him I depend;
      No sorrow brings he,
      And thankful I be   20
That his daddy once tied up my garter for me!

Julie-Jane

Sing; how 'a would sing!
How 'a would raise the tune
When we rode in the waggon from harvesting
        By the light o' the moon!

Dance; how 'a would dance!
If a fiddlestring did but sound
She would hold out her coats, give a slanting glance,°
        And go round and round.

Laugh; how 'a would laugh!
Her peony lips would part   10
As if none such a place for a lover to quaff
        At the deeps of a heart.

Julie, O girl of joy,
Soon, soon that lover he came.
Ah, yes; and gave thee a baby-boy,
        But never his name. . . .

—Tolling for her, as you guess;
And the baby too. . . . 'Tis well.
You knew her in maidhood likewise?—Yes,
        That's her burial bell.   20

'I suppose', with a laugh, she said,
'I should blush that I'm not a wife;
But how can it matter, so soon to be dead,
        What one does in life!'

When we sat making the mourning
By her death-bed side, said she,
'Dears, how can you keep from your lovers, adorning
        In honour of me!'

Bubbling and brightsome eyed!
But now—O never again.   30
She chose her bearers before she died
        From her fancy-men.

The Fiddler

The fiddler knows what's brewing
  To the lilt of his lyric wiles:
The fiddler knows what rueing
  Will come of this night's smiles!

He sees couples join them for dancing,
  And afterwards joining for life,
He sees them pay high for their prancing
  By a welter of wedded strife.

He twangs: 'Music hails from the devil,
  Though vaunted to come from heaven,
For it makes people do at a revel
  What multiplies sins by seven.

'There's many a heart now mangled,
  And waiting its time to go,
Whose tendrils were first entangled
  By my sweet viol and bow!'

10

A Church Romance

(Mellstock, *circa* 1835)

She turned in the high pew, until her sight
Swept the west gallery, and caught its row
Of music-men with viol, book, and bow
Against the sinking sad tower-window light.

She turned again; and in her pride's despite
One strenuous viol's inspirer seemed to throw
A message from his string to her below,
Which said: 'I claim thee as my own forthright!'

Thus their hearts' bond began, in due time signed.
And long years thence, when Age had scared Romance,
At some old attitude of his or glance

10

That gallery-scene would break upon her mind,
With him as minstrel, ardent, young, and trim,
Bowing 'New Sabbath' or 'Mount Ephraim'.

The Rash Bride

An Experience of the Mellstock Quire

I

We Christmas-carolled down the Vale, and up the Vale, and
    round the Vale,
We played and sang that night as we were yearly wont to do—
A carol in a minor key, a carol in the major D,
Then at each house: 'Good wishes: many Christmas joys to you!'

II

Next, to the widow's John and I and all the rest drew on. And I
Discerned that John could hardly hold the tongue of him for joy.
The widow was a sweet young thing whom John was bent on
    marrying,
And quiring at her casement seemed romantic to the boy.

III

'She'll make reply, I trust,' said he, 'to our salute? She must!'
    said he,
'And then I will accost her gently—much to her surprise!—   10
For knowing not I am with you here, when I speak up and call
    her dear
A tenderness will fill her voice, a bashfulness her eyes.'

IV

So, by her window-square we stood; ay, with our lanterns there
    we stood,
And he along with us,—not singing, waiting for a sign;
And when we'd quired her carols three a light was lit and out
    looked she,
A shawl about her bedgown, and her colour red as wine.

V

And sweetly then she bowed her thanks, and smiled, and spoke
    aloud her thanks;
When lo, behind her back there, in the room, a man appeared.
I knew him—one from Woolcomb way—Giles Swetman—
    honest as the day,
But eager, hasty; and I felt that some strange trouble neared.   20

VI

'How comes he there? . . . Suppose', said we, 'she's wed of late!
    Who knows?' said we.
—'She married yester-morning—only mother yet has known
The secret o't!' shrilled one small boy. 'But now I've told, let's
    wish 'em joy!'
A heavy fall aroused us: John had gone down like a stone.

VII

We rushed to him and caught him round, and lifted him, and
    brought him round,
When, hearing something wrong had happened, oped the win-
    dow she:
'Has one of you fallen ill?' she asked, 'by these night labours
    overtasked?'
None answered. That she'd done poor John a cruel turn felt we.

VIII

Till up spoke Michael: 'Fie, young dame! You've broke your
    promise, sly young dame,
By forming this new tie, young dame, and jilting John so true,   30
Who trudged to-night to sing to 'ee because he thought he'd
    bring to 'ee
Good wishes as your coming spouse. May ye such trifling rue!'

IX

Her man had said no word at all; but being behind had heard
    it all,
And now cried: 'Neighbours, on my soul I knew not 'twas like
    this!'
And then to her: 'If I had known you'd had in tow not me alone,
No wife should you have been of mine. It is a dear bought bliss!'

X

She changed death-white, and heaved a cry: we'd never heard
    so grieved a cry
As came from her at this from him: heartbroken quite seemed
    she;
And suddenly, as we looked on, she turned, and rushed; and
    she was gone,
Whither, her husband, following after, knew not; nor knew we.   40

XI

We searched till dawn about the house; within the house, with-
    out the house,
We searched among the laurel boughs that grew beneath the
    wall,
And then among the crocks and things, and stores for winter
    junketings,
In linhay, loft, and dairy; but we found her not at all.

XII

Then John rushed in: 'O friends,' he said, 'hear this, this, this!'
    and bends his head:
'I've—searched round by the—*well*, and find the cover open
    wide!
I am fearful that—I can't say what ... Bring lanterns, and some
    cords to knot.'
We did so, and we went and stood the deep dark hole beside.

XIII

And then they, ropes in hand, and I—ay, John, and all the band,
    and I
Let down a lantern to the depths—some hundred feet and more;   50
It glimmered like a fog-dimmed star; and there, beside its light,
    afar,
White drapery floated, and we knew the meaning that it bore.

XIV

The rest is naught ... We buried her o' Sunday. Neighbours
    carried her;
And Swetman—he who'd married her—now miserablest of men,

Walked mourning first; and then walked John; just quivering,
    but composed anon;
And we the quire formed round the grave, as was the custom
    then.

XV

Our old bass player, as I recall—his white hair blown—but why
    recall!—
His viol upstrapped, bent figure—doomed to follow her full
    soon—
Stood bowing, pale and tremulous; and next to him the rest of
    us. . . .
We sang the Ninetieth Psalm to her—set to 'Saint Stephen's'
    tune.   60

The Christening

Whose child is this they bring
    Into the aisle?—
At so superb a thing
The congregation smile
And turn their heads awhile.

Its eyes are blue and bright,
    Its cheeks like rose;
Its simple robes unite
Whitest of calicoes
With lawn, and satin bows.   10

A pride in the human race
    At this paragon
Of mortals, lights each face
While the old rite goes on;
But ah, they are shocked anon.

What girl is she who peeps
    From the gallery stair,
Smiles palely, redly weeps,
With feverish furtive air
As though not fitly there?   20

'I am the baby's mother;
  This gem of the race
The decent fain would smother,
And for my deep disgrace
I am bidden to leave the place.'

'Where is the baby's father?'—
  'In the woods afar.
He says there is none he'd rather
Meet under moon or star
Than me, of all that are.   30

'To clasp me in lovelike weather,
  Wish fixing when,
He says: To be together
At will, just now and then,
Makes him the blest of men;

'But chained and doomed for life
  To slovening
As vulgar man and wife,
He says, is another thing:
Yea: sweet Love's sepulchring!'   40

      1904.

The Roman Road

The Roman Road runs straight and bare
As the pale parting-line in hair
Across the heath. And thoughtful men
Contrast its days of Now and Then,
And delve, and measure, and compare;

Visioning on the vacant air
Helmed legionaries, who proudly rear
The Eagle, as they pace again
    The Roman Road.

But no tall brass-helmed legionnaire   10
Haunts it for me. Uprises there
A mother's form upon my ken,
Guiding my infant steps, as when
We walked that ancient thoroughfare,
            The Roman Road.

The Reminder

While I watch the Christmas blaze
Paint the room with ruddy rays,
Something makes my vision glide
To the frosty scene outside.

There, to reach a rotting berry,
Toils a thrush,—constrained to very
Dregs of food by sharp distress,
Taking such with thankfulness.

Why, O starving bird, when I
One day's joy would justify,   10
And put misery out of view,
Do you make me notice you!

Night in the Old Home

When the wasting embers redden the chimney-breast,
And Life's bare pathway looms like a desert track to me,
And from hall and parlour the living have gone to their rest,
My perished people who housed them here come back to me.

They come and seat them around in their mouldy places,
Now and then bending towards me a glance of wistfulness,
A strange upbraiding smile upon all their faces,
And in the bearing of each a passive tristfulness.

'Do you uphold me, lingering and languishing here,
A pale late plant of your once strong stock?' I say to them;   10
'A thinker of crooked thoughts upon Life in the sere,
And on That which consigns men to night after showing the day
    to them?'

'—O let be the Wherefore! We fevered our years not thus:
Take of Life what it grants, without question!' they answer me
    seemingly.
'Enjoy, suffer, wait: spread the table here freely like us,
And, satisfied, placid, unfretting, watch Time away beamingly!'

After the Last Breath

(J. H. 1813–1904)

There's no more to be done, or feared, or hoped;
None now need watch, speak low, and list, and tire;
No irksome crease outsmoothed, no pillow sloped
        Does she require.

Blankly we gaze. We are free to go or stay;
Our morrow's anxious plans have missed their aim;
Whether we leave to-night or wait till day
        Counts as the same.

The lettered vessels of medicaments
Seem asking wherefore we have set them here;   10
Each palliative its silly face presents
        As useless gear.

And yet we feel that something savours well;
We note a numb relief withheld before;
Our well-beloved is prisoner in the cell
        Of Time no more.

We see by littles now the deft achievement
Whereby she has escaped the Wrongers all,
In view of which our momentary bereavement
        Outshapes but small.   20

                                    1904.

The Pine Planters

(Marty South's Reverie)

I

We work here together
 In blast and breeze;
He fills the earth in,
 I hold the trees.

He does not notice
 That what I do
Keeps me from moving
 And chills me through.

He has seen one fairer
 I feel by his eye,   10
Which skims me as though
 I were not by.

And since she passed here
 He scarce has known
But that the woodland
 Holds him alone.

I have worked here with him
 Since morning shine,
He busy with his thoughts
 And I with mine.   20

I have helped him so many,
 So many days,
But never win any
 Small word of praise!

Shall I not sigh to him
 That I work on
Glad to be nigh to him
 Though hope is gone?

Nay, though he never
     Knew love like mine,   30
I'll bear it ever
     And make no sign!

                    II

From the bundle at hand here
     I take each tree,
And set it to stand, here
     Always to be;
When, in a second,
     As if from fear
Of Life unreckoned
     Beginning here,   40
It starts a sighing
     Through day and night,
Though while there lying
     'Twas voiceless quite.

It will sigh in the morning,
     Will sigh at noon,
At the winter's warning,
     In wafts of June;
Grieving that never
     Kind Fate decreed   50
It should for ever
     Remain a seed,
And shun the welter
     Of things without,
Unneeding shelter
     From storm and drought.

Thus, all unknowing
     For whom or what
We set it growing
     In this bleak spot,   60
It still will grieve here
     Throughout its time,
Unable to leave here,
     Or change its clime;

Or tell the story
Of us to-day
When, halt and hoary,
We pass away.

One We Knew

(M. H. 1772–1857)

She told how they used to form for the country dances—
'The Triumph', 'The New-rigged Ship'—
To the light of the guttering wax in the panelled manses,
And in cots to the blink of a dip.

She spoke of the wild 'poussetting' and 'allemanding'
On carpet, on oak, and on sod;
And the two long rows of ladies and gentlemen standing,
And the figures the couples trod.

She showed us the spot where the maypole was yearly planted,
And where the bandsmen stood   10
While breeched and kerchiefed partners whirled, and panted
To choose each other for good.

She told of that far-back day when they learnt astounded
Of the death of the King of France:
Of the Terror; and then of Bonaparte's unbounded
Ambition and arrogance.

Of how his threats woke warlike preparations
Along the southern strand,
And how each night brought tremors and trepidations
Lest morning should see him land.   20

She said she had often heard the gibbet creaking
As it swayed in the lightning flash,
Had caught from the neighbouring town a small child's shrieking
At the cart-tail under the lash. . . .

With cap-framed face and long gaze into the embers—
      We seated around her knees—
She would dwell on such dead themes, not as one who
            remembers,
      But rather as one who sees.

She seemed one left behind of a band gone distant
      So far that no tongue could hail: 30
Past things retold were to her as things existent,
      Things present but as a tale.

May 20, 1902.

A Wet Night

I pace along, the rain-shafts riddling me,
Mile after mile out by the moorland way,
And up the hill, and through the ewe-leaze gray
Into the lane, and round the corner tree;

Where, as my clothing clams me, mire-bestarred,
And the enfeebled light dies out of day,
Leaving the liquid shades to reign, I say,
'This is a hardship to be calendared!'

Yet sires of mine now perished and forgot,
When worse beset, ere roads were shapen here,   10
And night and storm were foes indeed to fear,
Times numberless have trudged across this spot
In sturdy muteness on their strenuous lot,
And taking all such toils as trifles mere.

New Year's Eve

'I have finished another year', said God,
      'In grey, green, white, and brown;
I have strewn the leaf upon the sod,
Sealed up the worm within the clod,
      And let the last sun down.'

'And what's the good of it?' I said.
　　'What reasons made you call
From formless void this earth we tread,
When nine-and-ninety can be read
　　Why nought should be at all?　　　　10

'Yea, Sire; why shaped you us, who "in
　　This tabernacle groan"—°
If ever a joy be found herein,
Such joy no man had wished to win
　　If he had never known!'

Then he: 'My labours—logicless—
　　You may explain; not I:
Sense-sealed I have wrought, without a guess
That I evolved a Consciousness
　　To ask for reasons why.　　　　20

'Strange that ephemeral creatures who
　　By my own ordering are,
Should see the shortness of my view,
Use ethic tests I never knew,
　　Or made provision for!'

He sank to raptness as of yore,
　　And opening New Year's Day
Wove it by rote as theretofore,
And went on working evermore
　　In his unweeting way.　　　　30

　　　　　　　　1906.

God's Education

I saw him steal the light away
　　That haunted in her eye:
It went so gently none could say
More than that it was there one day
　　And missing by-and-by.

I watched her longer, and he stole
  Her lily tincts and rose;
All her young sprightliness of soul
Next fell beneath his cold control,
  And disappeared like those.   10

I asked: 'Why do you serve her so?
  Do you, for some glad day,
Hoard these her sweets—?' He said, 'O no,
They charm not me; I bid Time throw
  Them carelessly away.'

Said I: 'We call that cruelty—
  We, your poor mortal kind.'
He mused. 'The thought is new to me.
Forsooth, though I men's master be
  Theirs is the teaching mind!'   20

The Unborn

I rose at night, and visited
  The Cave of the Unborn:
And crowding shapes surrounded me
For tidings of the life to be,
Who long had prayed the silent Head
  To haste its advent morn.

Their eyes were lit with artless trust,
  Hope thrilled their every tone;
'A scene the loveliest, is it not?
A pure delight, a beauty-spot   10
Where all is gentle, true and just,
  And darkness is unknown?'

My heart was anguished for their sake,
  I could not frame a word;
And they descried my sunken face,
And seemed to read therein, and trace
The news that pity would not break,
  Nor truth leave unaverred.

And as I silently retired
    I turned and watched them still,   20
And they came helter-skelter out,
Driven forward like a rabble rout
Into the world they had so desired
    By the all-immanent Will.

1905.

The Man He Killed

'Had he and I but met
    By some old ancient inn,
We should have sat us down to wet
    Right many a nipperkin!

'But ranged as infantry,
    And staring face to face,
I shot at him as he at me,
    And killed him in his place.

'I shot him dead because—
    Because he was my foe,   10
Just so: my foe of course he was;
    That's clear enough; although

'He thought he'd 'list, perhaps,
    Off-hand like—just as I—
Was out of work—had sold his traps—
    No other reason why.

'Yes; quaint and curious war is!
    You shoot a fellow down
You'd treat if met where any bar is,
    Or help to half-a-crown.'   20

1902.

One Ralph Blossom Soliloquizes

('It being deposed that vij women who were mayds before he knew them have
been brought upon the towne [rates?] by the fornicacions of one Ralph Blossom,
Mr Maior inquired why he should not contribute xiv pence weekly toward their
mayntenance. But it being shewn that the sayd R. B. was dying of a purple
feaver, no order was made.'—*Budmouth Borough Minutes*: 16—.)

When I am in hell or some such place,
A-groaning over my sorry case,
What will those seven women say to me
Who, when I coaxed them, answered 'Aye' to me?

'I did not understand your sign!'
Will be the words of Caroline;
While Jane will cry, 'If I'd had proof of you,
I should have learnt to hold aloof of you!'

'I won't reproach: it was to be!'
Will drily murmur Cicely;   10
And Rosa: 'I feel no hostility,
For I must own I lent facility.'

Lizzy says: 'Sharp was my regret,
And sometimes it is now! But yet
I joy that, though it brought notoriousness,
I knew Love once and all its gloriousness!'

Says Patience: 'Why are we apart?
Small harm did you, my poor Sweet Heart!
A manchild born, now tall and beautiful,
Was worth the ache of days undutiful.'   20

And Anne cries: 'O the time was fair,
So wherefore should you burn down there?
There is a deed under the sun, my Love,
And that was ours. What's done is done, my Love.
These trumpets here in Heaven are dumb to me
With you away. Dear, come, O come to me!'

George Meredith

1828–1909

Forty years back, when much had place
That since has perished out of mind,
I heard that voice and saw that face.

He spoke as one afoot will wind
A morning horn ere men awake;
His note was trenchant, turning kind.

He was of those whose wit can shake
And riddle to the very core
The counterfeits that Time will break. . . .

Of late, when we two met once more,   10
The luminous countenance and rare
Shone just as forty years before.

So that, when now all tongues declare
His shape unseen by his green hill,
I scarce believe he sits not there.

No matter. Further and further still
Through the world's vaporous vitiate air
His words wing on—as live words will.

May, 1909.

Yell'ham-Wood's Story

Coomb-Firtrees say that Life is a moan,
    And Clyffe-hill Clump says 'Yea!'
But Yell'ham says a thing of its own:
      It's not 'Gray, gray
      Is Life alway!'
     That Yell'ham says,
Nor that Life is for ends unknown.

It says that Life would signify
  A thwarted purposing:
That we come to live, and are called to die.   10
        Yes, that's the thing
        In fall, in spring,
        That Yell'ham says:—
      'Life offers—to deny!'

                              1902.

In Front of the Landscape

Plunging and labouring on in a tide of visions,
    Dolorous and dear,
Forward I pushed my way as amid waste waters
    Stretching around,
Through whose eddies there glimmered the customed landscape
    Yonder and near

Blotted to feeble mist. And the coomb and the upland
    Coppice-crowned,
Ancient chalk-pit, milestone, rills in the grass-flat
    Stroked by the light,   10
Seemed but a ghost-like gauze, and no substantial
    Meadow or mound.

What were the infinite spectacles featuring foremost
    Under my sight,
Hindering me to discern my paced advancement
    Lengthening to miles;
What were the re-creations killing the daytime
    As by the night?

O they were speechful faces, gazing insistent,
    Some as with smiles,   20
Some as with slow-born tears that brinily trundled
    Over the wrecked
Cheeks that were fair in their flush-time, ash now with anguish,
    Harrowed by wiles.

Yes, I could see them, feel them, hear them, address them—
    Halo-bedecked—
And, alas, onwards, shaken by fierce unreason,
    Rigid in hate,
Smitten by years-long wryness born of misprision,
    Dreaded, suspect.   30

Then there would breast me shining sights, sweet seasons
　　Further in date;
Instruments of strings with the tenderest passion
　　Vibrant, beside
Lamps long extinguished, robes, cheeks, eyes with the earth's
　　crust
　　Now corporate.

Also there rose a headland of hoary aspect
　　Gnawed by the tide,
Frilled by the nimb of the morning as two friends stood there
　　Guilelessly glad—
Wherefore they knew not—touched by the fringe of an ecstasy　　　40
　　Scantly descried.

Later images too did the day unfurl me,
　　Shadowed and sad,
Clay cadavers of those who had shared in the dramas,
　　Laid now at ease,
Passions all spent, chiefest the one of the broad brow
　　Sepulture-clad.

So did beset me scenes miscalled of the bygone,
　　Over the leaze,
Past the clump, and down to where lay the beheld ones;　　　　50
　　—Yea, as the rhyme
Sung by the sea-swell, so in their pleading dumbness
　　Captured me these.

For, their lost revisiting manifestations
　　In their live time
Much had I slighted, caring not for their purport,
　　Seeing behind
Things more coveted, reckoned the better worth calling
　　Sweet, sad, sublime.　　　　　　　　　　　　　　　60

Thus do they now show hourly before the intenser
　　Stare of the mind
As they were ghosts avenging their slights by my bypast
　　Body-borne eyes,
Show, too, with fuller translation than rested upon them
　　As living kind.

Hence wag the tongues of the passing people, saying
     In their surmise,
'Ah—whose is this dull form that perambulates, seeing nought
     Round him that looms   70
Whithersoever his footsteps turn in his farings,
     Save a few tombs?'

Channel Firing

     That night your great guns, unawares,
     Shook all our coffins as we lay,
     And broke the chancel window-squares,
     We thought it was the Judgment-day

     And sat upright. While drearisome
     Arose the howl of wakened hounds:
     The mouse let fall the altar-crumb,
     The worms drew back into the mounds,

     The glebe cow drooled. Till God called, 'No;
     It's gunnery practice out at sea   10
     Just as before you went below;
     The world is as it used to be:

     'All nations striving strong to make
     Red war yet redder. Mad as hatters
     They do no more for Christés sake
     Than you who are helpless in such matters.

     'That this is not the judgment-hour
     For some of them's a blessed thing,
     For if it were they'd have to scour
     Hell's floor for so much threatening. . . .   20

     'Ha, ha. It will be warmer when
     I blow the trumpet (if indeed
     I ever do; for you are men,
     And rest eternal sorely need).'

So down we lay again. 'I wonder,
Will the world ever saner be',
Said one, 'than when He sent us under
In our indifferent century!'

And many a skeleton shook his head.
'Instead of preaching forty year,'   30
My neighbour Parson Thirdly said,
'I wish I had stuck to pipes and beer.'

Again the guns disturbed the hour,
Roaring their readiness to avenge,
As far inland as Stourton Tower,
And Camelot, and starlit Stonehenge.

April 1914.

The Convergence of the Twain

(Lines on the loss of the *Titanic*)

I

In a solitude of the sea
Deep from human vanity,
And the Pride of Life that planned her, stilly couches she.

II

Steel chambers, late the pyres
Of her salamandrine fires,
Cold currents thrid, and turn to rhythmic tidal lyres.

III

Over the mirrors meant
To glass the opulent
The sea-worm crawls—grotesque, slimed, dumb, indifferent.

IV

Jewels in joy designed   10
To ravish the sensuous mind
Lie lightless, all their sparkles bleared and black and blind.

V

Dim moon-eyed fishes near
Gaze at the gilded gear
And query: 'What does this vaingloriousness down here?' ...

VI

Well: while was fashioning
This creature of cleaving wing,
The Immanent Will that stirs and urges everything

VII

Prepared a sinister mate
For her—so gaily great—   20
A Shape of Ice, for the time far and dissociate.

VIII

And as the smart ship grew
In stature, grace, and hue,
In shadowy silent distance grew the Iceberg too.

IX

Alien they seemed to be:
No mortal eye could see
The intimate welding of their later history,

X

Or sign that they were bent
By paths coincident
On being anon twin halves of one august event,   30

XI

Till the Spinner of the Years
Said 'Now!' And each one hears,
And consummation comes, and jars two hemispheres.

The Ghost of the Past

We two kept house, the Past and I,
        The Past and I;
Through all my tasks it hovered nigh,
        Leaving me never alone.
It was a spectral housekeeping
        Where fell no jarring tone,
As strange, as still a housekeeping
        As ever has been known.

As daily I went up the stair,
        And down the stair,   10
I did not mind the Bygone there—
        The Present once to me;
Its moving meek companionship
        I wished might ever be,
There was in that companionship
        Something of ecstasy.

It dwelt with me just as it was,
        Just as it was
When first its prospects gave me pause
        In wayward wanderings,   20
Before the years had torn old troths
        As they tear all sweet things,
Before gaunt griefs had torn old troths
        And dulled old rapturings.

And then its form began to fade,
        Began to fade,
Its gentle echoes faintlier played
        At eves upon my ear
Than when the autumn's look embrowned
        The lonely chambers here,   30
When autumn's settling shades embrowned
        Nooks that it haunted near.

And so with time my vision less,
        Yea, less and less
Makes of that Past my housemistress,

It dwindles in my eye;
It looms a far-off skeleton
    And not a comrade nigh,
A fitful far-off skeleton
    Dimming as days draw by.   40

After the Visit

(To F. E. D.)

Come again to the place
Where your presence was as a leaf that skims
Down a drouthy way whose ascent bedims
    The bloom on the farer's face.

Come again, with the feet
That were light on the green as a thistledown ball,
And those mute ministrations to one and to all
    Beyond a man's saying sweet.

Until then the faint scent
Of the bordering flowers swam unheeded away,   10
And I marked not the charm in the changes of day
    As the cloud-colours came and went.

Through the dark corridors
Your walk was so soundless I did not know
Your form from a phantom's of long ago
    Said to pass on the ancient floors,

Till you drew from the shade,
And I saw the large luminous living eyes
Regard me in fixed inquiring-wise
    As those of a soul that weighed,   20

Scarce consciously,
The eternal question of what Life was,
And why we were there, and by whose strange laws
    That which mattered most could not be.

The Difference

I

Sinking down by the gate I discern the thin moon,
And a blackbird tries over old airs in the pine,
But the moon is a sorry one, sad the bird's tune,
For this spot is unknown to that Heartmate of mine.

II

Did my Heartmate but haunt here at times such as now,
The song would be joyous and cheerful the moon;
But she will see never this gate, path, or bough,
Nor I find a joy in the scene or the tune.

The Sun on the Bookcase

(Student's Love-song: 1870)

Once more the cauldron of the sun
Smears the bookcase with winy red,
And here my page is, and there my bed,
And the apple-tree shadows travel along.
Soon their intangible track will be run,
    And dusk grow strong
    And they have fled.

Yes: now the boiling ball is gone,
And I have wasted another day. . . .
But wasted—*wasted*, do I say?   10
Is it a waste to have imaged one
Beyond the hills there, who, anon,
    My great deeds done
    Will be mine alway?

'When I set out for Lyonnesse'

(1870)

When I set out for Lyonnesse,
    A hundred miles away,
    The rime was on the spray,
And starlight lit my lonesomeness
When I set out for Lyonnesse
    A hundred miles away.

What would bechance at Lyonnesse
    While I should sojourn there
    No prophet durst declare,
Nor did the wisest wizard guess
What would bechance at Lyonnesse
    While I should sojourn there.

When I came back from Lyonnesse
    With magic in my eyes,
    All marked with mute surmise
My radiance rare and fathomless,
When I came back from Lyonnesse
    With magic in my eyes!

A Thunderstorm in Town

(A Reminiscence: 1893)

She wore a new 'terra-cotta' dress,
And we stayed, because of the pelting storm,
Within the hansom's dry recess,
Though the horse had stopped; yea, motionless
    We sat on, snug and warm.

Then the downpour ceased, to my sharp sad pain,
And the glass that had screened our forms before
Flew up, and out she sprang to her door:
I should have kissed her if the rain
    Had lasted a minute more.

Beyond the Last Lamp

(Near Tooting Common)

I

While rain, with eve in partnership,
Descended darkly, drip, drip, drip,
Beyond the last lone lamp I passed
    Walking slowly, whispering sadly,
    Two linked loiterers, wan, downcast:
Some heavy thought constrained each face,
And blinded them to time and place.

II

The pair seemed lovers, yet absorbed
In mental scenes no longer orbed
By love's young rays. Each countenance   10
    As it slowly, as it sadly
    Caught the lamplight's yellow glance
Held in suspense a misery
At things which had been or might be.

III

When I retrod that watery way
Some hours beyond the droop of day,
Still I found pacing there the twain
    Just as slowly, just as sadly,
    Heedless of the night and rain.
One could but wonder who they were   20
And what wild woe detained them there.

IV

Though thirty years of blur and blot
Have slid since I beheld that spot,
And saw in curious converse there
    Moving slowly, moving sadly
    That mysterious tragic pair,
Its olden look may linger on—
All but the couple; they have gone.

V

Whither? Who knows, indeed. . . . And yet
To me, when nights are weird and wet,   30
Without those comrades there at tryst
    Creeping slowly, creeping sadly,
     That lone lane does not exist.
There they seem brooding on their pain,
And will, while such a lane remain.

The Face at the Casement

    If ever joy leave
An abiding sting of sorrow,
So befell it on the morrow
    Of that May eve. . . .

    The travelled sun dropped
To the north-west, low and lower,
The pony's trot grew slower,
    Until we stopped.

    'This cosy house just by
I must call at for a minute,   10
A sick man lies within it
    Who soon will die.

    'He wished to—marry me,
So I am bound, when I drive near him
To inquire, if but to cheer him,
    How he may be.'

    A message was sent in,
And wordlessly we waited,
Till some one came and stated
    The bulletin.   20

    And that the sufferer said,
For her call no words could thank her;
As his angel he must rank her
    Till life's spark fled.

Slowly we drove away,
When I turned my head, although not
Called to; why I turned I know not
    Even to this day.

And lo, there in my view
Pressed against an upper lattice   30
Was a white face, gazing at us
    As we withdrew.

And well did I divine
It to be the man's there dying,
Who but lately had been sighing
    For her pledged mine.

Then I deigned a deed of hell;
It was done before I knew it;
What devil made me do it
    I cannot tell!   40

Yes, while he gazed above,
I put my arm about her
That he might see, nor doubt her
    My plighted Love.

The pale face vanished quick,
As if blasted, from the casement,
And my shame and self-abasement
    Began their prick.

And they prick on, ceaselessly,
For that stab in Love's fierce fashion   50
Which, unfired by lover's passion,
    Was foreign to me.

She smiled at my caress,
But why came the soft embowment
Of her shoulder at that moment
    She did not guess.

Long long years has he lain
In thy garth, O sad Saint Cleather:
What tears there, bared to weather,
    Will cleanse that stain!   60

Love is long-suffering, brave,
Sweet, prompt, precious as a jewel;
But jealousy is cruel,
    Cruel as the grave!°

Lost Love

I play my sweet old airs—
    The airs he knew
    When our love was true—
    But he does not balk
    His determined walk,
And passes up the stairs.

I sing my songs once more,
    And presently hear
    His footstep near
    As if it would stay;   10
    But he goes his way,
And shuts a distant door.

So I wait for another morn,
    And another night
    In this soul-sick blight;
    And I wonder much
    As I sit, why such
A woman as I was born!

'My spirit will not haunt the mound'

My spirit will not haunt the mound
　　Above my breast,
But travel, memory-possessed,
To where my tremulous being found
　　Life largest, best.

My phantom-footed shape will go
　　When nightfall grays
Hither and thither along the ways
I and another used to know
　　In backward days.　　　　　　　　　　　　10

And there you'll find me, if a jot
　　You still should care
For me, and for my curious air;
If otherwise, then I shall not,
　　For you, be there.

Wessex Heights

(1896)

There are some heights in Wessex, shaped as if by a kindly hand
For thinking, dreaming, dying on, and at crises when I stand,
Say, on Ingpen Beacon eastward, or on Wylls-Neck westwardly,
I seem where I was before my birth, and after death may be.

In the lowlands I have no comrade, not even the lone man's
　　friend—
Her who suffereth long and is kind; accepts what he is too weak
　　to mend:°
Down there they are dubious and askance; there nobody thinks
　　as I,
But mind-chains do not clank where one's next neighbour is the
　　sky.

In the towns I am tracked by phantoms having weird detective
    ways—
Shadows of beings who fellowed with myself of earlier days: 10
They hang about at places, and they say harsh heavy things—
Men with a wintry sneer, and women with tart disparagings.

Down there I seem to be false to myself, my simple self that was,
And is not now, and I see him watching, wondering what crass
    cause
Can have merged him into such a strange continuator as this,
Who yet has something in common with himself, my chrysalis.

I cannot go to the great grey Plain; there's a figure against the
    moon,
Nobody sees it but I, and it makes my breast beat out of tune;
I cannot go to the tall-spired town, being barred by the forms
    now passed°
For everybody but me, in whose long vision they stand there fast.   20

There's a ghost at Yell'ham Bottom chiding loud at the fall of
    the night,
There's a ghost in Froom-side Vale, thin lipped and vague, in a
    shroud of white,
There is one in the railway-train whenever I do not want it near,
I see its profile against the pane, saying what I would not hear.

As for one rare fair woman, I am now but a thought of hers,
I enter her mind and another thought succeeds me that she
    prefers;
Yet my love for her in its fulness she herself even did not know;
Well, time cures hearts of tenderness, and now I can let her go.

So I am found on Ingpen Beacon, or on Wylls-Neck to the west,
Or else on homely Bulbarrow, or little Pilsdon Crest,   30
Where men have never cared to haunt, nor women have walked
    with me,
And ghosts then keep their distance; and I know some liberty.

In Death Divided

I

I shall rot here, with those whom in their day
    You never knew,
And alien ones who, ere they chilled to clay,
    Met not my view,
Will in your distant grave-place ever neighbour you.

II

No shade of pinnacle or tree or tower,
    While earth endures,
Will fall on my mound and within the hour
    Steal on to yours;
One robin never haunt our two green covertures.   10

III

Some organ may resound on Sunday noons
    By where you lie,
Some other thrill the panes with other tunes
    Where moulder I;
No selfsame chords compose our common lullaby.

IV

The simply-cut memorial at my head
    Perhaps may take
A rustic form, and that above your bed
    A stately make;
No linking symbol show thereon for our tale's sake.   20

V

And in the monotonous moils of strained, hard-run
    Humanity,
The eternal tie which binds us twain in one
    No eye will see
Stretching across the miles that sever you from me.

189–.

A Singer Asleep

(Algernon Charles Swinburne, 1837–1909)

I

In this fair niche above the unslumbering sea,
That sentrys up and down all night, all day,
From cove to promontory, from ness to bay,
The Fates have fitly bidden that he should be
    Pillowed eternally.

II

—It was as though a garland of red roses
Had fallen about the hood of some smug nun
When irresponsibly dropped as from the sun,
In fulth of numbers freaked with musical closes,
Upon Victoria's formal middle time   10
    His leaves of rhythm and rhyme.

III

O that far morning of a summer day
When, down a terraced street whose pavements lay
Glassing the sunshine into my bent eyes,
I walked and read with a quick glad surprise
    New words, in classic guise,—

IV

The passionate pages of his earlier years,
Fraught with hot sighs, sad laughters, kisses, tears;
Fresh-fluted notes, yet from a minstrel who
Blew them not naïvely, but as one who knew   20
    Full well why thus he blew.

V

I still can hear the brabble and the roar
At those thy tunes, O still one, now passed through
That fitful fire of tongues then entered new!
Their power is spent like spindrift on this shore;
    Thine swells yet more and more.

VI

—His singing-mistress verily was no other
Than she the Lesbian, she the music-mother
Of all the tribe that feel in melodies;
Who leapt, love-anguished, from the Leucadian steep   30
Into the rambling world-encircling deep
       Which hides her where none sees.

VII

And one can hold in thought that nightly here
His phantom may draw down to the water's brim,
And hers come up to meet it, as a dim
Lone shine upon the heaving hydrosphere,
And mariners wonder as they traverse near,
       Unknowing of her and him.

VIII

One dreams him sighing to her spectral form:
'O teacher, where lies hid thy burning line;   40
Where are those songs, O poetess divine
Whose very orts are love incarnadine?'
And her smile back: 'Disciple true and warm,
       Sufficient now are thine.' . . .

IX

So here, beneath the waking constellations,
Where the waves peal their everlasting strains,
And their dull subterrene reverberations
Shake him when storms make mountains of their plains—
Him once their peer in sad improvisations,
And deft as wind to cleave their frothy manes—   50
I leave him, while the daylight gleam declines
       Upon the capes and chines.

                                   Bonchurch, 1910.

A Plaint to Man

When you slowly emerged from the den of Time,
And gained percipience as you grew,
And fleshed you fair out of shapeless slime,

Wherefore, O Man, did there come to you
The unhappy need of creating me—
A form like your own—for praying to?

My virtue, power, utility,
Within my maker must all abide,
Since none in myself can ever be,

One thin as a phasm on a lantern-slide   10
Shown forth in the dark upon some dim sheet,
And by none but its showman vivified.

'Such a forced device', you may say, 'is meet
For easing a loaded heart at whiles:
Man needs to conceive of a mercy-seat

'Somewhere above the gloomy aisles
Of this wailful world, or he could not bear
The irk no local hope beguiles.'

—But since I was framed in your first despair
The doing without me has had no play   20
In the minds of men when shadows scare;

And now that I dwindle day by day
Beneath the deicide eyes of seers
In a light that will not let me stay,

And to-morrow the whole of me disappears,
The truth should be told, and the fact be faced
That had best been faced in earlier years:

The fact of life with dependence placed
On the human heart's resource alone,
In brotherhood bonded close and graced   30

With loving-kindness fully blown,
And visioned help unsought, unknown.

1909–10.

God's Funeral

I

I saw a slowly-stepping train—
Lined on the brows, scoop-eyed and bent and hoar—
Following in files across a twilit plain
A strange and mystic form the foremost bore.

II

And by contagious throbs of thought
Or latent knowledge that within me lay
And had already stirred me, I was wrought
To consciousness of sorrow even as they.

III

The fore-borne shape, to my blurred eyes,
At first seemed man-like, and anon to change   10
To an amorphous cloud of marvellous size,
At times endowed with wings of glorious range.

IV

And this phantasmal variousness
Ever possessed it as they drew along:
Yet throughout all it symboled none the less
Potency vast and loving-kindness strong.

V

Almost before I knew I bent
Towards the moving columns without a word;
They, growing in bulk and numbers as they went,
Struck out sick thoughts that could be overheard:—   20

VI

'O man-projected Figure, of late
Imaged as we, thy knell who shall survive?
Whence came it we were tempted to create
One whom we can no longer keep alive?

VII

'Framing him jealous, fierce, at first,
We gave him justice as the ages rolled,
Will to bless those by circumstance accurst,
And longsuffering, and mercies manifold.

VIII

'And, tricked by our own early dream
And need of solace, we grew self-deceived,   30
Our making soon our maker did we deem,
And what we had imagined we believed.

IX

'Till, in Time's stayless stealthy swing,
Uncompromising rude reality
Mangled the Monarch of our fashioning,
Who quavered, sank; and now has ceased to be.

X

'So, toward our myth's oblivion,
Darkling, and languid-lipped, we creep and grope
Sadlier than those who wept in Babylon,
Whose Zion was a still abiding hope.   40

XI

'How sweet it was in years far hied
To start the wheels of day with trustful prayer,
To lie down liegely at the eventide
And feel a blest assurance he was there!

XII

'And who or what shall fill his place?
Whither will wanderers turn distracted eyes
For some fixed star to stimulate their pace
Towards the goal of their enterprise?' . . .

XIII

Some in the background then I saw,
Sweet women, youths, men, all incredulous,   50
Who chimed: 'This is a counterfeit of straw,
This requiem mockery! Still he lives to us!'

XIV

I could not buoy their faith: and yet
Many I had known: with all I sympathized;
And though struck speechless, I did not forget
That what was mourned for, I, too, long had prized.

XV

Still, how to bear such loss I deemed
The insistent question for each animate mind,
And gazing, to my growing sight there seemed
A pale yet positive gleam low down behind,   60

XVI

Whereof, to lift the general night,
A certain few who stood aloof had said,
'See you upon the horizon that small light—
Swelling somewhat?' Each mourner shook his head.

XVII

And they composed a crowd of whom
Some were right good, and many nigh the best. . . .
Thus dazed and puzzled 'twixt the gleam and gloom
Mechanically I followed with the rest.

1908–10.

'Ah, are you digging on my grave?'

'Ah, are you digging on my grave
    My loved one?—planting rue?'
—'No: yesterday he went to wed
One of the brightest wealth has bred.
"It cannot hurt her now", he said,
    "That I should not be true."'

'Then who is digging on my grave?
    My nearest dearest kin?'
—'Ah, no; they sit and think, "What use!
What good will planting flowers produce?   10
No tendance of her mound can loose
    Her spirit from Death's gin."'

'But some one digs upon my grave?
    My enemy?—prodding sly?'
—'Nay: when she heard you had passed the Gate
That shuts on all flesh soon or late,
She thought you no more worth her hate,
    And cares not where you lie.'

'Then, who is digging on my grave?
    Say—since I have not guessed!'   20
—'O it is I, my mistress dear,
Your little dog, who still lives near,
And much I hope my movements here
    Have not disturbed your rest?'

'Ah, yes! *You* dig upon my grave . . .
    Why flashed it not on me
That one true heart was left behind!
What feeling do we ever find
To equal among human kind
    A dog's fidelity!'   30

'Mistress, I dug upon your grave
        To bury a bone, in case
I should be hungry near this spot
When passing on my daily trot.
I am sorry, but I quite forgot
        It was your resting-place.'

The Discovery

I wandered to a crude coast
        Like a ghost;
Upon the hills I saw fires—
        Funeral pyres
Seemingly—and heard breaking
Waves like distant cannonades that set the land shaking.

And so I never once guessed
        A Love-nest,
Bowered and candle-lit, lay
        In my way,   10
Till I found a hid hollow,
Where I burst on her my heart could not but follow.

Tolerance

'It is a foolish thing', said I,
'To bear with such, and pass it by;
Yet so I do, I know not why!'

And at each cross I would surmise
That if I had willed not in that wise
I might have spared me many sighs.

But now the only happiness
In looking back that I possess—
Whose lack would leave me comfortless—

Is to remember I refrained 10
From masteries I might have gained,
And for my tolerance was disdained;

For see, a tomb. And if it were
I had bent and broke, I should not dare
To linger in the shadows there.

Before and After Summer

I

Looking forward to the spring
One puts up with anything.
On this February day
Though the winds leap down the street,
Wintry scourgings seem but play,
And these later shafts of sleet
—Sharper pointed than the first—
And these later snows—the worst—
Are as a half-transparent blind
Riddled by rays from sun behind. 10

II

Shadows of the October pine
Reach into this room of mine:
On the pine there swings a bird;
He is shadowed with the tree.
Mutely perched he bills no word;
Blank as I am even is he.
For those happy suns are past,
Fore-discerned in winter last.
When went by their pleasure, then?
I, alas, perceived not when. 20

At Day-Close in November

The ten hours' light is abating,
    And a late bird wings across,
Where the pines, like waltzers waiting,
    Give their black heads a toss.

Beech leaves, that yellow the noon-time,
    Float past like specks in the eye;
I set every tree in my June time,
    And now they obscure the sky.

And the children who ramble through here
    Conceive that there never has been   10
A time when no tall trees grew here,
    That none will in time be seen.

The Year's Awakening

How do you know that the pilgrim track
Along the belting zodiac
Swept by the sun in his seeming rounds
Is traced by now to the Fishes' bounds
And into the Ram, when weeks of cloud
Have wrapt the sky in a clammy shroud,
And never as yet a tinct of spring
Has shown in the Earth's apparelling;
    O vespering bird, how do you know,
      How do you know?   10

How do you know, deep underground,
Hid in your bed from sight and sound,
Without a turn in temperature,
With weather life can scarce endure,
That light has won a fraction's strength,
And day put on some moments' length,
Whereof in merest rote will come,
Weeks hence, mild airs that do not numb;
    O crocus root, how do you know.
      How do you know?   20

February 1910.

Under the Waterfall

'Whenever I plunge my arm, like this,
In a basin of water, I never miss
The sweet sharp sense of a fugitive day
Fetched back from its thickening shroud of gray.
      Hence the only prime
      And real love-rhyme
      That I know by heart,
      And that leaves no smart,
Is the purl of a little valley fall
About three spans wide and two spans tall   10
Over a table of solid rock,
And into a scoop of the self-same block;
The purl of a runlet that never ceases
In stir of kingdoms, in wars, in peaces;
With a hollow boiling voice it speaks
And has spoken since hills were turfless peaks.'

'And why gives this the only prime
Idea to you of a real love-rhyme?
And why does plunging your arm in a bowl
Full of spring water, bring throbs to your soul?'   20

'Well, under the fall, in a crease of the stone,
Though where precisely none ever has known,
Jammed darkly, nothing to show how prized,
And by now with its smoothness opalized,
      Is a drinking-glass:
      For, down that pass
      My lover and I
      Walked under a sky
Of blue with a leaf-wove awning of green,
In the burn of August, to paint the scene,   30
And we placed our basket of fruit and wine
By the runlet's rim, where we sat to dine;
And when we had drunk from the glass together,
Arched by the oak-copse from the weather,
I held the vessel to rinse in the fall,
Where it slipped, and sank, and was past recall,

Though we stooped and plumbed the little abyss
With long bared arms. There the glass still is.
And, as said, if I thrust my arm below
Cold water in basin or bowl, a throe   40
From the past awakens a sense of that time,
And the glass we used, and the cascade's rhyme.
The basin seems the pool, and its edge
The hard smooth face of the brook-side ledge,
And the leafy pattern of china-ware
The hanging plants that were bathing there.

'By night, by day, when it shines or lours,
There lies intact that chalice of ours,
And its presence adds to the rhyme of love
Persistently sung by the fall above.   50
No lip has touched it since his and mine
In turns therefrom sipped lovers' wine.'

POEMS OF 1912–13

Veteris vestigia flammae

The Going

Why did you give no hint that night
That quickly after the morrow's dawn,
And calmly, as if indifferent quite,
You would close your term here, up and be gone
    Where I could not follow
    With wing of swallow
To gain one glimpse of you ever anon!

    Never to bid good-bye,
    Or lip me the softest call,
Or utter a wish for a word, while I   10
Saw morning harden upon the wall,
    Unmoved, unknowing
    That your great going
Had place that moment, and altered all.

Why do you make me leave the house
And think for a breath it is you I see
At the end of the alley of bending boughs
Where so often at dusk you used to be;
     Till in darkening dankness
     The yawning blankness   20
Of the perspective sickens me!

     You were she who abode
     By those red-veined rocks far West,
You were the swan-necked one who rode
Along the beetling Beeny Crest,
     And, reining nigh me,
     Would muse and eye me,
While Life unrolled us its very best.

Why, then, latterly did we not speak,
Did we not think of those days long dead,   30
And ere your vanishing strive to seek
That time's renewal? We might have said,
     'In this bright spring weather
     We'll visit together
Those places that once we visited.'

     Well, well! All's past amend,
     Unchangeable. It must go.
I seem but a dead man held on end
To sink down soon. . . . O you could not know
     That such swift fleeing   40
     No soul foreseeing—
Not even I—would undo me so!

December 1912.

Your Last Drive

Here by the moorway you returned,
And saw the borough lights ahead
That lit your face—all undiscerned
To be in a week the face of the dead,
And you told of the charm of that haloed view
That never again would beam on you.

And on your left you passed the spot
Where eight days later you were to lie,
And be spoken of as one who was not;
Beholding it with a heedless eye   10
As alien from you, though under its tree
You soon would halt everlastingly.

I drove not with you. . . . Yet had I sat
At your side that eve I should not have seen
That the countenance I was glancing at
Had a last-time look in the flickering sheen,
Nor have read the writing upon your face,
'I go hence soon to my resting-place;

'You may miss me then. But I shall not know
How many times you visit me there,   20
Or what your thoughts are, or if you go
There never at all. And I shall not care.
Should you censure me I shall take no heed
And even your praises no more shall need.'

True: never you'll know. And you will not mind.
But shall I then slight you because of such?
Dear ghost, in the past did you ever find
The thought 'What profit', move me much?
Yet abides the fact, indeed, the same,—
You are past love, praise, indifference, blame.   30

December 1912.

The Walk

You did not walk with me
Of late to the hill-top tree
    By the gated ways,
    As in earlier days;
    You were weak and lame,
    So you never came,
And I went alone, and I did not mind,
Not thinking of you as left behind.

I walked up there to-day
    Just in the former way: 10
    Surveyed around
    The familiar ground
    By myself again:
    What difference, then?
Only that underlying sense
Of the look of a room on returning thence.

Rain on a Grave

Clouds spout upon her
    Their waters amain
    In ruthless disdain,—
Her who but lately
    Had shivered with pain
As at touch of dishonour
If there had lit on her
So coldly, so straightly
    Such arrows of rain.

One who to shelter   10
    Her delicate head
Would quicken and quicken
    Each tentative tread

If drops chanced to pelt her
  That summertime spills
  In dust-paven rills
When thunder-clouds thicken
  And birds close their bills.

Would that I lay there
  And she were housed here!   20
Or better, together
Were folded away there
Exposed to one weather
We both,—who would stray there
When sunny the day there,
  Or evening was clear
  At the prime of the year.

Soon will be growing
  Green blades from her mound,
And daisies be showing   30
  Like stars on the ground,
Till she form part of them—
Ay—the sweet heart of them,
Loved beyond measure
With a child's pleasure
  All her life's round.

Jan. 31, 1913.

'I found her out there'

I found her out there
On a slope few see,
That falls westwardly
To the salt-edged air,
Where the ocean breaks
On the purple strand,
And the hurricane shakes
The solid land.

I brought her here,
And have laid her to rest 10
In a noiseless nest
No sea beats near.
She will never be stirred
In her loamy cell
By the waves long heard
And loved so well.

So she does not sleep
By those haunted heights
The Atlantic smites
And the blind gales sweep, 20
Whence she often would gaze
At Dundagel's famed head,
While the dipping blaze
Dyed her face fire-red;

And would sigh at the tale
Of sunk Lyonnesse,
As a wind-tugged tress
Flapped her cheek like a flail;
Or listen at whiles
With a thought-bound brow 30
To the murmuring miles
She is far from now.

Yet her shade, maybe,
Will creep underground
Till it catch the sound
Of that western sea
As it swells and sobs
Where she once domiciled,
And joy in its throbs
With the heart of a child. 40

December 1912.

Without Ceremony

It was your way, my dear,
To vanish without a word
When callers, friends, or kin
Had left, and I hastened in
To rejoin you, as I inferred.

And when you'd a mind to career
Off anywhere—say to town—
You were all on a sudden gone
Before I had thought thereon,
Or noticed your trunks were down.   10

So, now that you disappear
For ever in that swift style,
Your meaning seems to me
Just as it used to be:
'Good-bye is not worth while!'

Lament

How she would have loved
A party to-day!—
Bright-hatted and gloved,
With table and tray
And chairs on the lawn
Her smiles would have shone
With welcomings. . . . But
She is shut, she is shut
    From friendship's spell
    In the jailing shell   10
    Of her tiny cell.

Or she would have reigned
At a dinner to-night
With ardours unfeigned,
And a generous delight;

All in her abode
She'd have freely bestowed
On her guests. . . . But alas,
She is shut under grass
      Where no cups flow,   20
      Powerless to know
      That it might be so.

And she would have sought
With a child's eager glance
The shy snowdrops brought
By the new year's advance,
And peered in the rime
Of Candlemas-time
For crocuses . . . chanced
It that she were not tranced   30
      From sights she loved best;
      Wholly possessed
      By an infinite rest!

And we are here staying
Amid these stale things
Who care not for gaying,
And those junketings
That used so to joy her,
And never to cloy her
As us they cloy! . . . But   40
She is shut, she is shut
      From the cheer of them, dead
      To all done and said
      In her yew-arched bed.

The Haunter

He does not think that I haunt here nightly:
      How shall I let him know
That whither his fancy sets him wandering
      I, too, alertly go?—

Hover and hover a few feet from him
        Just as I used to do,
But cannot answer the words he lifts me—
        Only listen thereto!

When I could answer he did not say them:
        When I could let him know   10
How I would like to join in his journeys
        Seldom he wished to go.
Now that he goes and wants me with him
        More than he used to do,
Never he sees my faithful phantom
        Though he speaks thereto.

Yes, I companion him to places
        Only dreamers know,
Where the shy hares print long paces,
        Where the night rooks go;   20
Into old aisles where the past is all to him,
        Close as his shade can do,
Always lacking the power to call to him,
        Near as I reach thereto!

What a good haunter I am, O tell him!
        Quickly make him know
If he but sigh since my loss befell him
        Straight to his side I go.
Tell him a faithful one is doing
        All that love can do   30
Still that his path may be worth pursuing,
        And to bring peace thereto.

The Voice

Woman much missed, how you call to me, call to me,
Saying that now you are not as you were
When you had changed from the one who was all to me,
But as at first, when our day was fair.

Can it be you that I hear? Let me view you, then,
Standing as when I drew near to the town
Where you would wait for me: yes, as I knew you then,
Even to the original air-blue gown!

Or is it only the breeze, in its listlessness
Travelling across the wet mead to me here,   10
You being ever dissolved to wan wistlessness,
Heard no more again far or near?

    Thus I; faltering forward,
    Leaves around me falling,
Wind oozing thin through the thorn from norward
    And the woman calling.

                      December 1912.

His Visitor

I come across from Mellstock while the moon wastes weaker
To behold where I lived with you for twenty years and more:
I shall go in the gray, at the passing of the mail-train,
And need no setting open of the long familiar door
    As before.

The change I notice in my once own quarters!
A formal-fashioned border where the daisies used to be,
The rooms new painted, and the pictures altered,
And other cups and saucers, and no cozy nook for tea
    As with me.   10

I discern the dim faces of the sleep-wrapt servants;
They are not those who tended me through feeble hours and
    strong,
But strangers quite, who never knew my rule here,
Who never saw me painting, never heard my softling song
    Float along.

So I don't want to linger in this re-decked dwelling,
I feel too uneasy at the contrasts I behold,
And I make again for Mellstock to return here never,
And rejoin the roomy silence, and the mute and manifold
        Souls of old.   20

                              1913.

A Circular

As 'legal representative'
I read a missive not my own,
On new designs the senders give
    For clothes, in tints as shown.

Here figure blouses, gowns for tea,
And presentation-trains of state,
Charming ball-dresses, millinery,
    Warranted up to date.

And this gay-pictured, spring-time shout
Of Fashion, hails what lady proud?   10
Her who before last year ebbed out
    Was costumed in a shroud.

A Dream or No

Why go to Saint-Juliot? What's Juliot to me?
    Some strange necromancy
    But charmed me to fancy
That much of my life claims the spot as its key.

Yes. I have had dreams of that place in the West,
    And a maiden abiding
    Thereat as in hiding;
Fair-eyed and white-shouldered, broad-browed and brown-
    tressed,

And of how, coastward bound on a night long ago,
    There lonely I found her, 10
    The sea-birds around her,
And other than nigh things uncaring to know.

So sweet her life there (in my thought has it seemed)
    That quickly she drew me
    To take her unto me,
And lodge her long years with me. Such have I dreamed.

But nought of that maid from Saint-Juliot I see;
    Can she ever have been here,
    And shed her life's sheen here,
The woman I thought a long housemate with me? 20

Does there even a place like Saint-Juliot exist?
    Or a Vallency Valley
    With stream and leafed alley,
Or Beeny, or Bos with its flounce flinging mist?

February 1913.

After a Journey

Hereto I come to view a voiceless ghost;
    Whither, O whither will its whim now draw me?
Up the cliff, down, till I'm lonely, lost,
    And the unseen waters' ejaculations awe me.
Where you will next be there's no knowing,
    Facing round about me everywhere,
        With your nut-coloured hair,
And gray eyes, and rose-flush coming and going.

Yes: I have re-entered your olden haunts at last;
    Through the years, through the dead scenes I have tracked
        you; 10
What have you now found to say of our past—

Scanned across the dark space wherein I have lacked you?
Summer gave us sweets, but autumn wrought division?
  Things were not lastly as firstly well
    With us twain, you tell?
But all's closed now, despite Time's derision.

I see what you are doing: you are leading me on
  To the spots we knew when we haunted here together,
The waterfall, above which the mist-bow shone
  At the then fair hour in the then fair weather,   20
And the cave just under, with a voice still so hollow
  That it seems to call out to me from forty years ago,
    When you were all aglow,
And not the thin ghost that I now frailly follow!

Ignorant of what there is flitting here to see,
  The waked birds preen and the seals flop lazily,
Soon you will have, Dear, to vanish from me,
  For the stars close their shutters and the dawn whitens hazily.
Trust me, I mind not, though Life lours,
  The bringing me here; nay, bring me here again!   30
    I am just the same as when
Our days were a joy, and our paths through flowers.

Pentargan Bay.

A Death-Day Recalled

Beeny did not quiver,
  Juliot grew not gray,
Thin Valency's river
  Held its wonted way.
Bos seemed not to utter
  Dimmest note of dirge,
Targan mouth a mutter
  To its creamy surge.

Yet though these, unheeding,
  Listless, passed the hour   10
Of her spirit's speeding,
  She had, in her flower,

Sought and loved the places—
   Much and often pined
For their lonely faces
   When in towns confined.

Why did not Valency
   In his purl deplore
One whose haunts were whence he
   Drew his limpid store?   20
Why did Bos not thunder,
   Targan apprehend
Body and breath were sunder
   Of their former friend?

Beeny Cliff

March 1870–March 1913

I

O the opal and the sapphire of that wandering western sea,
And the woman riding high above with bright hair flapping free—
The woman whom I loved so, and who loyally loved me.

II

The pale mews plained below us, and the waves seemed far away
In a nether sky, engrossed in saying their ceaseless babbling say,
As we laughed light-heartedly aloft on that clear-sunned March
   day.

III

A little cloud then cloaked us, and there flew an irised rain,
And the Atlantic dyed its levels with a dull misfeatured stain,
And then the sun burst out again, and purples prinked the main.

IV

—Still in all its chasmal beauty bulks old Beeny to the sky,   10
And shall she and I not go there once again now March is nigh,
And the sweet things said in that March say anew there by and
   by?

V

What if still in chasmal beauty looms that wild weird western
  shore,
The woman now is—elsewhere—whom the ambling pony bore,
And nor knows nor cares for Beeny, and will laugh there nevermore.

At Castle Boterel

As I drive to the junction of lane and highway,
    And the drizzle bedrenches the waggonette,
I look behind at the fading byway,
    And see on its slope, now glistening wet,
        Distinctly yet

Myself and a girlish form benighted
    In dry March weather. We climb the road
Beside a chaise. We had just alighted
    To ease the sturdy pony's load
        When he sighed and slowed.   10

What we did as we climbed, and what we talked of
    Matters not much, nor to what it led,—
Something that life will not be balked of
    Without rude reason till hope is dead,
        And feeling fled.

It filled but a minute. But was there ever
    A time of such quality, since or before,
In that hill's story? To one mind never,
    Though it has been climbed, foot-swift, foot-sore,
        By thousands more.   20

Primaeval rocks form the road's steep border,
    And much have they faced there, first and last,
Of the transitory in Earth's long order;
    But what they record in colour and cast
        Is—that we two passed.

And to me, though Time's unflinching rigour,
 In mindless rote, has ruled from sight
The substance now, one phantom figure
 Remains on the slope, as when that night
  Saw us alight.   30

I look and see it there, shrinking, shrinking,
 I look back at it amid the rain
For the very last time; for my sand is sinking,
 And I shall traverse old love's domain
  Never again.

March 1913.

Places

Nobody says: Ah, that is the place
Where chanced, in the hollow of years ago,
What none of the Three Towns cared to know—
The birth of a little girl of grace—
The sweetest the house saw, first or last;
  Yet it was so
  On that day long past.

Nobody thinks: There, there she lay
In a room by the Hoe, like the bud of a flower,
And listened, just after the bedtime hour,   10
To the stammering chimes that used to play
The quaint Old Hundred-and-Thirteenth tune
  In Saint Andrew's tower
  Night, morn, and noon.

Nobody calls to mind that here
Upon Boterel Hill, where the waggoners skid,
With cheeks whose airy flush outbid
Fresh fruit in bloom, and free of fear,
She cantered down, as if she must fall
  (Though she never did),   20
  To the charm of all.

Nay: one there is to whom these things,
That nobody else's mind calls back,
Have a savour that scenes in being lack,
And a presence more than the actual brings;
To whom to-day is beneaped and stale,
  And its urgent clack
  But a vapid tale.

Plymouth, March 1913.

The Phantom Horsewoman

I

Queer are the ways of a man I know:
  He comes and stands
  In a careworn craze,
  And looks at the sands
  And the seaward haze,
  With moveless hands
  And face and gaze,
  Then turns to go . . .
And what does he see when he gazes so?

II

They say he sees as an instant thing   10
  More clear than to-day,
  A sweet soft scene
  That was once in play
  By that briny green;
  Yes, notes alway
  Warm, real, and keen,
  What his back years bring—
A phantom of his own figuring.

III

Of this vision of his they might say more:
  Not only there   20
  Does he see this sight,
  But everywhere

In his brain—day, night,
As if on the air
It were drawn rose bright—
Yea, far from that shore
Does he carry this vision of heretofore:

IV

A ghost-girl-rider. And though, toil-tried,
He withers daily,
Time touches her not,   30
But she still rides gaily
In his rapt thought
On that shagged and shaly
Atlantic spot,
And as when first eyed
Draws rein and sings to the swing of the tide.

1913.

The Spell of the Rose

'I mean to build a hall anon,
And shape two turrets there,
And a broad newelled stair,
And a cool well for crystal water;
Yes; I will build a hall anon,
Plant roses love shall feed upon,
And apple trees and pear.'

He set to build the manor-hall,
And shaped the turrets there,
And the broad newelled stair,   10
And the cool well for crystal water;
He built for me that manor-hall,
And planted many trees withal,
But no rose anywhere.

And as he planted never a rose
       That bears the flower of love,
       Though other flowers throve
Some heart-bane moved our souls to sever
       Since he had planted never a rose;
       And misconceits raised horrid shows,   20
       And agonies came thereof.

'I'll mend these miseries,' then said I,
       And so, at dead of night,
       I went and, screened from sight,
That nought should keep our souls in severance,
       I set a rose-bush. 'This', said I,
       'May end divisions dire and wry,
       And long-drawn days of blight.'

But I was called from earth—yea, called
       Before my rose-bush grew;   30
       And would that now I knew
What feels he of the tree I planted,
       And whether, after I was called
       To be a ghost, he, as of old,
       Gave me his heart anew!

Perhaps now blooms that queen of trees
       I set but saw not grow,
       And he, beside its glow—
Eyes couched of the mis-vision that blurred me—
       Ay, there beside that queen of trees   40
       He sees me as I was, though sees
       Too late to tell me so!

St Launce's Revisited

       Slip back, Time!
       Yet again I am nearing
       Castle and keep, uprearing
       Gray, as in my prime.

At the inn
Smiling nigh, why is it
Not as on my visit
    When hope and I were twin?

Groom and jade
Whom I found here, moulder;   10
Strange the tavern-holder,
    Strange the tap-maid.

Here I hired
Horse and man for bearing
Me on my wayfaring
    To the door desired.

Evening gloomed
As I journeyed forward
To the faces shoreward,
    Till their dwelling loomed.   20

If again
Towards the Atlantic sea there
I should speed, they'd be there
    Surely now as then? . . .

Why waste thought,
When I know them vanished
Under earth; yea, banished
    Ever into nought!

Where the Picnic Was

Where we made the fire
In the summer time
Of branch and briar
On the hill to the sea,
I slowly climb
Through winter mire,
And scan and trace
The forsaken place
Quite readily.

Now a cold wind blows,   10
And the grass is gray,
But the spot still shows
As a burnt circle—aye,
And stick-ends, charred,
Still strew the sward
Whereon I stand,
Last relic of the band
Who came that day!

Yes, I am here
Just as last year,   20
And the sea breathes brine
From its strange straight line
Up hither, the same
As when we four came.
—But two have wandered far
From this grassy rise
Into urban roar
Where no picnics are,
And one—has shut her eyes
For evermore.   30

*　　*　　*

'She charged me'

She charged me with having said this and that
To another woman long years before,
In the very parlour where we sat,—

Sat on a night when the endless pour
Of rain on the roof and the road below
Bent the spring of the spirit more and more. . . .

—So charged she me; and the Cupid's bow
Of her mouth was hard, and her eyes, and her face,
And her white forefinger lifted slow.

Had she done it gently, or shown a trace 10
That not too curiously would she view
A folly flown ere her reign had place,

A kiss might have closed it. But I knew
From the fall of each word, and the pause between,
That the curtain would drop upon us two
Ere long, in our play of slave and queen.

Had You Wept

Had you wept; had you but neared me with a hazed uncertain
ray,
Dewy as the face of the dawn, in your large and luminous eye,
Then would have come back all the joys the tidings had slain
that day,
And a new beginning, a fresh fair heaven, have smoothed the
things awry.
But you were less feebly human, and no passionate need for
clinging
Possessed your soul to overthrow reserve when I came near;
Ay, though you suffer as much as I from storms the hours are
bringing
Upon your heart and mine, I never see you shed a tear.

The deep strong woman is weakest, the weak one is the strong;
The weapon of all weapons best for winning, you have not used; 10
Have you never been able, or would you not, through the evil
times and long?
Has not the gift been given you, or such gift have you refused?
When I bade me not absolve you on that evening or the morrow,
Why did you not make war on me with those who weep like
rain?
You felt too much, so gained no balm for all your torrid sorrow,
And hence our deep division, and our dark undying pain.

Bereft, She Thinks She Dreams

I dream that the dearest I ever knew
    Has died and been entombed.
I am sure it's a dream that cannot be true,
    But I am so overgloomed
By its persistence, that I would gladly
    Have quick death take me,
Rather than longer think thus sadly;
    So wake me, wake me!

It has lasted days, but minute and hour
    I expect to get aroused   10
And find him as usual in the bower
    Where we so happily housed.
Yet stays this nightmare too appalling,
    And like a web shakes me,
And piteously I keep on calling,
    And no one wakes me!

In the British Museum

'What do you see in that time-touched stone,
    When nothing is there
But ashen blankness, although you give it
    A rigid stare?

'You look not quite as if you saw,
    But as if you heard,
Parting your lips, and treading softly
    As mouse or bird.

'It is only the base of a pillar, they'll tell you,
    That came to us   10
From a far old hill men used to name
    Areopagus.'

—'I know no art, and I only view
    A stone from a wall,
But I am thinking that stone has echoed
    The voice of Paul,

'Paul as he stood and preached beside it
    Facing the crowd,
A small gaunt figure with wasted features,
    Calling out loud   20

'Words that in all their intimate accents
    Pattered upon
That marble front, and were wide reflected,
    And then were gone.

'I'm a labouring man, and know but little,
    Or nothing at all;
But I can't help thinking that stone once echoed
    The voice of Paul.'

In the Servants' Quarters

'Man, you too, aren't you, one of these rough followers of the
    criminal?
All hanging hereabout to gather how he's going to bear
Examination in the hall.' She flung disdainful glances on
The shabby figure standing at the fire with others there,
    Who warmed them by its flare.

'No indeed, my skipping maiden: I know nothing of the trial
    here,
Or criminal, if so he be.—I chanced to come this way,
And the fire shone out into the dawn, and morning airs are cold
    now;
I, too, was drawn in part by charms I see before me play,
    That I see not every day.'   10

'Ha, ha!' then laughed the constables who also stood to warm
    themselves,
The while another maiden scrutinized his features hard,
As the blaze threw into contrast every line and knot that
    wrinkled them,
Exclaiming, 'Why, last night when he was brought in by the
    guard,
       You were with him in the yard!'

'Nay, nay, you teasing wench, I say! You know you speak mis-
    takenly.
Cannot a tired pedestrian who has legged it long and far
Here on his way from northern parts, engrossed in humble
    marketings,
Come in and rest awhile, although judicial doings are
       Afoot by morning star?'   20

'O, come, come!' laughed the constables. 'Why, man, you speak
    the dialect
He uses in his answers; you can hear him up the stairs.
So own it. We sha'n't hurt ye. There he's speaking now! His
    syllables
Are those you sound yourself when you are talking unawares,
       As this pretty girl declares.'

'And you shudder when his chain clinks!' she rejoined. 'O yes,
    I noticed it.
And you winced, too, when those cuffs they gave him echoed to
    us here.
They'll soon be coming down, and you may then have to defend
    yourself
Unless you hold your tongue, or go away and keep you clear
       When he's led to judgment near!'   30

'No! I'll be damned in hell if I know anything about the man!
No single thing about him more than everybody knows!
Must not I even warm my hands but I am charged with blas-
    phemies?' . . .
—His face convulses as the morning cock that moment crows,
       And he droops, and turns, and goes.

'Regret not me'

Regret not me;
Beneath the sunny tree
I lie uncaring, slumbering peacefully.

Swift as the light
I flew my faery flight;
Ecstatically I moved, and feared no night.

I did not know
That heydays fade and go,
But deemed that what was would be always so.

I skipped at morn   10
Between the yellowing corn,
Thinking it good and glorious to be born.

I ran at eves
Among the piled-up sheaves,
Dreaming, 'I grieve not, therefore nothing grieves.'

Now soon will come
The apple, pear, and plum,
And hinds will sing, and autumn insects hum.

Again you will fare
To cider-makings rare,   20
And junketings; but I shall not be there.

Yet gaily sing
Until the pewter ring
Those songs we sang when we went gipsying.

And lightly dance
Some triple-timed romance
In coupled figures, and forget mischance;

And mourn not me
Beneath the yellowing tree;
For I shall mind not, slumbering peacefully.   30

The Moon Looks In

I

I have risen again,
And awhile survey
By my chilly ray
Through your window-pane
Your upturned face,
As you think, 'Ah—she
Now dreams of me
In her distant place!'

II

I pierce her blind
In her far-off home: 10
She fixes a comb,
And says in her mind,
'I start in an hour;
Whom shall I meet?
Won't the men be sweet,
And the women sour!'

The Moth-Signal

(On Egdon Heath)

'What are you still, still thinking,'
   He asked in vague surmise,
'That you stare at the wick unblinking
   With those deep lost luminous eyes?'

'O, I see a poor moth burning
   In the candle-flame,' said she,
'Its wings and legs are turning
   To a cinder rapidly.'

'Moths fly in from the heather',
   He said, 'now the days decline.'   10
'I know,' said she. 'The weather,
   I hope, will at last be fine.

'I think', she added lightly,
    'I'll look out at the door.
The ring the moon wears nightly
    May be visible now no more.'

She rose, and, little heeding,
    Her life-mate then went on
With his mute and museful reading
    In the annals of ages gone.   20

Outside the house a figure
    Came from the tumulus near,
And speedily waxed bigger,
    And clasped and called her Dear.

'I saw the pale-winged token
    You sent through the crack,' sighed she.
'That moth is burnt and broken
    With which you lured out me.

'And were I as the moth is
    It might be better far   30
For one whose marriage troth is
    Shattered as potsherds are!'

Then grinned the Ancient Briton
    From the tumulus treed with pine:
'So, hearts are thwartly smitten
    In these days as in mine!'

Seen by the Waits

Through snowy woods and shady
    We went to play a tune
To the lonely manor-lady
    By the light of the Christmas moon.

We violed till, upward glancing
    To where a mirror leaned,
It showed her airily dancing,
    Deeming her movements screened;

Dancing alone in the room there,
    Thin-draped in her robe of night;   10
Her postures, glassed in the gloom there,
    Were a strange phantasmal sight.

She had learnt (we heard when homing)
    That her roving spouse was dead;
Why she had danced in the gloaming
    We thought, but never said.

In the Days of Crinoline

A plain tilt-bonnet on her head
She took the path across the leaze.
—Her spouse the vicar, gardening, said,
'Too dowdy that, for coquetries,
        So I can hoe at ease.'

But when she had passed into the heath,
And gained the wood beyond the flat,
She raised her skirts, and from beneath
Unpinned and drew as from a sheath
        An ostrich-feathered hat.   10

And where the hat had hung she now
Concealed and pinned the dowdy hood,
And set the hat upon her brow,
And thus emerging from the wood
        Tripped on in jaunty mood.

The sun was low and crimson-faced
As two came that way from the town,
And plunged into the wood untraced. . . .
When severally therefrom they paced
        The sun had quite gone down.   20

The hat and feather disappeared,
The dowdy hood again was donned,
And in the gloom the fair one neared
Her home and husband dour, who conned
    Calmly his blue-eyed blonde.

'To-day', he said, 'you have shown good sense,
A dress so modest and so meek
Should always deck your goings hence
Alone.' And as a recompense
    He kissed her on the cheek.   30

The Roman Gravemounds

By Rome's dim relics there walks a man,
Eyes bent; and he carries a basket and spade;
I guess what impels him to scrape and scan;
Yea, his dreams of that Empire long decayed.

'Vast was Rome', he must muse, 'in the world's regard,
Vast it looms there still, vast it ever will be';
And he stoops as to dig and unmine some shard
Left by those who are held in such memory.

But no; in his basket, see, he has brought
A little white furred thing, stiff of limb,   10
Whose life never won from the world a thought;
It is this, and not Rome, that is moving him.

And to make it a grave he has come to the spot,
And he delves in the ancient dead's long home;
Their fames, their achievements, the man knows not;
The furred thing is all to him—nothing Rome!

'Here say you that Cæsar's warriors lie?—
But my little white cat was my only friend!
Could she but live, might the record die
Of Cæsar, his legions, his aims, his end!'   20

Well, Rome's long rule here is oft and again
A theme for the sages of history,
And the small furred life was worth no one's pen;
Yet its mourner's mood has a charm for me.

November 1910.

The Sacrilege

A Ballad-Tragedy

(*Circa* 182–)

PART I

'I have a Love I love too well
Where Dunkery frowns on Exon Moor;
I have a Love I love too well,
       To whom, ere she was mine,
"Such is my love for you", I said,
"That you shall have to hood your head
A silken kerchief crimson-red,
       Wove finest of the fine."

'And since this Love, for one mad moon,
On Exon Wild by Dunkery Tor,   10
Since this my Love for one mad moon
       Did clasp me as her king,
I snatched a silk-piece red and rare
From off a stall at Priddy Fair,
For handkerchief to hood her hair
       When we went gallanting.

'Full soon the four weeks neared their end
Where Dunkery frowns on Exon Moor;
And when the four weeks neared their end,
       And their swift sweets outwore,   20
I said, "What shall I do to own
Those beauties bright as tulips blown,
And keep you here with me alone
       As mine for evermore?"

'And as she drowsed within my van
On Exon Wild by Dunkery Tor—
And as she drowsed within my van,
        And dawning turned to day,
She heavily raised her sloe-black eyes
And murmured back in softest wise,   30
"One more thing, and the charms you prize
        Are yours henceforth for aye.

'"And swear I will I'll never go
While Dunkery frowns on Exon Moor
To meet the Cornish Wrestler Joe
        For dance and dallyings.
If you'll to yon cathedral shrine,
And finger from the chest divine
Treasure to buy me ear-drops fine,
        And richly jewelled rings."   40

'I said: "I am one who has gathered gear
From Marlbury Downs to Dunkery Tor,
Who has gathered gear for many a year
        From mansion, mart and fair;
But at God's house I've stayed my hand,
Hearing within me some command—
Curbed by a law not of the land
        From doing damage there!"

'Whereat she pouts, this Love of mine,
As Dunkery pouts to Exon Moor,   50
And still she pouts, this Love of mine,
        So cityward I go.
But ere I start to do the thing,
And speed my soul's imperilling
For one who is my ravishing
        And all the joy I know,

'I come to lay this charge on thee—
On Exon Wild by Dunkery Tor—
I come to lay this charge on thee
        With solemn speech and sign: 60

Should things go ill, and my life pay
For botchery in this rash assay,
You are to take hers likewise—yea,
  The month the law takes mine.

'For should my rival, Wrestler Joe,
Where Dunkery frowns on Exon Moor—
My reckless rival, Wrestler Joe,
  My Love's bedwinner be,
My rafted spirit would not rest,
But wander weary and distrest
Throughout the world in wild protest: 70
  The thought nigh maddens me!'

PART II

Thus did he speak—this brother of mine—
On Exon Wild by Dunkery Tor,
Born at my birth of mother of mine,
  And forthwith went his way
To dare the deed some coming night . . .
I kept the watch with shaking sight,
The moon at moments breaking bright,
  At others glooming gray.   80

For three full days I heard no sound
Where Dunkery frowns on Exon Moor,
I heard no sound at all around
  Whether his fay prevailed,
Or one more foul the master were,
Till some afoot did tidings bear
How that, for all his practised care,
  He had been caught and jailed.

They had heard a crash when twelve had chimed
By Mendip east of Dunkery Tor,
When twelve had chimed and moonlight climbed; . 90
  They watched, and he was tracked
By arch and aisle and saint and knight
Of sculptured stonework sheeted white
In the cathedral's ghostly light,
  And captured in the act.

Yes; for this Love he loved too well
Where Dunkery sights the Severn shore,
All for this Love he loved too well
      He burst the holy bars,   100
Seized golden vessels from the chest
To buy her ornaments of the best,
At her ill-witchery's request
      And lure of eyes like stars. . . .

When blustering March confused the sky
In Toneborough Town by Exon Moor,
When blustering March confused the sky
      They stretched him; and he died.
Down in the crowd where I, to see
The end of him, stood silently,   110
With a set face he lipped to me—
      'Remember.' 'Ay!' I cried.

By night and day I shadowed her
From Toneborough Deane to Dunkery Tor,
I shadowed her asleep, astir,
      And yet I could not bear—
Till Wrestler Joe anon began
To figure as her chosen man,
And took her to his shining van—
      To doom a form so fair!   120

He made it handsome for her sake—
And Dunkery smiled to Exon Moor—
He made it handsome for her sake,
      Painting it out and in;
And on the door of apple-green
A bright brass knocker soon was seen,
And window-curtains white and clean
      For her to sit within.

And all could see she clave to him
As cleaves a cloud to Dunkery Tor,   130
Yea, all could see she clave to him,
      And every day I said,

'A pity it seems to part those two
That hourly grow to love more true:
Yet she's the wanton woman who
          Sent one to swing till dead!'

That blew to blazing all my hate,
While Dunkery frowned on Exon Moor,
And when the river swelled, her fate
          Came to her pitilessly. . . .   140
I dogged her, crying: 'Across that plank
They use as bridge to reach yon bank
A coat and hat lie limp and dank;
          Your goodman's, can they be?'

She paled, and went, I close behind—
And Exon frowned to Dunkery Tor,
She went, and I came up behind
          And tipped the plank that bore
Her, fleetly flitting across to eye
What such might bode. She slid awry;   150
And from the current came a cry,
          A gurgle; and no more.

How that befell no mortal knew
From Marlbury Downs to Exon Moor;
No mortal knew that deed undue
          But he who schemed the crime,
Which night still covers. . . . But in dream
Those ropes of hair upon the stream
He sees, and he will hear that scream
          Until his judgment-time.   160

Exeunt Omnes

I

Everybody else, then, going,
And I still left where the fair was? . . .
Much have I seen of neighbour loungers
Making a lusty showing,
Each now past all knowing.

II

There is an air of blankness
In the street and the littered spaces;
Thoroughfare, steeple, bridge and highway
   Wizen themselves to lankness;
   Kennels dribble dankness.   10

III

Folk all fade. And whither,
As I wait alone where the fair was?
Into the clammy and numbing night-fog
   Whence they entered hither.
   Soon one more goes thither!

June 2, 1913.

SATIRES OF CIRCUMSTANCE

I

At Tea

The kettle descants in a cozy drone,
And the young wife looks in her husband's face,
And then at her guest's, and shows in her own
Her sense that she fills an envied place;
And the visiting lady is all abloom,
And says there was never so sweet a room.

And the happy young housewife does not know
That the woman beside her was first his choice,
Till the fates ordained it could not be so. . . .
Betraying nothing in look or voice   10
The guest sits smiling and sips her tea,
And he throws her a stray glance yearningly.

II

In Church

'And now to God the Father,' he ends,
And his voice thrills up to the topmost tiles:
Each listener chokes as he bows and bends,
And emotion pervades the crowded aisles.
Then the preacher glides to the vestry-door,
And shuts it, and thinks he is seen no more.

The door swings softly ajar meanwhile,
And a pupil of his in the Bible class,
Who adores him as one without gloss or guile,
Sees her idol stand with a satisfied smile   10
And re-enact at the vestry-glass
Each pulpit gesture in deft dumb-show
That had moved the congregation so.

III

By Her Aunt's Grave

'Sixpence a week', says the girl to her lover,
'Aunt used to bring me, for she could confide
In me alone, she vowed. 'Twas to cover
The cost of her headstone when she died.
And that was a year ago last June;
I've not yet fixed it. But I must soon.'

'And where is the money now, my dear?'
'O, snug in my purse . . . Aunt was *so* slow
In saving it—eighty weeks, or near.' . . .
'Let's spend it,' he hints. 'For she won't know.   10
There's a dance to-night at the Load of Hay.'
She passively nods. And they go that way.

IV

In the Room of the Bride-Elect

'Would it had been the man of our wish!'
Sighs her mother. To whom with vehemence she
In the wedding-dress—the wife to be—
'Then why were you so mollyish
As not to insist on him for me!'
The mother, amazed: 'Why, dearest one,
Because you pleaded for this or none!'

'But Father and you should have stood out strong!
Since then, to my cost, I have lived to find
That you were right and that I was wrong;   10
This man is a dolt to the one declined. . . .
Ah!—here he comes with his button-hole rose.
Good God—I must marry him I suppose!'

V

At a Watering-Place

They sit and smoke on the esplanade,
The man and his friend, and regard the bay
Where the far chalk cliffs, to the left displayed,
Smile sallowly in the decline of day.
And saunterers pass with laugh and jest—
A handsome couple among the rest.

'That smart proud pair', says the man to his friend,
'Are to marry next week. . . . How little he thinks
That dozens of days and nights on end
I have stroked her neck, unhooked the links   10
Of her sleeve to get at her upper arm. . . .
Well, bliss is in ignorance: what's the harm!'

VI

In the Cemetery

'You see those mothers squabbling there?'
Remarks the man of the cemetery.
'One says in tears, "*'Tis mine lies here!*"
Another, "*Nay, mine, you Pharisee!*"
Another, "*How dare you move my flowers
And put your own on this grave of ours!*"
But all their children were laid therein
At different times, like sprats in a tin.

'And then the main drain had to cross,
And we moved the lot some nights ago,   10
And packed them away in the general foss
With hundreds more. But their folks don't know,
And as well cry over a new-laid drain
As anything else, to ease your pain!'

VII

Outside the Window

'My stick!' he says, and turns in the lane
To the house just left, whence a vixen voice
Comes out with the firelight through the pane,
And he sees within that the girl of his choice
Stands rating her mother with eyes aglare
For something said while he was there.

'At last I behold her soul undraped!'
Thinks the man who had loved her more than himself;
'My God!—'tis but narrowly I have escaped.—
My precious porcelain proves it delf.'   10
His face has reddened like one ashamed,
And he steals off, leaving his stick unclaimed.

VIII

In the Study

He enters, and mute on the edge of a chair
Sits a thin-faced lady, a stranger there,
A type of decayed gentility;
And by some small signs he well can guess
That she comes to him almost breakfastless.

'I have called—I hope I do not err—
I am looking for a purchaser
Of some score volumes of the works
Of eminent divines I own,—
Left by my father—though it irks   10
My patience to offer them.' And she smiles
As if necessity were unknown;
'But the truth of it is that oftenwhiles
I have wished, as I am fond of art,
To make my rooms a little smart,
And these old books are so in the way.'
And lightly still she laughs to him,
As if to sell were a mere gay whim,
And that, to be frank, Life were indeed
To her not vinegar and gall,   20
But fresh and honey-like; and Need
No household skeleton at all.

IX

At the Altar-Rail

'My bride is not coming, alas!' says the groom,
And the telegram shakes in his hand. 'I own
It was hurried! We met at a dancing-room
When I went to the Cattle-Show alone,
And then, next night, where the Fountain leaps,
And the Street of the Quarter-Circle sweeps.

'Ay, she won me to ask her to be my wife—
'Twas foolish perhaps!—to forsake the ways
Of the flaring town for a farmer's life.
She agreed. And we fixed it. Now she says: 10
"*It's sweet of you, dear, to prepare me a nest,*
But a swift, short, gay life suits me best.
What I really am you have never gleaned;
I had eaten the apple ere you were weaned."'

X

In the Nuptial Chamber

'O that mastering tune!' And up in the bed
Like a lace-robed phantom springs the bride;
'And why?' asks the man she had that day wed,
With a start, as the band plays on outside.
'It's the townsfolks' cheery compliment
Because of our marriage, my Innocent.'

'O but you don't know! 'Tis the passionate air
To which my old Love waltzed with me,
And I swore as we spun that none should share
My home, my kisses, till death, save he!   10
And he dominates me and thrills me through,
And it's he I embrace while embracing you!'

XI

In the Restaurant

'But hear. If you stay, and the child be born,
It will pass as your husband's with the rest,
While, if we fly, the teeth of scorn
Will be gleaming at us from east to west;
And the child will come as a life despised;
I feel an elopement is ill-advised!'

'O you realize not what it is, my dear,
To a woman! Daily and hourly alarms
Lest the truth should out. How can I stay here,
And nightly take him into my arms!   10
Come to the child no name or fame,
Let's go, and face it, and bear the shame.'

XII

At the Draper's

'I stood at the back of the shop, my dear,
    But you did not perceive me.
Well, when they deliver what you were shown
    I shall know nothing of it, believe me!'

And he coughed and coughed as she paled and said,
    'O, I didn't see you come in there—
Why couldn't you speak?'—'Well, I didn't. I left
    That you should not notice I'd been there.

'You were viewing some lovely things. "*Soon required
    For a widow, of latest fashion*";   10
And I knew 'twould upset you to meet the man
    Who had to be cold and ashen

'And screwed in a box before they could dress you
    "*In the last new note in mourning*",
As they defined it. So, not to distress you,
    I left you to your adorning.'

XIII

On the Death-Bed

'I'll tell—being past all praying for—
Then promptly die. . . . He was out at the war,
And got some scent of the intimacy
That was under way between her and me;

And he stole back home, and appeared like a ghost
One night, at the very time almost
That I reached her house. Well, I shot him dead,
And secretly buried him. Nothing was said.

'The news of the battle came next day;
He was scheduled missing. I hurried away,   10
Got out there, visited the field,
And sent home word that a search revealed
He was one of the slain; though, lying alone
And stript, his body had not been known.

'But she suspected. I lost her love,
Yea, my hope of earth, and of Heaven above;
And my time's now come, and I'll pay the score.
Though it be burning for evermore.'

XIV

Over the Coffin

They stand confronting, the coffin between,
His wife of old, and his wife of late,
And the dead man whose they both had been
Seems listening aloof, as to things past date.
—'I have called,' says the first. 'Do you marvel or not?'
'In truth,' says the second, 'I do—somewhat.'

'Well, there was a word to be said by me! . . .
I divorced that man because of you—
It seemed I must do it, boundenly;
But now I am older, and tell you true,   10
For life is little, and dead lies he;
I would I had let alone you two!
And both of us, scorning parochial ways,
Had lived like the wives in the patriarchs' days.'

XV

In the Moonlight

'O lonely workman, standing there
In a dream, why do you stare and stare
At her grave, as no other grave there were?

'If your great gaunt eyes so importune
Her soul by the shine of this corpse-cold moon,
Maybe you'll raise her phantom soon!'

'Why, fool, it is what I would rather see
Than all the living folk there be;
But alas, there is no such joy for me!'

'Ah—she was one you loved, no doubt,
Through good and evil, through rain and drought,
And when she passed, all your sun went out?'

'Nay: she was the woman I did not love,
Whom all the others were ranked above,
Whom during her life I thought nothing of.'

Moments of Vision

That mirror
Which makes of men a transparency,
    Who holds that mirror
And bids us such a breast-bare spectacle see
    Of you and me?

That mirror
Whose magic penetrates like a dart,
    Who lifts that mirror
And throws our mind back on us, and our heart,
    Until we start?   10

That mirror
Works well in these night hours of ache;
    Why in that mirror
Are tincts we never see ourselves once take
    When the world is awake?

That mirror
Can test each mortal when unaware;
    Yea, that strange mirror
May catch his last thoughts, whole life foul or fair,
    Glassing it—where?   20

The Voice of Things

Forty Augusts—aye, and several more—ago,
    When I paced the headlands loosed from dull employ,
The waves huzza'd like a multitude below,
    In the sway of an all-including joy
        Without cloy.

Blankly I walked there a double decade after,
    When thwarts had flung their toils in front of me,
And I heard the waters wagging in a long ironic laughter
    At the lot of men, and all the vapoury
        Things that be.   10

Wheeling change has set me again standing where
    Once I heard the waves huzza at Lammas-tide;
But they supplicate now—like a congregation there
    Who murmur the Confession—I outside,
        Prayer denied.

'We sat at the window'

(Bournemouth, 1875)

We sat at the window looking out,
And the rain came down like silken strings
That Swithin's day. Each gutter and spout
Babbled unchecked in the busy way
    Of witless things:
Nothing to read, nothing to see
Seemed in that room for her and me
    On Swithin's day.

We were irked by the scene, by our own selves; yes,
For I did not know, nor did she infer   10
How much there was to read and guess
By her in me, and to see and crown
    By me in her.
Wasted were two souls in their prime,
And great was the waste, that July time
    When the rain came down.

Afternoon Service at Mellstock

(*Circa* 1850)

On afternoons of drowsy calm
    We stood in the panelled pew,
Singing one-voiced a Tate-and-Brady psalm
    To the tune of 'Cambridge New'.

We watched the elms, we watched the rooks,
    The clouds upon the breeze,
Between the whiles of glancing at our books,
    And swaying like the trees.

So mindless were those outpourings!—
    Though I am not aware   10
That I have gained by subtle thought on things
    Since we stood psalming there.

At the Wicket-Gate

There floated the sounds of church-chiming,
    But no one was nigh,
Till there came, as a break in the loneness,
    Her father, she, I.
And we slowly moved on to the wicket,
    And downlooking stood,
Till anon people passed, and amid them
    We parted for good.

Greater, wiser, may part there than we three
    Who parted there then,   10
But never will Fates colder-featured
    Hold sway there again.
Of the churchgoers through the still meadows
    No single one knew
What a play was played under their eyes there
    As thence we withdrew.

Apostrophe to an Old Psalm Tune

I met you first—ah, when did I first meet you?
When I was full of wonder, and innocent,
Standing meek-eyed with those of choric bent,
    While dimming day grew dimmer
      In the pulpit-glimmer.

Much riper in years I met you—in a temple
Where summer sunset streamed upon our shapes,
And you spread over me like a gauze that drapes,
    And flapped from floor to rafters,
      Sweet as angels' laughters.   10

But you had been stripped of some of your old vesture
By Monk, or another. Now you wore no frill,°
And at first you startled me. But I knew you still,
    Though I missed the minim's waver,
      And the dotted quaver.

I grew accustomed to you thus. And you hailed me
Through one who evoked you often. Then at last
Your raiser was borne off, and I mourned you had passed
    From my life with your late outsetter;
      Till I said, ' 'Tis better!'   20

But you waylaid me. I rose and went as a ghost goes,
And said, eyes-full: 'I'll never hear it again!
It is overmuch for scathed and memoried men
    When sitting among strange people
      Under their steeple.'

Now, a new stirrer of tones calls you up before me
And wakes your speech, as she of Endor did
(When sought by Saul who, in disguises hid,
    Fell down on the earth to hear it)
      Samuel's spirit.   30

So, your quired oracles beat till they make me tremble
As I discern your mien in the old attire,
Here in these turmoiled years of belligerent fire
        Living still on—and onward, maybe,
            Till Doom's great day be!

Sunday, August 13, 1916.

At the Word 'Farewell'

She looked like a bird from a cloud
        On the clammy lawn,
Moving alone, bare-browed
        In the dim of dawn.
The candles alight in the room
        For my parting meal
Made all things withoutdoors loom
        Strange, ghostly, unreal.

The hour itself was a ghost,
        And it seemed to me then   10
As of chances the chance furthermost
        I should see her again.
I beheld not where all was so fleet
        That a Plan of the past
Which had ruled us from birthtime to meet
        Was in working at last:

No prelude did I there perceive
        To a drama at all,
Or foreshadow what fortune might weave
        From beginnings so small;   20
But I rose as if quicked by a spur
        I was bound to obey,
And stepped through the casement to her
        Still alone in the gray.

'I am leaving you. . . . Farewell!' I said,
　　As I followed her on
By an alley bare boughs overspread;
　　'I soon must be gone!'
Even then the scale might have been turned
　　Against love by a feather,   30
—But crimson one cheek of hers burned
　　When we came in together.

First Sight of Her and After

A day is drawing to its fall
　　I had not dreamed to see;
The first of many to enthrall
　　My spirit, will it be?
Or is this eve the end of all
　　Such new delight for me?

I journey home: the pattern grows
　　Of moonshades on the way:
'Soon the first quarter, I suppose,'
　　Sky-glancing travellers say;   10
I realize that it, for those,
　　Has been a common day.

The Rival

I determined to find out whose it was—
　　The portrait he looked at so, and sighed;
Bitterly have I rued my meanness
　　And wept for it since he died!

I searched his desk when he was away,
　　And there was the likeness—yes, my own!
Taken when I was the season's fairest,
　　And time-lines all unknown.

I smiled at my image, and put it back,
  And he went on cherishing it, until   10
I was chafed that he loved not the me then living,
    But that past woman still.

Well, such was my jealousy at last,
  I destroyed that face of the former me;
Could you ever have dreamed the heart of woman
    Would work so foolishly!

Heredity

I am the family face;
Flesh perishes, I live on,
Projecting trait and trace
Through time to times anon,
And leaping from place to place
Over oblivion.

The years-heired feature that can
In curve and voice and eye
Despise the human span
Of durance—that is I;   10
The eternal thing in man,
That heeds no call to die.

'You were the sort that men forget'

You were the sort that men forget;
    Though I—not yet!—
Perhaps not ever. Your slighted weakness
  Adds to the strength of my regret!

You'd not the art—you never had
    For good or bad—
To make men see how sweet your meaning,
  Which, visible, had charmed them glad.

You would, by words inept let fall,
  Offend them all,   10
Even if they saw your warm devotion
  Would hold your life's blood at their call.

You lacked the eye to understand
  Those friends offhand
Whose mode was crude, though whose dim purport
  Outpriced the courtesies of the bland.

I am now the only being who
  Remembers you
It may be. What a waste that Nature
  Grudged soul so dear the art its due! 20

She, I, and They

  I was sitting,
  She was knitting,
And the portraits of our fore-folk hung around;
  When there struck on us a sigh;
  'Ah—what is that?' said I:
'Was it not you?' said she. 'A sigh did sound.'

  I had not breathed it,
  Nor the night-wind heaved it,
And how it came to us we could not guess;
  And we looked up at each face   10
  Framed and glazed there in its place,
Still hearkening; but thenceforth was silentness.

  Half in dreaming,
  'Then its meaning',
Said we, 'must be surely this; that they repine
  That we should be the last
  Of stocks once unsurpassed,
And unable to keep up their sturdy line.'

         1916.

Near Lanivet, 1872

There was a stunted handpost just on the crest,
    Only a few feet high:
She was tired, and we stopped in the twilight-time for her rest,
    At the crossways close thereby.

She leant back, being so weary, against its stem,
    And laid her arms on its own,
Each open palm stretched out to each end of them,
    Her sad face sideways thrown.

Her white-clothed form at this dim-lit cease of day
    Made her look as one crucified   10
In my gaze at her from the midst of the dusty way,
    And hurriedly 'Don't,' I cried.

I do not think she heard. Loosing thence she said,
    As she stepped forth ready to go,
'I am rested now.—Something strange came into my head;
    I wish I had not leant so!'

And wordless we moved onward down from the hill
    In the west cloud's murked obscure,
And looking back we could see the handpost still
    In the solitude of the moor.   20

'It struck her too,' I thought, for as if afraid
    She heavily breathed as we trailed;
Till she said, 'I did not think how 'twould look in the shade,
    When I leant there like one nailed.'

I, lightly: 'There's nothing in it. For *you*, anyhow!'
    —'O I know there is not,' said she ...
  'Yet I wonder ... If no one is bodily crucified now,
    In spirit one may be!'

And we dragged on and on, while we seemed to see
    In the running of Time's far glass   30
Her crucified, as she had wondered if she might be
    Some day.—Alas, alas!

Joys of Memory

When the spring comes round, and a certain day
Looks out from the brume by the eastern copsetrees
    And says, Remember,
    I begin again, as if it were new,
    A day of like date I once lived through,
    Whiling it hour by hour away;
      So shall I do till my December,
        When spring comes round.

I take my holiday then and my rest
Away from the dun life here about me,
    Old hours re-greeting
    With the quiet sense that bring they must
    Such throbs as at first, till I house with dust,
    And in the numbness my heartsome zest
      For things that were, be past repeating
        When spring comes round.

To the Moon

    'What have you looked at, Moon,
      In your time,
    Now long past your prime?'
'O, I have looked at, often looked at
      Sweet, sublime,
Sore things, shudderful, night and noon
      In my time.'

    'What have you mused on, Moon,
      In your day,
    So aloof, so far away?'
'O, I have mused on, often mused on
      Growth, decay,
Nations alive, dead, mad, aswoon,
      In my day!'

'Have you much wondered, Moon,
    On your rounds,
    Self-wrapt, beyond Earth's bounds?'
'Yea, I have wondered, often wondered
    At the sounds
Reaching me of the human tune   20
    On my rounds.'

'What do you think of it, Moon,
    As you go?
    Is Life much, or no?'
'O, I think of it, often think of it
    As a show
God ought surely to shut up soon,
    As I go.'

Copying Architecture in an Old Minster

(Wimborne)

How smartly the quarters of the hour march by
    That the jack-o'-clock never forgets;
Ding-dong; and before I have traced a cusp's eye,
Or got the true twist of the ogee over,
    A double ding-dong ricochetts.

Just so did he clang here before I came,
    And so will he clang when I'm gone
Through the Minster's cavernous hollows—the same
Tale of hours never more to be will he deliver
    To the speechless midnight and dawn!   10

I grow to conceive it a call to ghosts,
    Whose mould lies below and around.
Yes; the next 'Come, come,' draws them out from their posts,
And they gather, and one shade appears, and another,
    As the eve-damps creep from the ground.

See—a Courtenay stands by his quatrefoiled tomb,
   And a Duke and his Duchess near;
And one Sir Edmund in columned gloom,
And a Saxon king by the presbytery chamber;
     And shapes unknown in the rear.   20

Maybe they have met for a parle on some plan
   To better ail-stricken mankind;
I catch their cheepings, though thinner than
The overhead creak of a passager's pinion
     When leaving land behind.

Or perhaps they speak to the yet unborn,
   And caution them not to come
To a world so ancient and trouble-torn,
Of foiled intents, vain lovingkindness,
     And ardours chilled and numb.   30

They waste to fog as I stir and stand,
   And move from the arched recess,
And pick up the drawing that slipped from my hand,
And feel for the pencil I dropped in the cranny
     In a moment's forgetfulness.

To Shakespeare

After Three Hundred Years

Bright baffling Soul, least capturable of themes,
Thou, who display'dst a life of commonplace,
Leaving no intimate word or personal trace
Of high design outside the artistry
    Of thy penned dreams,
Still shalt remain at heart unread eternally.

Through human orbits thy discourse to-day,
Despite thy formal pilgrimage, throbs on
In harmonies that cow Oblivion,
And, like the wind, with all-uncared effect   10
    Maintain a sway
Not fore-desired, in tracks unchosen and unchecked.

And yet, at thy last breath, with mindless note
The borough clocks but samely tongued the hour,
The Avon just as always glassed the tower,
Thy age was published on thy passing-bell
        But in due rote
With other dwellers' deaths accorded a like knell.

And at the strokes some townsman (met, maybe,
And thereon queried by some squire's good dame   20
Driving in shopward) may have given thy name,
With, 'Yes, a worthy man and well-to-do;
        Though, as for me,
I knew him but by just a neighbour's nod, 'tis true.

'I' faith, few knew him much here, save by word,
He having elsewhere led his busier life;
Though to be sure he left with us his wife.'
—'Ah, one of the tradesmen's sons, I now recall. . . .
        Witty, I've heard. . . .
We did not know him. . . . Well, good-day. Death comes to all.'   30

So, like a strange bright bird we sometimes find
To mingle with the barn-door brood awhile,
Then vanish from their homely domicile—
Into man's poesy, we wot not whence,
        Flew thy strange mind,
Lodged there a radiant guest, and sped for ever thence.

                                                    1916.

Quid Hic Agis?

I

When I weekly knew
An ancient pew,
And murmured there
The forms of prayer
And thanks and praise
In the ancient ways,

And heard read out
During August drought
That chapter from Kings
Harvest-time brings;   10
—How the prophet, broken
By griefs unspoken,
Went heavily away
To fast and to pray,
And, while waiting to die,
The Lord passed by,
And a whirlwind and fire
Drew nigher and nigher,
And a small voice anon
Bade him up and be gone,—   20
I did not apprehend
As I sat to the end
And watched for her smile
Across the sunned aisle,
That this tale of a seer
Which came once a year
Might, when sands were heaping,
Be like a sweat creeping,
Or in any degree
Bear on her or on me!   30

II

When later, by chance
Of circumstance,
It befel me to read
On a hot afternoon
At the lectern there
The selfsame words
As the lesson decreed,
To the gathered few
From the hamlets near—
Folk of flocks and herds   40
Sitting half aswoon,
Who listened thereto
As women and men
Not overmuch
Concerned at such—

So, like them then,
I did not see
What drought might be
With me, with her,
As the Kalendar   50
Moved on, and Time
Devoured our prime.

III

But now, at last,
When our glory has passed,
And there is no smile
From her in the aisle,
But where it once shone
A marble, men say,
With her name thereon
Is discerned to-day;   60
And spiritless
In the wilderness
I shrink from sight
And desire the night,
(Though, as in old wise,
I might still arise,
Go forth, and stand
And prophesy in the land),
I feel the shake
Of wind and earthquake,   70
And consuming fire
Nigher and nigher,
And the voice catch clear,
'What doest thou here?'

The Spectator: 1916.

On a Midsummer Eve

I idly cut a parsley stalk,
And blew therein towards the moon;
I had not thought what ghosts would walk
With shivering footsteps to my tune.

I went, and knelt, and scooped my hand
As if to drink, into the brook,
And a faint figure seemed to stand
Above me, with the bygone look.

I lipped rough rhymes of chance, not choice,
I thought not what my words might be;   10
There came into my ear a voice
That turned a tenderer verse for me.

Before Knowledge

When I walked roseless tracks and wide,
Ere dawned your date for meeting me,
O why did you not cry Halloo
Across the stretch between, and say:

'We move, while years as yet divide,
On closing lines which—though it be
You know me not nor I know you—
Will intersect and join some day!'

    Then well I had borne
    Each scraping thorn;   10
    But the winters froze,
    And grew no rose;
    No bridge bestrode
    The gap at all;
    No shape you showed,
    And I heard no call!

The Blinded Bird

So zestfully canst thou sing?
And all this indignity,
With God's consent, on thee!
Blinded ere yet a-wing
By the red-hot needle thou,
I stand and wonder how
So zestfully thou canst sing!

Resenting not such wrong,
Thy grievous pain forgot,
Eternal dark thy lot,   10
Groping thy whole life long,
After that stab of fire;
Enjailed in pitiless wire;
Resenting not such wrong!

Who hath charity? This bird.
Who suffereth long and is kind,
Is not provoked, though blind
And alive ensepulchred?
Who hopeth, endureth all things?
Who thinketh no evil, but sings?   20
Who is divine? This bird.°

'The wind blew words'

The wind blew words along the skies,
    And these it blew to me
Through the wide dusk: 'Lift up your eyes,
    Behold this troubled tree,
Complaining as it sways and plies;
    It is a limb of thee.

'Yea, too, the creatures sheltering round—
    Dumb figures, wild and tame,
Yea, too, thy fellows who abound—
    Either of speech the same   10

Or far and strange—black, dwarfed, and browned,
   They are stuff of thy own frame.'

I moved on in a surging awe
   Of inarticulateness
At the pathetic Me I saw
   In all his huge distress,
Making self-slaughter of the law
   To kill, break, or suppress.

The Faded Face

How was this I did not see
Such a look as here was shown
Ere its womanhood had blown
Past its first felicity?—
That I did not know you young,
   Faded Face,
      Know you young!

Why did Time so ill bestead
That I heard no voice of yours
Hail from out the curved contours
Of those lips when rosy red;
Weeted not the songs they sung,
   Faded Face,
      Songs they sung!

By these blanchings, blooms of old,
And the relics of your voice—
Leavings rare of rich and choice
From your early tone and mould—
Let me mourn,—aye, over-wrung,
   Faded Face,
      Over-wrung!

To My Father's Violin

Does he want you down there
In the Nether Glooms where
The hours may be a dragging load upon him,
    As he hears the axle grind
       Round and round
    Of the great world, in the blind
       Still profound
Of the night-time? He might liven at the sound
Of your string, revealing you had not forgone him.

    In the gallery west the nave,   10
    But a few yards from his grave,
Did you, tucked beneath his chin, to his bowing
    Guide the homely harmony
       Of the quire
    Who for long years strenuously—
       Son and sire—
Caught the strains that at his fingering low or higher
From your four thin threads and eff-holes came outflowing.

    And, too, what merry tunes
    He would bow at nights or noons   20
That chanced to find him bent to lute a measure,
    When he made you speak his heart
       As in dream,
    Without book or music-chart,
       On some theme
Elusive as a jack-o'-lanthorn's gleam,
And the psalm of duty shelved for trill of pleasure.

    Well, you can not, alas,
    The barrier overpass
That screens him in those Mournful Meads hereunder,   30
    Where no fiddling can be heard
       In the glades
    Of silentness, no bird
       Thrills the shades;
Where no viol is touched for songs or serenades,
No bowing wakes a congregation's wonder.

He must do without you now,
  Stir you no more anyhow
To yearning concords taught you in your glory;
  While, your strings a tangled wreck,   40
      Once smart drawn,
  Ten worm-wounds in your neck,
      Purflings wan
With dust-hoar, here alone I sadly con
Your present dumbness, shape your olden story.

                 1916.

The Change

Out of the past there rises a week—
  Who shall read the years O!—
Out of the past there rises a week
  Enringed with a purple zone.
Out of the past there rises a week
When thoughts were strung too thick to speak,
And the magic of its lineaments remains with me alone.

In that week there was heard a singing—
  Who shall spell the years, the years!—
In that week there was heard a singing,   10
  And the white owl wondered why.
In that week, yea, a voice was ringing,
And forth from the casement were candles flinging
Radiance that fell on the deodar and lit up the path thereby.

Could that song have a mocking note?—
  Who shall unroll the years O!—
Could that song have a mocking note
  To the white owl's sense as it fell?
Could that song have a mocking note
As it trilled out warm from the singer's throat,   20
And who was the mocker and who the mocked when two felt all
    was well?

In a tedious trampling crowd yet later—
    Who shall bare the years, the years!—
In a tedious trampling crowd yet later,
    When silvery singings were dumb;
In a crowd uncaring what time might fate her,
Mid murks of night I stood to await her,
And the twanging of iron wheels gave out the signal that she was
    come.

She said with a travel-tired smile—
    Who shall lift the years O!—   30
She said with a travel-tired smile,
    Half scared by scene so strange;
She said, outworn by mile on mile,
The blurred lamps wanning her face the while,
'O Love, I am here; I am with you!' . . . Ah, that there should
    have come a change!

O the doom by someone spoken—
    Who shall unseal the years, the years!—
O the doom that gave no token,
    When nothing of bale saw we:
O the doom by someone spoken,   40
O the heart by someone broken,
The heart whose sweet reverberances are all time leaves to me.

Jan.–Feb. 1913.

The Young Churchwarden

When he lit the candles there,
And the light fell on his hand,
And it trembled as he scanned
Her and me, his vanquished air
Hinted that his dream was done,
And I saw he had begun
    To understand.

When Love's viol was unstrung,
Sore I wished the hand that shook
Had been mine that shared her book   10
While that evening hymn was sung,
His the victor's, as he lit
Candles where he had bidden us sit
    With vanquished look.

Now her dust lies listless there,
His afar from tending hand,
What avails the victory scanned?
Does he smile from upper air:
'Ah, my friend, your dream is done;
And 'tis *you* who have begun   20
    To understand!'

'*I travel as a phantom now*'

I travel as a phantom now,
For people do not wish to see
In flesh and blood so bare a bough
    As Nature makes of me.

And thus I visit bodiless
Strange gloomy households often at odds,
And wonder if Man's consciousness
    Was a mistake of God's.

And next I meet you, and I pause,
And think that if mistake it were,
As some have said, O then it was   10
    One that I well can bear!

               1915.

'*In the seventies*'

'Qui deridetur ab amico suo sicut ego.'—Job.

In the seventies I was bearing in my breast,
          Penned tight,
Certain starry thoughts that threw a magic light
On the worktimes and the soundless hours of rest
In the seventies; aye, I bore them in my breast
          Penned tight.

In the seventies when my neighbours—even my friend—
          Saw me pass,
Heads were shaken, and I heard the words, 'Alas,
For his onward years and name unless he mend!'   10
In the seventies, when my neighbours and my friend
          Saw me pass.

In the seventies those who met me did not know
          Of the vision
That immuned me from the chillings of misprision
And the damps that choked my goings to and fro
In the seventies; yea, those nodders did not know
          Of the vision.

In the seventies nought could darken or destroy it,
          Locked in me,   20
Though as delicate as lamp-worm's lucency;
Neither mist nor murk could weaken or alloy it
In the seventies!—could not darken or destroy it,
          Locked in me.

Where They Lived

Dishevelled leaves creep down
          Upon that bank to-day,
Some green, some yellow, and some pale brown;
          The wet bents bob and sway;
The once warm slippery turf is sodden
          Where we laughingly sat or lay.

The summerhouse is gone,
　　Leaving a weedy space;
The bushes that veiled it once have grown
　　Gaunt trees that interlace,
Through whose lank limbs I see too clearly
　　The nakedness of the place.

And where were hills of blue,
　　Blind drifts of vapour blow,
And the names of former dwellers few,
　　If any, people know,
And instead of a voice that called, 'Come in, Dears,'
　　Time calls, 'Pass below!'

The Occultation

When the cloud shut down on the morning shine,
　　And darkened the sun,
I said, 'So ended that joy of mine
　　Years back begun.'

But day continued its lustrous roll
　　In upper air;
And did my late irradiate soul
　　Live on somewhere?

Life Laughs Onward

Rambling I looked for an old abode
Where, years back, one had lived I knew;
Its site a dwelling duly showed,
　　But it was new.

I went where, not so long ago,
The sod had riven two breasts asunder;
Daisies throve gaily there, as though
　　No grave were under.

I walked along a terrace where
Loud children gambolled in the sun;   10
The figure that had once sat there
     Was missed by none.

Life laughed and moved on unsubdued,
I saw that Old succumbed to Young:
'Twas well. My too regretful mood
     Died on my tongue.

'Something tapped'

Something tapped on the pane of my room
     When there was never a trace
Of wind or rain, and I saw in the gloom
     My weary Belovéd's face.

'O I am tired of waiting', she said,
     'Night, morn, noon, afternoon;
So cold it is in my lonely bed,
     And I thought you would join me soon!'

I rose and neared the window-glass,
     But vanished thence had she: 10
Only a pallid moth, alas,
     Tapped at the pane for me.

                         August 1913.

The Wound

I climbed to the crest,
     And, fog-festooned,
The sun lay west
     Like a crimson wound:

Like that wound of mine
     Of which none knew,
For I'd given no sign
     That it pierced me through.

A Merrymaking in Question

'I will get a new string for my fiddle,
　　And call to the neighbours to come,
And partners shall dance down the middle
　　Until the old pewter-wares hum:
　　And we'll sip the mead, cyder, and rum!'

From the night came the oddest of answers:
　　A hollow wind, like a bassoon,
And headstones all ranged up as dancers,
　　And cypresses droning a croon,
　　And gurgoyles that mouthed to the tune.　　10

A January Night

(1879)

The rain smites more and more,
The east wind snarls and sneezes;
Through the joints of the quivering door
　　The water wheezes.

The tip of each ivy-shoot
Writhes on its neighbour's face;
There is some hid dread afoot
　　That we cannot trace.

Is it the spirit astray
Of the man at the house below　　　　　　　　10
Whose coffin they took in to-day?
　　We do not know.

The Announcement

They came, the brothers, and took two chairs
      In their usual quiet way;
And for a time we did not think
      They had much to say.

And they began and talked awhile
      Of ordinary things,
Till spread that silence in the room
      A pent thought brings.

And then they said: 'The end has come.
      Yes: it has come at last.'
And we looked down, and knew that day   10
      A spirit had passed.

The Oxen

Christmas Eve, and twelve of the clock.
      'Now they are all on their knees,'
An elder said as we sat in a flock
      By the embers in hearthside ease.

We pictured the meek mild creatures where
      They dwelt in their strawy pen,
Nor did it occur to one of us there
      To doubt they were kneeling then.

So fair a fancy few would weave
      In these years! Yet, I feel,   10
If someone said on Christmas Eve,
      'Come; see the oxen kneel

'In the lonely barton by yonder coomb
      Our childhood used to know,'
I should go with him in the gloom,
      Hoping it might be so.

                              1915.

An Anniversary

It was at the very date to which we have come,
   In the month of the matching name,
When, at a like minute, the sun had upswum,
   Its couch-time at night being the same.
And the same path stretched here that people now follow,
   And the same stile crossed their way,
And beyond the same green hillock and hollow
   The same horizon lay;
And the same man pilgrims now hereby who pilgrimed here that
   day.

Let so much be said of the date-day's sameness;   10
   But the tree that neighbours the track,
And stoops like a pedlar afflicted with lameness,
   Knew of no sogged wound or wind-crack.
And the joints of that wall were not enshrouded
   With mosses of many tones,
And the garth up afar was not overcrowded
   With a multitude of white stones,
And the man's eyes then were not so sunk that you saw the
   socket-bones.

Kingston-Maurward Ewelease.

The Pink Frock

'O my pretty pink frock,
I shan't be able to wear it!
Why is he dying just now?
   I hardly can bear it!

'He might have contrived to live on;
But they say there's no hope whatever:
And must I shut myself up,
   And go out never?

'O my pretty pink frock,
Puff-sleeved and accordion-pleated!   10
He might have passed in July,
    And not so cheated!'

Transformations

Portion of this yew
Is a man my grandsire knew,
Bosomed here at its foot:
This branch may be his wife,
A ruddy human life
Now turned to a green shoot.

These grasses must be made
Of her who often prayed,
Last century, for repose;
And the fair girl long ago   10
Whom I vainly tried to know
May be entering this rose.

So, they are not underground,
But as nerves and veins abound
In the growths of upper air,
And they feel the sun and rain,
And the energy again
That made them what they were!

In her Precincts

Her house looked cold from the foggy lea,
And the square of each window a dull black blur
    Where showed no stir:
Yes, her gloom within at the lack of me
Seemed matching mine at the lack of her.

The black squares grew to be squares of light
As the eveshade swathed the house and lawn,
  And viols gave tone;
There was glee within. And I found that night
The gloom of severance mine alone.   10

       Kingston-Maurward Park.

The Last Signal

(*Oct.* 11, 1886)

A MEMORY OF WILLIAM BARNES

Silently I footed by an uphill road
That led from my abode to a spot yew-boughed;
Yellowly the sun sloped low down to westward,
  And dark was the east with cloud.

Then, amid the shadow of that livid sad east,
Where the light was least, and a gate stood wide,
Something flashed the fire of the sun that was facing it,
  Like a brief blaze on that side.

Looking hard and harder I knew what it meant—
The sudden shine sent from the livid east scene;   10
It meant the west mirrored by the coffin of my friend there,
  Turning to the road from his green,

To take his last journey forth—he who in his prime
Trudged so many a time from that gate athwart the land!
Thus a farewell to me he signalled on his grave-way,
  As with a wave of his hand.

      Winterborne–Came Path.

The House of Silence

'That is a quiet place—
That house in the trees with the shady lawn.'
'—If, child, you knew what there goes on
You would not call it a quiet place.
Why, a phantom abides there, the last of its race,
　　And a brain spins there till dawn.'

'But I see nobody there,—
Nobody moves about the green,
Or wanders the heavy trees between.'
'—Ah, that's because you do not bear　　　　　10
The visioning powers of souls who dare
　　To pierce the material screen.

'Morning, noon, and night,
Mid those funereal shades that seem
The uncanny scenery of a dream,
Figures dance to a mind with sight,
And music and laughter like floods of light
　　Make all the precincts gleam.

'It is a poet's bower,
Through which there pass, in fleet arrays,　　　20
Long teams of all the years and days,
Of joys and sorrows, of earth and heaven,
That meet mankind in its ages seven,
　　An aeon in an hour.'

Great Things

Sweet cyder is a great thing,
　A great thing to me,
Spinning down to Weymouth town
　By Ridgway thirstily,

And maid and mistress summoning
   Who tend the hostelry:
O cyder is a great thing,
   A great thing to me!

The dance it is a great thing,
   A great thing to me,   10
With candles lit and partners fit
   For night-long revelry;
And going home when day-dawning
   Peeps pale upon the lea:
O dancing is a great thing,
   A great thing to me!

Love is, yea, a great thing,
   A great thing to me,
When, having drawn across the lawn
   In darkness silently,   20
A figure flits like one a-wing
   Out from the nearest tree:
O love is, yes, a great thing,
   A great thing to me!

Will these be always great things,
   Great things to me? . . .
Let it befall that One will call,
   'Soul, I have need of thee':
What then? Joy-jaunts, impassioned flings,
   Love, and its ecstasy,   30
Will always have been great things,
   Great things to me!

The Chimes

That morning when I trod the town
The twitching chimes of long renown
   Played out to me
The sweet Sicilian sailors' tune,
And I knew not if late or soon
   My day would be:

A day of sunshine beryl-bright
And windless; yea, think as I might,
    I could not say,
Even to within years' measure, when   10
One would be at my side who then
    Was far away.

When hard utilitarian times
Had stilled the sweet Saint-Peter's chimes
    I learnt to see
That bale may spring where blisses are,
And one desired might be afar
    Though near to me.

The Figure in the Scene

It pleased her to step in front and sit
    Where the cragged slope was green,
While I stood back that I might pencil it
    With her amid the scene.
      Till it gloomed and rained;
But I kept on, despite the drifting wet
    That fell and stained
My draught, leaving for curious quizzings yet
    The blots engrained.

And thus I drew her there alone,   10
    Seated amid the gauze
Of moisture, hooded, only her outline shown,
    With rainfall marked across.
      —Soon passed our stay;
Yet her rainy form is the Genius still of the spot,
    Immutable, yea,
Though the place now knows her no more, and has known her not
    Ever since that day.

From an old note.

'Why did I sketch'

Why did I sketch an upland green,
    And put the figure in
    Of one on the spot with me?—
For now that one has ceased to be seen
    The picture waxes akin
    To a wordless irony.

If you go drawing on down or cliff
    Let no soft curves intrude
    Of a woman's silhouette,
But show the escarpments stark and stiff   10
    As in utter solitude;
    So shall you half forget.

Let me sooner pass from sight of the sky
    Than again on a thoughtless day
    Limn, laugh, and sing, and rhyme
With a woman sitting near, whom I
    Paint in for love, and who may
    Be called hence in my time!

                              From an old note.

The Blow

That no man schemed it is my hope—
Yea, that it fell by will and scope
    Of That Which some enthrone,
And for whose meaning myriads grope.

For I would not that of my kind
There should, of his unbiassed mind,
    Have been one known
Who such a stroke could have designed;

Since it would augur works and ways
Below the lowest that man assays   10
    To have hurled that stone
Into the sunshine of our days!

And if it prove that no man did,
And that the Inscrutable, the Hid,
    Was cause alone
Of this foul crash our lives amid,

I'll go in due time, and forget
In some deep graveyard's oubliette
    The thing whereof I groan,
And cease from troubling; thankful yet   20

Time's finger should have stretched to show
No aimful author's was the blow
    That swept us prone,
But the Immanent Doer's That doth not know,

Which in some age unguessed of us
May lift Its blinding incubus,
    And see, and own:
'It grieves me I did thus and thus!'

Love the Monopolist

(Young Lover's Reverie)

The train draws forth from the station-yard,
    And with it carries me.
I rise, and stretch out, and regard
    The platform left, and see
An airy slim blue form there standing,
    And know that it is she.

While with strained vision I watch on,
    The figure turns round quite
To greet friends gaily; then is gone. . . .
    The import may be slight,   10

But why remained she not hard gazing
    Till I was out of sight?

'O do not chat with others there,'
    I brood. 'They are not I.
O strain your thoughts as if they were
    Gold bands between us; eye
All neighbour scenes as so much blankness
    Till I again am by!

'A troubled soughing in the breeze
    And the sky overhead   20
Let yourself feel; and shadeful trees,
    Ripe corn, and apples red,
Read as things barren and distasteful
    While we are separated!

'When I come back uncloak your gloom,
    And let in lovely day;
Then the long dark as of the tomb
    Can well be thrust away
With sweet things I shall have to practise,
    And you will have to say!'   30

                Begun 1871: finished ——.

At Middle-Field Gate in February

The bars are thick with drops that show
    As they gather themselves from the fog
Like silver buttons ranged in a row,
And as evenly spaced as if measured, although
    They fall at the feeblest jog.

They load the leafless hedge hard by,
    And the blades of last year's grass,
While the fallow ploughland turned up nigh
In raw rolls clammy and clogging lie—
    Too clogging for feet to pass.   10

How dry it was on a far-back day
    When straws hung the hedge and around,
When amid the sheaves in amorous play
In curtained bonnets and light array
    Bloomed a bevy now underground!

Bockhampton Lane.

The Head above the Fog

    Something do I see
Above the fog that sheets the mead,
A figure like to life indeed,
Moving along with spectre-speed,
    Seen by none but me.

    O the vision keen!—
Tripping along to me for love
As in the flesh it used to move,
Only its hat and plume above
    The evening fog-fleece seen.   10

    In the day-fall wan,
When nighted birds break off their song,
Mere ghostly head it skims along,
Just as it did when warm and strong,
    Body seeming gone.

    Such it is I see
Above the fog that sheets the mead—
Yea, that which once could breathe and plead!—
Skimming along with spectre-speed
    To a last tryst with me.   20

Overlooking the River Stour

The swallows flew in the curves of an eight
    Above the river-gleam
    In the wet June's last beam:
Like little crossbows animate
The swallows flew in the curves of an eight
    Above the river-gleam.

Planing up shavings of crystal spray
    A moor-hen darted out
    From the bank thereabout,
And through the stream-shine ripped his way;   10
Planing up shavings of crystal spray
    A moor-hen darted out.

Closed were the kingcups; and the mead
    Dripped in monotonous green,
    Though the day's morning sheen
Had shown it golden and honeybee'd;
Closed were the kingcups; and the mead
    Dripped in monotonous green.

And never I turned my head, alack,
    While these things met my gaze   20
    Through the pane's drop-drenched glaze,
To see the more behind my back. . . .
O never I turned, but let, alack,
    These less things hold my gaze!

On Sturminster Foot-Bridge

(Onomatopoeic)

Reticulations creep upon the slack stream's face
    When the wind skims irritably past,
The current clucks smartly into each hollow place
That years of flood have scrabbled in the pier's sodden base;
    The floating-lily leaves rot fast.

On a roof stand the swallows ranged in wistful waiting rows,
    Till they arrow off and drop like stones
Among the eyot-withies at whose foot the river flows;
And beneath the roof is she who in the dark world shows
    As a lattice-gleam when midnight moans.   10

Old Furniture

I know not how it may be with others
    Who sit amid relics of householdry
That date from the days of their mothers' mothers,
        But well I know how it is with me
            Continually.

I see the hands of the generations
    That owned each shiny familiar thing
In play on its knobs and indentations,
        And with its ancient fashioning
            Still dallying: 10

Hands behind hands, growing paler and paler,
    As in a mirror a candle-flame
Shows images of itself, each frailer
    As it recedes, though the eye may frame
        Its shape the same.

On the clock's dull dial a foggy finger,
    Moving to set the minutes right
With tentative touches that lift and linger
    In the wont of a moth on a summer night,
        Creeps to my sight.   20

On this old viol, too, fingers are dancing—
    As whilom—just over the strings by the nut,
The tip of a bow receding, advancing
    In airy quivers, as if it would cut
        The plaintive gut.

And I see a face by that box for tinder,
 Glowing forth in fits from the dark,
And fading again, as the linten cinder
 Kindles to red at the flinty spark,
  Or goes out stark.   30

Well, well. It is best to be up and doing,
 The world has no use for one to-day
Who eyes things thus—no aim pursuing!
 He should not continue in this stay,
  But sink away.

A Thought in Two Moods

I saw it—pink and white—revealed
 Upon the white and green;
The white and green was a daisied field,
 The pink and white Ethleen.

And as I looked it seemed in kind
 That difference they had none;
The two fair bodiments combined
 As varied miens of one.

A sense that, in some mouldering year,
 As one they both would lie,   10
Made me move quickly on to her
 To pass the pale thought by.

She laughed and said: 'Out there, to me,
 You looked so weather-browned,
And brown in clothes, you seemed to be
 Made of the dusty ground!'

The Last Performance

'I am playing my oldest tunes,' declared she,
    'All the old tunes I know,—
Those I learnt ever so long ago.'
—Why she should think just then she'd play them
    Silence cloaks like snow.

When I returned from the town at nightfall
    Notes continued to pour
As when I had left two hours before:
'It's the very last time,' she said in closing;
    'From now I play no more.'   10

A few morns onward found her fading,
    And, as her life outflew,
I thought of her playing her tunes right through;
And I felt she had known of what was coming,
    And wondered how she knew.

                                        1912.

The Interloper

'And I saw the figure and visage of Madness seeking for a home.'

There are three folk driving in a quaint old chaise,
And the cliff-side track looks green and fair;
I view them talking in quiet glee
As they drop down towards the puffins' lair
    By the roughest of ways;
But another with the three rides on, I see,
    Whom I like not to be there!

No: it's not anybody you think of. Next
A dwelling appears by a slow sweet stream
Where two sit happy and half in the dark: 10
They read, helped out by a frail-wick'd gleam,
    Some rhythmic text;
But one sits with them whom they don't mark,
    One I'm wishing could not be there.

No: not whom you knew and name. And now
I discern gay diners in a mansion-place,
And the guests dropping wit—pert, prim, or choice,
And the hostess's tender and laughing face,
    And the host's bland brow;
But I cannot help hearing a hollow voice,   20
    And I'd fain not hear it there.

No: it's not from the stranger you met once. Ah,
Yet a goodlier scene than that succeeds;
People on a lawn—quite a crowd of them. Yes,
And they chatter and ramble as fancy leads;
    And they say, 'Hurrah!'
To a blithe speech made; save one, mirthless,
    Who ought not to be there.

Nay: it's not the pale Form your imagings raise,
That waits on us all at a destined time,   30
It is not the Fourth Figure the Furnace showed;°
O that it were such a shape sublime
    In these latter days!
It is that under which best lives corrode;
    Would, would it could not be there!

Logs on the Hearth

A Memory of a Sister

    The fire advances along the log
        Of the tree we felled,
Which bloomed and bore striped apples by the peck
   Till its last hour of bearing knelled.

    The fork that first my hand would reach
        And then my foot
In climbings upward inch by inch, lies now
   Sawn, sapless, darkening with soot.

Where the bark chars is where, one year,
    It was pruned, and bled—   10
Then overgrew the wound. But now, at last,
    Its growings all have stagnated.

My fellow-climber rises dim
    From her chilly grave—
Just as she was, her foot near mine on the bending limb,
    Laughing, her young brown hand awave.

December 1915.

The Sunshade

Ah—it's the skeleton of a lady's sunshade,
    Here at my feet in the hard rock's chink,
    Merely a naked sheaf of wires!—
    Twenty years have gone with their livers and diers
    Since it was silked in its white or pink.

Noonshine riddles the ribs of the sunshade,
    No more a screen from the weakest ray;
    Nothing to tell us the hue of its dyes,
    Nothing but rusty bones as it lies
    In its coffin of stone, unseen till to-day.   10

Where is the woman who carried that sunshade
    Up and down this seaside place?—
    Little thumb standing against its stem,
    Thoughts perhaps bent on a love-stratagem,
    Softening yet more the already soft face!

Is the fair woman who carried that sunshade
    A skeleton just as her property is,
    Laid in the chink that none may scan?
    And does she regret—if regret dust can—
    The vain things thought when she flourished this?   20

Swanage Cliffs.

The Ageing House

When the walls were red
That now are seen
To be overspread
With a mouldy green,
A fresh fair head
Would often lean
From the sunny casement
And scan the scene,
While blithely spoke the wind to the little sycamore tree.

But storms have raged   10
Those walls about,
And the head has aged
That once looked out;
And zest is suaged
And trust grows doubt,
And slow effacement
Is rife throughout,
While fiercely girds the wind at the long-limbed sycamore tree!

The Five Students

The sparrow dips in his wheel-rut bath,
    The sun grows passionate-eyed,
And boils the dew to smoke by the paddock-path;
    As strenuously we stride,—
Five of us; dark He, fair He, dark She, fair She, I,
    All beating by.

The air is shaken, the high-road hot,
    Shadowless swoons the day,
The greens are sobered and cattle at rest; but not
    We on our urgent way,—   10
Four of us; fair She, dark She, fair He, I, are there,
    But one—elsewhere.

Autumn moulds the hard fruit mellow,
   And forward still we press
Through moors, briar-meshed plantations, clay-pits yellow,
   As in the spring hours—yes,
Three of us; fair He, fair She, I, as heretofore,
   But—fallen one more.

The leaf drops: earthworms draw it in
   At night-time noiselessly,   20
The fingers of birch and beech are skeleton-thin,
   And yet on the beat are we,—
Two of us; fair She, I. But no more left to go
   The track we know.

Icicles tag the church-aisle leads,
   The flag-rope gibbers hoarse,
The home-bound foot-folk wrap their snow-flaked heads,
   Yet I still stalk the course,—
One of us. . . . Dark and fair He, dark and fair She, gone:
   The rest—anon.   30

The Wind's Prophecy

I travel on by barren farms,
And gulls glint out like silver flecks
Against a cloud that speaks of wrecks,
And bellies down with black alarms.
I say: 'Thus from my lady's arms
I go; those arms I love the best!'
The wind replies from dip and rise,
'Nay; toward her arms thou journeyest.'

A distant verge morosely gray
Appears, while clots of flying foam   10
Break from its muddy monochrome,
And a light blinks up far away.
I sigh: 'My eyes now as all day
Behold her ebon loops of hair!'
Like bursting bonds the wind responds,
'Nay, wait for tresses flashing fair!'

From tides the lofty coastlines screen
Come smitings like the slam of doors,
Or hammerings on hollow floors,
As the swell cleaves through caves unseen.   20
Say I: 'Though broad this wild terrene,
Her city home is matched of none!'
From the hoarse skies the wind replies:
'Thou shouldst have said her sea-bord one.'

The all-prevailing clouds exclude
The one quick timorous transient star;
The waves outside where breakers are
Huzza like a mad multitude.
'Where the sun ups it, mist-imbued,'
I cry, 'there reigns the star for me!'   30
The wind outshrieks from points and peaks:
'Here, westward, where it downs, mean ye!'

Yonder the headland, vulturine,
Snores like old Skrymer in his sleep,˘
And every chasm and every steep
Blackens as wakes each pharos-shine.
'I roam, but one is safely mine,'
I say. 'God grant she stay my own!'
Low laughs the wind as if it grinned:
'Thy Love is one thou'st not yet known.'   40

Rewritten from an old copy.

During Wind and Rain

They sing their dearest songs—
He, she, all of them—yea,
Treble and tenor and bass,
    And one to play;
With the candles mooning each face. . . .
    Ah, no; the years O!
How the sick leaves reel down in throngs!

They clear the creeping moss—
Elders and juniors—aye,
Making the pathways neat   10
    And the garden gay;
And they build a shady seat. . . .
     Ah, no; the years, the years;
See, the white storm-birds wing across.

They are blithely breakfasting all—
Men and maidens—yea,
Under the summer tree,
    With a glimpse of the bay,
While pet fowl come to the knee. . . .
     Ah, no; the years O!   20
And the rotten rose is ript from the wall.

They change to a high new house,
He, she, all of them—aye,
Clocks and carpets and chairs
    On the lawn all day,
And brightest things that are theirs. . . .
     Ah, no; the years, the years;
Down their carved names the rain-drop ploughs.

He Prefers Her Earthly

This after-sunset is a sight for seeing,
Cliff-heads of craggy cloud surrounding it.
    —And dwell you in that glory-show?
You may; for there are strange strange things in being,
     Stranger than I know.

Yet if that chasm of splendour claim your presence
Which glows between the ash cloud and the dun,
    How changed must be your mortal mould!
Changed to a firmament-riding earthless essence
     From what you were of old: 10

All too unlike the fond and fragile creature
Then known to me. . . . Well, shall I say it plain?
   I would not have you thus and there,
But still would grieve on, missing you, still feature
   You as the one you were.

Molly Gone

No more summer for Molly and me;
   There is snow on the tree,
And the blackbirds plump large as the rooks are, almost,
   And the water is hard
Where they used to dip bills at the dawn ere her figure was lost
   To these coasts, now my prison close-barred.

No more planting by Molly and me
   Where the beds used to be
Of sweet-william; no training the clambering rose
   By the framework of fir   10
Now bowering the pathway, whereon it swings gaily and blows
   As if calling commendment from her.

No more jauntings by Molly and me
   To the town by the sea,
Or along over Whitesheet to Wynyard's green Gap,
   Catching Montacute Crest
To the right against Sedgmoor, and Corton-Hill's far-distant cap,
   And Pilsdon and Lewsdon to west.

No more singing by Molly to me
   In the evenings when she   20
Was in mood and in voice, and the candles were lit,
   And past the porch-quoin
The rays would spring out on the laurels; and dumbledores hit
   On the pane, as if wishing to join.

Where, then, is Molly, who's no more with me?
  —As I stand on this lea,
Thinking thus, there's a many-flamed star in the air,
  That tosses a sign
That her glance is regarding its face from her home, so that there
  Her eyes may have meetings with mine.   30

A Backward Spring

The trees are afraid to put forth buds,
And there is timidity in the grass;
The plots lie gray where gouged by spuds,
  And whether next week will pass
Free of sly sour winds is the fret of each bush
  Of barberry waiting to bloom.

Yet the snowdrop's face betrays no gloom,
And the primrose pants in its heedless push,
Though the myrtle asks if it's worth the fight
  This year with frost and rime   10
  To venture one more time
On delicate leaves and buttons of white
From the selfsame bough as at last year's prime,
And never to ruminate on or remember
What happened to it in mid-December.

        April 1917.

Looking Across

I

It is dark in the sky,
And silence is where
Our laughs rang high;
And recall do I
That One is out there.°

II

The dawn is not nigh,
And the trees are bare,
And the waterways sigh
That a year has drawn by,
And Two are out there.   10

III

The wind drops to die
Like the phantom of Care
Too frail for a cry,
And heart brings to eye
That Three are out there.

IV

This Life runs dry
That once ran rare
And rosy in dye,
And fleet the days fly,
And Four are out there.   20

V

Tired, tired am I
Of this earthly air,
And my wraith asks: Why,
Since these calm lie,
Are not Five out there?

December 1915.

The Glimpse

She sped through the door
And, following in haste,
And stirred to the core,
I entered hot-faced;
But I could not find her,
No sign was behind her.

'Where is she?' I said:
—'Who?' they asked that sat there;
'Not a soul's come in sight.'
—'A maid with red hair.'   10
—'Ah.' They paled. 'She is dead.
People see her at night,
But you are the first
On whom she has burst
In the keen common light.'

It was ages ago,
When I was quite strong:
I have waited since,—O,
I have waited so long!
—Yea, I set me to own   20
The house, where now lone
I dwell in void rooms
Booming hollow as tombs!
But I never come near her,
Though nightly I hear her.
And my cheek has grown thin
And my hair has grown gray
With this waiting therein;
But she still keeps away!

'Who's in the next room?'

'Who's in the next room?—who?
        I seemed to see
Somebody in the dawning passing through,
        Unknown to me.'
'Nay: you saw nought. He passed invisibly.'

'Who's in the next room?—who?
        I seem to hear
Somebody muttering firm in a language new
        That chills the ear.'
'No: you catch not his tongue who has entered there.'   10

'Who's in the next room?—who?
                I seem to feel
His breath like a clammy draught, as if it drew
                From the Polar Wheel.'
'No: none who breathes at all does the door conceal.'

'Who's in the next room?—who?
                A figure wan
With a message to one in there of something due?
                Shall I know him anon?'
'Yea he; and he brought such; and you'll know him anon.' 20

At a Country Fair

At a bygone Western country fair
I saw a giant led by a dwarf
With a red string like a long thin scarf;
How much he was the stronger there
                The giant seemed unaware.

And then I saw that the giant was blind,
And the dwarf a shrewd-eyed little thing;
The giant, mild, timid, obeyed the string
As if he had no independent mind,
                Or will of any kind. 10

Wherever the dwarf decided to go
At his heels the other trotted meekly,
(Perhaps—I know not—reproaching weakly)
Like one Fate bade that it must be so,
                Whether he wished or no.

Various sights in various climes
I have seen, and more I may see yet,
But that sight never shall I forget,
And have thought it the sorriest of pantomimes,
                If once, a hundred times! 20

Paying Calls

I went by footpath and by stile
    Beyond where bustle ends,
Strayed here a mile and there a mile
    And called upon some friends.

On certain ones I had not seen
    For years past did I call,
And then on others who had been
    The oldest friends of all.

It was the time of midsummer
    When they had used to roam;   10
But now, though tempting was the air,
    I found them all at home.

I spoke to one and other of them
    By mound and stone and tree
Of things we had done ere days were dim,
    But they spoke not to me.

The Upper Birch-Leaves

Warm yellowy-green
In the blue serene,
How they skip and sway
On this autumn day!
They cannot know
What has happened below,—
That their boughs down there
Are already quite bare,
That their own will be
When a week has passed,—   10
For they jig as in glee
To this very last.

But no; there lies
At times in their tune
A note that cries
What at first I fear
I did not hear:
'O we remember
At each wind's hollo—
Though life holds yet—   20
We go hence soon,
For 'tis November;
—But that *you* follow
You may forget!'

'*It never looks like summer*'

'It never looks like summer here
    On Beeny by the sea.'
But though she saw its look as drear,
    Summer it seemed to me.

It never looks like summer now
    Whatever weather's there;
But ah, it cannot anyhow,
    On Beeny or elsewhere!

                Boscastle,
          March 8, 1913.

Everything Comes

'The house is bleak and cold
    Built so new for me!
All the winds upon the wold
    Search it through for me;
No screening trees abound,
And the curious eyes around
    Keep on view for me.'

'My Love, I am planting trees
　　As a screen for you
Both from winds, and eyes that tease　　　　10
　　And peer in for you.
Only wait till they have grown,
No such bower will be known
　　As I mean for you.'

'Then I will bear it, Love,
　　And will wait,' she said.
—So, with years, there grew a grove.
　　'Skill how great!' she said.
'As you wished, Dear?'—'Yes, I see!
But—I'm dying; and for me　　　　20
　　'Tis too late,' she said.

The Man with a Past

　　There was merry-making
　　When the first dart fell
　　As a heralding,—
Till grinned the fully bared thing,
　　And froze like a spell—
　　　Like a spell.

　　Innocent was she,
　　Innocent was I,
　　Too simple we!
Before us we did not see,　　　　10
　　Nearing, aught wry—
　　　Aught wry!

　　I can tell it not now,
　　It was long ago;
　　And such things cow;
But that is why and how
　　Two lives were so—
　　　Were so.

Yes, the years matured,
And the blows were three   20
That time ensured
On her, which she dumbly endured;
And one on me—
One on me.

He Fears His Good Fortune

There was a glorious time
At an epoch of my prime;
Mornings beryl-bespread,
And evenings golden-red;
    Nothing gray:
And in my heart I said,
'However this chanced to be,
It is too full for me,
Too rare, too rapturous, rash,
Its spell must close with a crash   10
    Some day!'

The radiance went on
Anon and yet anon,
And sweetness fell around
Like manna on the ground.
    'I've no claim',
Said I, 'to be thus crowned:
I am not worthy this:—
Must it not go amiss?—
Well ... let the end foreseen   20
Come duly!—I am serene.'
    —And it came.

Jubilate

'The very last time I ever was here', he said,
'I saw much less of the quick than I saw of the dead.'
—He was a man I had met with somewhere before,
But how or when I now could recall no more.

'The hazy mazy moonlight at one in the morning
Spread out as a sea across the frozen snow,
Glazed to live sparkles like the great breastplate adorning
The priest of the Temple, with Urim and Thummim aglow.

'The yew-tree arms, glued hard to the stiff stark air,
Hung still in the village sky as theatre-scenes   10
When I came by the churchyard wall, and halted there
At a shut-in sound of fiddles and tambourines.

'And as I stood harkening, dulcimers, hautboys, and shawms,
And violoncellos, and a three-stringed double-bass,
Joined in, and were intermixed with a singing of psalms;
And I looked over at the dead men's dwelling-place.

'Through the shine of the slippery snow I now could see,
As it were through a crystal roof, a great company
Of the dead minueting in stately step underground
To the tune of the instruments I had before heard sound.   20

'It was "Eden New", and dancing they sang in a chore,
"We are out of it all!—yea, in Little-Ease cramped no more!"
And their shrouded figures pacing with joy I could see
As you see the stage from the gallery. And they had no heed of
    me.

'And I lifted my head quite dazed from the churchyard wall
And I doubted not that it warned I should soon have my call.
But—' . . . Then in the ashes he emptied the dregs of his cup,
And onward he went, and the darkness swallowed him up.

He Revisits His First School

I should not have shown in the flesh,
I ought to have gone as a ghost;
It was awkward, unseemly almost,
Standing solidly there as when fresh,
    Pink, tiny, crisp-curled,
    My pinions yet furled
From the winds of the world.

After waiting so many a year
To wait longer, and go as a sprite
From the tomb at the mid of some night
Was the right, radiant way to appear;
    Not as one wanzing weak
    From life's roar and reek,
    His rest still to seek:

Yea, beglimpsed through the quaint quarried glass
Of green moonlight, by me greener made,
When they'd cry, perhaps, 'There sits his shade
In his olden haunt—just as he was
    When in Walkingame he
    Conned the grand Rule-of-Three
    With the bent of a bee.'

But to show in the afternoon sun,
With an aspect of hollow-eyed care,
When none wished to see me come there,
Was a garish thing, better undone.
    Yes; wrong was the way;
    But yet, let me say,
    I may right it—some day.

'I thought, my Heart'

I thought, my Heart, that you had healed
Of those sore smartings of the past,
And that the summers had oversealed
        All mark of them at last.
But closely scanning in the night
I saw them standing crimson-bright
            Just as she made them:
            Nothing could fade them;
            Yea, I can swear
            That there they were—   10
            They still were there!

Then the Vision of her who cut them came,
And looking over my shoulder said,
'I am sure you deal me all the blame
        For those sharp smarts and red;
But meet me, dearest, to-morrow night,
In the churchyard at the moon's half-height,
            And so strange a kiss
            Shall be mine, I wis,
            That you'll cease to know   20
            If the wounds you show
            Be there or no!'

Midnight on the Great Western

In the third-class seat sat the journeying boy,
        And the roof-lamp's oily flame
Played down on his listless form and face,
Bewrapt past knowing to what he was going,
            Or whence he came.

In the band of his hat the journeying boy
        Had a ticket stuck; and a string
Around his neck bore the key of his box,
That twinkled gleams of the lamp's sad beams
            Like a living thing.   10

What past can be yours, O journeying boy
    Towards a world unknown,
Who calmly, as if incurious quite
On all at stake, can undertake
      This plunge alone?

Knows your soul a sphere, O journeying boy,
    Our rude realms far above,
Whence with spacious vision you mark and mete
This region of sin that you find you in,
      But are not of?   20

Honeymoon-Time at an Inn

At the shiver of morning, a little before the false dawn,
    The moon was at the window-square,
    Deedily brooding in deformed decay—
The curve hewn off her cheek as by an adze;
At the shiver of morning a little before the false dawn
    So the moon looked in there.

Her speechless eyeing reached across the chamber,
    Where lay two souls opprest,
    One a white lady sighing, 'Why am I sad!'
    To him who sighed back, 'Sad, my Love, am I!'   10
And speechlessly the old moon conned the chamber,
    And these two reft of rest.

While their large-pupilled vision swept the scene there,
    Nought seeming imminent,
    Something fell sheer, and crashed, and from the floor
    Lay glittering at the pair with a shattered gaze,
While their large-pupilled vision swept the scene there,
    And the many-eyed thing outleant.

With a start they saw that it was an old-time pier-glass
    Which had stood on the mantel near,   20
    Its silvering blemished,—yes, as if worn away

By the eyes of the countless dead who had smirked at it
Ere these two ever knew that old-time pier-glass
    And its vague and vacant leer.

As he looked, his bride like a moth skimmed forth, and kneeling
    Quick, with quivering sighs,
  Gathered the pieces under the moon's sly ray,
  Unwitting as an automaton what she did;
Till he entreated, hasting to where she was kneeling,
    'Let it stay where it lies!'   30

'Long years of sorrow this means!' breathed the lady
    As they retired. 'Alas!'
  And she lifted one pale hand across her eyes.
  'Don't trouble, Love; it's nothing,' the bridegroom said.
'Long years of sorrow for us!' murmured the lady,
    'Or ever this evil pass!'

And the Spirits Ironic laughed behind the wainscot,
    And the Spirits of Pity sighed.
  'It's good', said the Spirits Ironic, 'to tickle their minds
  With a portent of their wedlock's after-grinds.'   40
And the Spirits of Pity sighed behind the wainscot,
    'It's a portent we cannot abide!

'More, what shall happen to prove the truth of the portent?'
    —'Oh; in brief, they will fade till old,
  And their loves grow numbed ere death, by the cark of care.'
  —'But nought see we that asks for portents there?—
'Tis the lot of all.'—'Well, no less true is a portent
    That it fits all mortal mould.'

In a Waiting-Room

On a morning sick as the day of doom
    With the drizzling gray
    Of an English May,
There were few in the railway waiting-room.
About its walls were framed and varnished
Pictures of liners, fly-blown, tarnished.
The table bore a Testament
For travellers' reading, if suchwise bent.

    I read it on and on,
And, thronging the Gospel of Saint John,   10
    Were figures—additions, multiplications—
By some one scrawled, with sundry emendations;
    Not scoffingly designed,
    But with an absent mind,—
Plainly a bagman's counts of cost,
What he had profited, what lost;
And whilst I wondered if there could have been
    Any particle of a soul
    In that poor man at all,
    To cypher rates of wage   20
    Upon that printed page,
    There joined in the charmless scene
And stood over me and the scribbled book
    (To lend the hour's mean hue
    A smear of tragedy too)
A soldier and wife, with haggard look
Subdued to stone by strong endeavour;
    And then I heard
    From a casual word
They were parting as they believed for ever.   30

    But next there came
    Like the eastern flame
Of some high altar, children—a pair—
Who laughed at the fly-blown pictures there.

'Here are the lovely ships that we,
Mother, are by and by going to see!
When we get there it's 'most sure to be fine,
And the band will play, and the sun will shine!'

It rained on the skylight with a din
As we waited and still no train came in;   40
But the words of the child in the squalid room
Had spread a glory through the gloom.

The Clock-Winder

It is dark as a cave,
Or a vault in the nave
When the iron door
Is closed, and the floor
Of the church relaid
With trowel and spade.

But the parish-clerk
Cares not for the dark
As he winds in the tower
At a regular hour   10
The rheumatic clock,
Whose dilatory knock
You can hear when praying
At the day's decaying,
Or at any lone while
From a pew in the aisle.

Up, up from the ground
Around and around
In the turret stair
He clambers, to where   20
The wheelwork is,
With its tick, click, whizz,

Reposefully measuring
Each day to its end
That mortal men spend
In sorrowing and pleasuring.
Nightly thus does he climb
To the trackway of Time.

Him I followed one night
To this place without light,   30
And, ere I spoke, heard
Him say, word by word,
At the end of his winding,
The darkness unminding:—

'So I wipe out one more,
My Dear, of the sore
Sad days, that still be,
Like a drying Dead Sea,
Between you and me!'

Who she was no man knew: 40
He had long borne him blind
To all womankind;
And was ever one who
Kept his past out of view.

Old Excursions

'What's the good of going to Ridgeway,
      Cerne, or Sydling Mill,
      Or to Yell'ham Hill,
Blithely bearing Casterbridge-way
      As we used to do?
She will no more climb up there,
Or be visible anywhere
      In those haunts we knew.

But to-night, while walking weary,
    Near me seemed her shade,   10
    Come as 'twere to upbraid
This my mood in deeming dreary
    Scenes that used to please;
And, if she did come to me
Still solicitous, there may be
    Good in going to these.

So, I'll care to roam to Ridgeway,
    Cerne, or Sydling Mill,
    Or to Yell'ham Hill,
Blithely bearing Casterbridge-way   20
    As we used to do,
Since her phasm may flit out there,
And may greet me anywhere
    In those haunts we knew.

April 1913.

The Something that Saved Him

    It was when
Whirls of thick waters laved me
    Again and again,
That something arose and saved me;
    Yea, it was then.

    In that day
Unseeing the azure went I
    On my way,
And to white winter bent I,
    Knowing no May.   10

    Reft of renown,
Under the night clouds beating
    Up and down,
In my needfulness greeting
    Cit and clown.

Long there had been
Much of a murky colour
In the scene,
Dull prospects meeting duller;
Nought between.   20

Last, there loomed
A closing-in blind alley,
Though there boomed
A feeble summons to rally
Where it gloomed.

The clock rang;
The hour brought a hand to deliver;
I upsprang,
And looked back at den, ditch and river,
And sang.   30

On the Doorstep

The rain imprinted the step's wet shine
With target-circles that quivered and crossed
As I was leaving this porch of mine;
When from within there swelled and paused
            A song's sweet note;
        And back I turned, and thought,
            'Here I'll abide.'

The step shines wet beneath the rain,
Which prints its circles as heretofore;
I watch them from the porch again,   10
But no song-notes within the door
            Now call to me
        To shun the dripping lea;
            And forth I stride.

                                    Jan. 1914.

Signs and Tokens

Said the red-cloaked crone
In a whispered moan:

'The dead man was limp
When laid in his chest;
Yea, limp; and why
But to signify
That the grave will crimp
Ere next year's sun
Yet another one
Of those in that house—   10
It may be the best—
For its endless drowse!'

Said the brown-shawled dame
To confirm the same:

'And the slothful flies
On the rotting fruit
Have been seen to wear
While crawling there
Crape scarves, by eyes
That were quick and acute;   20
As did those that had pitched
On the cows by the pails,
And with flaps of their tails
Were far away switched.'

Said the third in plaid,
Each word being weighed:

'And trotting does
In the park, in the lane,
And just outside
The shuttered pane,   30
Have also been heard—
Quick feet as light
As the feet of a sprite—

And the wise mind knows
What things may betide
When such has occurred.'

Cried the black-craped fourth,
Cold faced as the north:

'O, though giving such
Some head-room, I smile   40
At your falterings
When noting those things
Round your domicile!
For what, what can touch
One whom, riven of all
That makes life gay,
No hints can appal
Of more takings away!'

At the Piano

A woman was playing,
   A man looking on;
    And the mould of her face,
    And her neck, and her hair,
   Which the rays fell upon
   Of the two candles there,
Sent him mentally straying
   In some fancy-place
   Where pain had no trace.

A cowled Apparition   10
   Came pushing between;
    And her notes seemed to sigh,
    And the lights to burn pale,
   As a spell numbed the scene.
   But the maid saw no bale,
And the man no monition;
   And Time laughed awry,
   And the Phantom hid nigh.

The Shadow on the Stone

I went by the Druid stone
That broods in the garden white and lone,
And I stopped and looked at the shifting shadows
That at some moments fall thereon
From the tree hard by with a rhythmic swing,
And they shaped in my imagining
To the shade that a well-known head and shoulders
Threw there when she was gardening.

I thought her behind my back,
Yea, her I long had learned to lack,   10
And I said: 'I am sure you are standing behind me,
Though how do you get into this old track?'
And there was no sound but the fall of a leaf
As a sad response; and to keep down grief
I would not turn my head to discover
That there was nothing in my belief.

Yet I wanted to look and see
That nobody stood at the back of me;
But I thought once more: 'Nay, I'll not unvision
A shape which, somehow, there may be.'   20
So I went on softly from the glade,
And left her behind me throwing her shade,
As she were indeed an apparition—
My head unturned lest my dream should fade.

Begun 1913: finished 1916.

In the Garden

(M. H.)

We waited for the sun
To break its cloudy prison
(For day was not yet done,
And night still unbegun)
Leaning by the dial.

After many a trial—
We all silent there—
It burst as new-arisen,
Shading its finger where
Time travelled at that minute.   10

Little saw we in it,
But this much I know,
Of lookers on that shade,
Her towards whom it made
Soonest had to go.

                                    1915.

An Upbraiding

Now I am dead you sing to me
    The songs we used to know,
But while I lived you had no wish
    Or care for doing so.

Now I am dead you come to me
    In the moonlight, comfortless;
Ah, what would I have given alive
    To win such tenderness!

When you are dead, and stand to me
    Not differenced, as now,   10
But like again, will you be cold
    As when we lived, or how?

Looking at a Picture on an Anniversary

But don't you know it, my dear,
    Don't you know it,
That this day of the year
(What rainbow-rays embow it!)
We met, strangers confessed,
    But parted—blest?

Though at this query, my dear,
 There in your frame
Unmoved you still appear,
You must be thinking the same,
But keep that look demure
 Just to allure.

And now at length a trace
 I surely vision
Upon that wistful face
Of old-time recognition,
Smiling forth, 'Yes, as you say,
 It is the day.'

For this one phase of you
 Now left on earth
This great date must endue
With pulsings of rebirth!—
I see them vitalize
 Those two deep eyes!

But if this face I con
 Does not declare
Consciousness living on
Still in it, little I care
To live myself, my dear,
 Lone-labouring here!

Spring 1913.

The Choirmaster's Burial

He often would ask us
That, when he died,
After playing so many
To their last rest,
If out of us any
Should here abide,
And it would not task us,

We would with our lutes
Play over him
By his grave-brim   10
The psalm he liked best—
The one whose sense suits
'Mount Ephraim'—
And perhaps we should seem
To him, in Death's dream,
Like the seraphim.

As soon as I knew
That his spirit was gone
I thought this his due,
And spoke thereupon.   20

'I think', said the vicar,
'A read service quicker
Than viols out-of-doors
In these frosts and hoars.
That old-fashioned way
Requires a fine day,
And it seems to me
It had better not be.'

Hence, that afternoon,
Though never knew he   30
That his wish could not be,
To get through it faster
They buried the master
Without any tune.

But 'twas said that, when
At the dead of next night
The vicar looked out,
There struck on his ken
Thronged roundabout,
Where the frost was graying   40
The headstoned grass,

A band all in white
Like the saints in church-glass,
Singing and playing
The ancient stave
By the choirmaster's grave.

Such the tenor man told
When he had grown old.

While Drawing in a Churchyard

'It is sad that so many of worth,
    Still in the flesh', soughed the yew,
'Misjudge their lot whom kindly earth
        Secludes from view.

'They ride their diurnal round
    Each day-span's sum of hours
In peerless ease, without jolt or bound
        Or ache like ours.

'If the living could but hear
    What is heard by my roots as they creep   10
Round the restful flock, and the things said there,
        No one would weep.'

'"Now set among the wise,"
    They say: "Enlarged in scope,
That no God trumpet us to rise
        We truly hope."'

I listened to his strange tale
    In the mood that stillness brings,
And I grew to accept as the day wore pale
        That show of things.   20

'For Life I had never cared greatly'

For Life I had never cared greatly,
   As worth a man's while;
   Peradventures unsought,
Peradventures that finished in nought,
Had kept me from youth and through manhood till lately
   Unwon by its style.

In earliest years—why I know not—
   I viewed it askance;
   Conditions of doubt,
Conditions that leaked slowly out,   10
May haply have bent me to stand and to show not
   Much zest for its dance.

With symphonies soft and sweet colour
   It courted me then,
   Till evasions seemed wrong,
Till evasions gave in to its song,
And I warmed, until living aloofly loomed duller
   Than life among men.

Anew I found nought to set eyes on,
   When, lifting its hand,   20
   It uncloaked a star,
Uncloaked it from fog-damps afar,
And showed its beams burning from pole to horizon
   As bright as a brand.

And so, the rough highway forgetting,
   I pace hill and dale
   Regarding the sky,
Regarding the vision on high,
And thus re-illumed have no humour for letting
   My pilgrimage fail.   30

POEMS OF WAR AND PATRIOTISM

'Men who march away'

(Song of the Soldiers)

What of the faith and fire within us
   Men who march away
   Ere the barn-cocks say
   Night is growing gray,
Leaving all that here can win us;
What of the faith and fire within us
   Men who march away?

Is it a purblind prank, O think you,
   Friend with the musing eye,   10
   Who watch us stepping by
   With doubt and dolorous sigh?
Can much pondering so hoodwink you!
It is a purblind prank, O think you,
   Friend with the musing eye?

Nay. We well see what we are doing
   Though some may not see—
   Dalliers as they be:—
   England's need are we;   20
Her distress would leave us rueing:
Nay. We well see what we are doing,
   Though some may not see!

In our heart of hearts believing
   Victory crowns the just,
   And that braggarts must
   Surely bite the dust,
Press we to the field ungrieving,
In our heart of hearts believing
   Victory crowns the just.

Hence the faith and fire within us
Men who march away
Ere the barn-cocks say
Night is growing gray,
Leaving all that here can win us;
Hence the faith and fire within us
Men who march away.

September 5, 1914.

The Pity of It

I walked in loamy Wessex lanes, afar
From rail-track and from highway, and I heard
In field and farmstead many an ancient word
Of local lineage like 'Thu bist', 'Er war',

'Ich woll', 'Er sholl', and by-talk similar,
Nigh as they speak who in this month's moon gird
At England's very loins, thereunto spurred
By gangs whose glory threats and slaughters are.

Then seemed a Heart crying: 'Whosoever they be
At root and bottom of this, who flung this flame   10
Between kin folk kin tongued even as are we,

'Sinister, ugly, lurid, be their fame;
May their familiars grow to shun their name,
And their brood perish everlastingly.'

April 1915.

In Time of 'the Breaking of Nations'

I

Only a man harrowing clods
   In a slow silent walk
With an old horse that stumbles and nods
   Half asleep as they stalk.

II

Only thin smoke without flame
   From the heaps of couch-grass;
Yet this will go onward the same
   Though Dynasties pass.

III

Yonder a maid and her wight
   Come whispering by: 10
War's annals will cloud into night
   Ere their story die.

1915.

Before Marching and After

(In Memoriam F. W. G.)

Orion swung southward aslant
Where the starved Egdon pine-trees had thinned,
The Pleiads aloft seemed to pant
With the heather that twitched in the wind;
But he looked on indifferent to sights such as these,
Unswayed by love, friendship, home joy or home sorrow,
And wondered to what he would march on the morrow.

The crazed household-clock with its whirr
Rang midnight within as he stood,
He heard the low sighing of her   10
Who had striven from his birth for his good;

But he still only asked the spring starlight, the breeze,
What great thing or small thing his history would borrow
From that Game with Death he would play on the morrow.

    When the heath wore the robe of late summer,
    And the fuchsia-bells, hot in the sun,
    Hung red by the door, a quick comer
    Brought tidings that marching was done
For him who had joined in that game over-seas
Where Death stood to win, though his name was to borrow   20
A brightness therefrom not to fade on the morrow.

September 1915.

A New Year's Eve in War Time

I

    Phantasmal fears,
    And the flap of the flame,
    And the throb of the clock,
    And a loosened slate,
    And the blind night's drone,
Which tiredly the spectral pines intone!

II

    And the blood in my ears
    Strumming always the same,
    And the gable-cock
    With its fitful grate,   10
    And myself, alone.

III

    The twelfth hour nears
    Hand-hid, as in shame;
    I undo the lock,
    And listen, and wait
    For the Young Unknown.

IV

In the dark there careers—
As if Death astride came
To numb all with his knock—
A horse at mad rate   20
Over rut and stone.

V

No figure appears,
No call of my name,
No sound but 'Tic-toc'
Without check. Past the gate
It clatters—is gone.

VI

What rider it bears
There is none to proclaim;
And the Old Year has struck,
And, scarce animate,   30
The New makes moan.

VII

Maybe that 'More Tears!—
More Famine and Flame—
More Severance and Shock!'
Is the order from Fate
That the Rider speeds on
To pale Europe; and tiredly the pines intone.

                                        1915–1916.

The Coming of the End

How it came to an end!
The meeting afar from the crowd,
And the love-looks and laughters unpenned,
The parting when much was avowed,
        How it came to an end!

It came to an end;
Yes, the outgazing over the stream,
With the sun on each serpentine bend,
Or, later, the luring moon-gleam;
It came to an end.   10

It came to an end,
The housebuilding, furnishing, planting,
As if there were ages to spend
In welcoming, feasting, and jaunting;
It came to an end.

It came to an end,
That journey of one day a week:
('It always goes on', said a friend,
'Just the same in bright weathers or bleak';)
But it came to an end.   20

'*How* will come to an end
This orbit so smoothly begun,
Unless some convulsion attend?'
I often said. 'What will be done
When it comes to an end?'

Well, it came to an end
Quite silently—stopped without jerk;
Better close no prevision could lend;
Working out as One planned it should work
Ere it came to an end.   30

Afterwards

When the Present has latched its postern behind my tremulous stay,
    And the May month flaps its glad green leaves like wings,
Delicate-filmed as new-spun silk, will the neighbours say,
    'He was a man who used to notice such things'?

If it be in the dusk when, like an eyelid's soundless blink,
   The dewfall-hawk comes crossing the shades to alight
Upon the wind-warped upland thorn, a gazer may think,
   'To him this must have been a familiar sight.'

If I pass during some nocturnal blackness, mothy and warm,
   When the hedgehog travels furtively over the lawn,   10
One may say, 'He strove that such innocent creatures should
     come to no harm,
   But he could do little for them; and now he is gone.'

If, when hearing that I have been stilled at last, they stand at
     the door,
   Watching the full-starred heavens that winter sees,
Will this thought rise on those who will meet my face no more,
   'He was one who had an eye for such mysteries'?

And will any say when my bell of quittance is heard in the gloom,
   And a crossing breeze cuts a pause in its outrollings,
Till they swell again, as they were a new bell's boom,
   'He hears it not now, but used to notice such things'?   20

from LATE LYRICS AND EARLIER

APOLOGY

ABOUT half the verses that follow were written quite lately. The rest are older, having been held over in MS. when past volumes were published, on considering that these would contain a sufficient number of pages to offer readers at one time, more especially during the distractions of the war. The unusually far back poems to be found here are, however, but some that were overlooked in gathering previous collections. A freshness in them, now unattainable, seemed to make up for their inexperience and to justify their inclusion. A few are dated; the dates of others are not discoverable.

The launching of a volume of this kind in neo-Georgian days by one who began writing in mid-Victorian, and has published nothing to speak of for some years, may seem to call for a few words of excuse or explanation. Whether or no, readers may feel assured that a new book is submitted to them with great hesitation at so belated a date. Insistent practical reasons, however, among which were requests from some illustrious men of letters who are in sympathy with my productions, the accident that several of the poems have already seen the light, and that dozens of them have been lying about for years, compelled the course adopted, in spite of the natural disinclination of a writer whose works have been so frequently regarded askance by a pragmatic section here and there, to draw attention to them once more.

I do not know that it is necessary to say much on the contents of the book, even in deference to suggestions that will be mentioned presently. I believe that those readers who care for my poems at all—readers to whom no passport is required—will care for this new instalment of them, perhaps the last, as much as for any that have preceded them. Moreover, in the eyes of a less friendly class the pieces, though a very mixed collection indeed, contain, so far as I am able to see, little or nothing in technic or teaching that can be considered a Star-Chamber matter, or so much as agitating to a ladies' school; even though, to use Wordsworth's observation in his Preface to *Lyrical Ballads*, such readers may suppose 'that by the act of writing in verse an author makes a formal engagement that he will gratify certain known habits of association: that he not only thus apprises the reader that certain classes of ideas and expressions will be found in his book, but that others will be carefully excluded.'

It is true, nevertheless, that some grave, positive, stark delineations are interspersed among those of the passive, lighter, and traditional sort presumably nearer to stereotyped tastes. For—while I am quite aware that a thinker is not expected, and, indeed, is scarcely allowed, now more than heretofore, to state all that crosses his mind concerning existence in this universe, in his attempts to explain or excuse the presence of evil and the incongruity of penalizing the irresponsible—it must be obvious to open intelligences that, without denying the beauty and faithful service of certain venerable cults, such disallowance of 'obstinate questionings' and 'blank misgivings'° tends to a paralysed intellectual stalemate. Heine observed nearly a hundred years ago that the soul has her eternal rights; that she will not be darkened by statutes, nor lullabied by the music of bells. And what is to-day, in allusions to the present author's pages, alleged to be 'pessimism' is, in truth, only such 'questionings' in the exploration of reality, and is the first step towards the soul's betterment, and the body's also.

If I may be forgiven for quoting my own old words, let me repeat what I printed in this relation more than twenty years ago, and wrote much· earlier, in a poem entitled 'In Tenebris':

If way to the Better there be, it exacts a full look at the Worst:

that is to say, by the exploration of reality, and its frank recognition stage by stage along the survey, with an eye to the best consummation possible: briefly, evolutionary meliorism. But it is called pessimism nevertheless; under which word, expressed with condemnatory emphasis, it is re-garded by many as some pernicious new thing (though so old as to underlie the Gospel scheme, and even to permeate the Greek drama); and the subject is charitably left to decent silence, as if further comment were needless.

Happily there are some who feel such Levitical passing-by to be, alas, by no means a permanent dismissal of the matter; that comment on where the world stands is very much the reverse of needless in these disordered years of our prematurely afflicted century: that amendment and not madness lies that way. And looking down the future these few hold fast to the same: that whether the human and kindred animal races survive till the exhaustion or destruction of the globe, or whether these races perish and are succeeded by others before that conclusion comes, pain to all upon it, tongued or dumb, shall be kept down to a minimum by loving-kindness, operating through scientific knowledge, and actuated by the modicum of free will conjecturally possessed by organic life when the mighty necessitating forces—unconscious or other—that have 'the balancings of the clouds',° happen to be in equilibrium, which may or may not be often.

To conclude this question I may add that the argument of the so-called optimists is neatly summarized in a stern pronouncement against me by my friend Mr Frederic Harrison in a late essay of his, in the words: 'This view of life is not mine.'° The solemn declaration does not seem to me to be so annihilating to the said 'view' (really a series of fugitive impressions which I have never tried to co-ordinate) as is complacently assumed. Surely it embodies a too human fallacy quite familiar in logic. Next, a knowing reviewer, apparently a Roman Catholic young man, speaks, with some rather gross instances of the *suggestio falsi* in his whole article, of 'Mr Hardy refusing consolation', the 'dark gravity of his ideas', and so on. When a Positivist and a Romanist° agree there must be something wonderful in it, which should make a poet sit up. But . . . O that 'twere possible!

I would not have alluded in this place or anywhere else to such casual personal criticisms—for casual and unreflecting they must be—but for the satisfaction of two or three friends in whose opinion a short answer was deemed desirable, on account of the continual repetition of these criticisms, or more precisely, quizzings. After all, the serious and truly literary inquiry in this connection is: Should a shaper of such stuff as dreams are made on disregard considerations of what is customary and expected, and apply himself to the real function of poetry, the application of ideas to life (in Matthew Arnold's familiar phrase)?° This bears more particularly on what has been called the 'philosophy' of these poems—usually reproved as 'queer'. Whoever the author may be that undertakes such application of ideas in this 'philosophic' direction—where it is specially required—glacial judgments must inevitably fall upon him amid opinion whose arbiters largely decry individuality, to whom *ideas* are oddities to smile at, who are moved by a yearning the reverse of that of the Athenian inquirers on Mars Hill;° and stiffen their features not only at sound of a new thing, but at a restatement of old things in new terms. Hence should anything of this sort in the following adumbrations seem 'queer'—should any of them seem to good Panglossians to embody strange and disrespectful conceptions of this best of all possible worlds, I apologize; but cannot help it.

Such divergences, which, though piquant for the nonce, it would be affectation to say are not saddening and discouraging likewise, may, to be sure, arise sometimes from superficial aspect only, writer and reader seeing the same thing at different angles. But in palpable cases of divergence they arise, as already said, whenever a serious effort is made towards that which the authority I have cited—who would now be called old-fashioned, possibly even parochial—affirmed to be what no good critic could deny as the poet's province, the application of ideas to life. One might shrewdly guess, by the by, that in such recommendation the famous writer may have overlooked the cold-shouldering results upon an enthusiastic disciple that would be pretty certain to follow his putting the high aim in practice and have forgotten the disconcerting experience of Gil Blas with the Archbishop.

To add a few more words to what has already taken up too many, there is a contingency liable to miscellanies of verse that I have never seen mentioned, so far as I can remember; I mean the chance little shocks that may be caused over a book of various character like the present and its predecessors by the juxtaposition of unrelated, even discordant, effusions; poems perhaps years apart in the making, yet facing each other. An odd result of this has been that dramatic anecdotes of a satirical and humorous intention following verse in graver voice, have been read as misfires because they raise the smile that they were intended to raise, the journalist, deaf to the sudden change of key, being unconscious that he is laughing with the author and not at him. I admit that I did not foresee such contingencies as I ought to have done, and that people might not perceive when the tone altered. But the difficulties of arranging the themes in a graduated kinship of moods would have been so great that irrelation was almost unavoidable with efforts so diverse. I must trust for right note-catching to those finely-touched spirits who can divine without half a whisper, whose intuitiveness is proof against all the accidents of inconsequence. In respect of the less alert, however, should any one's train of thought be thrown out of gear by a consecutive piping of vocal reeds in jarring tonics, without a semiquaver's rest between, and be led thereby to miss the writer's aim and meaning in one out of two contiguous compositions, I shall deeply regret it.

Having at last, I think, finished with the personal points that I was recommended to notice, I will forsake the immediate object of this Preface; and, leaving *Late Lyrics* to whatever fate it deserves, digress for a few moments to more general considerations. The thoughts of any man of letters concerned to keep poetry alive cannot but run uncomfortably on the precarious prospects of English verse at the present day. Verily the hazards and casualties surrounding the birth and setting forth of almost every modern creation in numbers are ominously like those of one of Shelley's paper-boats on a windy lake. And a forward conjecture scarcely permits the hope of a better time, unless men's tendencies should change. So indeed of all art, literature, and 'high thinking' nowadays. Whether owing to the barbarizing of taste in the younger minds by the dark madness of the late war, the unabashed cultivation of selfishness in all classes, the plethoric growth of knowledge simultaneously with the stunting of wisdom, 'a degrading thirst after outrageous stimulation' (to quote Wordsworth again),° or from any other cause, we seem threatened with a new Dark Age.

I formerly thought, like other much exercised writers, that so far as literature was concerned a partial cause might be impotent or mischievous criticism; the satirizing of individuality, the lack of whole-seeing in contemporary estimates of poetry and kindred work, the knowingness affected by junior reviewers, the overgrowth of meticulousness in their peerings for an opinion, as if it were a cultivated habit in them to scrutinize the tool-marks and be blind to the building, to hearken for the key-creaks and be deaf to the diapason, to judge the landscape by a nocturnal exploration with a flash-lantern. In other words, to carry on the old game of sampling the poem or drama by quoting the worst line or worst passage only, in ignorance or not of Coleridge's proof that a versification of any length neither can be nor ought to be all poetry;° of reading meanings into a book that its author never dreamt of writing there. I might go on interminably.

But I do not now think any such temporary obstructions to be the cause of the hazard, for these negligences and ignorances, though they may have stifled a few true poets in the run of generations, disperse like stricken leaves before the wind of next week, and are no more heard of again in the region of letters than their writers themselves. No: we may be convinced that something of the deeper sort mentioned must be the cause.

In any event poetry, pure literature in general, religion—I include religion, in its essential and undogmatic sense, because poetry and religion touch each other, or rather modulate into each other; are, indeed, often but different names for the same thing—these, I say, the visible signs of mental and emotional life, must like all other things keep moving, becoming; even though at present, when belief in witches of Endor is displacing the Darwinian theory and 'the truth that shall make you free', men's minds appear, as above noted, to be moving backwards rather than on. I speak somewhat sweepingly, and should except many thoughtful writers in verse and prose; also men in certain worthy but small bodies of various denominations, and perhaps in the homely quarter where advance might have been the very least expected a few years back—the English Church—if one reads it rightly as showing evidence of 'removing those things that are shaken',° in accordance with the wise Epistolary recommendation to the Hebrews. For since the historic and once august hierarchy of Rome some generation ago lost its chance of being the religion of the future by doing otherwise, and throwing over the little band of New Catholics who were making a struggle for continuity by applying the principle of evolution to their own faith, joining hands with modern science, and outflanking the hesitating English instinct towards liturgical restatement (a flank march which I at the time quite expected to witness, with the gathering of many millions of waiting agnostics into its fold); since then, one may ask, what other purely English establishment than the Church, of sufficient dignity and footing, with such strength of old association, such scope for transmutability, such architectural spell, is left in this country to keep the shreds of morality together?°

It may indeed be a forlorn hope, a mere dream, that of an alliance between religion, which must be retained unless the world is to perish, and complete rationality, which must come, unless also the world is to perish, by means of the interfusing effect of poetry—'the breath and finer spirit of all knowledge; the impassioned expression of science', as it was defined by an English poet who was quite orthodox in his ideas.° But if it be true, as Comte argued,° that advance is never in a straight line, but in a looped orbit, we may, in the aforesaid ominous moving backward, be doing it *pour mieux sauter*, drawing back for a spring. I repeat that I forlornly hope so, notwithstanding the supercilious regard of hope by Schopenhauer, von Hartmann, and other philosophers down to Einstein who have my respect. But one dares not prophesy. Physical, chronological, and other contingencies keep me in these days from critical studies and literary circles

> Where once we held debate, a band
> Of youthful friends, on mind and art°

(if one may quote Tennyson in this century). Hence I cannot know how things are going so well as I used to know them, and the aforesaid limitations must quite prevent my knowing henceforward.

I have to thank the editors and owners of *The Times*, *Fortnightly*, *Mercury*, and other periodicals in which a few of the poems have appeared for kindly assenting to their being reclaimed for collected publication.

T. H.

February 1922.

Weathers

I

This is the weather the cuckoo likes,
    And so do I;
When showers betumble the chestnut spikes,
    And nestlings fly:
And the little brown nightingale bills his best,
And they sit outside at 'The Travellers' Rest',
And maids come forth sprig-muslin drest,
And citizens dream of the south and west,
    And so do I.

II

This is the weather the shepherd shuns,   10
    And so do I;
When beeches drip in browns and duns,
    And thresh, and ply;
And hill-hid tides throb, throe on throe,
And meadow rivulets overflow,
And drops on gate-bars hang in a row,
And rooks in families homeward go,
    And so do I.

Summer Schemes

When friendly summer calls again,
    Calls again
Her little fifers to these hills,
We'll go—we two—to that arched fane
Of leafage where they prime their bills
Before they start to flood the plain
With quavers, minims, shakes, and trills.
    '—We'll go,' I sing; but who shall say
    What may not chance before that day!

And we shall see the waters spring,   10
     Waters spring
From chinks the scrubby copses crown;
And we shall trace their oncreeping
To where the cascade tumbles down
And sends the bobbing growths aswing,
And ferns not quite but almost drown.
     '—We shall,' I say; but who may sing
     Of what another moon will bring!

Faintheart in a Railway Train

At nine in the morning there passed a church,
At ten there passed me by the sea,
At twelve a town of smoke and smirch,
At two a forest of oak and birch,
     And then, on a platform, she:

A radiant stranger, who saw not me.
I said, 'Get out to her do I dare?'
But I kept my seat in my search for a plea,
And the wheels moved on. O could it but be
     That I had alighted there!   10

The Garden Seat

Its former green is blue and thin,
And its once firm legs sink in and in;
Soon it will break down unaware,
Soon it will break down unaware.

At night when reddest flowers are black
Those who once sat thereon come back;
Quite a row of them sitting there,
Quite a row of them sitting there.

With them the seat does not break down,
Nor winter freeze them, nor floods drown,   10
For they are as light as upper air,
They are as light as upper air!

Jezreel

On its seizure by the English under
Allenby, September 1918

Did they catch as it were in a Vision at shut of the day—
When their cavalry smote through the ancient Esdraelon Plain,
And they crossed where the Tishbite stood forth in his enemy's
    way—
His gaunt mournful Shade as he bade the King haste off amain?

On war-men at this end of time—even on Englishmen's eyes—
Who slay with their arms of new might in that long-ago place,
Flashed he who drove furiously? . . . Ah, did the phantom arise
Of that queen, of that proud Tyrian woman who painted her face?

Faintly marked they the words 'Throw her down!' from the
    Night eerily,
Spectre-spots of the blood of her body on some rotten wall?   10
And the thin note of pity that came: 'A King's daughter is she,'
As they passed where she trodden was once by the chargers'
    footfall?

Could such be the hauntings of men of to-day, at the cease
Of pursuit, at the dusk-hour, ere slumber their senses could seal?
Enghosted seers, kings—one on horseback who asked 'Is it
    peace?' . . .
Yea, strange things and spectral may men have beheld in Jezreel!

September 24, 1918.

'The curtains now are drawn'

(Song)

I

The curtains now are drawn,
And the spindrift strikes the glass,
Blown up the jaggèd pass
By the surly salt sou'-west,
And the sneering glare is gone
Behind the yonder crest,
   While she sings to me:
'O the dream that thou art my Love, be it thine,
And the dream that I am thy Love, be it mine,
And death may come, but loving is divine.'   10

II

I stand here in the rain,
With its smite upon her stone,
And the grasses that have grown
Over women, children, men,
And their texts that 'Life is vain';
But I hear the notes as when
   Once she sang to me:
'O the dream that thou art my Love, be it thine,
And the dream that I am thy Love, be it mine,
And death may come, but loving is divine.'   20

1913.

'According to the Mighty Working'

I

When moiling seems at cease
   In the vague void of night-time,
   And heaven's wide roomage stormless
   Between the dusk and light-time,
   And fear at last is formless,
We call the allurement Peace.

II

Peace, this hid riot, Change,
   This revel of quick-cued mumming,
   This never truly being,
   This evermore becoming,   10
   This spinner's wheel onfleeing
Outside perception's range.

                   1917.

Welcome Home

   Back to my native place
   Bent upon returning,
   Bosom all day burning
   To be where my race
Well were known, 'twas keen with me
There to dwell in amity.

   Folk had sought their beds,
   But I hailed: to view me
   Under the moon, out to me
   Several pushed their heads,   10
And to each I told my name,
Plans, and that therefrom I came.

   'Did you? . . . Ah, 'tis true,'
   Said they, 'back a long time,
   Here had spent his young time,
   Some such man as you . . .
Good-night.' The casement closed again,
And I was left in the frosty lane.

Going and Staying

I

The moving sun-shapes on the spray,
The sparkles where the brook was flowing,
Pink faces, plightings, moonlit May,
These were the things we wished would stay;
       But they were going.

II

Seasons of blankness as of snow,
The silent bleed of a world decaying,
The moan of multitudes in woe,
These were the things we wished would go;
       But they were staying.   10

III

Then we looked closelier at Time,
And saw his ghostly arms revolving
To sweep off woeful things with prime,
Things sinister with things sublime
       Alike dissolving.

Read by Moonlight

I paused to read a letter of hers
    By the moon's cold shine,
Eyeing it in the tenderest way,
And edging it up to catch each ray
    Upon her light-penned line.
I did not know what years would flow
    Of her life's span and mine
Ere I read another letter of hers
    By the moon's cold shine!

I chance now on the last of hers,   10
    By the moon's cold shine;
It is the one remaining page
Out of the many shallow and sage
    Whereto she set her sign.

Who could foresee there were to be
Such missives of pain and pine
Ere I should read this last of hers
By the moon's cold shine!

At a House in Hampstead

Sometime the Dwelling of John Keats

O Poet, come you haunting here
Where streets have stolen up all around,
And never a nightingale pours one
    Full-throated sound?

Drawn from your drowse by the Seven famed Hills,
Thought you to find all just the same
Here shining, as in hours of old,
    If you but came?

What will you do in your surprise
At seeing that changes wrought in Rome   10
Are wrought yet more on the misty slope
    One time your home?

Will you wake wind-wafts on these stairs?
Swing the doors open noisily?
Show as an umbraged ghost beside
    Your ancient tree?

Or will you, softening, the while
You further and yet further look,
Learn that a laggard few would fain
    Preserve your nook? . . .   20

—Where the Piazza steps incline,
And catch late light at eventide,
I once stood, in that Rome, and thought,
    ''Twas here he died.'

I drew to a violet-sprinkled spot,
Where day and night a pyramid keeps
Uplifted its white hand, and said,
　　' 'Tis there he sleeps.'

Pleasanter now it is to hold
That here, where sang he, more of him　　30
Remains than where he, tuneless, cold,
　　Passed to the dim.

　　　　　　　　　　　July 1920.

Her Song

I sang that song on Sunday,
　To witch an idle while,
I sang that song on Monday,
　As fittest to beguile;
I sang it as the year outwore,
　　And the new slid in;
I thought not what might shape before
　Another would begin.

I sang that song in summer,
　All unforeknowingly,　　　　　　　　　10
To him as a new-comer
　From regions strange to me:
I sang it when in afteryears
　　The shades stretched out,
And paths were faint; and flocking fears
　Brought cup-eyed care and doubt.

Sings he that song on Sundays
　In some dim land afar,
On Saturdays, or Mondays,
　As when the evening star　　　　　　　20
Glimpsed in upon his bending face
　　And my hanging hair,
And time untouched me with a trace
　Of soul-smart or despair?

A Wet August

Nine drops of water bead the jessamine,
And nine-and-ninety smear the stones and tiles:
—'Twas not so in that August—full-rayed, fine—
When we lived out-of-doors, sang songs, strode miles.

Or was there then no noted radiancy
Of summer? Were dun clouds, a dribbling bough,
Gilt over by the light I bore in me,
And was the waste world just the same as now?

It can have been so: yea, that threatenings
Of coming down-drip on the sunless gray,   10
By the then golden chances seen in things
Were wrought more bright than brightest skies to-day.

                                        1920.

'A man was drawing
near to me'

On that gray night of mournful drone,
Apart from aught to hear, to see,
I dreamt not that from shires unknown
          In gloom, alone,
          By Halworthy,
A man was drawing near to me.

I'd no concern at anything,
No sense of coming pull-heart play;
Yet, under the silent outspreading
          Of even's wing   10
          Where Otterham lay,
A man was riding up my way.

I thought of nobody—not of one,
But only of trifles—legends, ghosts—
Though, on the moorland dim and dun
       That travellers shun
       About these coasts,
The man had passed Tresparret Posts.

There was no light at all inland,
Only the seaward pharos-fire,   20
Nothing to let me understand
       That hard at hand
       By Hennett Byre
The man was getting nigh and nigher.

There was a rumble at the door,
A draught disturbed the drapery,
And but a minute passed before,
       With gaze that bore
       My destiny,
The man revealed himself to me.   30

The Strange House

(Max Gate, AD 2000)

'I hear the piano playing—
   Just as a ghost might play.'
'—O, but what are you saying?
   There's no piano to-day;
Their old one was sold and broken;
   Years past it went amiss.'
'—I heard it, or shouldn't have spoken:
      A strange house, this!

'I catch some undertone here,
   From someone out of sight.'   10
'—Impossible; we are alone here,
   And shall be through the night.'

'—The parlour-door—what stirred it?'
 '—No one: no soul's in range.'
'—But, anyhow, I heard it,
  And it seems strange!

'Seek my own room I cannot—
 A figure is on the stair!'
'—What figure? Nay, I scan not
 Anyone lingering there.
A bough outside is waving,
 And that's its shade by the moon.'   20
'—Well, all is strange! I am craving
  Strength to leave soon.'

'—Ah, maybe you've some vision
 Of showings beyond our sphere;
Some sight, sense, intuition
 Of what once happened here?
The house is old; they've hinted
 It once held two love-thralls,   30
And they may have imprinted
  Their dreams on its walls?

'They were—I think 'twas told me—
 Queer in their works and ways;
The teller would often hold me
 With weird tales of those days.
Some folk can not abide here,
 But we—we do not care
Who loved, laughed, wept, or died here,
  Knew joy, or despair.'   40

The Contretemps

A forward rush by the lamp in the gloom,
 And we clasped, and almost kissed;
But she was not the woman whom
I had promised to meet in the thawing brume
On that harbour-bridge; nor was I he of her tryst.

So loosening from me swift she said:
   'O why, why feign to be
The one I had meant!—to whom I have sped
To fly with, being so sorrily wed!'
—'Twas thus and thus that she upbraided me.   10

My assignation had struck upon
   Some others' like it, I found.
And her lover rose on the night anon;
And then her husband entered on
The lamplit, snowflaked, sloppiness around.

'Take her and welcome, man!' he cried:
   'I wash my hands of her.
I'll find me twice as good a bride!'
—All this to me, whom he had eyed,
'Twas clear, as his wife's planned deliverer.   20

And next the lover: 'Little I knew,
   Madam, you had a third!
Kissing here in my very view!'
—Husband and lover then withdrew.
I let them; and I told them not they erred.

Why not? Well, there faced she and I—
   Two strangers who'd kissed, or near,
Chancewise. To see stand weeping by
A woman once embraced, will try
The tension of a man the most austere.   30

So it began; and I was young,
   She pretty, by the lamp,
As flakes came waltzing down among
The waves of her clinging hair, that hung
Heavily on her temples, dark and damp.

And there alone still stood we two;
   She one cast off for me,
Or so it seemed: while night ondrew,
Forcing a parley what should do
We twain hearts caught in one catastrophe.   40

In stranded souls a common strait
　　Wakes latencies unknown,
Whose impulse may precipitate
A life-long leap. The hour was late,
And there was the Jersey boat with its funnel agroan.

'Is wary walking worth much pother?'
　　It grunted, as still it stayed.
'One pairing is as good as another
Where all is venture! Take each other,
And scrap the oaths that you have aforetime made.'. . .   50

—Of the four involved there walks but one
　　On earth at this late day.
And what of the chapter so begun?
In that odd complex what was done?
Well; happiness comes in full to none:
Let peace lie on lulled lips: I will not say.

　　　　　　　　　　　　　　Weymouth.

A Night in November

I marked when the weather changed,
And the panes began to quake,
And the winds rose up and ranged,
That night, lying half-awake.

Dead leaves blew into my room,
And alighted upon my bed,
And a tree declared to the gloom
Its sorrow that they were shed.

One leaf of them touched my hand,
And I thought that it was you   10
There stood as you used to stand,
And saying at last you knew!

　　　　　　　　　(?) 1913.

'Where three roads joined'

Where three roads joined it was green and fair,
And over a gate was the sun-glazed sea,
And life laughed sweet when I halted there;
Yet there I never again would be.

I am sure those branchways are brooding now,
With a wistful blankness upon their face,
While the few mute passengers notice how
Spectre-beridden is the place;

Which nightly sighs like a laden soul,
And grieves that a pair, in bliss for a spell   10
Not far from thence, should have let it roll
Away from them down a plumbless well

While the phasm of him who fared starts up,
And of her who was waiting him sobs from near,
As they haunt there and drink the wormwood cup
They filled for themselves when their sky was clear.

Yes, I see those roads—now rutted and bare,
While over the gate is no sun-glazed sea;
And though life laughed when I halted there,
It is where I never again would be.   20

'And there was a Great Calm'

(On the Signing of The Armistice, Nov. 11, 1918)

I

There had been years of Passion—scorching, cold,
And much Despair, and Anger heaving high,
Care whitely watching, Sorrows manifold,
Among the young, among the weak and old,
And the pensive Spirit of Pity whispered, 'Why?'

II

Men had not paused to answer. Foes distraught
Pierced the thinned peoples in a brute-like blindness,
Philosophies that sages long had taught,
And Selflessness, were as an unknown thought,
And 'Hell!' and 'Shell!' were yapped at Lovingkindness.   10

III

The feeble folk at home had grown full-used
To 'dug-outs', 'snipers', 'Huns', from the war-adept
In the mornings heard, and at evetides perused;
To day-dreamt men in millions, when they mused—
To nightmare-men in millions when they slept.

IV

Waking to wish existence timeless, null,
Sirius they watched above where armies fell;
He seemed to check his flapping when, in the lull
Of night a boom came thencewise, like the dull
Plunge of a stone dropped into some deep well.   20

V

So, when old hopes that earth was bettering slowly
Were dead and damned, there sounded 'War is done!'
One morrow. Said the bereft, and meek, and lowly,
'Will men some day be given to grace? yea, wholly,
And in good sooth, as our dreams used to run?'

VI

Breathless they paused. Out there men raised their glance
To where had stood those poplars lank and lopped,
As they had raised it through the four years' dance
Of Death in the now familiar flats of France;
And murmured, 'Strange, this! How? All firing stopped?'   30

VII

Aye; all was hushed. The about-to-fire fired not,
The aimed-at moved away in trance-lipped song.
One checkless regiment slung a clinching shot
And turned. The Spirit of Irony smirked out, 'What?
Spoil peradventures woven of Rage and Wrong?'

VIII

Thenceforth no flying fires inflamed the gray,
No hurtlings shook the dewdrop from the thorn,
No moan perplexed the mute bird on the spray;
Worn horses mused: 'We are not whipped to-day';
No weft-winged engines blurred the moon's thin horn.   40

IX

Calm fell. From Heaven distilled a clemency;
There was peace on earth, and silence in the sky;
Some could, some could not, shake off misery:
The Sinister Spirit sneered: 'It had to be!'
And again the Spirit of Pity whispered, 'Why?'

Haunting Fingers

A Phantasy in a Museum of Musical Instruments

'Are you awake,
    Comrades, this silent night?
Well 'twere if all of our glossy gluey make
Lay in the damp without, and fell to fragments quite!'

'O viol, my friend,
    I watch, though Phosphor nears,
And I fain would drowse away to its utter end
This dumb dark stowage after our loud melodious years!'

And they felt past handlers clutch them,
    Though none was in the room,   10
Old players' dead fingers touch them,
        Shrunk in the tomb.

''Cello, good mate,
    You speak my mind as yours:
Doomed to this voiceless, crippled, corpselike state,
Who, dear to famed Amphion, trapped here, long endures?'

'Once I could thrill
  The populace through and through,
Wake them to passioned pulsings past their will.' . . .
(A contra-basso spake so, and the rest sighed anew.)   20

And they felt old muscles travel
  Over their tense contours,
And with long skill unravel
    Cunningest scores.

  'The tender pat
  Of her aery finger-tips
Upon me daily—I rejoiced thereat!'
(Thuswise a harpsichord, as 'twere from dampered lips.)

  'My keys' white shine,
  Now sallow, met a hand   30
Even whiter. . . . Tones of hers fell forth with mine
In sowings of sound so sweet no lover could withstand!'

And its clavier was filmed with fingers
  Like tapering flames—wan, cold—
Or the nebulous light that lingers
    In charnel mould.

  'Gayer than most
  Was I,' reverbed a drum;
'The regiments, marchings, throngs, hurrahs! What a host
I stirred—even when crape mufflings gagged me well-nigh
    dumb!'   40

  Trilled an aged viol:
  'Much tune have I set free
To spur the dance, since my first timid trial
Where I had birth—far hence, in sun-swept Italy!'

And he feels apt touches on him
  From those that pressed him then;
Who seem with their glance to con him,
    Saying, 'Not again!'

'A holy calm',
    Mourned a shawm's voice subdued,   50
  'Steeped my Cecilian rhythms when hymn and psalm
Poured from devout souls met in Sabbath sanctitude.'

'I faced the sock
    Nightly', twanged a sick lyre,
  'Over ranked lights! O charm of life in mock,
O scenes that fed love, hope, wit, rapture, mirth, desire!'

Thus they, till each past player
    Stroked thinner and more thin,
And the morning sky grew grayer,
    And day crawled in.   60

'If it's ever spring again'

(Song)

If it's ever spring again,
    Spring again,
I shall go where went I when
Down the moor-cock splashed, and hen,
Seeing me not, amid their flounder,
Standing with my arm around her;
If it's ever spring again,
    Spring again,
I shall go where went I then.

If it's ever summer-time,   10
    Summer-time,
With the hay crop at the prime,
And the cuckoos—two—in rhyme,
As they used to be, or seemed to,
We shall do as long we've dreamed to,
If it's ever summer-time,
    Summer-time,
With the hay, and bees achime.

The Two Houses

In the heart of night,
  When farers were not near,
The left house said to the house on the right,
'I have marked your rise, O smart newcomer here.'

    Said the right, cold-eyed:
      'Newcomer here I am,
Hence haler than you with your cracked old hide,
Loose casements, wormy beams, and doors that jam.

    'Modern my wood,
      My hangings fair of hue;   10
While my windows open as they should,
And water-pipes thread all my chambers through.

    'Your gear is gray,
      Your face wears furrows untold.'
'—Yours might', mourned the other, 'if you held, brother,
The Presences from aforetime that I hold.

    'You have not known
      Men's lives, deaths, toils, and teens;
You are but a heap of stick and stone:
A new house has no sense of the have-beens.   20

    'Void as a drum
      You stand: I am packed with these,
Though, strangely, living dwellers who come
See not the phantoms all my substance sees!

    'Visible in the morning
      Stand they, when dawn drags in;
Visible at night; yet hint or warning
Of these thin elbowers few of the inmates win.

    'Babes new-brought-forth
      Obsess my rooms; straight-stretched   30
Lank corpses, ere outborne to earth;
Yea, throng they as when first from the 'Byss upfetched.

'Dancers and singers
  Throb in me now as once;
Rich-noted throats and gossamered flingers
Of heels; the learned in love-lore and the dunce.

'Note here within
  The bridegroom and the bride,
Who smile and greet their friends and kin,
And down my stairs depart for tracks untried.   40

'Where such inbe,
  A dwelling's character
Takes theirs, and a vague semblancy
To them in all its limbs, and light, and atmosphere.

'Yet the blind folk
  My tenants, who come and go
In the flesh mid these, with souls unwoke,
Of such sylph-like surrounders do not know.'

'—Will the day come',
  Said the new one, awestruck, faint,   50
'When I shall lodge shades dim and dumb—
And with such spectral guests become acquaint?'

'—That will it, boy;
  Such shades will people thee,
Each in his misery, irk, or joy,
And print on thee their presences as on me.'

On Stinsford Hill at Midnight

I glimpsed a woman's muslined form
    Sing-songing airily
Against the moon; and still she sang,
    And took no heed of me.

Another trice, and I beheld
  What first I had not scanned,
That now and then she tapped and shook
  A timbrel in her hand.

So late the hour, so white her drape,
  So strange the look it lent   10
To that blank hill, I could not guess
  What phantastry it meant.

Then burst I forth: 'Why such from you?
  Are you so happy now?'
Her voice swam on; nor did she show
  Thought of me anyhow.

I called again: 'Come nearer; much
  That kind of note I need!'
The song kept softening, loudening on,
  In placid calm unheed.   20

'What home is yours now?' then I said;
  'You seem to have no care.'
But the wild wavering tune went forth
  As if I had not been there.

'This world is dark, and where you are',
  I said, 'I cannot be!'
But still the happy one sang on,
  And had no heed of me.

The Fallow Deer at the Lonely House

   One without looks in to-night
         Through the curtain-chink
   From the sheet of glistening white;
   One without looks in to-night
         As we sit and think
         By the fender-brink.

We do not discern those eyes
　　　Watching in the snow;
Lit by lamps of rosy dyes
We do not discern those eyes　　　　　　　10
　　　Wondering, aglow,
　　　Fourfooted, tiptoe.

The Selfsame Song

A bird sings the selfsame song,
With never a fault in its flow,
That we listened to here those long
　　　Long years ago.

A pleasing marvel is how
A strain of such rapturous rote
Should have gone on thus till now
　　　Unchanged in a note!

—But it's not the selfsame bird.—
No: perished to dust is he. . . .　　　　　　10
As also are those who heard
　　　That song with me.

The Wanderer

There is nobody on the road
　　　But I,
And no beseeming abode
　　　I can try
For shelter, so abroad
　　　I must lie.

The stars feel not far up,
　　　And to be
The lights by which I sup
　　　Glimmeringly,　　　　　　　　　　　10
Set out in a hollow cup
　　　Over me.

They wag as though they were
    Panting for joy
Where they shine, above all care,
    And annoy,
And demons of despair—
    Life's alloy.

Sometimes outside the fence
    Feet swing past,   20
Clock-like, and then go hence,
    Till at last
There is a silence, dense,
    Deep, and vast.

A wanderer, witch-drawn
    To and fro,
To-morrow, at the dawn,
    On I go,
And where I rest anon
    Do not know!   30

Yet it's meet—this bed of hay
    And roofless plight;
For there's a house of clay,
    My own, quite,
To roof me soon, all day
    And all night.

At Lulworth Cove a Century Back

Had I but lived a hundred years ago
I might have gone, as I have gone this year,
By Warmwell Cross on to a Cove I know,
And Time have placed his finger on me there:

'*You see that man?*'—I might have looked, and said,
'O yes: I see him. One that boat has brought
Which dropped down Channel round Saint Alban's Head.
So commonplace a youth calls not my thought.'

'*You see that man?*'—'Why yes; I told you; yes:
Of an idling town-sort; thin; hair brown in hue;   10
And as the evening light scants less and less
He looks up at a star, as many do.'

'*You see that man?*'—'Nay, leave me!' then I plead,
'I have fifteen miles to vamp across the lea,
And it grows dark, and I am weary-kneed:
I have said the third time; yes, that man I see!'

'Good. That man goes to Rome—to death, despair;
And no one notes him now but you and I:
A hundred years, and the world will follow him there,
And bend with reverence where his ashes lie.'   20

September 1920.

The Wedding Morning

Tabitha dressed for her wedding:—
    'Tabby, why look so sad?'
'—O I feel a great gloominess spreading, spreading,
    Instead of supremely glad! . . .

    'I called on Carry last night,
    And he came whilst I was there,
Not knowing I'd called. So I kept out of sight,
    And I heard what he said to her:

'"—Ah, I'd far liefer marry
    You, Dear, to-morrow!" he said,   10
"But that cannot be."—O I'd give him to Carry,
    And willingly see them wed,

"But how can I do it when
    His baby will soon be born?
After that I hope I may die. And then
    She can have him. I shall not mourn!'

The Chimes Play 'Life's a Bumper!'

'Awake! I'm off to cities far away,'
I said; and rose, on peradventures bent.
The chimes played 'Life's a Bumper!' long that day
To the measure of my walking as I went:
Their sweetness frisked and floated on the lea,
As they played out 'Life's a Bumper!' there to me.

'Awake!' I said. 'I go to take a bride!'
—The sun arose behind me ruby-red
As I journeyed townwards from the countryside,
The chiming bells saluting near ahead.   10
Their sweetness swelled in tripping tings of glee
As they played out 'Life's a Bumper!' there to me.

'Again arise.' I seek a turfy slope,
And go forth slowly on an autumn noon,
And there I lay her who has been my hope,
And think, 'O may I follow hither soon!'
While on the wind the chimes come cheerily,
Playing out 'Life's a Bumper!' there to me.

                                    1913.

At the Railway Station, Upway

   'There is not much that I can do,
For I've no money that's quite my own!'
   Spoke up the pitying child—
A little boy with a violin
At the station before the train came in,—
'But I can play my fiddle to you,
And a nice one 'tis, and good in tone!'

   The man in the handcuffs smiled;
The constable looked, and he smiled, too,
   As the fiddle began to twang;   10
And the man in the handcuffs suddenly sang

With grimful glee:
'This life so free
Is the thing for me!'
And the constable smiled, and said no word,
As if unconscious of what he heard;
And so they went on till the train came in—
The convict, and boy with the violin.

Side by Side

So there sat they,
The estranged two,
Thrust in one pew
By chance that day;
Placed so, breath-nigh,
Each comer unwitting
Who was to be sitting
In touch close by.

Thus side by side
Blindly alighted,   10
They seemed united
As groom and bride,
Who'd not communed
For many years—
Lives from twain spheres
With hearts distuned.

Her fringes brushed
His garment's hem
As the harmonies rushed
Through each of them: 20
Her lips could be heard
In the creed and psalms,
And their fingers neared
At the giving of alms.

And women and men,
The matins ended,
By looks commended
Them, joined again.
Quickly said she,
'Don't undeceive them—   30
Better thus leave them':
'Quite so,' said he.

Slight words!—the last
Between them said,
Those two, once wed,
Who had not stood fast.
Diverse their ways
From the western door,
To meet no more
In their span of days.   40

The Child and the Sage

You say, O Sage, when weather-checked,
  'I have been favoured so
With cloudless skies, I must expect
  This dash of rain or snow.'

'Since health has been my lot', you say,
  'So many months of late,
I must not chafe that one short day
  Of sickness mars my state.'

You say, 'Such bliss has been my share
  From Love's unbroken smile,   10
It is but reason I should bear
  A cross therein awhile.'

And thus you do not count upon
  Continuance of joy;
But, when at ease, expect anon
  A burden of annoy.

But, Sage—this Earth—why not a place
    Where no reprisals reign,
Where never a spell of pleasantness
    Makes reasonable a pain?   20

December 21, 1908.

An Autumn Rain-Scene

There trudges one to a merrymaking
    With a sturdy swing,
  On whom the rain comes down.

To fetch the saving medicament
    Is another bent,
  On whom the rain comes down.

One slowly drives his herd to the stall
    Ere ill befall,
  On whom the rain comes down.

This bears his missives of life and death   10
    With quickening breath,
  On whom the rain comes down.

One watches for signals of wreck or war
    From the hill afar,
  On whom the rain comes down.

Careless to gain a shelter or none,
    Unhired moves one,
  On whom the rain comes down.

And another knows nought of its chilling fall
    Upon him at all,   20
  On whom the rain comes down.

October 1904.

An Experience

Wit, weight, or wealth there was not
   In anything that was said,
   In anything that was done;
All was of scope to cause not
   A triumph, dazzle, or dread
   To even the subtlest one,
      My friend,
   To even the subtlest one.

But there was a new afflation—
   An aura zephyring round,   10
   That care infected not:
It came as a salutation,
   And, in my sweet astound,
   I scarcely witted what
      Might pend,
   I scarcely witted what.

The hills in samewise to me
   Spoke, as they grayly gazed,
   —First hills to speak so yet!
The thin-edged breezes blew me   20
   What I, though cobwebbed, crazed,
   Was never to forget,
      My friend,
   Was never to forget!

The Wood Fire

(A Fragment)

'This is a brightsome blaze you've lit, good friend, to-night!'
'—Aye, it has been the bleakest spring I have felt for years,
And nought compares with cloven logs to keep alight:
I buy them bargain-cheap of the executioners,
As I dwell near; and they wanted the crosses out of sight
By Passover, not to affront the eyes of visitors.

'Yes, they're from the crucifixions last week-ending
At Kranion. We can sometimes use the poles again,
But they get split by the nails, and 'tis quicker work than
    mending
To knock together new; though the uprights now and then   10
Serve twice when they're let stand. But if a feast's impending,
As lately, you've to tidy up for the comers' ken.

'Though only three were impaled, you may know it didn't pass
    off
So quietly as was wont? That Galilee carpenter's son
Who boasted he was king, incensed the rabble to scoff:
I heard the noise from my garden. This piece is the one he was
    on. . . .
Yes, it blazes up well if lit with a few dry chips and shroff;
And it's worthless for much else, what with cuts and stains
    thereon.'

On the Tune Called the
Old-Hundred-and-Fourth

We never sang together
    Ravenscroft's terse old tune
On Sundays or on weekdays,
In sharp or summer weather,
    At night-time or at noon.

Why did we never sing it,
    Why never so incline
On Sundays or on weekdays,
Even when soft wafts would wing it
    From your far floor to mine?   10

Shall we that tune, then, never
    Stand voicing side by side
On Sundays or on weekdays? . . .
Or shall we, when for ever
    In Sheol we abide,

Sing it in desolation,
   As we might long have done
On Sundays or on weekdays
With love and exultation
   Before our sands had run?   20

The Rift

(Song: Minor Mode)

'Twas just at gnat and cobweb-time,
When yellow begins to show in the leaf,
That your old gamut changed its chime
From those true tones—of span so brief!—
That met my beats of joy, of grief,
   As rhyme meets rhyme.

So sank I from my high sublime!
We faced but chancewise after that,
And never I knew or guessed my crime. . . .
Yes; 'twas the date—or nigh thereat—   10
Of the yellowing leaf; at moth and gnat
   And cobweb-time.

Voices from Things
Growing in a Churchyard

These flowers are I, poor Fanny Hurd,
   Sir or Madam,
A little girl here sepultured.
Once I flit-fluttered like a bird
Above the grass, as now I wave
In daisy shapes above my grave,
   All day cheerily,
   All night eerily!

—I am one Bachelor Bowring, 'Gent',
     Sir or Madam;   10
In shingled oak my bones were pent;
Hence more than a hundred years I spent
In my feat of change from a coffin-thrall
To a dancer in green as leaves on a wall,
     All day cheerily,
     All night eerily!

—I, these berries of juice and gloss,
     Sir or Madam,
Am clean forgotten as Thomas Voss;
Thin-urned, I have burrowed away from the moss   20
That covers my sod, and have entered this yew,
And turned to clusters ruddy of view,
     All day cheerily,
     All night eerily!

—The Lady Gertrude, proud, high-bred,
     Sir or Madam,
Am I—this laurel that shades your head;
Into its veins I have stilly sped,
And made them of me; and my leaves now shine,
As did my satins superfine,   30
     All day cheerily,
     All night eerily!

—I, who as innocent withwind climb,
     Sir or Madam,
Am one Eve Greensleeves, in olden time
Kissed by men from many a clime,
Beneath sun, stars, in blaze, in breeze,
As now by glowworms and by bees,
     All day cheerily,
     All night eerily!

                    40

—I'm old Squire Audeley Grey, who grew,
     Sir or Madam,
Aweary of life, and in scorn withdrew;
Till anon I clambered up anew

As ivy-green, when my ache was stayed,
And in that attire I have longtime gayed
    All day cheerily,
    All night eerily!

—And so these maskers breathe to each
      Sir or Madam   50
Who lingers there, and their lively speech
Affords an interpreter much to teach,
As their murmurous accents seem to come
Thence hitheraround in a radiant hum,
    All day cheerily,
    All night eerily!

On the Way

The trees fret fitfully and twist,
Shutters rattle and carpets heave,
Slime is the dust of yestereve,
    And in the streaming mist
Fishes might seem to fin a passage if they list.

    But to his feet,
    Drawing nigh and nigher
    A hidden seat,
    The fog is sweet
    And the wind a lyre.   10

A vacant sameness grays the sky,
A moisture gathers on each knop
Of the bramble, rounding to a drop,
    That greets the goer-by
With the cold listless lustre of a dead man's eye.

    But to her sight,
    Drawing nigh and nigher
    Its deep delight,
    The fog is bright
    And the wind a lyre.   20

'She did not turn'

She did not turn,
But passed foot-faint with averted head
In her gown of green, by the bobbing fern,
Though I leaned over the gate that led
From where we waited with table spread;
　　　　But she did not turn:
Why was she near there if love had fled?

　　　　She did not turn,
Though the gate was whence I had often sped
In the mists of morning to meet her, and learn　　10
Her heart, when its moving moods I read
As a book—she mine, as she sometimes said;
　　　　But she did not turn,
And passed foot-faint with averted head.

Growth in May

I enter a daisy-and-buttercup land,
　　And thence thread a jungle of grass:
Hurdles and stiles scarce visible stand
　　Above the lush stems as I pass.

Hedges peer over, and try to be seen,
　　And seem to reveal a dim sense
That amid such ambitious and elbow-high green
　　They make a mean show as a fence.

Elsewhere the mead is possessed of the neats,
　　That range not greatly above　　　　10
The rich rank thicket which brushes their teats,
　　And *her* gown, as she waits for her Love.

Near Chard.

The Children and Sir Nameless

Sir Nameless, once of Athelhall, declared:
'These wretched children romping in my park
Trample the herbage till the soil is bared,
And yap and yell from early morn till dark!
Go keep them harnessed to their set routines:
Thank God I've none to hasten my decay;
For green remembrance there are better means
Than offspring, who but wish their sires away.'

Sir Nameless of that mansion said anon:
'To be perpetuate for my mightiness   10
Sculpture must image me when I am gone.'
—He forthwith summoned carvers there express
To shape a figure stretching seven-odd feet
(For he was tall) in alabaster stone,
With shield, and crest, and casque, and sword complete:
When done a statelier work was never known.

Three hundred years hied; Church-restorers came,
And, no one of his lineage being traced,
They thought an effigy so large in frame
Best fitted for the floor. There it was placed,   20
Under the seats for schoolchildren. And they
Kicked out his name, and hobnailed off his nose;
And, as they yawn through sermon-time, they say,
'Who was this old stone man beneath our toes?'

A Two-Years' Idyll

Yes; such it was;
Just those two seasons unsought,
Sweeping like summertide wind on our ways;
Moving, as straws,
Hearts quick as ours in those days;
Going like wind, too, and rated as nought
Save as the prelude to plays
Soon to come—larger, life-fraught:
Yes; such it was.

'Nought' it was called,　　　　　　　　　　10
Even by ourselves—that which springs
Out of the years for all flesh, first or last,
　　　　Commonplace, scrawled
　　　Dully on days that go past.
Yet, all the while, it upbore us like wings
　　　Even in hours overcast:
　　　Aye, though this best thing of things,
　　　　'Nought' it was called!

　　　　What seems it now?
　　　Lost: such beginning was all;　　　　　20
Nothing came after: romance straight forsook
　　　　Quickly somehow
　　　Life when we sped from our nook,
Primed for new scenes with designs smart and tall. . . .
　　　—A preface without any book,
　　　A trumpet uplipped, but no call;
　　　　That seems it now.

By Henstridge Cross at the Year's End

(From this centuries-old cross-road the highway leads east to London, north to Bristol and Bath, west to Exeter and the Land's End, and south to the Channel coast.)

　　　Why go the east road now? . . .
　　That way a youth went on a morrow
　　After mirth, and he brought back sorrow
　　　　Painted upon his brow:
　　　Why go the east road now?

　　　Why go the north road now?
　Torn, leaf-strewn, as if scoured by foemen,
　Once edging fiefs of my forefolk yeomen,
　　　Fallows fat to the plough:
　　　Why go the north road now?　　　　　10

Why go the west road now?
Thence to us came she, bosom-burning,
Welcome with joyousness returning. . . .
    She sleeps under the bough:
    Why go the west road now?

    Why go the south road now?
That way marched they some are forgetting,
Stark to the moon left, past regretting
    Loves who have falsed their vow. . . .
    Why go the south road now?   20

    Why go any road now?
White stands the handpost for brisk onbearers,
'Halt!' is the word for wan-cheeked farers
    Musing on Whither, and How. . . .
    Why go any road now?

    'Yea: we want new feet now'
Answer the stones. 'Want chit-chat, laughter:
Plenty of such to go hereafter
    By our tracks, we trow!
    We are for new feet now.'   30

During the War.

Penance

'Why do you sit, O pale thin man,
    At the end of the room
By that harpsichord, built on the quaint old plan?
    —It is cold as a tomb,
And there's not a spark within the grate;
    And the jingling wires
    Are as vain desires
    That have lagged too late.'

'Why do I? Alas, far times ago
  A woman lyred here   10
In the evenfall; one who fain did so
  From year to year;
And, in loneliness bending wistfully,
   Would wake each note
   In sick sad rote,
  None to listen or see!

'I would not join. I would not stay,
  But drew away,
Though the winter fire beamed brightly. . . . Aye!
  I do to-day   20
What I would not then; and the chill old keys,
   Like a skull's brown teeth
   Loose in their sheath,
  Freeze my touch; yes, freeze.'

'I look in her face'

(Song: Minor)

I look in her face and say,
'Sing as you used to sing
About Love's blossoming';
But she hints not Yea or Nay.

'Sing, then, that Love's a pain,
If, Dear, you think it so,
Whether it be or no';
But dumb her lips remain.

I go to a far-off room,
A faint song ghosts my ear;   10
Which song I cannot hear,
But it seems to come from a tomb.

'*If you had known*'

     If you had known
When listening with her to the far-down moan
Of the white-selvaged and empurpled sea,
And rain came on that did not hinder talk,
Or damp your flashing facile gaiety
In turning home, despite the slow wet walk
By crooked ways, and over stiles of stone;
     If you had known

     You would lay roses,
Fifty years thence, on her monument, that discloses   10
Its graying shape upon the luxuriant green;
Fifty years thence to an hour, by chance led there,
What might have moved you?—yea, had you foreseen
That on the tomb of the selfsame one, gone where
The dawn of every day is as the close is,
     You would lay roses!

              1920.

At the Entering of the New Year

I

(Old Style)

Our songs went up and out the chimney,
And roused the home-gone husbandmen;
Our allemands, our heys, poussettings,
Our hands-across and back again,
Sent rhythmic throbbings through the casements
    On to the white highway,
Where nighted farers paused and muttered,
    'Keep it up well, do they!'

The contrabasso's measured booming
Sped at each bar to the parish bounds,   10
To shepherds at their midnight lambings,
To stealthy poachers on their rounds;

And everybody caught full duly
   The notes of our delight,
As Time unrobed the Youth of Promise
   Hailed by our sanguine sight.

II

(New Style)

We stand in the dusk of a pine-tree limb,
As if to give ear to the muffled peal,
Brought or withheld at the breeze's whim;
But our truest heed is to words that steal   20
From the mantled ghost that looms in the gray,
And seems, so far as our sense can see,
To feature bereaved Humanity,
As it sighs to the imminent year its say:—

'O stay without, O stay without,
Calm comely Youth, untasked, untired;
Though stars irradiate thee about
Thy entrance here is undesired.
Open the gate not, mystic one;
Must we avow what we would close confine?   30
With thee, good friend, we would have converse none,
   Albeit the fault may not be thine.'

                         December 31. During the War.

They Would Not Come

I travelled to where in her lifetime
   She'd knelt at morning prayer,
   To call her up as if there;
But she paid no heed to my suing,
As though her old haunt could win not
   A thought from her spirit, or care.

I went where my friend had lectioned
  The prophets in high declaim,
  That my soul's ear the same
Full tones should catch as aforetime;   10
But silenced by gear of the Present
  Was the voice that once there came!

Where the ocean had sprayed our banquet
  I stood, to recall it as then:
  The same eluding again!
No vision. Shows contingent
Affrighted it further from me
  Even than from my home-den.

When I found them no responders,
  But fugitives prone to flee   20
  From where they had used to be,
It vouched I had been led hither
As by night wisps in bogland,
  And bruised the heart of me!

After a Romantic Day

The railway bore him through
An earthen cutting out from a city:
  There was no scope for view,
Though the frail light shed by a slim young moon
  Fell like a friendly tune.

  Fell like a liquid ditty,
And the blank lack of any charm
  Of landscape did no harm.
The bald steep cutting, rigid, rough,
  And moon-lit, was enough   10
For poetry of place: its weathered face
Formed a convenient sheet whereon
The visions of his mind were drawn.

'I knew a lady'

(Club Song)

I knew a lady when the days
   Grew long, and evenings goldened;
   But I was not emboldened
By her prompt eyes and winning ways.

And when old Winter nipt the haws,
   'Another's wife I'll be,
   And then you'll care for me',
She said, 'and think how sweet I was!'

And soon she shone as another's wife:
   As such I often met her,   10
   And sighed, 'How I regret her!
My folly cuts me like a knife!'

And then, to-day, her husband came,
   And moaned, 'Why did you flout her?
   Well could I do without her!
For both our burdens you are to blame!'

A Procession of Dead Days

I see the ghost of a perished day;
I know his face, and the feel of his dawn:
'Twas he who took me far away
   To a spot strange and gray:
Look at me, Day, and then pass on,
But come again: yes, come anon!

Enters another into view;
His features are not cold or white,
But rosy as a vein seen through:
   Too soon he smiles adieu.   10
Adieu, O ghost-day of delight;
But come and grace my dying sight.

Enters the day that brought the kiss:
He brought it in his foggy hand
To where the mumbling river is,
   And the high clematis;
It lent new colour to the land,
And all the boy within me manned.

Ah, this one. Yes, I know his name,
He is the day that wrought a shine   20
Even on a precinct common and tame,
   As 'twere of purposed aim.
He shows him as a rainbow sign
Of promise made to me and mine.

The next stands forth in his morning clothes,
And yet, despite their misty blue,
They mark no sombre custom-growths
   That joyous living loathes,
But a meteor act, that left in its queue
A train of sparks my lifetime through.   30

I almost tremble at his nod—
This next in train—who looks at me
As I were slave, and he were god
   Wielding an iron rod.
I close my eyes; yet still is he
In front there, looking mastery.

In semblance of a face averse
The phantom of the next one comes:
I did not know what better or worse
   Chancings might bless or curse   40
When his original glossed the thrums
Of ivy, bringing that which numbs.

Yes; trees were turning in their sleep
Upon their windy pillows of gray
When he stole in. Silent his creep
   On the grassed eastern steep. . . .
I shall not soon forget that day,
And what his third hour took away!

He Follows Himself

In a heavy time I dogged myself
    Along a louring way,
Till my leading self to my following self
    Said: 'Why do you hang on me
      So harassingly?'

'I have watched you, Heart of mine,' I cried,
    'So often going astray
And leaving me, that I have pursued,
    Feeling such truancy
      Ought not to be.'   10

He said no more, and I dogged him on
    From noon to the dun of day
By prowling paths, until anew
    He begged: 'Please turn and flee!—
      What do you see?'

'Methinks I see a man', said I,
    'Dimming his hours to gray.
I will not leave him while I know
    Part of myself is he
      Who dreams such dree!'   20

'I go to my old friend's house,' he urged,
    'So do not watch me, pray!'
'Well, I will leave you in peace,' said I,
    'Though of this poignancy
      You should fight free:

'Your friend, O other me, is dead;
    You know not what you say.'
—'That do I! And at his green-grassed door
    By night's bright galaxy
      I bend a knee.'   30

—The yew-plumes moved like mockers' beards,
    Though only boughs were they,
And I seemed to go; yet still was there,
    And am, and there haunt we
        Thus bootlessly.

The Singing Woman

There was a singing woman
    Came riding across the mead
At the time of the mild May weather,
    Tameless, tireless;
This song she sung: 'I am fair, I am young!'
    And many turned to heed.

And the same singing woman
    Sat crooning in her need
At the time of the winter weather;
    Friendless, fireless,   10
She sang this song: 'Life, thou'rt too long!'
    And there was none to heed.

'O I won't lead a homely life'

(To an old air)

'O I won't lead a homely life
As father's Jack and mother's Jill,
But I will be a fiddler's wife,
    With music mine at will!
        Just a little tune,
        Another one soon,
    As I merrily fling my fill!'

And she became a fiddler's Dear,
And merry all day she strove to be;
And he played and played afar and near,   10
    But never at home played he
        Any little tune
        Or late or soon;
    And sunk and sad was she!

In the Small Hours

I lay in my bed and fiddled
    With a dreamland viol and bow,
And the tunes flew back to my fingers
    I had melodied years ago.
It was two or three in the morning
    When I fancy-fiddled so
Long reels and country-dances,
    And hornpipes swift and slow.

And soon anon came crossing
    The chamber in the gray   10
Figures of jigging fieldfolk—
    Saviours of corn and hay—
To the air of 'Haste to the Wedding',
    As after a wedding-day;
Yea, up and down the middle
    In windless whirls went they!

There danced the bride and bridegroom,
    And couples in a train,
Gay partners time and travail
    Had longwhiles stilled amain! . . .   20
It seemed a thing for weeping
    To find, at slumber's wane
And morning's sly increeping,
    That Now, not Then, held reign.

The Little Old Table

Creak, little wood thing, creak,
When I touch you with elbow or knee;
That is the way you speak
Of one who gave you to me!

You, little table, she brought—
Brought me with her own hand,
As she looked at me with a thought
That I did not understand.

—Whoever owns it anon,
And hears it, will never know   10
What a history hangs upon
This creak from long ago.

Vagg Hollow

Vagg Hollow is a marshy spot on the old Roman Road near Ilchester, where 'things' are seen. Merchandise was formerly fetched inland from the canal-boats at Load-Bridge by waggons this way.

'What do you see in Vagg Hollow,
Little boy, when you go
In the morning at five on your lonely drive?'
'—I see men's souls, who follow
Till we've passed where the road lies low,
When they vanish at our creaking!

'They are like white faces speaking
Beside and behind the waggon—
One just as father's was when here.
The waggoner drinks from his flagon,   10
(Or he'd flinch when the Hollow is near)
But he does not give me any.

'Sometimes the faces are many;
But I walk along by the horses,
He asleep on the straw as we jog;

And I hear the loud water-courses,
And the drops from the trees in the fog,
And watch till the day is breaking,

'And the wind out by Tintinhull waking;
I hear in it father's call   20
As he called when I saw him dying,
And he sat by the fire last Fall,
And mother stood by sighing;
But I'm not afraid at all!'

The Dream is—Which?

I am laughing by the brook with her,
    Splashed in its tumbling stir;
And then it is a blankness looms
    As if I walked not there,
Nor she, but found me in haggard rooms,
    And treading a lonely stair.

With radiant cheeks and rapid eyes
    We sit where none espies;
Till a harsh change comes edging in
    As no such scene were there,   10
But winter, and I were bent and thin,
    And cinder-gray my hair.

We dance in heys around the hall,
    Weightless as thistleball;
And then a curtain drops between,
    As if I danced not there,
But wandered through a mounded green
    To find her, I knew where.

March 1913.

The Country Wedding

(A Fiddler's Story)

Little fogs were gathered in every hollow,
But the purple hillocks enjoyed fine weather
As we marched with our fiddles over the heather
—How it comes back!—to their wedding that day.

Our getting there brought our neighbours and all, O!
Till, two and two, the couples stood ready.
And her father said: 'Souls, for God's sake, be steady!'
And we strung up our fiddles, and sounded out 'A'.

The groomsman he stared, and said, 'You must follow!'
But we'd gone to fiddle in front of the party,   10
(Our feelings as friends being true and hearty)
And fiddle in front we did—all the way.

Yes, from their door by Mill-tail-Shallow,
And up Styles Lane, and by Front-Street houses,
Where stood maids, bachelors, and spouses,
Who cheered the songs that we knew how to play.

I bowed the treble before her father,
Michael the tenor in front of the lady,
The bass-viol Reub—and right well played he!—
The serpent Jim; ay, to church and back.   20

I thought the bridegroom was flurried rather,
As we kept up the tune outside the chancel,
Wile they were swearing things none can cancel
Inside the walls to our drumstick's whack.

'Too gay!' she pleaded. 'Clouds may gather,
And sorrow come.' But she gave in, laughing,
And by supper-time when we'd got to the quaffing
Her fears were forgot, and her smiles weren't slack.

A grand wedding 'twas! And what would follow
We never thought. Or that we should have buried her   30
On the same day with the man that married her,
A day like the first, half hazy, half clear.

Yes: little fogs were in every hollow,
Though the purple hillocks enjoyed fine weather,
When we went to play 'em to church together,
And carried 'em there in an after year.

Lonely Days

Lonely her fate was,
Environed from sight
In the house where the gate was
Past finding at night.
None there to share it,
No one to tell:
Long she'd to bear it,
And bore it well.

Elsewhere just so she
Spent many a day;   10
Wishing to go she
Continued to stay.
And people without
Basked warm in the air,
But none sought her out,
Or knew she was there.
Even birthdays were passed so,
Sunny and shady:
Years did it last so
For this sad lady.   20
Never declaring it,
No one to tell,
Still she kept bearing it—
Bore it well.

The days grew chillier,
And then she went
To a city, familiar
In years forespent,
When she walked gaily
Far to and fro,   30

But now, moving frailly,
Could nowhere go.
The cheerful colour
Of houses she'd known
Had died to a duller
And dingier tone.
Streets were now noisy
Where once had rolled
A few quiet coaches,
Or citizens strolled.   40
Through the party-wall
Of the memoried spot
They danced at a ball
Who recalled her not.
Tramlines lay crossing
Once gravelled slopes,
Metal rods clanked,
And electric ropes.
So she endured it all,
Thin, thinner wrought,   50
Until time cured it all,
And she knew nought.

Versified from a Diary.

The Master and the Leaves

I

We are budding, Master, budding,
    We of your favourite tree;
March drought and April flooding
    Arouse us merrily,
Our stemlets newly studding;
    And yet you do not see!

II

We are fully woven for summer
    In stuff of limpest green,
The twitterer and the hummer
    Here rest of nights, unseen,   10

While like a long-roll drummer
  The nightjar thrills the treen.

III

We are turning yellow, Master,
  And next we are turning red,
And faster then and faster
  Shall seek our rooty bed,
All wasted in disaster!
  But you lift not your head.

IV

—'I mark your early going,
  And that you'll soon be clay,   20
I have seen your summer showing
  As in my youthful day;
But why I seem unknowing
  Is too sunk in to say!'

                                        1917.

Last Words to a Dumb Friend

Pet was never mourned as you,
Purrer of the spotless hue,
Plumy tail, and wistful gaze
While you humoured our queer ways,
Or outshrilled your morning call
Up the stairs and through the hall—
Foot suspended in its fall—
While, expectant, you would stand
Arched, to meet the stroking hand;
Till your way you chose to wend   10
Yonder, to your tragic end.

Never another pet for me!
Let your place all vacant be;
Better blankness day by day
Than companion torn away.
Better bid his memory fade,
Better blot each mark he made,
Selfishly escape distress
By contrived forgetfulness,
Than preserve his prints to make   20
Every morn and eve an ache.

From the chair whereon he sat
Sweep his fur, nor wince thereat;
Rake his little pathways out
Mid the bushes roundabout;
Smooth away his talons' mark
From the claw-worn pine-tree bark,
Where he climbed as dusk embrowned,
Waiting us who loitered round.

Strange it is this speechless thing,   30
Subject to our mastering,
Subject for his life and food
To our gift, and time, and mood;
Timid pensioner of us Powers,
His existence ruled by ours,
Should—by crossing at a breath
Into safe and shielded death,
By the merely taking hence
Of his insignificance—
Loom as largened to the sense,   40
Shape as part, above man's will,
Of the Imperturbable.

As a prisoner, flight debarred,
Exercising in a yard,
Still retain I, troubled, shaken,
Mean estate, by him forsaken;
And this home, which scarcely took
Impress from his little look,
By his faring to the Dim
Grows all eloquent of him.   50

Housemate, I can think you still
Bounding to the window-sill,
Over which I vaguely see
Your small mound beneath the tree,
Showing in the autumn shade
That you moulder where you played.

October 2, 1904.

A Drizzling Easter Morning

And he is risen? Well, be it so. . . .
And still the pensive lands complain,
And dead men wait as long ago,
As if, much doubting, they would know
What they are ransomed from, before
They pass again their sheltering door.

I stand amid them in the rain,
While blusters vex the yew and vane;
And on the road the weary wain
Plods forward, laden heavily;   10
And toilers with their aches are fain
For endless rest—though risen is he.

On One Who Lived and Died
Where He Was Born

When a night in November
    Blew forth its bleared airs
An infant descended
    His birth-chamber stairs
    For the very first time,
    At the still, midnight chime;
All unapprehended
    His mission, his aim.—
Thus, first, one November,
An infant descended   10
    The stairs.

On a night in November
   Of weariful cares,
A frail aged figure
   Ascended those stairs
   For the very last time:
   All gone his life's prime,
All vanished his vigour,
   And fine, forceful frame:
Thus, last, one November   20
Ascended that figure
     Upstairs.

On those nights in November—
   Apart eighty years—
The babe and the bent one
   Who traversed those stairs
   From the early first time
   To the last feeble climb—
That fresh and that spent one—
   Were even the same: 30
Yea, who passed in November
As infant, as bent one,
     Those stairs.

Wise child of November!
   From birth to blanched hairs
Descending, ascending,
   Wealth-wantless, those stairs;
   Who saw quick in time
   As a vain pantomime
Life's tending, its ending,   40
   The worth of its fame.
Wise child of November,
Descending, ascending
     Those stairs!

On a Discovered Curl of Hair

When your soft welcomings were said,
This curl was waving on your head,
And when we walked where breakers dinned
It sported in the sun and wind,
And when I had won your words of grace
It brushed and clung about my face.
Then, to abate the misery
Of absentness, you gave it me.

Where are its fellows now? Ah, they
For brightest brown have donned a gray,   10
And gone into a caverned ark,
Ever unopened, always dark!

Yet this one curl, untouched of time,
Beams with live brown as in its prime,
So that it seems I even could now
Restore it to the living brow
By bearing down the western road
Till I had reached your old abode.

February 1913.

Her Apotheosis

'Secretum meum mihi'

(Faded Woman's Song)

There were years vague of measure,
    Needless the asking when;
No honours, praises, pleasure
    Reached common maids from men.

And hence no lures bewitched them,
    No hand was stretched to raise,
No gracious gifts enriched them,
    No voices sang their praise.

Yet an iris at that season
   Amid the accustomed slight   10
From denseness, dull unreason,
   Ringed me with living light.

The Lament of the Looking-Glass

Words from the mirror softly pass
   To the curtains with a sigh:
'Why should I trouble again to glass
   These smileless things hard by,
Since she I pleasured once, alas,
   Is now no longer nigh!

'I've imaged shadows of coursing cloud,
   And of the plying limb
On the pensive pine when the air is loud
   With its aerial hymn;   10
But never do they make me proud
   To catch them within my rim!

'I flash back phantoms of the night
   That sometimes flit by me,
I echo roses red and white—
   The loveliest blooms that be—
But now I never hold to sight
   So sweet a flower as she.'

Best Times

We went a day's excursion to the stream,
Basked by the bank, and bent to the ripple-gleam,
     And I did not know
     That life would show,
However it might flower, no finer glow.

I walked in the Sunday sunshine by the road
That wound towards the wicket of your abode,
          And I did not think
          That life would shrink
To nothing ere it shed a rosier pink.   10

Unlooked for I arrived on a rainy night,
And you hailed me at the door by the swaying light,
          And I full forgot
          That life might not
Again be touching that ecstatic height.

And that calm eve when you walked up the stair,
After a gaiety prolonged and rare,
          No thought soever
          That you might never
Walk down again, struck me as I stood there.   20

                    Rewritten from an old draft.

Intra Sepulchrum

          What curious things we said,
          What curious things we did
Up there in the world we walked till dead
          Our kith and kin amid!

          How we played at love,
          And its wildness, weakness, woe;
Yes, played thereat far more than enough
          As it turned out, I trow!

          Played at believing in gods
          And observing the ordinances,   10
I for your sake in impossible codes
          Right ready to acquiesce.

          Thinking our lives unique,
          Quite quainter than usual kinds,
We held that we could not abide a week
          The tether of typic minds.

    —Yet people who day by day
      Pass by and look at us
From over the wall in a casual way
    Are of this unconscious.   20

    And feel, if anything,
      That none can be buried here
Removed from commonest fashioning,
    Or lending note to a bier:

    No twain who in heart-heaves proved
      Themselves at all adept,
Who more than many laughed and loved,
    Who more than many wept,

    Or were as sprites or elves
      Into blind matter hurled,   30
Or ever could have been to themselves
    The centre of the world.

Just the Same

    I sat. It all was past;
    Hope never would hail again;
    Fair days had ceased at a blast,
    The world was a darkened den.

    The beauty and dream were gone,
    And the halo in which I had hied
    So gaily gallantly on
    Had suffered blot and died!

    I went forth, heedless whither,
    In a cloud too black for name: 10
    —People frisked hither and thither;
    The world was just the same.

The Last Time

The kiss had been given and taken,
    And gathered to many past:
It never could reawaken;
    But I heard none say: 'It's the last!'

The clock showed the hour and the minute,
    But I did not turn and look:
I read no finis in it,
    As at closing of a book.

But I read it all too rightly
    When, at a time anon,   10
A figure lay stretched out whitely,
    And I stood looking thereon.

The Sun's Last Look on the Country Girl

(M. H.)

The sun threw down a radiant spot
    On the face in the winding-sheet—
The face it had lit when a babe's in its cot;
And the sun knew not, and the face knew not
    That soon they would no more meet.

Now that the grave has shut its door,
    And lets not in one ray,
Do they wonder that they meet no more—
That face and its beaming visitor—
    That met so many a day?   10

December 1915.

In a London Flat

I

'You look like a widower,' she said
Through the folding-doors with a laugh from the bed,
As he sat by the fire in the outer room,
Reading late on a night of gloom,
And a cab-hack's wheeze, and the clap of its feet
In its breathless pace on the smooth wet street,
Were all that came to them now and then. . . .
'You really do!' she quizzed again.

II

And the Spirits behind the curtains heard,
And also laughed, amused at her word,   10
And at her light-hearted view of him.
'Let's get him made so—just for a whim!'
Said the Phantom Ironic. ' "Twould serve her right
If we coaxed the Will to do it some night.'
'O pray not!' pleaded the younger one,
The Sprite of the Pities. 'She said it in fun!'

III

But so it befell, whatever the cause,
That what she had called him he next year was;
And on such a night, when she lay elsewhere,
He, watched by those Phantoms, again sat there,   20
And gazed, as if gazing on far faint shores,
At the empty bed through the folding-doors
As he remembered her words; and wept
That she had forgotten them where she slept.

Drawing Details in an Old Church

I hear the bell-rope sawing,
And the oil-less axle grind,
As I sit alone here drawing
What some Gothic brain designed;

And I catch the toll that follows
        From the lagging bell,
Ere it spreads to hills and hollows
        Where people dwell.

I ask not whom it tolls for,
Incurious who he be;   10
So, some morrow, when those knolls for
One unguessed, sound out for me,
A stranger, loitering under
        In nave or choir,
May think, too, 'Whose, I wonder?'
        But not inquire.

The Colour

(The following lines are partly original, partly remembered from
a Wessex folk-rhyme)

'What shall I bring you?
Please will white do
Best for your wearing
        The long day through?'
'—White is for weddings,
Weddings, weddings,
White is for weddings,
        And that won't do.'

'What shall I bring you?
Please will red do   10
Best for your wearing
        The long day through?'
'—Red is for soldiers,
Soldiers, soldiers,
Red is for soldiers,
        And that won't do.'

'What shall I bring you?
Please will blue do
Best for your wearing
    The long day through?'   20
'—Blue is for sailors,
Sailors, sailors,
Blue is for sailors,
    And that won't do.'

'What shall I bring you?
Please will green do
Best for your wearing
    The long day through?'
'—Green is for mayings,
Mayings, mayings,   30
Green is for mayings,
    And that won't do.'

'What shall I bring you
Then? Will black do
Best for your wearing
    The long day through?'
'—Black is for mourning,
Mourning, mourning,
Black is for mourning,
    And black will do.'   40

Epitaph

I never cared for Life: Life cared for me,
And hence I owed it some fidelity.
It now says, 'Cease; at length thou hast learnt to grind
Sufficient toll for an unwilling mind,
And I dismiss thee—not without regard
That thou didst ask no ill-advised reward,
Nor sought in me much more than thou couldst find.'

An Ancient to Ancients

Where once we danced, where once we sang,
        Gentlemen,
The floors are sunken, cobwebs hang,
And cracks creep; worms have fed upon
The doors. Yea, sprightlier times were then
Than now, with harps and tabrets gone,
        Gentlemen!

Where once we rowed, where once we sailed,
        Gentlemen,
And damsels took the tiller, veiled   10
Against too strong a stare (God wot
Their fancy, then or anywhen!)
Upon that shore we are clean forgot,
        Gentlemen!

We have lost somewhat, afar and near,
        Gentlemen,
The thinning of our ranks each year
Affords a hint we are nigh undone,
That we shall not be ever again
The marked of many, loved of one,   20
        Gentlemen.

In dance the polka hit our wish,
        Gentlemen,
The paced quadrille, the spry schottische,
'Sir Roger'.—And in opera spheres
The 'Girl' (the famed 'Bohemian'),
And 'Trovatore', held the ears,
        Gentlemen.

This season's paintings do not please,
        Gentlemen,   30
Like Etty, Mulready, Maclise;
Throbbing romance has waned and wanned;
No wizard wields the witching pen
Of Bulwer, Scott, Dumas, and Sand,
        Gentlemen.

The bower we shrined to Tennyson,
     Gentlemen,
Is roof-wrecked; damps there drip upon
Sagged seats, the creeper-nails are rust,
The spider is sole denizen;   40
Even she who voiced those rhymes is dust,
     Gentlemen!

We who met sunrise sanguine-souled,
     Gentlemen,
Are wearing weary. We are old;
These younger press; we feel our rout
Is imminent to Aïdes' den,—
That evening shades are stretching out,
     Gentlemen!

And yet, though ours be failing frames,   50
     Gentlemen,
So were some others' history names,
Who trode their track light limbed and fast
As these youth, and not alien
From enterprise, to their long last,
     Gentlemen.

Sophocles, Plato, Socrates,
     Gentlemen,
Pythagoras, Thucydides,
Herodotus, and Homer,—yea,   60
Clement, Augustin, Origen,
Burnt brightlier towards their setting-day,
     Gentlemen.

And ye, red-lipped and smooth-browed; list,
     Gentlemen;
Much is there waits you we have missed;
Much lore we leave you worth the knowing,
Much, much has lain outside our ken:
Nay, rush not: time serves: we are going,
     Gentlemen.   70

Surview

'Cogitavi vias meas'°

A cry from the green-grained sticks of the fire
    Made me gaze where it seemed to be:
'Twas my own voice talking therefrom to me
On how I had walked when my sun was higher—
    My heart in its arrogancy.

'*You held not to whatsoever was true,*'
    Said my own voice talking to me:
'*Whatsoever was just you were slack to see;*
Kept not things lovely and pure in view,'
    Said my own voice talking to me.   10

'*You slighted her that endureth all,*'
    Said my own voice talking to me;
'*Vaunteth not, trusteth hopefully;*
That suffereth long and is kind withal,'
    Said my own voice talking to me.

'*You taught not that which you set about,*'
    Said my own voice talking to me;
'*That the greatest of things is Charity. . . .*'°
—And the sticks burnt low, and the fire went out,
    And my voice ceased talking to me.   20

Waiting Both

A star looks down at me,
And says: 'Here I and you
Stand, each in his degree:
What do you mean to do,—
　　Mean to do?'

I say: 'For all I know,
Wait, and let Time go by,
Till my change come.'—'Just so,'°
The star says: 'So mean I:—
　　So mean I.'　　　　　　　　10

A Bird-Scene at a Rural Dwelling

When the inmate stirs, the birds retire discreetly
From the window-ledge, whereon they whistled sweetly
　　And on the step of the door,
　　In the misty morning hoar;
　But now the dweller is up they flee
　　To the crooked neighbouring codlin-tree;
And when he comes fully forth they seek the garden,
And call from the lofty costard, as pleading pardon
　　For shouting so near before
　　In their joy at being alive:—　　　　　10
Meanwhile the hammering clock within goes five.

I know a domicile of brown and green,
Where for a hundred summers there have been
Just such enactments, just such daybreaks seen.

'Any little old song'

Any little old song
   Will do for me,
Tell it of joys gone long,
   Or joys to be,
Or friendly faces best
   Loved to see.

Newest themes I want not
   On subtle strings,
And for thrillings pant not
   That new song brings: 10
I only need the homeliest
   Of heartstirrings.

A Cathedral Façade at Midnight

Along the sculptures of the western wall
   I watched the moonlight creeping:
It moved as if it hardly moved at all,
   Inch by inch thinly peeping
Round on the pious figures of freestone, brought
And poised there when the Universe was wrought
To serve its centre, Earth, in mankind's thought.

The lunar look skimmed scantly toe, breast, arm,
   Then edged on slowly, slightly,
To shoulder, hand, face; till each austere form   10
   Was blanched its whole length brightly
Of prophet, king, queen, cardinal in state,
That dead men's tools had striven to simulate;
And the stiff images stood irradiate.

A frail moan from the martyred saints there set
   Mid others of the erection
Against the breeze, seemed sighings of regret
   At the ancient faith's rejection

Under the sure, unhasting, steady stress
Of Reason's movement, making meaningless   20
The coded creeds of old-time godliness.

                                        Salisbury

Last Week in October

The trees are undressing, and fling in many places—
On the gray road, the roof, the window-sill—
Their radiant robes and ribbons and yellow laces;
A leaf each second so is flung at will,
Here, there, another and another, still and still.

A spider's web has caught one while downcoming,
That stays there dangling when the rest pass on;
Like a suspended criminal hangs he, mumming
In golden garb, while one yet green, high yon,
Trembles, as fearing such a fate for himself anon.   10

The Later Autumn

Gone are the lovers, under the bush
        Stretched at their ease;
        Gone the bees,
Tangling themselves in your hair as they rush
        On the line of your track,
        Leg-laden, back
        With a dip to their hive
        In a prepossessed dive.

Toadsmeat is mangy, frosted, and sere;
        Apples in grass   10
        Crunch as we pass,
And rot ere the men who make cyder appear.
        Couch-fires abound
        On fallows around,
        And shades far extend
        Like lives soon to end.

Spinning leaves join the remains shrunk and brown
  Of last year's display
  That lie wasting away,
On whose corpses they earlier as scorners gazed down 20
  From their aery green height:
  Now in the same plight
  They huddle; while yon
  A robin looks on.

Green Slates

(Penpethy)

It happened once, before the duller
  Loomings of life defined them,
I searched for slates of greenish colour
  A quarry where men mined them;

And saw, the while I peered around there,
  In the quarry standing
A form against the slate background there,
  Of fairness eye-commanding.

And now, though fifty years have flown me,
  With all their dreams and duties, 10
And strange-pipped dice my hand has thrown me,
  And dust are all her beauties,

Green slates—seen high on roofs, or lower
  In waggon, truck, or lorry—
Cry out: 'Our home was where you saw her
  Standing in the quarry!'

At Rushy-Pond

On the frigid face of the heath-hemmed pond
  There shaped the half-grown moon:
Winged whiffs from the north with a husky croon
  Blew over and beyond.

And the wind flapped the moon in its float on the pool,
    And stretched it to oval form;
Then corkscrewed it like a wriggling worm;
    Then wanned it weariful.

And I cared not for conning the sky above
    Where hung the substant thing,   10
For my thought was earthward sojourning
    On the scene I had vision of.

Since there it was once, in a secret year,
    I had called a woman to me
From across this water, ardently—
    And practised to keep her near;

Till the last weak love-words had been said,
    And ended was her time,
And blurred the bloomage of her prime,
    And white the earlier red.   20

And the troubled orb in the pond's sad shine
    Was her very wraith, as scanned
When she withdrew thence, mirrored, and
    Her days dropped out of mine.

Four in the Morning

    At four this day of June I rise:
    The dawn-light strengthens steadily;
    Earth is a cerule mystery,
    As if not far from Paradise
            At four o'clock,

    Or else near the Great Nebula,
    Or where the Pleiads blink and smile:
    (For though we see with eyes of guile
    The grisly grin of things by day,
            At four o'clock   10

They show their best.) . . . In this vale's space
I am up the first, I think. Yet, no,
A whistling? and the to-and-fro
Wheezed whettings of a scythe apace
    At four o'clock? . . .

—Though pleasure spurred, I rose with irk:
Here is one at compulsion's whip
Taking his life's stern stewardship
With blithe uncare, and hard at work
    At four o'clock!   20

         Bockhampton.

On the Esplanade

Midsummer: 10 p.m.

The broad bald moon edged up where the sea was wide,
  Mild, mellow-faced;
Beneath, a tumbling twinkle of shines, like dyed,
  A trackway traced
To the shore, as of petals fallen from a rose to waste,
  In its overblow,
And fluttering afloat on inward heaves of the tide:—
All this, so plain; yet the rest I did not know.

The horizon gets lost in a mist new-wrought by the night:
  The lamps of the Bay   10
That reach from behind me round to the left and right
  On the sea-wall way
For a constant mile of curve, make a long display
  As a pearl-strung row,
Under which in the waves they bore their gimlets of light:—
All this was plain; but there was a thing not so.

Inside a window, open, with undrawn blind,
    There plays and sings
A lady unseen a melody undefined:
    And where the moon flings   20
Its shimmer a vessel crosses, whereon to the strings
    Plucked sweetly and low
Of a harp, they dance. Yea, such did I mark. That, behind,
My Fate's masked face crept near me I did not know!

Coming Up Oxford Street: Evening

    The sun from the west glares back,
    And the sun from the watered track,
    And the sun from the sheets of glass,
    And the sun from each window-brass;
    Sun-mirrorings, too, brighten
    From show-cases beneath
    The laughing eyes and teeth
    Of ladies who rouge and whiten.
    And the same warm god explores
    Panels and chinks of doors;   10
    Problems with chymists' bottles
    Profound as Aristotle's
    He solves, and with good cause,
    Having been ere man was.

Also he dazzles the pupils of one who walks west,
A city-clerk, with eyesight not of the best,
Who sees no escape to the very verge of his days
From the rut of Oxford Street into open ways;
And he goes along with head and eyes flagging forlorn,
Empty of interest in things, and wondering why he was born. 20

                        As seen *July* 4, 1872.

A Last Journey

'Father, you seem to have been sleeping fair?'
The child uncovered the dimity-curtained window-square
    And looked out at the dawn,
    And back at the dying man nigh gone,
    And propped up in his chair,
Whose breathing a robin's 'chink' took up in antiphon.

    The open fireplace spread
  Like a vast weary yawn above his head,
Its thin blue blower waved against his whitening crown,
    For he could not lie down: 10
He raised him on his arms so emaciated:—

   'Yes; I've slept long, my child. But as for rest,
    Well, that I cannot say.
The whole night have I footed field and turnpike-way—
   A regular pilgrimage—as at my best
    And very briskest day!

   ''Twas first to Weatherb'ry, to see them there,
    And thence to King's-Stag, where
I joined in a jolly trip to Weydon-Priors Fair:
   I shot for nuts, bought gingerbreads, cream-cheese;   20
    And, not content with these,
I went to London: heard the watchmen cry the hours.

'I soon was off again, and found me in the bowers
    Of father's apple-trees,
  And he shook the apples down: they fell in showers,
Whereon he turned, smiled strange at me, as ill at ease;
   And then you pulled the curtain; and, ah me,
   I found me back where I wished not to be!'

'Twas told the child next day: 'Your father's dead.'
    And, struck, she questioned, 'O,   30
That journey, then, did father really go?—
Buy nuts, and cakes, and travel at night till dawn was red,
   And tire himself with journeying, as he said,
    To see those old friends that he cared for so?'

Singing Lovers

I rowed: the dimpled tide was at the turn,
And mirth and moonlight spread upon the bay:
There were two singing lovers in the stern;
     But mine had gone away,—
     Whither, I shunned to say!

The houses stood confronting us afar,
A livid line against the evening glare;
The small lamps livened; then out-stole a star;
     But my Love was not there,—
     Vanished, I sorrowed where!   10

His arm was round her, both full facing me
With no reserve. Theirs was not love to hide;
He held one tiller-rope, the other she;
     I pulled—the merest glide,—
     Looked on at them, and sighed.

The moon's glassed glory heaved as we lay swinging
Upon the undulations. Shoreward, slow,
The plash of pebbles joined the lovers' singing,
     But she of a bygone vow
     Joined in the song not now!   20

                    Weymouth.

The Month's Calendar

Tear off the calendar
Of this month past,
And all its weeks that are
Flown, to be cast
To oblivion fast!

Darken that day
On which we met,
With its words of gay
Half-felt regret
That you'll forget!   10

The second day, too;
The noon I nursed
Well—thoughts; yes, through
To the thirty-first;
That was the worst.

For then it was
You let me see
There was good cause
Why you could not be
Aught ever to me!   20

When Dead

To ——

It will be much better when
    I am under the bough;
I shall be more myself, Dear, then,
    Than I am now.

No sign of querulousness
    To wear you out
Shall I show there: strivings and stress
    Be quite without.

This fleeting life-brief blight
    Will have gone past   10
When I resume my old and right
    Place in the Vast.

And when you come to me
    To show you true,
Doubt not I shall infallibly
    Be waiting you.

Sine Prole

(Latin Sequence-Metre)

Forth from ages thick in mystery,
Through the morn and noon of history,
 To the moment where I stand
Has my line wound: I the last one
Outcome of each spectral past one
 Of that file, so many-manned!

Nothing in its time-trail marred it:
As one long life I regard it
 Throughout all the years till now,
When it fain—the close seen coming—   10
After annals past all plumbing—
 Makes to Being its parting bow.

Unlike Jahveh's ancient nation,
Little in their line's cessation
 Moderns see for surge of sighs:
They have been schooled by lengthier vision,
View Life's lottery with misprision,
 And its dice that fling no prize!

Ten Years Since

 'Tis ten years since
 I saw her on the stairs,
 Heard her in house-affairs,
 And listened to her cares;
And the trees are ten feet taller,
And the sunny spaces smaller
Whose bloomage would enthrall her;
And the piano wires are rustier,
The smell of bindings mustier,
And lofts and lumber dustier   10

Than when, with casual look
And ear, light note I took
Of what shut like a book
Those ten years since!

Nov. 1922.

Every Artemisia

'Your eye-light wanes with an ail of care,
Frets freeze gray your face and hair.'

　　'I was the woman who met him,
　　　　Then cool and keen,
　　　　Whiling away
Time, with its restless scene on scene
　　　　Every day.'

'Your features fashion as in a dream
Of things that were, or used to seem.'

　　'I was the woman who won him:　　　　　10
　　　　Steadfast and fond
　　　　Was he, while I
Tepidly took what he gave, nor conned
　　　　Wherefore or why.'

'Your house looks blistered by a curse,
As if a wraith ruled there, or worse.'

　　'I was the woman who slighted him:
　　　　Far from my town
　　　　Into the night
He went. . . . My hair, then auburn-brown,　　20
　　　　Pangs have wanned white.'

'Your ways reflect a monstrous gloom;
Your voice speaks from within a tomb.'

'I was the woman who buried him:
My misery
God laughed to scorn:
The people said: "'Twere well if she
Had not been born!"'

'You plod to pile a monument
So madly that your breath is spent.'   30

'I am the woman who god him:
I build, to ease
My scalding fires,
A temple topping the Deities'
Fanes of my sires.'

The Best She Could

Nine leaves a minute
Swim down shakily;
Each one fain would spin it
Straight to earth; but, see,
How the sharp airs win it
Slantwise away!—Hear it say,
'Now we have finished our summer show
Of what we knew the way to do:
Alas, not much! But, as things go,
As fair as any. And night-time calls,   10
And the curtain falls!'

Sunlight goes on shining
As if no frost were here,
Blackbirds seem designing
Where to build next year;
Yet is warmth declining:
And still the day seems to say,
'Saw you how Dame Summer drest?
Of all God taught her she bethought her!
Alas, not much! And yet the best   20
She could, within the too short time
Granted her prime.'

Nov. 8, 1923.

The Graveyard of Dead Creeds

I lit upon the graveyard of dead creeds
In wistful wanderings through old wastes of thought,
Where bristled fennish fungi, fruiting nought,
Amid the sepulchres begirt with weeds,

Which stone by stone recorded sanct, deceased
Catholicons that had, in centuries flown,
Physicked created man through his long groan,
Ere they went under, all their potence ceased.

When in a breath-while, lo, their spectres rose
Like wakened winds that autumn summons up:—   10
'Out of us cometh an heir, that shall disclose
New promise!' cried they. 'And the caustic cup

'We ignorantly upheld to men, be filled
With draughts more pure than those we ever distilled,
That shall make tolerable to sentient seers
The melancholy marching of the years.'

'There seemed a strangeness'

A Phantasy

There seemed a strangeness in the air,
Vermilion light on the land's lean face;
I heard a Voice from I knew not where:—
'The Great Adjustment is taking place!

'I set thick darkness over you,
And fogged you all your years therein;
    At last I uncloud your view,
Which I am weary of holding in.

'Men have not heard, men have not seen
Since the beginning of the world°   10
    What earth and heaven mean;
But now their curtains shall be furled,

'And they shall see what is, ere long,
Not through a glass, but face to face;°
And Right shall disestablish Wrong:
The Great Adjustment is taking place.'

A Night of Questionings

On the eve of All-Souls' Day
I heard the dead men say
Who lie by the tottering tower,
To the dark and doubling wind
At the midnight's turning hour,
When other speech had thinned:
  'What of the world now?'
The wind whiffed back: 'Men still
Who are born, do good, do ill
Here, just as in your time: 10
Till their years the locust hath eaten,°
Leaving them bare, downbeaten;
Somewhiles in springtide rime,
Somewhiles in summer glow,
Somewhiles in winter snow:—
    No more I know.'

The same eve I caught cry
To the selfsame wind, those dry
As dust beneath the aisles
Of old cathedral piles,   20
Walled up in vaulted biers
Through many Christian years:
  'What of the world now?'
Sighed back the circuiteer:
'Men since your time (shrined here
By deserved ordinance,
Their own craft, or by chance,
Which follows men from birth
Even until under earth)

But little difference show   30
When ranged in sculptured row,
Different as dyes although:—
    No more I know.'

On the selfsame eve, too, said
Those swayed in the sunk sea-bed
To the selfsame wind as it played
With the tide in the starless shade
From Comorin to Horn,
And round by Wrath forlorn:
    'What of the world now?'   40
And the wind for a second ceased,
Then whirred: 'Men west and east,
As each sun soars and dips,
Go down to the sea in ships°
As you went—hither and thither;
See the wonders of the deep,
As you did, ere they sleep;
But few at home care whither
They wander to and fro;
Themselves care little also!—   50
    No more I know.'

Said, too, on the selfsame eve
The troubled skulls that heave
And fust in the flats of France,
To the wind wayfaring over
Listlessly as in trance
From the Ardennes to Dover,
    'What of the world now?'
And the farer moaned: 'As when
You mauled these fields, do men   60
Set them with dark-drawn breaths
To knave their neighbours' deaths
In periodic spasms!
Yea, fooled by foul phantasms,
In a strange cyclic throe
Backward to type they go:—
    No more I know.'

That night, too, men whose crimes
Had cut them off betimes,
Who lay within the pales   70
Of town and county jails
With the rope-groove on them yet,
Said to the same wind's fret
   'What of the world now?'
And the blast in its brooding tone
Returned: 'Men have not shown,
Since you were stretched that morning,
A white cap your adorning,
More lovely deeds or true
In thus neck-knotting you;   80
Or that they purer grow,
Or ever will, I trow!—
   No more I know.'

Life and Death at Sunrise

(Near Dogbury Gate, 1867)

The hills uncap their tops
Of woodland, pasture, copse,
And look on the layers of mist
At their foot that still persist:
They are like awakened sleepers on one elbow lifted,
Who gaze around to learn if things during night have shifted.

A waggon creaks up from the fog
With a laboured leisurely jog;
Then a horseman from off the hill-tip
Comes clapping down into the dip;   10
While woodlarks, finches, sparrows, try to entune at one time,
And cocks and hens and cows and bulls take up the chime.

With a shouldered basket and flagon
A man meets the one with the waggon,
And both the men halt of long use.
   'Well,' the waggoner says, 'what's the news?'
'—'Tis a boy this time. You've just met the doctor trotting back.
She's doing very well. And we think we shall call him "Jack".'

'And what have you got covered there?'
He nods to the waggon and mare.   20
'Oh, a coffin for old John Thinn:
We are just going to put him in.'
'—So he's gone at last. He always had a good constitution.'
'—He was ninety-odd. He could call up the French Revolution.'

Night-Time in Mid-Fall

It is a storm-strid night, winds footing swift
　　　　Through the blind profound;
　　I know the happenings from their sound;
Leaves totter down still green, and spin and drift;
The tree-trunks rock to their roots, which wrench and lift
The loam where they run onward underground.

The streams are muddy and swollen; eels migrate
　　　　To a new abode;
　　Even cross, 'tis said, the turnpike-road;
(Men's feet have felt their crawl, homecoming late):   10
The westward fronts of towers are saturate,
Church-timbers crack, and witches ride abroad.

A Sheep Fair

　　The day arrives of the autumn fair,
　　　　　　And torrents fall,
　　Though sheep in throngs are gathered there,
　　　　　　Ten thousand all,
　　Sodden, with hurdles round them reared:
　　And, lot by lot, the pens are cleared,
　　And the auctioneer wrings out his beard,
　　And wipes his book, bedrenched and smeared,
And rakes the rain from his face with the edge of his hand,
　　　　　　As torrents fall.   10

The wool of the ewes is like a sponge
    With the daylong rain:
Jammed tight, to turn, or lie, or lunge,
    They strive in vain.
Their horns are soft as finger-nails,
Their shepherds reek against the rails,
The tied dogs soak with tucked-in tails,
The buyers' hat-brims fill like pails,
Which spill small cascades when they shift their stand
    In the daylong rain.   20

POSTSCRIPT

Time has trailed lengthily since met
    At Pummery Fair
Those panting thousands in their wet
    And woolly wear:
And every flock long since has bled,
And all the dripping buyers have sped,
And the hoarse auctioneer is dead,
Who 'Going—going!' so often said,
As he consigned to doom each meek, mewed band
    At Pummery Fair.   30

Snow in the Suburbs

Every branch big with it,
    Bent every twig with it;
Every fork like a white web-foot;
Every street and pavement mute:
Some flakes have lost their way, and grope back upward, when
Meeting those meandering down they turn and descend again.
    The palings are glued together like a wall,
    And there is no waft of wind with the fleecy fall.

A sparrow enters the tree,
    Whereon immediately   10
A snow-lump thrice his own slight size
Descends on him and showers his head and eyes,

And overturns him,
And near inurns him,
And lights on a nether twig, when its brush
Starts off a volley of other lodging lumps with a rush.

The steps are a blanched slope,
Up which, with feeble hope,
A black cat comes, wide-eyed and thin;
And we take him in.   20

A Light Snow-Fall after Frost

On the flat road a man at last appears:
How much his whitening hairs
Owe to the settling snow's mute anchorage,
And how much to a life's rough pilgrimage,
One cannot certify.

The frost is on the wane,
And cobwebs hanging close outside the pane
Pose as festoons of thick white worsted there,
Of their pale presence no eye being aware
Till the rime made them plain.   10

A second man comes by;
His ruddy beard brings fire to the pallid scene:
His coat is faded green;
Hence seems it that his mien
Wears something of the dye
Of the berried holm-trees that he passes nigh.

The snow-feathers so gently swoop that though
But half an hour ago
The road was brown, and now is starkly white,
A watcher would have failed defining quite   20
When it transformed it so.

                                        Near Surbiton.

Winter Night in Woodland

(Old Time)

The bark of a fox rings, sonorous and long:—
Three barks, and then silentness; 'wong, wong, wong!'
In quality horn-like, yet melancholy,
As from teachings of years; for an old one is he.
The hand of all men is against him, he knows; and yet, why?
That he knows not,—will never know, down to his death-halloo
    cry.

With clap-nets and lanterns off start the bird-baiters,
In trim to make raids on the roosts in the copse,
Where they beat the boughs artfully, while their awaiters
Grow heavy at home over divers warm drops. 10
The poachers, with swingels, and matches of brimstone, outcreep
To steal upon pheasants and drowse them a-perch and asleep.

Out there, on the verge, where a path wavers through,
Dark figures, filed singly, thrid quickly the view,
Yet heavily laden: land-carriers are they
In the hire of the smugglers from some nearest bay.
Each bears his two 'tubs', slung across, one in front, one behind,
To a further snug hiding, which none but themselves are to find.

And then, when the night has turned twelve, the air brings
From dim distance, a rhythm of voices and strings: 20
'Tis the quire, just afoot on their long yearly rounds,
To rouse by worn carols each house in their bounds;
Robert Penny, the Dewys, Mail, Voss, and the rest; till anon°
Tired and thirsty, but cheerful, they home to their beds in the
    dawn.

Ice on the Highway

Seven buxom women abreast, and arm in arm,
   Trudge down the hill, tip-toed,
     And breathing warm;
They must perforce trudge thus, to keep upright
   On the glassy ice-bound road,
And they must get to market whether or no,
   Provisions running low
   With the nearing Saturday night,
While the lumbering van wherein they mostly ride
    Can nowise go: 10
Yet loud their laughter as they stagger and slide!

                       Yell'ham Hill.

Music in a Snowy Street

   The weather is sharp,
   But the girls are unmoved:
   One wakes from a harp,
   The next from a viol,
   A strain that I loved
   When life was no trial.

   The tripletime beat
   Bounds forth on the snow,
   But the spry springing feet
   Of a century ago,   10
   And the arms that enlaced
   As the couples embraced,
   Are silent old bones
   Under graying gravestones.

   The snow-feathers sail
   Across the harp-strings,
   Whose throbbing threads wail
   Like love-satiate things.
   Each lyre's grimy mien,

With its rout-raising tune,   20
Against the new white
Of the flake-laden noon,
Is incongruous to sight,
Hinting years they have seen
Of revel at night
Ere these damsels became
Possessed of their frame.

O bygone whirls, heys,
Crotchets, quavers, the same
That were danced in the days   30
Of grim Bonaparte's fame,
Or even by the toes
Of the fair Antoinette,—
Yea, old notes like those
Here are living on yet!—
But of their fame and fashion
How little these know
Who strum without passion
For pence, in the snow!

The Frozen Greenhouse

(St Juliot)

'There was a frost
Last night!' she said,
'And the stove was forgot
When we went to bed,
And the greenhouse plants
Are frozen dead!'

By the breakfast blaze
Blank-faced spoke she,
Her scared young look
Seeming to be   10
The very symbol
Of tragedy.

The frost is fiercer
Than then to-day,
As I pass the place
Of her once dismay,
But the greenhouse stands
Warm, tight, and gay,

While she who grieved
At the sad lot   20
Of her pretty plants—
Cold, iced, forgot—
Herself is colder,
And knows it not.

No Buyers

A Street Scene

A load of brushes and baskets and cradles and chairs
        Labours along the street in the rain:
With it a man, a woman, a pony with whiteybrown hairs.—
        The man foots in front of the horse with a shambling sway
            At a slower tread than a funeral train,
        While to a dirge-like tune he chants his wares,
Swinging a Turk's-head brush (in a drum-major's way
            When the bandsmen march and play).

A yard from the back of the man is the whiteybrown pony's nose:
He mirrors his master in every item of pace and pose: 10
            He stops when the man stops, without being told,
        And seems to be eased by a pause; too plainly he's old,
            Indeed, not strength enough shows
            To steer the disjointed waggon straight,
        Which wriggles left and right in a rambling line,
        Deflected thus by its own warp and weight,
And pushing the pony with it in each incline.

The woman walks on the pavement verge,
  Parallel to the man:
She wears an apron white and wide in span,   20
And carries a like Turk's-head, but more in nursing-wise:
  Now and then she joins in his dirge,
  But as if her thoughts were on distant things.
  The rain clams her apron till it clings.—
So, step by step, they move with their merchandize,
  And nobody buys.

The Weary Walker

A plain in front of me,
  And there's the road
Upon it. Wide country,
  And, too, the road!

Past the first ridge another,
  And still the road
Creeps on. Perhaps no other
  Ridge for the road?

Ah! Past that ridge a third,
  Which still the road   10
Has to climb furtherward—
  The thin white road!

Sky seems to end its track;
  But no. The road
Trails down the hill at the back.
  Ever the road!

Last Love-Word

(Song)

This is the last; the very, very last!
　　Anon, and all is dead and dumb,
　　Only a pale shroud over the past,
　　　　That cannot be
　　　　Of value small or vast,
　　　　　Love, then to me!

I can say no more: I have even said too much.
　　I did not mean that this should come:
　　I did not know 'twould swell to such—
　　　　Nor, perhaps, you—　　　　　　　　10
　　　　When that first look and touch,
　　　　　Love, doomed us two!

　　　　　　　　　　189-.

Nobody Comes

Tree-leaves labour up and down,
　　And through them the fainting light
　　Succumbs to the crawl of night.
Outside in the road the telegraph wire
　　To the town from the darkening land
Intones to travellers like a spectral lyre
　　Swept by a spectral hand.

A car comes up, with lamps full-glare,
　　That flash upon a tree:
　　It has nothing to do with me,　　　　　10
And whangs along in a world of its own,
　　Leaving a blacker air;
And mute by the gate I stand again alone,
　　And nobody pulls up there.

　　　　　　　　　October 9, 1924.

The Last Leaf

'The leaves throng thick above:—
Well, I'll come back, dear Love,
    When they all are down!'

She watched that August tree,
(None now scorned summer as she),
    Till it broidered it brown.

And then October came blowing,
And the leaves showed signs they were going,
    And she saw up through them.

O how she counted them then!   10
—November left her but ten,
    And started to strew them.

'Ah, when they all are gone,
And the skeleton-time comes on,
    Whom shall I see!'

—When the fifteenth spread its sky
That month, her upturned eye
    Could count but three.

And at the close of the week
A flush flapped over her cheek: 20
    The last one fell.

But—he did not come. And, at length,
Her hope of him lost all strength,
    And it was as a knell. . . .

When he did come again,
Years later, a husband then,
    Heavy somewhat,

With a smile she reminded him:
And he cried: 'Ah, that vow of our whim!—
   Which I forgot,   30

'As one does!—And was that the tree?
So it was!—Dear me, dear me:
   Yes: I forgot.'

A Second Attempt

Thirty years after
I began again
An old-time passion:
And it seemed as fresh as when
The first day ventured on:
When mutely I would waft her
In Love's past fashion
Dreams much dwelt upon,
Dreams I wished she knew.

I went the course through,   10
From Love's fresh-found sensation—
Remembered still so well—
To worn words charged anew,
That left no more to tell:
Thence to hot hopes and fears,
And thence to consummation,
And thence to sober years,
Markless, and mellow-hued.

Firm the whole fabric stood,
Or seemed to stand, and sound   20
As it had stood before.
But nothing backward climbs,
And when I looked around
As at the former times,
There was Life—pale and hoar;
And slow it said to me,
'Twice-over cannot be!'

The Absolute Explains

I

'O no,' said It: 'her lifedoings
    Time's touch hath not destroyed:
They lie their length, with the throbbing things
    Akin them, down the Void,
        Live, unalloyed.

II

'Know, Time is toothless, seen all through;
    The Present, that men but see,
Is phasmal: since in a sane purview
    All things are shaped to be
        Eternally.   10

III

'Your "Now" is just a gleam, a glide
    Across your gazing sense:
With me, "Past", "Future", ever abide:
    They come not, go not, whence
        They are never hence.

IV

'As one upon a dark highway,
    Plodding by lantern-light,
Finds but the reach of its frail ray
    Uncovered to his sight,
        Though mid the night   20

V

'The road lies all its length the same,
    Forwardly as at rear,
So, outside what you "Present" name,
    Future and Past stand sheer,
        Cognate and clear.'

VI

—Thus It: who straightway opened then
　　The vista called the Past,
Wherein were seen, as fair as when
　　They seemed they could not last,
　　　　Small things and vast.　　　　　　30

VII

There were those songs, a score times sung,
　　With all their tripping tunes,
There were the laughters once that rung,
　　There those unmatched full moons,
　　　　Those idle noons!

VIII

There fadeless, fixed, were dust-dead flowers
　　Remaining still in blow;
Elsewhere, wild love-makings in bowers;
　　Hard by, that irised bow
　　　　Of years ago.　　　　　　　　40

IX

There were my ever memorable
　　Glad days of pilgrimage,
Coiled like a precious parchment fell,
　　Illumined page by page,
　　　　Unhurt by age.

X

'—Here you see spread those mortal ails
　　So powerless to restrain
Your young life's eager hot assails,
　　With hazards then not plain
　　　　Till past their pain.　　　　　　50

XI

'Here you see her who, by these laws
　　You learn of, still shines on,
As pleasing-pure as erst she was,
　　Though you think she lies yon,
　　　　Graved, glow all gone.

XII

'Here are those others you used to prize.—
    But why go further we?
The Future?—Well, I would advise
    You let the future be,
        Unshown by me!   60

XIII

''Twould harrow you to see undraped
    The scenes in ripe array
That wait your globe—all worked and shaped;
    And I'll not, as I say,
        Bare them to-day.

XIV

'In fine, Time is a mock,—yea, such!—
    As he might well confess:
Yet hath he been believed in much,
    Though lately, under stress
        Of science, less.   70

XV

'And hence, of her you asked about
    At your first speaking: she
Hath, I assure you, not passed out
    Of continuity,
        But is in me.

XVI

'So thus doth Being's length transcend
    Time's ancient regal claim
To see all lengths begin and end.
    "The Fourth Dimension" fame
        Bruits as its name.'   80

New Year's Eve, 1922.

An Inquiry

A Phantasy

Circumdederunt me dolores mortis.—Ps. xviii.°

I said to It: 'We grasp not what you meant,
(Dwelling down here, so narrowly pinched and pent)
By crowning Death the King of the Firmament:
        —The query I admit to be
        One of unwonted size,
    But it is put you sorrowingly,
        And not in idle-wise.'

'Sooth, since you ask me gravely,' It replied,
'Though too incisive questions I have decried,
This shows some thought, and may be justified.   10
        I'll gauge its value as I go
        Across the Universe,
    And bear me back in a moment or so
        And say, for better or worse.'

Many years later, when It came again,
'That matter an instant back which brought you pain',
It said, 'and you besought me to explain:
        Well, my forethoughtless modes to you
        May seem a shameful thing,
    But—I'd no meaning, that I knew,   20
        In crowning Death as King!'

The Pair He Saw Pass

    O sad man, now a long dead man,
        To whom it was so real,
    I picture, as 'twere yesterday,
        How you would tell the tale!

Just wived were you, you sad dead man,
   And 'settling down', you'd say,
And had rigged the house you had reared for yourself
   And the mate now yours alway.

You had eyed and tried each door and lock,
   And cupboard, and bell, and glass,
When you glanced across to the road without,   10
   And saw a carriage pass.

It bowled along from the old town-gate;
   Two forms its freight, and those
Were a just-joined pair, as you discerned
   By the favours and the bows.

And one of the pair you saw was a Fair
   Whom you had wooed awhile,
And the other you saw, with a creeping awe,
   Was yourself, in bridegroom style.   20

'And there we rode as man and wife
   In the broad blaze of the sun,'
Would you aver; yea, you with her
   You had left for another one.

'The morning', you said, my friend long dead,
   'Was ordinary and fine;
And yet there gleamed, it somehow seemed,
   At moments, a strange shine.'

You hailed a boy from your garden-plot,
   And sent him along the way   30
To the parish church; whence word was brought
   No marriage had been that day.

You mused, you said; till you heard anon
   That at that hour she died
Whom once, instead of your living wife,
   You had meant to make your bride. . . .

You, dead man, dwelt in your new-built house
    With no great spirit or will,
And after your soon decease your spouse
    Re-mated: she lives there still.   40

Which should be blamed, if either can,
    The teller does not know
For your mismatch, O weird-wed man,
    Or what you thought was so.

From an old draft.

Last Look Round St Martin's Fair

The sun is like an open furnace door,
Whose round revealed retort confines the roar
    Of fires beyond terrene;
The moon presents the lustre-lacking face
    Of a brass dial gone green,
    Whose hours no eye can trace.
The unsold heathcroppers are driven home
To the shades of the Great Forest whence they come
By men with long cord-waistcoats in brown monochrome.
    The stars break out, and flicker in the breeze,   10
        It seems, that twitches the trees.—
        From its hot idol soon
The fickle unresting earth has turned to a fresh patroon—
    The cold, now brighter, moon.

The woman in red, at the nut-stall with the gun,
    Lights up, and still goes on:
She's redder in the flare-lamp than the sun
    Showed it ere it was gone.
Her hands are black with loading all the day,
And yet she treats her labour as 'twere play,   20
    Tosses her ear-rings, and talks ribaldry
To the young men around as natural gaiety,
    And not a weary work she'd readily stay,
        And never again nut-shooting see,
            Though crying, 'Fire away!'

A Leader of Fashion

Never has she known
The way a robin will skip and come,
With an eye half bold, half timorsome,
To the table's edge for a breakfast crumb:

Nor has she seen
A streak of roseate gently drawn
Across the east, that means the dawn,
When, up and out, she foots it on:

Nor has she heard
The rustle of the sparrow's tread   10
To roost in roof-holes near her head
When dusk bids her, too, seek her bed:

Nor has she watched
Amid a stormy eve's turmoil
The pipkin slowly come to boil,
In readiness for one at toil:

Nor has she hearkened
Through the long night-time, lone and numb,
For sounds of sent-for help to come
Ere the swift-sinking life succumb: 20

Nor has she ever
Held the loved-lost one on her arm,
Attired with care his straightened form,
As if he were alive and warm:

Yea, never has she
Known, seen, heard, felt, such things as these,
Haps of so many in their degrees
Throughout their count of calvaries!

Midnight on Beechen, 187–

On Beechen Cliff self-commune I
This night of mid-June, mute and dry;
When darkness never rises higher
Than Bath's dim concave, towers, and spire,
Last eveglow loitering in the sky

To feel the dawn, close lurking by,
The while the lamps as glow-worms lie
In a glade, myself their lonely eyer
　　　　　　On Beechen Cliff:

The city sleeps below. I sigh,　　　　　　　　　　10
For there dwells one, all testify,
To match the maddest dream's desire:
What swain with her would not aspire
To walk the world, yea, sit but nigh
　　　　　　On Beechen Cliff!

The Prospect

The twigs of the birch imprint the December sky
　Like branching veins upon a thin old hand;
I think of summer-time, yes, of last July,
　When she was beneath them, greeting a gathered band
　　Of the urban and bland.

Iced airs wheeze through the skeletoned hedge from the north,
　With steady snores, and a numbing that threatens snow,
And skaters pass; and merry boys go forth
　To look for slides. But well, well do I know
　　Whither I would go!　　　　　　　　　　10

December 1912.

The Fading Rose

I saw a rose, in bloom, but sad,
Shedding the petals that still it had,
And I heard it say: 'O where is she
Who used to come and muse on me?

'The pruner says she comes no more
Because she loves another flower,
The weeder says she's tired of me
Because I droop so suddenly.

'Because of a sweetheart she comes not,
Declares the man with the watering-pot;   10
"She does not come", says he with the rake,
"Because all women are fickle in make."

'He with the spade and humorous leer
Says: "Know, I delve elsewhere than here,
Mid text-writ stones and grassy heaps,
Round which a curious silence creeps.

'"She must get to you underground
If any way at all be found,
For, clad in her beauty, marble's kin,
'Tis there I have laid her and trod her in."'   20

When Oats Were Reaped

That day when oats were reaped, and wheat was ripe, and barley
          ripening,
     The road-dust hot, and the bleaching grasses dry,
          I walked along and said,
While looking just ahead to where some silent people lie:

'I wounded one who's there, and now know well I wounded her;
     But, ah, she does not know that she wounded me!'
          And not an air stirred,
Nor a bill of any bird; and no response accorded she.

August 1913.

Louie

I am forgetting Louie the buoyant;
Why not raise her phantom, too,
    Here in daylight
    With the elect one's?
She will never thrust the foremost figure out of view!

Mid this heat, in gauzy muslin
See I Louie's life-lit brow
    Here in daylight
    By the elect one's.—
Long two strangers they and far apart; such neighbours now!   10

July 1913.

'She opened the door'

She opened the door of the West to me,
    With its loud sea-lashings,
    And cliff-side clashings
Of waters rife with revelry.

She opened the door of Romance to me,
    The door from a cell
    I had known too well,
Too long, till then, and was fain to flee.

She opened the door of a Love to me,
    That passed the wry   10
    World-welters by
As far as the arching blue the lea.

She opens the door of the Past to me,
    Its magic lights,
    Its heavenly heights,
When forward little is to see!

1913.

The Harbour Bridge

From here, the quay, one looks above to mark
The bridge across the harbour, hanging dark
Against the day's-end sky, fair-green in glow
Over and under the middle archway's bow:
It draws its skeleton where the sun has set,
Yea, clear from cutwater to parapet;
On which mild glow, too, lines of rope and spar
    Trace themselves black as char.

Down here in shade we hear the painters shift
Against the bollards with a drowsy lift,   10
As moved by the incoming stealthy tide.
High up across the bridge the burghers glide
As cut black-paper portraits hastening on
In conversation none knows what upon:
Their sharp-edged lips move quickly word by word
    To speech that is not heard.

There trails the dreamful girl, who leans and stops,
There presses the practical woman to the shops,
There is a sailor, meeting his wife with a start,
And we, drawn nearer, judge they are keeping apart.   20
Both pause. She says: 'I've looked for you. I thought
We'd make it up.' Then no words can be caught.
At last: 'Won't you come home?' She moves still nigher:
    ''Tis comfortable, with a fire.'

'No,' he says gloomily. 'And, anyhow,
I can't give up the other woman now:
You should have talked like that in former days,
When I was last home.' They go different ways.
And the west dims, and yellow lamplights shine:
And soon above, like lamps more opaline,   30
White stars ghost forth, that care not for men's wives,
    Or any other lives.

                              Weymouth.

Vagrant's Song

(With an Old Wessex Refrain)

I

When a dark-eyed dawn
Crawls forth, cloud-drawn,
And starlings doubt the night-time's close;
And 'three months yet',
They seem to fret,
'Before we cease us slaves of snows,
And sun returns
To loose the burns,
And this wild woe called Winter goes!'—
O a hollow tree   10
Is as good for me
As a house where the back-brand glows!°
Che-hane, mother; che-hane, mother,°
As a house where the back-brand glows!

II

When autumn brings
A whirr of wings
Among the evergreens around,
And sundry thrills
About their quills
Awe rooks, and misgivings abound,   20
And the joyless pines
In leaning lines
Protect from gales the lower ground,
O a hollow tree
Is as good for me
As a house of a thousand pound!
Che-hane, mother; che-hane, mother,°
As a house of a thousand pound!

Farmer Dunman's Funeral

'Bury me on a Sunday,'
   He said; 'so as to see
Poor folk there. 'Tis their one day
   To spare for following me.'

With forethought of that Sunday,
   He wrote, while he was well,
On ten rum-bottles one day,
   '*Drink for my funeral.*'

They buried him on a Sunday,
   That folk should not be balked   10
His wish, as 'twas their one day:
   And forty couple walked.

They said: 'To have it Sunday
   Was always his concern;
His meaning being that one day
   He'd do us a good turn.

'We must, had it been Monday,
   Have got it over soon,
But now we gain, being Sunday,
   A jolly afternoon.'   20

The Sexton at Longpuddle

He passes down the churchyard track
   On his way to toll the bell;
And stops, and looks at the graves around,
And notes each finished and greening mound
     Complacently,
     As their shaper he,
And one who can do it well.

And, with a prosperous sense of his doing,
    Thinks he'll not lack
Plenty such work in the long ensuing   10
    Futurity.
    For people will always die,
    And he will always be nigh
      To shape their cell.

The Harvest-Supper

(*Circa* 1850)

Nell and the other maids danced their best
    With the Scotch-Greys in the barn;
These had been asked to the harvest-feast;
    Red shapes amid the corn.

Nell and the other maids sat in a row
    Within the benched barn-nook;
Nell led the songs of long ago
    She'd learnt from never a book.

She sang of the false Sir John of old,
    The lover who witched to win,
And the parrot, and cage of glittering gold;   10
    And the other maids joined in.

Then whispered to her a gallant Grey,
    'Dear, sing that ballet again!
For a bonnier mouth in a bonnier way
    Has sung not anywhen!'

As she loosed her lips anew there sighed
    To Nell through the dark barn-door
The voice of her Love from the night outside,
    Who was buried the month before: 20

'O Nell, can you sing ballets there,
  And I out here in the clay,
Of lovers false of yore, nor care
  What you vowed to me one day!

'O can you dance with soldiers bold,
  Who kiss when dancing's done,
Your little waist within their hold,
  As ancient troth were none!'

She cried: 'My heart is pierced with a wound!
  There's something outside the wall   30
That calls me forth to a greening mound:
  I can sing no more at all!

'My old Love rises from the worms,
  Just as he used to be,
And I must let gay gallants' arms
  No more encircle me!'

They bore her home from the merrymaking;
  Bad dreams disturbed her bed:
'Nevermore will I dance and sing,'
  Mourned Nell; 'and never wed!'   40

At a Pause in a Country Dance

(Middle of Last Century)

They stood at the foot of the figure,
And panted: they'd danced it down through—
That 'Dashing White Serjeant' they loved so:—
A window, uncurtained, was nigh them
That end of the room. Thence in view

Outside it a valley updrew,
Where the frozen moon lit frozen snow:
At the furthermost reach of the valley
A light from a window shone low.
'They are inside that window,' said she,   10

As she looked. 'They sit up there for me;
And baby is sleeping there, too.'
He glanced. 'Yes,' he said. 'Never mind.
Let's foot our way up again; do!
'Tis "The Dashing White Serjeant" we love so.
Let's dance down the line as before.

'What's the world to us, meeting once more!'
'—Not much, when my husband full trusts me,
And thinks the child his that I bore!'
He was silent. The fiddlers six-eighted   20
With even more passionate vigour.

The pair swept again up the figure,
The child's cuckoo-father and she,
And the next couples threaded below,
And the twain wove their way to the top
Of 'The Dashing White Serjeant' they loved so,
Restarting: right, left, to and fro.

—From the homestead, seen yon, the small glow
Still adventured forth over the white,
Where the child slept, unknowing who sired it,   30
In the cradle of wicker tucked tight,
And its grandparents, nodding, admired it
In elbow-chairs through the slow night.

On the Portrait of a Woman
about to be Hanged

Comely and capable one of our race,
Posing there in your gown of grace,
    Plain, yet becoming;
        Could subtlest breast
        Ever have guessed
What was behind that innocent face,
        Drumming, drumming!

Would that your Causer, ere knoll your knell
For this riot of passion, might deign to tell
     Why, since It made you   10
        Sound in the germ,
        It sent a worm
To madden Its handiwork, when It might well
     Not have assayed you,

Not have implanted, to your deep rue,
The Clytaemnestra spirit in you,
     And with purblind vision
        Sowed a tare
        In a field so fair,
And a thing of symmetry, seemly to view,   20
     Brought to derision!

                January 6, 1923.

'Not only I'

     Not only I
     Am doomed awhile to lie
In this close bin with earthen sides;
But the things I thought, and the songs I sang,
And the hopes I had, and the passioned pang
        For people I knew
        Who passed before me,
     Whose memory barely abides;
        And the visions I drew
        That daily upbore me!   10

     And the joyous springs and summers,
     And the jaunts with blithe new-comers,
And my plans and appearances; drives and rides
That fanned my face to a lively red:
        And the grays and blues
        Of the far-off views,
That nobody else discerned outspread;
And little achievements for blame or praise;
Things left undone; things left unsaid;
        In brief, my days!   20

Compressed here in six feet by two,
　　　In secrecy
　　　To lie with me
　　　Till the Call shall be,
　　Are all these things I knew,
　　Which cannot be handed on;
Strange happenings quite unrecorded,
Lost to the world and disregarded,
That only thinks: 'Here moulders till Doom's-dawn
　　A woman's skeleton.'　　　　　　　　　　30

Once at Swanage

The spray sprang up across the cusps of the moon,
　　　And all its light loomed green
　　　As a witch-flame's weirdsome sheen
At the minute of an incantation scene;
And it greened our gaze—that night at demilune.

Roaring high and roaring low was the sea
　　　Behind the headland shores:
　　　It symboled the slamming of doors,
Or a regiment hurrying over hollow floors. . . .
And there we two stood, hands clasped; I and she!　　10

The Flower's Tragedy

In the bedchamber window, near the glass,
Stood the little flower in the little vase,
　　　Unnoticed quite
　　　For a whole fortnight,
And withered for lack of watering
To a skeleton mere—a mummied thing.

But it was not much, mid a world of teen,
That a flower should waste in a nook unseen!

One needed no thought to ascertain
How it happened; that when she went in the rain   10
  To return here not,
  She was mindless what
She had left here to perish.—Ah, well: for an hour
I wished I had not found the flower!

Yet it was not much. And she never had known
Of the flower's fate; nor it of her own.

A Watcher's Regret

J. E.'s Story

I slept across the front of the clock,
 Close to the long case-door;
The hours were brought by their brazen knock
 To my ear as the slow nights wore.

Thus did I, she being sick to death,
 That each hour as it belled
Should wake me to rise, and learn by her breath
 Whether her strength still held.

Yet though throughout life's midnights all
 I would have watched till spent   10
For her dear sake, I missed the call
 Of the hour in which she went.

The Missed Train

  How I was caught
 Hieing home, after days of allure,
And forced to an inn—small, obscure—
  At the junction, gloom-fraught.

How civil my face
To get them to chamber me there—
A roof I had scorned, scarce aware
    That it stood at the place.

And how all the night
I had dreams of the unwitting cause   10
Of my lodgment. How lonely I was;
    How consoled by her sprite!

Thus onetime to me . . .
Dim wastes of dead years bar away
Then from now. But such happenings to-day
    Fall to lovers, may be!

Years, years as shoaled seas,
Truly, stretch now between! Less and less
Shrink the visions then vast in me.—Yes,
    Then in me: Now in these.   20

Under High-Stoy Hill

Four climbed High-Stoy from Ivel-wards,
Where hedge meets hedge, and cart-ruts wind,
    Chattering like birds,
And knowing not what lay behind.

We laughed beneath the moonlight blink,
Said supper would be to our mind,
    And did not think
Of Time, and what might lie behind. . . .

The moon still meets that tree-tipped height,
The road—as then—still trails inclined;   10
    But since that night
We have well learnt what lay behind!

For all of the four then climbing here
But one are ghosts, and he brow-lined;
    With him they fare,
Yet speak not of what lies behind.

At the Mill

O Miller Knox, whom we knew well,
  And the mill, and the floury floors,
And the corn,—and those two women,
    And infants—yours!

The sun was shining when you rode
  To market on that day:
The sun was set when home-along
  You ambled in the gray,
And gathered what had taken place
    While you were away.   10

O Miller Knox, 'twas grief to see
  Your good wife hanging there
By her own rash and passionate hand,
    In a throe of despair;

And those two children, one by her,
  And one by the waiting-maid,
Borne the same hour, and you afar,
    And she past aid.

And though sometimes you walk of nights,
  Sleepless, to Yalbury Brow,
And glance the graveyard way, and grunt,
    ''Twas not much, anyhow:
She shouldn't ha' minded!' nought it helps
    To say that now.   20

And the water dribbles down your wheel,
  Your mead blooms green and gold,
And birds 'twit in your apple-boughs
    Just as of old.

Alike And Unlike

(Great-Orme's Head)

We watched the selfsame scene on that long drive,
Saw the magnificent purples, as one eye,
Of those near mountains; saw the storm arrive;
Laid up the sight in memory, you and I,
As if for joint recallings by and by.

But our eye-records, like in hue and line,
Had superimposed on them, that very day,
Gravings on your side deep, but slight on mine!—
Tending to sever us thenceforth alway;
Mine commonplace; yours tragic, gruesome, gray.   10

The Thing Unplanned

The white winter sun struck its stroke on the bridge,
    The meadow-rills rippled and gleamed
As I left the thatched post-office, just by the ridge,
And dropped in my pocket her long tender letter,
With: 'This must be snapped! it is more than it seemed;
    And now is the opportune time!'

But against what I willed worked the surging sublime
    Of the thing that I did—the thing better!

The Sheep-Boy

    A yawning, sunned concave
    Of purple, spread as an ocean wave
Entroughed on a morning of swell and sway
After a night when wind-fiends have been heard to rave:
    Thus was the Heath called 'Draäts', on an August day.

Suddenly there intunes a hum:
 This side, that side, it seems to come.
 From the purple in myriads rise the bees
With consternation mid their rapt employ.
So headstrongly each speeds him past, and flees,   10
 As to strike the face of the shepherd-boy.
Awhile he waits, and wonders what they mean;
Till none is left upon the shagged demesne.

To learn what ails, the sheep-boy looks around;
 Behind him, out of the sea in swirls
Flexuous and solid, clammy vapour-curls
Are rolling over Pokeswell Hills to the inland ground.
  Into the heath they sail,
  And travel up the vale
Like the moving pillar of cloud raised by the Israelite:—   20
In a trice the lonely sheep-boy seen so late ago,
  Draäts'-Hollow in gorgeous blow,
  And Kite-Hill's regal glow,
Are viewless—folded into those creeping scrolls of white.

On Rainbarrows.

Retty's Phases

I

Retty used to shake her head,
 Look with wicked eye;
Say, 'I'd tease you, simple Ned,
 If I cared to try!'
Then she'd hot-up scarlet red,
 Stilly step away,
Much afraid that what she'd said
 Sounded bold to say.

II

Retty used to think she loved
   (Just a little) me.
Not untruly, as it proved
   Afterwards to be.
For, when weakness forced her rest
   If we walked a mile,
She would whisper she was blest
   By my clasp awhile.

10

III

Retty used at last to say
   When she neared the Vale,
'Mind that you, Dear, on that day
   Ring my wedding peal!'
And we all, with pulsing pride,
   Vigorous sounding gave
Those six bells, the while outside
   John filled in her grave.

20

IV

Retty used to draw me down
   To the turfy heaps,
Where, with yeoman, squire, and clown
   Noticeless she sleeps.
Now her silent slumber-place
   Seldom do I know,
For when last I saw her face
   Was so long ago!

30

From an old draft of 1868.

A Poor Man and a Lady

We knew it was not a valid thing,
And only sanct in the sight of God
(To use your phrase), as with fervent nod
You swore your assent when I placed the ring

On your pale slim hand. Our whispering
Was soft as the fan of a turtledove
That round our heads might have seemed to wing;
So solemn were we; so sincere our love.

We could do no better; and thus it stood
Through a time of timorous secret bliss,   10
Till we were divided, and never a kiss
Of mine could touch you, or likelihood
Illumed our sky that we might, or should
Be each to each in the world's wide eye
What we were unviewed; and our vows make good
In the presence of parents and standers by.

I was a striver with deeds to do,
And little enough to do them with,
And a comely woman of noble kith,
With a courtly match to make, were you;   20
And we both were young; and though sterling-true
You had proved to our pledge under previous strains,
Our 'union', as we called it, grew
Less grave to your eyes in your town campaigns.

Well: the woeful neared, you needn't be told:
The current news-sheets clarioned soon
That you would be wived on a summer noon
By a man of illustrious line and old:
Nor better nor worse than the manifold
Of marriages made, had there not been   30
Our faith-swearing when fervent-souled,
Which, to me, seemed a breachless bar between.

We met in a Mayfair church, alone:
(The request was mine, which you yielded to.)
'But we were not married at all!' urged you:
'Why, of course we were!' I said. Your tone,
I noted, was world-wise. You went on:
''Twas sweet while it lasted. But you well know
That law is law. He'll be, anon,
My husband *really*. You, Dear, weren't so.'   40

'I wished—but to learn if—' faltered I,
And stopped. 'But I'll sting you not. Farewell!'
And we parted.—Do you recall the bell
That tolled by chance as we said good-bye? . . .
I saw you no more. The track of a high,
Sweet, liberal lady you've doubtless trod.
—All's past! No heart was burst thereby,
And no one knew, unless it was God.

Cynic's Epitaph

A race with the sun as he downed
  I ran at evetide,
Intent who should first gain the ground
  And there hide.

He beat me by some minutes then,
  But I triumphed anon,
For when he'd to rise up again
  I stayed on.

The Peace Peal

(After Four Years of Silence)

Said a wistful daw in Saint Peter's tower,
High above Casterbridge slates and tiles,
'Why do the walls of my Gothic bower
Shiver, and shrill out sounds for miles?
  This gray old rubble
  Has scorned such din
  Since I knew trouble
  And joy herein.

How still did abide them
These bells now swung,   10
While our nest beside them
Securely clung! . . .
It means some snare
For our feet or wings;
But I'll be ware
Of such baleful things!'
And forth he flew from his louvred niche
To take up life in a damp dark ditch.
—So mortal motives are misread,
And false designs attributed,   20
In upper spheres of straws and sticks,
Or lower, of pens and politics.

At the end of the War.

A Popular Personage at Home

'I live here: "Wessex" is my name:
I am a dog known rather well:
I guard the house; but how that came
To be my whim I cannot tell.

'With a leap and a heart elate I go
At the end of an hour's expectancy
To take a walk of a mile or so
With the folk I let live here with me.

'Along the path, amid the grass
I sniff, and find out rarest smells   10
For rolling over as I pass
The open fields towards the dells.

'No doubt I shall always cross this sill,
And turn the corner, and stand steady,
Gazing back for my mistress till
She reaches where I have run already,

'And that this meadow with its brook,
And bulrush, even as it appears
As I plunge by with hasty look,
Will stay the same a thousand years.'   20

Thus 'Wessex'. But a dubious ray
At times informs his steadfast eye,
Just for a trice, as though to say,
'Yet, will this pass, and pass shall I?'

1924.

Inscriptions for a Peal of Eight Bells

After a Restoration

I. Thomas Tremble new-made me
    Eighteen hundred and fifty-three:
    Why he did I fail to see.

II. I was well-toned by William Brine,
    Seventeen hundred and twenty-nine;
    Now, re-cast, I weakly whine!

III. Fifteen hundred used to be
     My date, but since they melted me
     'Tis only eighteen fifty-three.

IV. Henry Hopkins got me made,   10
    And I summon folk as bade;
    Not to much purpose, I'm afraid!

V. I likewise; for I bang and bid
    In commoner metal than I did,
    Some of me being stolen and hid.

VI. I, too, since in a mould they flung me,
    Drained my silver, and rehung me,
    So that in tin-like tones I tongue me.

VII. In nineteen hundred, so 'tis said,
    They cut my canon off my head,   20
    And made me look scalped, scraped, and dead.

VIII. I'm the peal's tenor still, but rue it!
    Once it took two to swing me through it:
    Now I'm rehung, one dolt can do it.

A Refusal

Said the grave Dean of Westminster:
Mine is the best minster
Seen in Great Britain,
As many have written:
So therefore I cannot
Rule here if I ban not
Such liberty-taking
As movements for making
Its grayness environ
The memory of Byron,   10
Which some are demanding
Who think them of standing,
But in my own viewing
Require some subduing
For tendering suggestions
On Abbey-wall questions
That must interfere here
With my proper sphere here,
And bring to disaster
This fane and its master,   20
Whose dict is but Christian
Though nicknamed Philistian.

A lax Christian charity—
No mental clarity
Ruling its movements
For fabric improvements—
Demands admonition
And strict supervision

When bent on enshrining
Rapscallions, and signing   30
Their names on God's stonework,
As if like His own work
Were their lucubrations:
And passed is my patience
That such a creed-scorner
(Not mentioning horner)
Should claim Poet's Corner.

'Tis urged that some sinners
Are here for worms' dinners
Already in person;   40
That he could not worsen
The walls by a name mere
With men of such fame here.
Yet nay; they but leaven
The others in heaven
In just true proportion,
While more mean distortion.

'Twill next be expected
That I get erected
To Shelley a tablet   50
In some niche or gablet.
Then—what makes my skin burn,
Yea, forehead to chin burn—
That I ensconce Swinburne!

August 1924.

Epitaph on a Pessimist

I'm Smith of Stoke, aged sixty-odd,
    I've lived without a dame
From youth-time on; and would to God
    My dad had done the same.

From the French and Greek.

'Known had I'

(Song)

Known had I what I knew not
  When we met eye to eye,
That thenceforth I should view not
  Again beneath the sky
So truefooted a farer
  As you who faced me then,
My path had been a rarer
  Than it figures among men!

I would have trod beside you
  To guard your feet all day,
And borne at night to guide you
  A lantern on your way:
Would not have left you lonely
  With wringing doubt, to cow
Old hope, if I could only
  Have known what I know now.

10

Bags of Meat

'Here's a fine bag of meat,'
  Says the master-auctioneer,
As the timid, quivering steer,
  Starting a couple of feet
At the prod of a drover's stick,
  And trotting lightly and quick,
A ticket stuck on his rump,
Enters with a bewildered jump.

'Where he's lived lately, friends,
  I'd live till lifetime ends:
They've a whole life everyday
  Down there in the Vale, have they!
He'd be worth the money to kill
And give away Christmas for good-will.'

10

'Now here's a heifer—worth more
Than bid, were she bone-poor;
Yet she's round as a barrel of beer';
'She's a plum,' said the second auctioneer.

'Now this young bull—for thirty pound?
Worth that to manure your ground!'   20
'Or to stand', chimed the second one,
'And have his picter done!'
The beast was rapped on the horns and snout
To make him turn about.
'Well,' cried a buyer, 'another crown—
Since I've dragged here from Taunton Town!'

'That calf, she sucked three cows,
Which is not matched for bouse
In the nurseries of high life
By the first-born of a nobleman's wife!'   30
The stick falls, meaning, 'A true tale's told,'
On the buttock of the creature sold,
And the buyer leans over and snips
His mark on one of the animal's hips.

Each beast, when driven in,
Looks round at the ring of bidders there
With a much-amazed reproachful stare,
As at unnatural kin,
For bringing him to a sinister scene
So strange, unhomelike, hungry, mean;   40
His fate the while suspended between
A butcher, to kill out of hand,
And a farmer, to keep on the land;
One can fancy a tear runs down his face
When the butcher wins, and he's driven from the place.

The Sundial on a Wet Day

I drip, drip here
In Atlantic rain,
Falling like handfuls
Of winnowed grain,
Which, tear-like, down
My gnomon drain,
And dim my numerals
With their stain,—
Till I feel useless,
And wrought in vain!   10

And then I think
In my despair
That, though unseen,
He is still up there,
And may gaze out
Anywhen, anywhere;
Not to help clockmen
Quiz and compare,
But in kindness to let me
My trade declare.   20

St Juliot.

Her Haunting-Ground

Can it be so? It must be so,
That visions have not ceased to be
In this the chiefest sanctuary
Of her whose form we used to know.
—Nay, but her dust is far away,
And 'where her dust is, shapes her shade,
If spirit clings to flesh,' they say:
Yet here her life-parts most were played!

Her voice explored this atmosphere,
Her foot impressed this turf around,   10
Her shadow swept this slope and mound,
Her fingers fondled blossoms here;
And so, I ask, why, why should she
Haunt elsewhere, by a slighted tomb,
When here she flourished sorrow-free,
And, save for others, knew no gloom?

A Parting-Scene

The two pale women cried,
  But the man seemed to suffer more,
    Which he strove hard to hide.
They stayed in the waiting-room, behind the door,
Till startled by the entering engine-roar,
As if they could not bear to have unfurled
Their misery to the eyes of all the world.

A soldier and his young wife
  Were the couple; his mother the third,
    Who had seen the seams of life.   10
He was sailing for the East I later heard.
—They kissed long, but they did not speak a word;
Then, strained, he went. To the elder the wife in tears
'Too long; too long!' burst out. ('Twas for five years.)

Shortening Days at the Homestead

The first fire since the summer is lit, and is smoking into the
        room:
  The sun-rays thread it through, like woof-lines in a loom.
  Sparrows spurt from the hedge, whom misgivings appal
That winter did not leave last year for ever, after all.
    Like shock-headed urchins, spiny-haired,
    Stand pollard willows, their twigs just bared.

Who is this coming with pondering pace,
Black and ruddy, with white embossed,
His eyes being black, and ruddy his face,
And the marge of his hair like morning frost?   10
    It's the cider-maker,
    And appletree-shaker,
And behind him on wheels, in readiness,
His mill, and tubs, and vat, and press.

Days to Recollect

    Do you recall
    That day in Fall
When we walked towards Saint Alban's Head,
On thistledown that summer had shed,
    Or must I remind you?
Winged thistle-seeds which hitherto
Had lain as none were there, or few,
But rose at the brush of your petticoat-seam
(As ghosts might rise of the recent dead),
And sailed on the breeze in a nebulous stream   10
    Like a comet's tail behind you:
    You don't recall
    That day in Fall?

    Then do you remember
    That sad November
When you left me never to see me more,
And looked quite other than theretofore,
    As if it could not *be* you?
And lay by the window whence you had gazed
So many times when blamed or praised,   20
Morning or noon, through years and years,
Accepting the gifts that Fortune bore,
Sharing, enduring, joys, hopes, fears!
    Well: I never more did see you.—
    Say you remember
    That sad November!

The High-School Lawn

Gray prinked with rose,
White tipped with blue,
Shoes with gay hose,
Sleeves of chrome hue;
Fluffed frills of white,
Dark bordered light;
Such shimmerings through
Trees of emerald green are eyed
This afternoon, from the road outside.

They whirl around:
Many laughters run
With a cascade's sound;
Then a mere one.

A bell: they flee:
Silence then:—
So it will be
Some day again
With them,—with me.

The Paphian Ball

Another Christmas Experience of The Mellstock Quire

We went our Christmas rounds once more,
With quire and viols as theretofore.

Our path was near by Rushy-Pond,
Where Egdon-Heath outstretched beyond.

There stood a figure against the moon,
Tall, spare, and humming a weirdsome tune.

'You tire of Christian carols,' he said:
'Come and lute at a ball instead.

' 'Tis to your gain, for it ensures
That many guineas will be yours.   10

'A slight condition hangs on't, true,
But you will scarce say nay thereto:

'That you go blindfold; that anon
The place may not be gossiped on.'

We stood and argued with each other:
'Why sing from one house to another

'These ancient hymns in the freezing night,
And all for nought? 'Tis foolish, quite!'

'—'Tis serving God, and shunning evil:
Might not elsedoing serve the devil?'   20

'But grand pay!' . . . We were lured by his call,
Agreeing to go blindfold all.

We walked, he guiding, some new track,
Doubting to find the pathway back.

In a strange hall we found us when
We were unblinded all again.

Gilded alcoves, great chandeliers,
Voluptuous paintings ranged in tiers,

In brief, a mansion large and rare,
With rows of dancers waiting there.   30

We tuned and played; the couples danced;
Half-naked women tripped, advanced,

With handsome partners footing fast,
Who swore strange oaths, and whirled them past.

And thus and thus the hours onbore us:
While shone our guineas heaped before us.

Drowsy at length, in lieu of the dance
'*While Shepherds watched* . . .' we bowed by chance;

And in a moment, at a blink,
There flashed a change; ere we could think   40

The ball-room vanished and all its crew:
Only the well-known heath we view—

The spot of our crossing overnight,
When wheedled by the stranger's sleight.

There, east, the Christmas dawn hung red,
And dark Rainbarrow with its dead

Bulged like a sleeping negress' breast
Against Clyffe-Clump's faint far-off crest.

Yea; the rare mansion, gorgeous, bright,
The ladies, gallants, gone were quite.   50

The heaped-up guineas, too, were gone
With the gold table they were on.

'Why did not grasp we what was owed!'
Cried some, as homeward, shamed, we strode.

Now comes the marvel and the warning:
When we had dragged to church next morning,

With downcast heads and scarce a word,
We were astound at what we heard.

Praises from all came forth in showers
For how we'd cheered the midnight hours.   60

'We've heard you many times,' friends said,
'But like *that* never have you played!

'*Rejoice ye tenants of the earth,*
And celebrate your Saviour's birth,

'Never so thrilled the darkness through,
Or more inspired us so to do!' ...

—The man who used to tell this tale
Was the tenor-viol, Michael Mail;

Yes; Mail the tenor, now but earth.—
I give it for what it may be worth.   70

That Moment

The tragedy of that moment
    Was deeper than the sea,
When I came in that moment
    And heard you speak to me!

What I could not help seeing
    Covered life as a blot;
Yes, that which I was seeing,
    And knew that you were not!

Premonitions

'The bell went heavy to-day
At afternoon service, they say,
And a screech-owl cried in the boughs,
And a raven flew over the house,
And Betty's old clock with one hand,
That's worn out, as I understand,
And never goes now, never will,
Struck twelve when the night was dead still,
Just as when my last loss came to me....
Ah! I wonder who next it will be!'   10

This Summer and Last

Unhappy summer you,
        Who do not see
What your yester-summer saw!
Never, never will you be
        Its match to me,
    Never, never draw
    Smiles your forerunner drew,
        Know what it knew!

Divine things done and said
        Illumined it,   10
Whose rays crept into corn-brown curls,
Whose breezes heard a humorous wit
        Of fancy flit.—
    Still the alert brook purls,
    Though feet that there would tread
        Elsewhere have sped.

So, bran-new summer, you
        Will never see
All that yester-summer saw!
Never, never will you be   20
        In memory
    Its rival, never draw
    Smiles your forerunner drew,
        Know what it knew!

                                        1913?

The Six Boards

    Six boards belong to me:
  I do not know where they may be;
  If growing green, or lying dry
        In a cockloft nigh.

Some morning I shall claim them,
And who may then possess will aim them
To bring to me those boards I need
   With thoughtful speed.

But though they hurry so
To yield me mine, I shall not know   10
How well my want they'll have supplied
   When notified.

Those boards and I—how much
In common we, of feel and touch
Shall share thence on,—earth's far core-quakings,
   Hill-shocks, tide-shakings—

Yea, hid where none will note,
The once live tree and man, remote
From mundane hurt as if on Venus, Mars,
   Or furthest stars.   20

Before My Friend Arrived

I sat on the eve-lit weir,
  Which gurgled in sobs and sighs;
I looked across the meadows near
   To the towered church on the rise.
   Overmuch cause had my look!
   I pulled out pencil and book,
  And drew a white chalk mound,
  Outthrown on the sepulchred ground.

Why did I pencil that chalk?
  It was fetched from the waiting grave,   10
  And would return there soon,
   Of one who had stilled his walk
   And sought oblivion's cave.
He was to come on the morrow noon
And take a good rest in the bed so hewn.

He came, and there he is now, although
This was a wondrous while ago.
And the sun still dons a ruddy dye;
    The weir still gurgles nigh;
    The tower is dark on the sky.   20

The Lady of Forebodings

'What do you so regret, my lady,
    Sitting beside me here?
    Are there not days as clear
As this to come—ev'n shaped less shady?'
'O no,' said she. 'Come what delight
    To you, by voice or pen,
To me will fall such day, such night,
      Not, not again!'

The lamps above and round were fair,
    The tables were aglee,   10
    As if 'twould ever be
That we should smile and sit on there.
But yet she said, as though she must,
    'Yes: it will soon be gone,
And all its dearness leave but dust
      To muse upon.'

A Leaving

  Knowing what it bore
I watched the rain-smitten back of the car—
(Brown-curtained, such as the old ones were)—
When it started forth for a journey afar
Into the sullen November air,
And passed the glistening laurels and round the bend.

I have seen many gayer vehicles turn that bend
   In autumn, winter, and summer air,
   Bearing for journeys near or afar
   Many who now are not, but were,   10
   But I don't forget that rain-smitten car,
     Knowing what it bore!

Song to an Old Burden

The feet have left the wormholed flooring,
    That danced to the ancient air,
    The fiddler, all-ignoring,
Sleeps by the gray-grassed 'cello player:
Shall I then foot around around around,
    As once I footed there!

The voice is heard in the room no longer
    That trilled, none sweetlier,
    To gentle stops or stronger,
Where now the dust-draped cobwebs stir: 10
Shall I then sing again again again,
    As once I sang with her!

The eyes that beamed out rapid brightness
    Have longtime found their close,
    The cheeks have wanned to whiteness
That used to sort with summer rose:
Shall I then joy anew anew anew,
    As once I joyed in those!

O what's to me this tedious Maying,
    What's to me this June?   20
    O why should viols be playing
To catch and reel and rigadoon?
Shall I sing, dance around around around,
    When phantoms call the tune!

from WINTER WORDS

[This volume, though prepared for the press, would have undergone further revision, had the author lived to issue it on the birthday of which he left the number uninserted below.]

INTRODUCTORY NOTE

So far as I am aware, I happen to be the only English poet who has brought out a new volume of his verse on his . . . birthday, whatever may have been the case with the ancient Greeks, for it must be remembered that poets did not die young in those days.

This, however, is not the point of the present few preliminary words. My last volume of poems was pronounced wholly gloomy and pessimistic by reviewers—even by some of the more able class. My sense of the oddity of this verdict may be imagined when, in selecting them, I had been, as I thought, rather too liberal in admitting flippant, not to say farcical, pieces into the collection. However, I did not suppose that the licensed tasters had wilfully misrepresented the book, and said nothing, knowing well that they could not have read it.

As labels stick, I foresee readily enough that the same perennial inscription will be set on the following pages, and therefore take no trouble to argue on the proceeding, notwithstanding the surprises to which I could treat my critics by uncovering a place here and there to them in the volume.

This being probably my last appearance on the literary stage, I would say, more seriously, that though, alas, it would be idle to pretend that the publication of these poems can have much interest for me, the track having been adventured so many times before to-day, the pieces themselves have been prepared with reasonable care, if not quite with the zest of a young man new to print.

I also repeat what I have often stated on such occasions, that no harmonious philosophy is attempted in these pages—or in any bygone pages of mine, for that matter.

T. H.

The New Dawn's Business

What are you doing outside my walls,
    O Dawn of another day?
I have not called you over the edge
      Of the heathy ledge,
    So why do you come this way,
With your furtive footstep without sound here,
    And your face so deedily gray?

'I show a light for killing the man
    Who lives not far from you,
And for bringing to birth the lady's child,   10
      Nigh domiciled,
    And for earthing a corpse or two,
And for several other such odd jobs round here
    That Time to-day must do.

'But you he leaves alone (although,
    As you have often said,
You are always ready to pay the debt
      You don't forget
      You owe for board and bed:)
The truth is, when men willing are found here   20
    He takes those loth instead.'

Proud Songsters

The thrushes sing as the sun is going,
And the finches whistle in ones and pairs,
And as it gets dark loud nightingales
    In bushes
Pipe, as they can when April wears,
    As if all Time were theirs.

These are brand new birds of twelvemonths' growing,
Which a year ago, or less than twain,
No finches were, nor nightingales,
      Nor thrushes,   10
But only particles of grain,
    And earth, and air, and rain.

'I am the one'

I am the one whom ringdoves see
    Through chinks in boughs
    When they do not rouse
    In sudden dread,
But stay on cooing, as if they said:
    'Oh; it's only he.'

I am the passer when up-eared hares,
    Stirred as they eat
    The new-sprung wheat,
    Their munch resume   10
As if they thought: 'He is one for whom
    Nobody cares.'

Wet-eyed mourners glance at me
    As in train they pass
    Along the grass
    To a hollowed spot,
And think: 'No matter; he quizzes not
    Our misery.'

I hear above: 'We stars must lend
    No fierce regard   20
    To his gaze, so hard
    Bent on us thus,—
Must scathe him not. He is one with us
    Beginning and end.'

A Wish for Unconsciousness

If I could but abide
As a tablet on a wall,
Or a hillock daisy-pied,
Or a picture in a hall,
And as nothing else at all,
I should feel no doleful achings,
I should hear no judgment-call,
Have no evil dreams or wakings,
No uncouth or grisly care;
In a word, no cross to bear.   10

To Louisa in the Lane

Meet me again as at that time
    In the hollow of the lane;
I will not pass as in my prime
    I passed at each day's wane.
        —Ah, I remember!
To do it you will have to see
Anew this sorry scene wherein you have ceased to be!

But I will welcome your aspen form
    As you gaze wondering round
And say with spectral frail alarm,   10
    'Why am I still here found?
        —Ah, I remember!
It is through him with blitheful brow
Who did not love me then, but loves and draws me now!'

And I shall answer: 'Sweet of eyes,
    Carry me with you, Dear,
To where you donned this spirit-guise;
    It's better there than here!'
        —Till I remember
Such is a deed you cannot do: 20
Wait must I, till with flung-off flesh I follow you.

The Love-Letters

(IN MEMORIAM H. R.)

I met him quite by accident
In a bye-path that he'd frequent.
And, as he neared, the sunset glow
Warmed up the smile of pleasantry
Upon his too thin face, while he
Held a square packet up to me,
      Of what, I did not know.

'Well,' said he then; 'they are my old letters.
Perhaps she—rather felt them fetters. . . .
You see, I am in a slow decline,   10
And she's broken off with me. Quite right
To send them back, and true foresight;
I'd got too fond of her! To-night
      I burn them—stuff of mine!'

He laughed in the sun—an ache in his laughter—
And went. I heard of his death soon after.

An Unkindly May

A shepherd stands by a gate in a white smock-frock:
He holds the gate ajar, intently counting his flock.

The sour spring wind is blurting boisterous-wise,
And bears on it dirty clouds across the skies;
Plantation timbers creak like rusty cranes,
And pigeons and rooks, dishevelled by late rains,
Are like gaunt vultures, sodden and unkempt,
And song-birds do not end what they attempt:
The buds have tried to open, but quite failing
Have pinched themselves together in their quailing.   10
The sun frowns whitely in eye-trying flaps

Through passing cloud-holes, mimicking audible taps.
'Nature, you're not commendable to-day!'
I think. 'Better to-morrow!' she seems to say.

That shepherd still stands in that white smock-frock,
Unnoting all things save the counting his flock.

Unkept Good Fridays

There are many more Good Fridays
    Than this, if we but knew
The names, and could relate them,
    Of men whom rulers slew
For their goodwill, and date them
    As runs the twelvemonth through.

These nameless Christs' Good Fridays,
    Whose virtues wrought their end,
Bore days of bonds and burning,
    With no man to their friend,   10
Of mockeries, and spurning;
    Yet they are all unpenned.

When they had their Good Fridays
    Of bloody sweat and strain
Oblivion hides. We quote not
    Their dying words of pain,
Their sepulchres we note not,
    Unwitting where they have lain.

No annual Good Fridays
    Gained they from cross and cord,   20
From being sawn asunder,
    Disfigured and abhorred,
Smitten and trampled under:
    Such dates no hands have scored.

Let be. Let lack Good Fridays
   These Christs of unwrit names;
The world was not even worthy
   To taunt their hopes and aims,
As little of earth, earthy,
   As his mankind proclaims.   30

Good Friday, 1927.

The Mound

   For a moment pause:—
   Just here it was;
And through the thin thorn hedge, by the rays of the moon,
I can see the tree in the field, and beside it the mound—
Now sheeted with snow—whereon we sat that June
   When it was green and round,
And she crazed my mind by what she coolly told—
   The history of her undoing,
(As I saw it), but she called 'comradeship,'
   That bred in her no rueing: 10
   And saying she'd not be bound
For life to one man, young, ripe-yeared, or old,
Left me—an innocent simpleton to her viewing;
For, though my accompt of years outscored her own,
   Hers had more hotly flown . . . .
We never met again by this green mound,
To press as once so often lip on lip,
   And palter, and pause:—
   Yes; here it was!

Christmastide

The rain-shafts splintered on me
　As despondently I strode;
The twilight gloomed upon me
　And bleared the blank high-road.
Each bush gave forth, when blown on
　By gusts in shower and shower,
A sigh, as it were sown on
　In handfuls by a sower.

A cheerful voice called, nigh me,
　'A merry Christmas, friend!'—　　　　10
There rose a figure by me,
　Walking with townward trend,
A sodden tramp's, who, breaking
　Into thin song, bore straight
Ahead, direction taking
　Toward the Casuals' gate.

Reluctant Confession

'What did you do? Cannot you let me know?'
'Don't ask! . . . 'Twas midnight, and I'd lost at cards.'
'Ah. Was it crime—or seemed it to be so?'
　'No—not till afterwards.'
　'But *what*, then, did you do?'
'Well—that was the beginning—months ago;
You see, I had lost, and could not pay but—so.
And there flashed from him strange and strong regards
That you only see when scruples smash to shards;
And thus it happened—O it rained and blew!—　　　　10
But I can't tell. 'Twas all so lurid in hue!
And what was worst came after, when I knew
　What first crossed not my mind,
　And he has never divined!' . . .
'But he must have, if he proposed it you?'
'I mean, that—I got rid of what resulted
In a way a woman told me I consulted:

'Tis that he does not know;
Great God, it harrows me so!
I did not mean to. Every night—   20
    In hell-dark dreams
I see an appealing figure in white—
    That somehow seems
A newborn child in the clothes I set to make,
But left off, for my own depraved name's sake!'

Expectation and Experience

'I had a holiday once,' said the woman—
    Her name I did not know—
'And I thought that where I'd like to go,
Of all the places for being jolly,
And getting rid of melancholy,
    Would be to a good big fair:
And I went. And it rained in torrents, drenching
Every horse, and sheep, and yeoman,
    And my shoulders, face, and hair;
And I found that I was the single woman   10
    In the field—and looked quite odd there!
Everything was spirit-quenching:
I crept and stood in the lew of a wall
To think, and could not tell at all
    What on earth made me plod there!'

Evening Shadows

The shadows of my chimneys stretch afar
Across the plot, and on to the privet bower,
And even the shadows of their smokings show,
And nothing says just now that where they are
They will in future stretch at this same hour,
Though in my earthen cyst I shall not know.

And at this time the neighbouring Pagan mound,
Whose myths the Gospel news now supersede,
Upon the greensward also throws its shade,
And nothing says such shade will spread around   10
Even as to-day when men will no more heed
The Gospel news than when the mound was made.

The Three Tall Men

THE FIRST TAPPING

'What's that tapping at night: tack, tack,
In some house in the street at the back?'

'O, 'tis a man who, when he has leisure,
Is making himself a coffin to measure.
He's so very tall that no carpenter
Will make it long enough, he's in fear.
His father's was shockingly short for his limb—
And it made a deep impression on him.'

THE SECOND TAPPING

'That tapping has begun again,
Which ceased a year back, or near then?'   10

'Yes, 'tis the man you heard before
Making his coffin. The first scarce done
His brother died—his only one—
And, being of his own height, or more,
He used it for him; for he was afraid
He'd not get a long enough one quick made.
He's making a second now, to fit
Himself when there shall be need for it.
Carpenters work so by rule of thumb
That they make mistakes when orders come.'   20

THE THIRD TAPPING

'It's strange, but years back, when I was here,
I used to notice a tapping near;
A man was making his coffin at night,
And he made a second, if I am right?
I have heard again the self-same tapping—
Yes, late last night—or was I napping?'

'O no. It's the same man. He made one
Which his brother had; and a second was done—
For himself, as he thought. But lately his son,
As tall as he, died; aye, and as trim,   30
And his sorrowful father bestowed it on him.
And now the man is making a third,
To be used for himself when he is interred.'

Many years later was brought to me
News that the man had died at sea.

The Lodging-House Fuchsias

Mrs Masters's fuchsias hung
Higher and broader, and brightly swung,
     Bell-like, more and more
Over the narrow garden-path,
Giving the passer a sprinkle-bath
     In the morning.

She put up with their pushful ways,
And made us tenderly lift their sprays,
     Going to her door:
But when her funeral had to pass   10
They cut back all the flowery mass
     In the morning.

Throwing a Tree

New Forest

The two executioners stalk along over the knolls,
Bearing two axes with heavy heads shining and wide,
And a long limp two-handled saw toothed for cutting great
  boles,
And so they approach the proud tree that bears the death-mark
  on its side.

Jackets doffed they swing axes and chop away just above
  ground,
And the chips fly about and lie white on the moss and
  fallen leaves;
Till a broad deep gash in the bark is hewn all the way
  round,
And one of them tries to hook upward a rope, which at last he
  achieves.

The saw then begins, till the top of the tall giant shivers:
The shivers are seen to grow greater each cut than before: 10
They edge out the saw, tug the rope; but the tree only
  quivers,
And kneeling and sawing again, they step back to try pulling
  once more.

Then, lastly, the living mast sways, further sways: with a
  shout
Job and Ike rush aside. Reached the end of its long staying
  powers
The tree crashes downward: it shakes all its neighbours
  throughout,
And two hundred years' steady growth has been ended in less
  than two hours.

The War-Wife of Catknoll

'What crowd is this in Catknoll Street,
　　Now I am just come home?
What crowd is this in my old street,
　　That flings me such a glance?
A stretcher—and corpse? A sobering sight
To greet me, when my heart is light
With thoughts of coming cheer to-night
　　Now I am back from France.'

'O 'tis a woman, soldier-man,
　　Who seems to be new come: 10
O 'tis a woman, soldier-man,
　　Found in the river here,
Whither she went and threw her in,
And now they are carrying her within:
She's drowned herself for a sly sin
　　Against her husband dear.

''A said to me, who knew her well,
　　"O why was I so weak!"
'A said to me, who knew her well,
　　And have done all her life,   20
With a downcast face she said to me,
"O why did I keep company
Wi' them that practised gallantry
　　When vowed a faithful wife!"

'"O God, I'm driven mad!" she said,
　　"To hear he's coming back;
I'm fairly driven mad!" she said:
　　"He's been two years agone,
And now he'll find me in this state,
And not forgive me. Had but fate   30
Kept back his coming three months late,
　　Nothing of it he'd known!"

'We did not think she meant so much,
        And said: "He may forgive."
O never we thought she meant so much
        As to go doing this.
And now she must be crowned!—so fair!—°
Who drew men's eyes so everywhere!—
And love-letters beyond compare
        For coaxing to a kiss.   40

'She kept her true a year or more
        Against the young men all;
Yes, kept her true a year or more,
        And they were most to blame.
There was Will Peach who plays the flute,
And Waywell with the dandy suit,
And Nobb, and Knight. . . . But she's been mute
        As to the father's name.'

Concerning his Old Home

MOOD I

I wish to see it never—
        That dismal place
        With cracks in its floor—
I would forget it ever!

MOOD II

To see it once, that sad
        And memoried place—
        Yes, just once more—
I should be faintly glad!

MOOD III

To see it often again—
        That friendly place   10
        With its green low door—
I'm willing anywhen!

MOOD IV

I'll haunt it night and day—
        That loveable place,
        With its flowers' rich store
That drives regret away!

Her Second Husband Hears Her Story

'Still, Dear, it is incredible to me
        That here, alone,
You should have sewed him up until he died,
And in this very bed. I do not see
How you could do it, seeing what might betide.'

'Well, he came home one midnight, liquored deep—
        Worse than I'd known—
And lay down heavily, and soundly slept:
Then, desperate driven, I thought of it, to keep
Him from me when he woke. Being an adept   10

'With needle and thimble, as he snored, click-click
        An hour I'd sewn,
Till, had he roused, he couldn't have moved from bed,
So tightly laced in sheet and quilt and tick
He lay. And in the morning he was dead.

'Ere people came I drew the stitches out,
        And thus 'twas shown
To be a stroke.'—'It's a strange tale!' said he.
'And this same bed?'—'Yes, here it came about.'
'Well, it sounds strange—told here and now to me.   20

'Did you intend his death by your tight lacing?'
        'O, that I cannot own.
I could not think of else that would avail
When he should wake up, and attempt embracing.'—
        'Well, it's a cool queer tale!'

Yuletide in a Younger World

We believed in highdays then,
    And could glimpse at night
      On Christmas Eve
Imminent oncomings of radiant revel—
    Doings of delight:—
    Now we have no such sight.

We had eyes for phantoms then,
    And at bridge or stile
      On Christmas Eve
Clear beheld those countless ones who had crossed it   10
    Cross again in file:—
    Such has ceased longwhile!

We liked divination then,
    And, as they homeward wound
      On Christmas Eve,
We could read men's dreams within them spinning
    Even as wheels spin round:—
    Now we are blinker-bound.

We heard still small voices then,
    And, in the dim serene   20
      Of Christmas Eve,
Caught the fartime tones of fire-filled prophets
    Long on earth unseen. . . .
    —Can such ever have been?

After the Death of a Friend

You died, and made but little of it!—
Why then should I, when called to doff it,
Drop, and renounce this worm-holed raiment,
Shrink edgewise off from its grey claimant?
Rather say, when I am Time-outrun,
As you did: Take me, and have done,
Inexorable, insatiate one!

Lying Awake

You, Morningtide Star, now are steady-eyed, over the east,
    I know it as if I saw you;
You, Beeches, engrave on the sky your thin twigs, even the least;
    Had I paper and pencil I'd draw you.

You, Meadow, are white with your counterpane cover of dew,
    I see it as if I were there;
You, Churchyard, are lightening faint from the shade of the yew,
    The names creeping out everywhere.

Childhood among the Ferns

I sat one sprinkling day upon the lea,
Where tall-stemmed ferns spread out luxuriantly,
And nothing but those tall ferns sheltered me.

The rain gained strength, and damped each lopping frond,
Ran down their stalks beside me and beyond,
And shaped slow-creeping rivulets as I conned,

With pride, my spray-roofed house. And though anon
Some drops pierced its green rafters, I sat on,
Making pretence I was not rained upon.

The sun then burst, and brought forth a sweet breath   10
From the limp ferns as they dried underneath:
I said: 'I could live on here thus till death';

And queried in the green rays as I sate:
'Why should I have to grow to man's estate,
And this afar-noised World perambulate?'

A Countenance

Her laugh was not in the middle of her face quite,
    As a gay laugh springs,
It was plain she was anxious about some things
    I could not trace quite.
Her curls were like fir-cones—piled up, brown—
    Or rather like tight-tied sheaves:
It seemed they could never be taken down. . . .

And her lips were too full, some might say:
I did not think so. Anyway,
The shadow her bottom one would cast   10
Was green in hue whenever she passed
    Bright sun on midsummer leaves.
Alas, I knew not much of her,
And lost all sight and touch of her!

If otherwise, should I have minded
The shy laugh not in the middle of her mouth quite,
And would my kisses have died of drouth quite
    As love became unblinded?

                                        1884.

Silences

There is the silence of a copse or croft
        When the wind sinks dumb,
        And of a belfry-loft
When the tenor after tolling stops its hum.

And there's the silence of a lonely pond
        Where a man was drowned,
        Nor nigh nor yond
A newt, frog, toad, to make the merest sound.

But the rapt silence of an empty house
      Where oneself was born,   10
      Dwelt, held carouse
With friends, is of all silences most forlorn!

Past are remembered songs and music-strains
      Once audible there:
      Roof, rafters, panes
Look absent-thoughted, tranced, or locked in prayer.

It seems no power on earth can waken it
      Or rouse its rooms,
      Or its past permit
The present to stir a torpor like a tomb's.   20

'I watched a blackbird'

I watched a blackbird on a budding sycamore
One Easter Day, when sap was stirring twigs to the core;
  I saw his tongue, and crocus-coloured bill
  Parting and closing as he turned his trill;
  Then he flew down, seized on a stem of hay,
And upped to where his building scheme was under way,
As if so sure a nest were never shaped on spray.

A Nightmare, and the Next Thing

On this decline of Christmas Day
The empty street is fogged and blurred:
The house-fronts all seem backwise turned
As if the outer world were spurned:
Voices and songs within are heard,
Whence red rays gleam when fires are stirred,
Upon this nightmare Christmas Day.

The lamps, just lit, begin to outloom
Like dandelion-globes in the gloom;
The stonework, shop-signs, doors, look bald;   10
Curious crude details seem installed,

And show themselves in their degrees
As they were personalities
Never discerned when the street was bustling
With vehicles, and farmers hustling.
Three clammy casuals wend their way
To the Union House. I hear one say:
'Jimmy, this is a treat! Hay-hay!'

Six laughing mouths, six rows of teeth,
Six radiant pairs of eyes, beneath   20
Six yellow hats, looking out at the back
Of a waggonette on its slowed-down track
Up the steep street to some gay dance,
Suddenly interrupt my glance.

They do not see a gray nightmare
Astride the day, or anywhere.

The Felled Elm and She

When you put on that inmost ring
She, like you, was a little thing:
When your circles reached their fourth,
Scarce she knew life's south from north:
When your year-zones counted twenty
She had fond admirers plenty:
When you'd grown your twenty-second
She and I were lovers reckoned:
When you numbered twenty-three
She went everywhere with me: 10
When you, at your fortieth line,
Showed decay, she seemed to pine:
When you were quite hollow within
She was felled—mere bone and skin:
You too, lacking strength to grow
Further trunk-rings, were laid low,
Matching her; both unaware
That your lives formed such a pair.

He Did Not Know Me

(Woman's Sorrow Song)

He said: 'I do not know you;
You are not she who came
And made my heart grow tame?'
    I laughed: 'The same!'

Still said he: 'I don't know you.'
    —'But I am your Love!' laughed I:
'Yours—faithful ever—till I die,
    And pulseless lie!'

Yet he said: 'I don't know you.'
Freakful, I went away,   10
And met pale Time, with 'Pray,
    What means his Nay?'

Said Time: 'He does not know you
In your mask of Comedy.'
—'But', said I, 'that I have chosen to be:
    Tragedy he.'

    —'True; hence he did not know you.'
    —'But him I could recognize?'
    —'Yea. Tragedy is true guise,
        Comedy lies.'   20

The Clasped Skeletons

Surmised Date 1800 B.C.

(In an Ancient British Barrow near the Writer's House)

O why did we uncover to view
    So closely clasped a pair?
Your chalky bedclothes over you,
    This long time here!

Ere Paris lay with Helena—
   The poets' dearest Dear—
Ere David bedded Bathsheba
   You two were bedded here.

Aye, even before the beauteous Jael
   Bade Sisera doff his gear   10
And lie in her tent; then drove the nail,
   You two lay here.

Wicked Aholah, in her youth,
   Colled Loves from far and near
Until they slew her without ruth;
   But you had long colled here.

Aspasia lay with Pericles,
   And Philip's son found cheer
At eves in lying on Thais' knees
   While you lay here.   20

Cleopatra with Antony,
   Resigned to dalliance sheer,
Lay, fatuous he, insatiate she,
   Long after you'd lain here.

Pilate by Procula his wife
   Lay tossing at her tear
Of pleading for an innocent life;
   You tossed not here.

Ages before Monk Abélard
   Gained tender Héloise' ear,   30
And loved and lay with her till scarred,
   Had you lain loving here.

So long, beyond chronology,
   Lovers in death as 'twere,
So long in placid dignity
   Have you lain here!

Yet what is length of time? But dream!
　　Once breathed this atmosphere
Those fossils near you, met the gleam
　　Of day as you did here;   40

But so far earlier theirs beside
　　Your life-span and career,
That they might style of yestertide
　　Your coming here!

After the Burial

The family had buried him,
　　Their bread-bringer, their best:
They had returned to the house, whose hush a dim
　　Vague vacancy expressed.

There sat his sons, mute, rigid-faced,
　　His daughters, strained, red-eyed,
His wife, whose wan, worn features, vigil-traced,
　　Bent over him when he died.

At once a peal bursts from the bells
　　Of a large tall tower hard by: 10
Along the street the jocund clangour swells,
　　And upward to the sky.

Probably it was a wedding-peal,
　　Or possibly for a birth,
Or townsman knighted for political zeal,
　　This resonant mark of mirth.

The mourners, heavy-browed, sat on
　　Motionless. Well they heard,
They could not help it; nevertheless thereon
　　Spoke not a single word,   20

Nor window did they close, to numb
　　The bells' insistent calls
Of joy; but suffered the harassing din to come
　　And penetrate their souls.

An Evening in Galilee

She looks far west towards Carmel, shading her eyes with her
    hand,
And she then looks east to the Jordan, and the smooth Tiberias'
    strand.
'Is my son mad?' she asks; and never an answer has she,
Save from herself, aghast at the possibility.
'He professes as his firm faiths things far too grotesque to be
    true,
And his vesture is odd—too careless for one of his fair young
    hue! . . .

'He lays down doctrines as if he were old—aye, fifty at least:
In the Temple he terrified me, opposing the very High-Priest!
Why did he say to me, "Woman, what have I to do with thee?"
O it cuts to the heart that a child of mine thus spoke to me!   10
And he said, too, "Who is my mother?"—when he knows so
    very well.
He might have said, "Who is my father?"—and I'd found it
    hard to tell!
That no one knows but Joseph and—one other, nor ever will;
One who'll not see me again. . . . How it chanced!—I dreaming
    no ill! . . .

'Would he'd not mix with the lowest folk—like those fisher-
    men—
The while so capable, culling new knowledge, beyond our
    ken! . . .
That woman of no good character, ever following him,
Adores him if I mistake not: his wish of her is but a whim
Of his madness, it may be, outmarking his lack of coherency;
After his "Keep the Commandments!" to smile upon such as
    she!   20
It is just what all those do who are wandering in their wit.
I don't know—dare not say—what harm may grow from it.
O a mad son is a terrible thing; it even may lead
To arrest, and death! . . . And how he can preach, expound, and
    read!

'Here comes my husband. Shall I unveil him this tragedy-brink?
No. He has nightmares enough. I'll pray, and think, and think.' . . .
She remembers she's never put on any pot for his evening meal,
And pondering a plea looks vaguely to south of her—towards
    Jezreel.

The Brother

O know you what I have done
To avenge our sister? She,
I thought, was wantoned with
By a man of levity:

And I lay in wait all day,
All day did I wait for him,
And dogged him to Bollard Head
When twilight dwindled dim,

And hurled him over the edge
And heard him fall below: 10
O would I were lying with him,
For the truth I did not know!

'O where's my husband?' she asked,
As evening wore away:
'Best you had one, forsooth,
But never had you!' I say.

'Yes, but I have!' says she,
'My Love made it up with me,
And we churched it yesterday
And mean to live happily.'   20

And now I go in haste
To the Head, before she's aware,
To join him in death for the wrong
I've done them both out there!

We Field-Women

How it rained
When we worked at Flintcomb-Ash,
And could not stand upon the hill
Trimming swedes for the slicing-mill.
The wet washed through us—plash, plash, plash:
How it rained!

How it snowed
When we crossed from Flintcomb-Ash
To the Great Barn for drawing reed,
Since we could nowise chop a swede.—
Flakes in each doorway and casement-sash:
How it snowed!

How it shone
When we went from Flintcomb-Ash
To start at dairywork once more
In the laughing meads, with cows threescore,
And pails, and songs, and love—too rash:
How it shone!

A Practical Woman

'O who'll get me a healthy child:—
        I should prefer a son—
Seven have I had in thirteen years,
        Sickly every one!

'Three mope about as feeble shapes;
        Weak; white; they'll be no good.
One came deformed; an idiot next;
        And two are crass as wood.

'I purpose one not only sound
        In flesh, but bright in mind:
And duly for producing him
        A means I've now to find.'

She went away. She disappeared,
    Years, years. Then back she came:
In her hand was a blooming boy
    Mentally and in frame.

'I found a father at last who'd suit
    The purpose in my head,
And used him till he'd done his job,'
    Was all thereon she said.   20

Squire Hooper

Hooper was ninety. One September dawn
    He sent a messenger
For his physician, who asked thereupon
    What ailed the sufferer
Which he might circumvent, and promptly bid begone.

'Doctor, I summoned you,' the squire replied—
    'Pooh-pooh me though you may—
To ask what's happened to me—burst inside,
    It seems—not much, I'd say—
But awkward with a house-full here for a shoot to-day.'   10

And he described the symptoms. With bent head
    The listener looked grave.
'H'm. . . . *You're a dead man in six hours*,' he said.—
    'I speak out, since you are brave—
And best 'tis you should know, that last things may be sped.'

'Right,' said the squire. 'And now comes—what to do?
    One thing: on no account
Must I now spoil the sport I've asked them to—
    My guests are paramount—
They must scour scrub and stubble; and big bags bring as due.'   20

He downed to breakfast, and bespoke his guests:—
   'I find I have to go
An unexpected journey, and it rests
   With you, my friends, to show
The shoot can go off gaily, whether I'm there or no.'

   Thus blandly spoke he; and to the fields they went,
     And Hooper up the stair.
   They had a glorious day; and stiff and spent
     Returned as dusk drew near.—
'Gentlemen,' said the doctor, 'he's not back as meant,   30

   'To his deep regret!'—So they took leave, each guest
     Observing: 'I dare say
Business detains him in the town: 'tis best
     We should no longer stay
Just now. We'll come again anon'; and they went their way.

   Meeting two men in the obscurity
     Shouldering a box a thin
Cloth-covering wrapt, one sportsman cried: 'Damn me,
     I thought them carrying in,
At first, a coffin; till I knew it could not be.'   40

'*A Gentleman's Second-hand Suit*'

   Here it is hanging in the sun
     By the pawn-shop door,
A dress-suit—all its revels done
     Of heretofore.
Long drilled to the waltzers' swing and sway,
     As its tokens show:
What it has seen, what it could say
     If it did but know!

   The sleeve bears still a print of powder
     Rubbed from her arms   10
When she warmed up as the notes swelled louder
     And livened her charms—

Or rather theirs, for beauties many
    Leant there, no doubt,
Leaving these tell-tale traces when he
    Spun them about.

Its cut seems rather in bygone style
    On looking close,
So it mayn't have bent it for some while
    To the dancing pose: 20
Anyhow, often within its clasp
    Fair partners hung,
Assenting to the wearer's grasp
    With soft sweet tongue.

Where is, alas, the gentleman
    Who wore this suit?
And where are his ladies? Tell none can:
    Gossip is mute.
Some of them may forget him quite
    Who smudged his sleeve,   30
Some think of a wild and whirling night
    With him, and grieve.

'We say we shall not meet'

We say we shall not meet
Again beneath this sky,
And turn with heavy feet,
    Murmuring 'Good-bye!'

But laugh at how we rued
Our former time's adieu
When those who went for good
    Are met anew.

We talk in lightest vein
On trifles talked before,   10
And part to meet again,
    But meet no more.

Seeing the Moon Rise

We used to go to Froom-hill Barrow
    To see the round moon rise
    Into the heath-rimmed skies,
Trudging thither by plough and harrow
Up the pathway, steep and narrow,
      Singing a song.
Now we do not go there. Why?
    Zest burns not so high!

Latterly we've only conned her
    With a passing glance   10
    From window or door by chance,
Hoping to go again, high yonder,
As we used, and gaze, and ponder,
      Singing a song.
Thitherward we do not go:
    Feet once quick are slow!

August 1927.

Song to Aurore

We'll not begin again to love,
    It only leads to pain;
The fire we now are master of
    Has seared us not in vain.
Any new step of yours I'm fain
    To hear of from afar,
And even in such may find a gain
    While lodged not where you are.

No: that must not be done anew
    Which has been done before;   10
I scarce could bear to seek, or view,
    Or clasp you any more!
Life is a labour, death is sore,
    And lonely living wrings;
But go your courses, sweet Aurore,
    Kisses are caresome things!

He Never Expected Much

[or]

A CONSIDERATION

[A reflection] On my Eighty-Sixth Birthday

Well, World, you have kept faith with me,
       Kept faith with me;
Upon the whole you have proved to be
       Much as you said you were.
Since as a child I used to lie
Upon the leaze and watch the sky,
Never, I own, expected I
       That life would all be fair.

'Twas then you said, and since have said,
       Times since have said,   10
In that mysterious voice you shed
       From clouds and hills around:
'Many have loved me desperately,
Many with smooth serenity,
While some have shown contempt of me
       Till they dropped underground.

'I do not promise overmuch,
       Child; overmuch;
Just neutral-tinted haps and such,'
       You said to minds like mine.   20
Wise warning for your credit's sake!
Which I for one failed not to take,
And hence could stem such strain and ache
       As each year might assign.

Standing by the Mantelpiece

(H. M. M., 1873)

This candle-wax is shaping to a shroud
To-night. (They call it that, as you may know)—
By touching it the claimant is avowed,
And hence I press it with my finger—so.

To-night. To me twice night, that should have been
The radiance of the midmost tick of noon,
And close around me wintertime is seen
That might have shone the veriest day of June!

But since all's lost, and nothing really lies
Above but shade, and shadier shade below,   10
Let me make clear, before one of us dies,
My mind to yours, just now embittered so.

Since you agreed, unurged and full-advised,
And let warmth grow without discouragement,
Why do you bear you now as if surprised,
When what has come was clearly consequent?

Since you have spoken, and finality
Closes around, and my last movements loom,
I say no more: the rest must wait till we
Are face to face again, yonside the tomb.   20

And let the candle-wax thus mould a shape
Whose meaning now, if hid before, you know,
And how by touch one present claims its drape,
And that it's I who press my finger—so.

Boys Then and Now

'More than one cuckoo?'
And the little boy
Seemed to lose something
Of his spring joy.

When he'd grown up
He told his son
He'd used to think
There was only one,

Who came each year
With the trees' new trim   10
On purpose to please
England and him:

And his son—old already
In life and its ways—
Said yawning: 'How foolish
Boys were in those days!'

That Kiss in the Dark

Recall it you?—
Say you do!—
When you went out into the night,
In an impatience that would not wait,
From that lone house in the woodland spot,
And when I, thinking you had gone
For ever and ever from my sight,
Came after, printing a kiss upon
      Black air
      In my despair,   10

And my two lips lit on your cheek
As you leant silent against a gate,
Making my woman's face flush hot
At what I had done in the dark, unware
You lingered for me but would not speak:
Yes, kissed you, thinking you were not there!
         Recall it you?—
         Say you do!

A Necessitarian's Epitaph

A world I did not wish to enter
Took me and poised me on my centre,
Made me grimace, and foot, and prance,
As cats on hot bricks have to dance
Strange jigs to keep them from the floor,
Till they sink down and feel no more.

Suspense

A clamminess hangs over all like a clout,
The fields are a water-colour washed out,
The sky at its rim leaves a chink of light,
Like the lid of a pot that will not close tight.

She is away by the groaning sea,
Strained at the heart, and waiting for me:
Between us our foe from a hid retreat
Is watching, to wither us if we meet. . . .

But it matters little, however we fare—
Whether we meet, or I get not there;
The sky will look the same thereupon,
And the wind and the sea go groaning on.

10

The Second Visit

Clack, clack, clack, went the mill-wheel as I came,
And she was on the bridge with the thin hand-rail,
And the miller at the door, and the ducks at mill-tail;
I come again years after, and all there seems the same.

And so indeed it is: the apple-tree'd old house,
And the deep mill pond, and the wet wheel clacking,
And a woman on the bridge, and white ducks quacking,
And the miller at the door, powdered pale from boots to brows.

But it's not the same miller whom long ago I knew,
Nor are they the same apples, nor the same drops that dash   10
Over the wet wheel, nor the ducks below that splash,
Nor the woman who to fond plaints replied, 'You know I do!'

Faithful Wilson

'I say she's handsome, by all laws
Of beauty, if wife ever was!'
Wilson insists thus, though each day
The years fret Fanny towards decay.
'She *was* once beauteous as a jewel,'
Hint friends; 'but Time, of course, is cruel.'
Still Wilson does not quite feel how,
Once fair, she can be different now.

Partly from Strato of Sardis.

A Forgotten Miniature

There you are in the dark,
Deep in a box
Nobody ever unlocks,
Or even turns to mark;
—Out of mind stark.

Yet there you have not been worsed
    Like your sitter
By Time, the Fair's hard-hitter;
Your beauties, undispersed,
    Glow as at first.   10

Shut in your case for years,
    Never an eye
Of the many passing nigh,
Fixed on their own affairs,
    Thinks what it nears!

—While you have lain in gloom,
    A form forgot,
Your reign remembered not,
Much life has come to bloom
    Within this room.   20

Yea, in Time's cyclic sweep
    Unrest has ranged:
Women and men have changed:
Some you knew slumber deep;
    Some wait for sleep.

Whispered at the Church-Opening

In the bran-new pulpit the bishop stands,
And gives out his text, as his gaze expands
To the people, the aisles, the roof's new frame,
And the arches, and ashlar with coloured bands.

'Why—he's the man', says one, 'who came
To preach in my boyhood—a fashion then—
In a series of sermons to working-men
On week-day evenings, a novelty
Which brought better folk to hear and see.
They preached each one each week, by request: 10
Some were eloquent speakers, among the best
Of the lot being this, as all confessed.'

'I remember now. And reflection brings
Back one in especial, sincerest of all;
Whose words, though unpicked, gave the essence of things;—
And where is he now, whom I well recall?'

'Oh, he'd no touches of tactic skill:
His mind ran on charity and good will:
He's but as he was, a vicar still.'

In Weatherbury Stocks

(1850)

'I sit here in these stocks,
And Saint-Mary's moans eleven;
The sky is dark and cold:
I would I were in heaven!

'What footsteps do I hear?
Ah, you do not forget,
My Sophy! O, my dear,
We may be happy yet!

'But—. Mother, is't your voice?
You who have come to me?—   10
It did not cross my thought:
I was thinking it was she.'

'She! Foolish simple son!
She says: "I've finished quite
With him or any one
Put in the stocks to-night."

'She's gone to Blooms-End dance,
And will not come back yet:
Her new man sees his chance,
And is teaching her to forget.   20

'Jim, think no other woman
To such a fellow is true
But the mother you have grieved so,
Or cares for one like you!'

A Placid Man's Epitaph

As for my life, I've led it
With fair content and credit:
It said: 'Take this.' I took it:
Said: 'Leave.' And I forsook it.
If I had done without it
None would have cared about it,
Or said: 'One has refused it
Who might have meetly used it.'

1925.

The Musing Maiden

'Why so often, silent one,
Do you steal away alone?'
Starting, half she turned her head,
    And guiltily she said:—

'When the vane points to his far town
I go upon the hog-backed down,
And think the breeze that stroked his lip
    Over my own may slip.

'When he walks at close of day
I ramble on the white highway,   10
And think it reaches to his feet:
    A meditation sweet!

'When coasters hence to London sail
I watch their puffed wings waning pale;
His window opens near the quay;
    Their coming he can see.

'I go to meet the moon at night;
To mark the moon was our delight;
Up there our eyesights touch at will
    If such he practise still.'   20

16 Westbourne Park Villas
October 1866 (recopied).

A Daughter Returns

I like not that dainty-cut raiment, those earrings of pearl,
   I like not the light in that eye;
I like not the note of that voice. Never so was the girl
   Who a year ago bade me good-bye!

Hadst but come bare and moneyless, worn in the vamp, weather-
      gray,
   But innocent still as before,
How warmly I'd lodged thee! But sport thy new gains far away;
   I pray thee now—come here no more!

And yet I'll not try to blot out every memory of thee;
   I'll think of thee—yes, now and then: 10
One who's watched thee since Time called thee out o' thy
      mother and me
   Must think of thee; aye, I know when! . . .

When the cold sneer of dawn follows night-shadows black as a
      hearse,
   And the rain filters down the fruit tree,
And the tempest mouths into the flue-top a word like a curse,
   Then, then I shall think, think of thee!

                        Dec. 17, 1901.

The Third Kissing-Gate

    She foots it forward down the town,
      Then leaves the lamps behind,
    And trots along the eastern road
      Where elms stand double-lined.

    She clacks the first dim kissing-gate
      Beneath the storm-strained trees,
    And passes to the second mead
      That fringes Mellstock Leaze.

She swings the second kissing-gate
  Next the gray garden-wall,   10
And sees the third mead stretching down
  Towards the waterfall.

And now the third-placed kissing-gate
  Her silent shadow nears,
And touches with; when suddenly
  Her person disappears.

What chanced by that third kissing-gate
  When the hushed mead grew dun?
Lo—two dark figures clasped and closed
  As if they were but one.   20

Drinking Song

Once on a time when thought began
    Lived Thales: he
    Was said to see
Vast truths that mortals seldom can;
    It seems without
    A moment's doubt
That everything was made for man.

Chorus. Fill full your cups: feel no distress
         That thoughts so great should now be less!

Earth mid the sky stood firm and flat,   10
    He held, till came
    A sage by name
Copernicus, and righted that.
    We trod, he told,
    A globe that rolled
Around a sun it warmed it at.

Chorus. Fill full your cups: feel no distress;
         'Tis only one great thought the less!

But still we held, as Time flew by
    And wit increased,   20
    Ours was, at least,
The only world whose rank was high:
    Till rumours flew
    From folk who knew
Of globes galore about the sky.

Chorus. Fill full your cups: feel no distress;
       'Tis only one great thought the less!

And that this earth, our one estate,
    Was no prime ball,
    The best of all,   30
But common, mean; indeed, tenth-rate:
    And men, so proud,
    A feeble crowd,
Unworthy any special fate.

Chorus. Fill full your cups: feel no distress;
       'Tis only one great thought the less!

Then rose one Hume, who could not see,
    If earth were such,
    Required were much
To prove no miracles could be: 40
    'Better believe
    The eyes deceive
Than that God's clockwork jolts,' said he.

Chorus. Fill full your cups: feel no distress;
       'Tis only one great thought the less!

Next this strange message Darwin brings,
    (Though saying his say
    In a quiet way);
We all are one with creeping things;
    And apes and men   50
    Blood-brethren,
And likewise reptile forms with stings.

Chorus. Fill full your cups: feel no distress;
    'Tis only one great thought the less!

And when this philosoph had done
    Came Doctor Cheyne:
    Speaking plain he
Proved no virgin bore a son.
    'Such tale, indeed,
    Helps not our creed,'   60
He said. 'A tale long known to none.'

Chorus. Fill full your cups: feel no distress;
    'Tis only one great thought the less!

And now comes Einstein with a notion—
    Not yet quite clear
    To many here—
That there's no time, no space, no motion,
    Nor rathe nor late,
    Nor square nor straight,
But just a sort of ether-ocean.   70

Chorus. Fill full your cups: feel no distress;
    'Tis only one great thought the less!

So here we are, in piteous case:
    Like butterflies
    Of many dyes
Upon an Alpine glacier's face:
    To fly and cower
    In some warm bower
Our chief concern in such a place.

Chorus. Fill full your cups; feel no distress   80
    At all our great thoughts shrinking less:
    We'll do a good deed nevertheless!

The Destined Pair

Two beings were drifting
Each one to the other:
No moment's veil-lifting
Or hint from another
  Led either to weet
  That the tracks of their feet
  Were arcs that would meet.

One moved in a city,
And one in a village,
Where many a ditty   10
He tongued when at tillage
  On dreams of a dim
  Figure fancy would limn
  That was viewless to him.

Would Fate have been kinder
To keep night between them?—
Had he failed to find her
And time never seen them
  Unite; so that, caught
  In no burning love-thought,   20
  She had faded unsought?

A Musical Incident

When I see the room it hurts me
 As with a pricking blade,
Those women being the memoried reason why my cheer deserts
  me.—
 'Twas thus. One of them played
To please her friend, not knowing
That friend was speedily growing,
 Behind the player's chair,
 Somnolent, unaware
 Of any music there.

I saw it, and it distressed me,   10
   For I had begun to think
I loved the drowsy listener, when this arose to test me
   And tug me from love's brink.
   'Beautiful!' said she, waking
   As the music ceased. 'Heart-aching!'
   Though never a note she'd heard
   To judge of as averred—
   Save that of the very last word.

All would have faded in me,
   But that the sleeper brought   20
News a week thence that her friend was dead. It stirred within me
   Sense of injustice wrought
   That dead player's poor intent—
   So heartily, kindly meant—
   As blandly added the sigher:
   'How glad I am I was nigh her,
   To hear her last tune!'—'Liar!'
   I lipped.—This gave love pause,
   And killed it, such as it was.

June Leaves and Autumn

I

   Lush summer lit the trees to green;
      But in the ditch hard by
   Lay dying boughs some hand unseen
   Had lopped when first with festal mien
      They matched their mates on high.
   It seemed a melancholy fate
   That leaves but brought to birth so late
      Should rust there, red and numb,
   In quickened fall, while all their race
   Still joyed aloft in pride of place   10
      With store of days to come.

II

At autumn-end I fared that way,
　And traced those boughs fore-hewn
Whose leaves, awaiting their decay
In slowly browning shades, still lay
　Where they had lain in June.
And now, no less embrowned and curst
Than if they had fallen with the first,
　Nor known a morning more,
Lay there alongside, dun and sere,   20
Those that at my last wandering here
　Had length of days in store.

Nov. 19, 1898.

No Bell-Ringing

A Ballad of Durnover

The little boy legged on through the dark,
　To hear the New-Year's ringing:
The three-mile road was empty, stark,
　No sound or echo bringing.

When he got to the tall church tower
　Standing upon the hill,
Although it was hard on the midnight hour
　The place was, as elsewhere, still;

Except that the flag-staff rope, betossed
　By blasts from the nor'-east,   10
Like a dead man's bones on a gibbet-post
　Tugged as to be released.

'Why is there no ringing to-night?'
　Said the boy to a moveless one
On a tombstone where the moon struck white;
　But he got answer none.

'No ringing in of New Year's Day,'
  He mused as he dragged back home;
And wondered till his head was gray
  Why the bells that night were dumb.   20

And often thought of the snowy shape
  That sat on the moonlit stone,
Nor spoke nor moved, and in mien and drape
  Seemed like a sprite thereon.

And then he met one left of the band
  That had treble-bobbed when young,
And said: 'I never could understand
  Why, that night, no bells rung.'

'True. There'd not happened such a thing
  For half a century; aye,   30
And never I've told why they did not ring
  From that time till to-day. . . .

'Through the week in bliss at *The Hit or Miss*
  We had drunk—not a penny left;
What then we did—well, now 'tis hid,—
  But better we'd stooped to theft!

'Yet, since none other remains who can,
  And few more years are mine,
I may tell you,' said the cramped old man.
  'We—swilled the Sacrament-wine.   40

'Then each set-to with the strength of two,
  Every man to his bell;
But something was wrong we found ere long
  Though what, we could not tell.

'We pulled till the sweat-drops fell around,
  As we'd never pulled before,
An hour by the clock, but not one sound
  Came down through the bell-loft floor.

'On the morrow all folk of the same thing spoke,
   They had stood at the midnight time   50
On their doorsteps near with a listening ear,
   But there reached them never a chime.

'We then could read the dye of our deed,
   And we knew we were accurst;
But we broke to none the thing we had done,
   And since then never durst.'

'I looked back'

I looked back as I left the house,
And, past the chimneys and neighbour tree,
The moon upsidled through the boughs:—
I thought: 'I shall a last time see
This picture; when will that time be?'

I paused amid the laugh-loud feast,
And selfward said: 'I am sitting where,
Some night, when ancient songs have ceased,
"Now is the last time I shall share
Such cheer," will be the thought I bear.'   10

An eye-sweep back at a look-out corner
Upon a hill, as forenight wore,
Stirred me to think: 'Ought I to warn her
That, though I come here times threescore,
One day 'twill be I come no more?'

Anon I reasoned there had been,
Ere quite forsaken was each spot,
Bygones whereon I'd lastly seen
That house, that feast, that maid forgot;
But when?—Ah, I remembered not!   20

Christmas: *1924*

'Peace upon earth!' was said. We sing it,
And pay a million priests to bring it.
After two thousand years of mass
We've got as far as poison-gas.

                                        1924.

Dead 'Wessex' the Dog to the Household

Do you think of me at all,
        Wistful ones?
Do you think of me at all
        As if nigh?
Do you think of me at all
At the creep of evenfall,
Or when the sky-birds call
        As they fly?

Do you look for me at times,
        Wistful ones?   10
Do you look for me at times
        Strained and still?
Do you look for me at times,
When the hour for walking chimes,
On that grassy path that climbs
        Up the hill?

You may hear a jump or trot,
        Wistful ones,
You may hear a jump or trot—
        Mine, as 'twere—   20
You may hear a jump or trot
On the stair or path or plot;
But I shall cause it not,
        Be not there.

Should you call as when I knew you,
　　Wistful ones,
Should you call as when I knew you,
　　Shared your home;
Should you call as when I knew you,
I shall not turn to view you,
I shall not listen to you,
　　Shall not come.

30

Family Portraits

Three picture-drawn people stepped out of their frames—
　　The blast, how it blew!
And the white-shrouded candles flapped smoke-headed flames;
—Three picture-drawn people came down from their frames,
And dumbly in lippings they told me their names,
　　Full well though I knew.

The first was a maiden of mild wistful tone,
　　Gone silent for years,
The next a dark woman in former time known;
But the first one, the maiden of mild wistful tone,
So wondering, unpractised, so vague and alone,
　　Nigh moved me to tears.

10

The third was a sad man—a man of much gloom;
　　And before me they passed
In the shade of the night, at the back of the room,
The dark and fair woman, the man of much gloom,
Three persons, in far-off years forceful, but whom
　　Death now fettered fast.

They set about acting some drama, obscure,
　　The women and he,
With puppet-like movements of mute strange allure;
Yea, set about acting some drama, obscure,
Till I saw 'twas their own lifetime's tragic amour,
　　Whose course begot me;

20

Yea—a mystery, ancestral, long hid from my reach
    In the perished years past,
That had mounted to dark doings each against each
In those ancestors' days, and long hid from my reach;
Which their restless enghostings, it seemed, were to teach
    Me in full, at this last.   30

But fear fell upon me like frost, of some hurt
    If they entered anew
On the orbits they smartly had swept when expert
In the law-lacking passions of life,—of some hurt
To their souls—and thus mine—which I fain would avert;
    So, in sweat cold as dew,

'Why wake up all this?' I cried out. 'Now, so late!
    Let old ghosts be laid!'
And they stiffened, drew back to their frames and numb state,
Gibbering: 'Thus are your own ways to shape, know too late!' 40
Then I grieved that I'd not had the courage to wait
    And see the play played.

I have grieved ever since: to have balked future pain,
    My blood's tendance foreknown,
Had been triumph. Nights long stretched awake I have lain
Perplexed in endeavours to balk future pain
By uncovering the drift of their drama. In vain,
    Though therein lay my own.

A Private Man on Public Men

When my contemporaries were driving
Their coach through Life with strain and striving,
And raking riches into heaps,
And ably pleading in the Courts
With smart rejoinders and retorts,
Or where the Senate nightly keeps
Its vigils, till their fames were fanned
By rumour's tongue throughout the land,

I lived in quiet, screened, unknown,
Pondering upon some stick or stone,   10
Or news of some rare book or bird
Latterly bought, or seen, or heard,
Not wishing ever to set eyes on
The surging crowd beyond the horizon,
Tasting years of moderate gladness
Mellowed by sundry days of sadness,
Shut from the noise of the world without,
Hearing but dimly its rush and rout,
Unenvying those amid its roar,
Little endowed, not wanting more.   20

Christmas in the Elgin Room

British Museum: early last century

'What is the noise that shakes the night,
And seems to soar to the Pole-star height?'
    —'Christmas bells,
    The watchman tells
Who walks this hall that blears us captives with its blight.'

'And what, then, mean such clangs, so clear?'
    —''Tis said to have been a day of cheer,
    And source of grace
    To the human race
Long ere their woven sails winged us to exile here.   10

'We are those whom Christmas overthrew
Some centuries after Pheidias knew
    How to shape us
    And bedrape us
And to set us in Athena's temple for men's view.

'O it is sad now we are sold—
We gods! for Borean people's gold,
    And brought to the gloom
    Of this gaunt room
Which sunlight shuns, and sweet Aurore but enters cold.   20

'For all these bells, would I were still
Radiant as on Athenai's Hill.'
    —'And I, and I!'
    The others sigh,
'Before this Christ was known, and we had men's good will.'

Thereat old Helios could but nod,
Throbbed, too, the Ilissus River-god,
    And the torsos there
    Of deities fair,
Whose limbs were shards beneath some Acropolitan clod: 30

Demeter too, Poseidon hoar,
Persephone, and many more
    Of Zeus' high breed,—
    All loth to heed
What the bells sang that night which shook them to the core.

                1905 and 1926.

He Resolves to Say No More

O my soul, keep the rest unknown!°
It is too like a sound of moan
    When the charnel-eyed
    Pale Horse has nighed:°
Yea, none shall gather what I hide!

Why load men's minds with more to bear
That bear already ails to spare?
    From now alway
    Till my last day
What I discern I will not say.   10

Let Time roll backward if it will;
(Magians who drive the midnight quill
    With brain aglow
    Can see it so,)
What I have learnt no man shall know.

And if my vision range beyond
The blinkered sight of souls in bond,
　　　—By truth made free—°
　　　I'll let all be,
And show to no man what I see.　　　　　20

UNCOLLECTED POEMS

Domicilium

It faces west, and round the back and sides
High beeches, bending, hang a veil of boughs,
And sweep against the roof. Wild honeysucks
Climb on the walls, and seem to sprout a wish
(If we may fancy wish of trees and plants)
To overtop the apple-trees hard by.

Red roses, lilacs, variegated box
Are there in plenty, and such hardy flowers
As flourish best untrained. Adjoining these
Are herbs and esculents; and farther still   10
A field; then cottages with trees, and last
The distant hills and sky.

Behind, the scene is wilder. Heath and furze
Are everything that seems to grow and thrive
Upon the uneven ground. A stunted thorn
Stands here and there, indeed; and from a pit
An oak uprises, springing from a seed
Dropped by some bird a hundred years ago.

                           In days bygone—
Long gone—my father's mother, who is now   20
Blest with the blest, would take me out to walk.
At such a time I once inquired of her
How looked the spot when first she settled here.
The answer I remember. 'Fifty years
Have passed since then, my child, and change has marked
The face of all things. Yonder garden-plots
And orchards were uncultivated slopes
O'ergrown with bramble bushes, furze and thorn:
That road a narrow path shut in by ferns,
Which, almost trees, obscured the passer-by.   30

'Our house stood quite alone, and those tall firs
And beeches were not planted. Snakes and efts
Swarmed in the summer days, and nightly bats
Would fly about our bedrooms. Heathcroppers
Lived on the hills, and were our only friends;
So wild it was when first we settled here.'

On the Doorstep

She sits in her nightdress without the door,
And her father comes up: 'He at it again?'
He mournfully cries. 'Poor girlie!' and then
Comes her husband to fetch her in, shamed and sore.
The elder strikes him. He falls head-bare
On the edge of the step, and lies senseless there.

She, seeing him stretched like a corpse at length,
Cries out to her father, who stands aghast,
'I hate you with all my soul and strength!
You've killed him. And if this word's my last
I hate you.... O my husband dear—
Live—do as you will! None shall interfere!'

    10

FROM *THE DYNASTS*

The Night of Trafalgár

(Boatman's Song)

I

In the wild October night-time, when the wind raved round the
    land,
And the Back-sea met the Front-sea, and our doors were
    blocked with sand,°
And we heard the drub of Dead-man's Bay, where bones of
    thousands are,
We knew not what the day had done for us at Trafalgár.
         Had done,
         Had done,
      For us at Trafalgár!

II

'Pull hard, and make the Nothe, or down we go!' one says, says
    he.
We pulled; and bedtime brought the storm; but snug at home
    slept we.
Yet all the while our gallants after fighting through the day,   10
Were beating up and down the dark, sou'-west of Cadiz Bay.
        The dark,
        The dark,
    Sou'-west of Cadiz Bay!

III

The victors and the vanquished then the storm it tossed and tore,
As hard they strove, those worn-out men, upon that surly shore;
Dead Nelson and his half-dead crew, his foes from near and far,
Were rolled together on the deep that night at Trafalgár!
        The deep,
        The deep,   20
    That night at Trafalgár!

Albuera

They come, beset by riddling hail;
They sway like sedges in a gale;
They fail, and win, and win, and fail. Albuera!

They gain the ground there, yard by yard,
Their brows and hair and lashes charred,
Their blackened teeth set firm and hard.

Their mad assailants rave and reel,
And face, as men who scorn to feel,
The close-lined, three-edged prongs of steel.

Till faintness follows closing-in,   10
When, faltering headlong down, they spin
Like leaves. But those pay well who win Albuera.

Out of six thousand souls that sware
To hold the mount, or pass elsewhere,
But eighteen hundred muster there.

Pale Colonels, Captains, ranksmen lie,
Facing the earth or facing sky;—
They strove to live, they stretch to die.

Friends, foemen, mingle; heap and heap.—
Hide their hacked bones, Earth!—deep, deep, deep,   20
Where harmless worms caress and creep.

Hide their hacked bones, Earth!—deep, deep, deep,
Where harmless worms caress and creep.—
What man can grieve? what woman weep?
Better than waking is to sleep! Albuera!

Hussar's Song

BUDMOUTH DEARS

I

When we lay where Budmouth Beach is,
O, the girls were fresh as peaches,
With their tall and tossing figures and their eyes of blue and
brown!
And our hearts would ache with longing
As we paced from our sing-songing,
With a smart *Clink! Clink!* up the Esplanade and down.

II

They distracted and delayed us
By the pleasant pranks they played us,
And what marvel, then, if troopers, even of regiments of re-
nown,
On whom flashed those eyes divine, O,   10
Should forget the countersign, O,
As we tore *Clink! Clink!* back to camp above the town.

III

Do they miss us much, I wonder,
Now that war has swept us sunder,
And we roam from where the faces smile to where the faces
    frown?
And no more behold the features
Of the fair fantastic creatures,
And no more *Clink! Clink!* past the parlours of the town?

IV

Shall we once again there meet them?
Falter fond attempts to greet them?
Will the gay sling-jacket glow again beside the muslin gown?—°   20
Will they archly quiz and con us
With a sideway glance upon us,
While our spurs *Clink! Clink!* up the Esplanade and down?

'My Love's gone a-fighting'

(Country-girl's Song)

I

My Love's gone a-fighting
   Where war-trumpets call,
The wrongs o' men righting
   Wi' carbine and ball,
And sabre for smiting,
   And charger, and all!

II

Of whom does he think there
   Where war-trumpets call?
To whom does he drink there,
   Wi' carbine and ball   10
On battle's red brink there,
   And charger, and all?

III

Her, whose voice he hears humming
   Where war-trumpets call,
'I wait, Love, thy coming
   Wi' carbine and ball,
And bandsmen a-drumming
   Thee, charger and all!'

The Eve of Waterloo

(Chorus of Phantoms)

The eyelids of eve fall together at last,
And the forms so foreign to field and tree
Lie down as though native, and slumber fast!

Sore are the thrills of misgiving we see
In the artless champaign at this harlequinade,
Distracting a vigil where calm should be!

The green seems opprest, and the Plain afraid
Of a Something to come, whereof these are the proofs,—
Neither earthquake, nor storm, nor eclipse's shade!

Yea, the coneys are scared by the thud of hoofs,   10
And their white scuts flash at their vanishing heels,
And swallows abandon the hamlet-roofs.

The mole's tunnelled chambers are crushed by wheels,
The lark's eggs scattered, their owners fled;
And the hedgehog's household the sapper unseals.

The snail draws in at the terrible tread,
But in vain; he is crushed by the felloe-rim;
The worm asks what can be overhead,

And wriggles deep from a scene so grim,
And guesses him safe; for he does not know   20
What a foul red flood will be soaking him!

Beaten about by the heel and toe
Are butterflies, sick of the day's long rheum,
To die of a worse than the weather-foe.

Trodden and bruised to a miry tomb
Are ears that have greened but will never be gold,
And flowers in the bud that will never bloom.

So the season's intent, ere its fruit unfold,
Is frustrate, and mangled, and made succumb,
Like a youth of promise struck stark and cold! ...   30

And what of these who to-night have come?
—The young sleep sound; but the weather awakes
In the veterans, pains from the past that numb;

Old stabs of Ind, old Peninsular aches,
Old Friedland chills, haunt their moist mud bed;
Cramps from Austerlitz; till their slumber breaks.

And each soul sighs as he shifts his head
On the loam he's to lease with the other dead
From to-morrow's mist-fall till Time be sped!

Chorus of the Pities

(After the Battle)

Semichorus I

To Thee whose eye all Nature owns,
Who hurlest Dynasts from their thrones,
And liftest those of low estate
We sing, with Her men consecrate!

II

Yea, Great and Good, Thee, Thee we hail,
Who shak'st the strong, Who shield'st the frail,
Who hadst not shaped such souls as we
If tendermercy lacked in Thee!

I

Though times be when the mortal moan
Seems unascending to Thy throne,   10
Though seers do not as yet explain
Why Suffering sobs to Thee in vain;

II

We hold that Thy unscanted scope
Affords a food for final Hope,
That mild-eyed Prescience ponders nigh
Life's loom, to lull it by and by.

I

Therefore we quire to highest height
The Wellwiller, the kindly Might
That balances the Vast for weal,
That purges as by wounds to heal.   20

II

The systemed suns the skies enscroll
Obey Thee in their rhythmic roll,
Ride radiantly at Thy command,
Are darkened by Thy Masterhand!

I

And these pale panting multitudes
Seen surging here, their moils, their moods,
All shall 'fulfil their joy' in Thee,
In Thee abide eternally!

II

Exultant adoration give
The Alone, through Whom all living live,   30
The Alone, in Whom all dying die,
Whose means the End shall justify! Amen.

Last Chorus

Semichorus I *of the Years*

Last as first the question rings
Of the Will's long travailings;
    Why the All-mover,
    Why the All-prover
Ever urges on and measures out the chordless chime of Things.

II

    Heaving dumbly
    As we deem,
    Moulding numbly
    As in dream,
Apprehending not how fare the sentient subjects of Its scheme.   10

Semichorus I *of the Pities*

Nay;—shall not Its blindness break?
Yea, must not Its heart awake,
    Promptly tending
    To Its mending
In a genial germing purpose, and for lovingkindness' sake?

II

    Should It never
    Curb or cure
    Aught whatever
    Those endure
Whom It quickens, let them darkle to extinction swift and sure.   20

Chorus

But—a stirring thrills the air
Like to sounds of joyance there
    That the rages
    Of the ages
Shall be cancelled, and deliverance offered from the darts that
        were,
Consciousness the Will informing, till It fashion all things fair!

23 Aug. 1865. The poetry of a scene varies with the minds of the perceivers. Indeed, it does not lie in the scene at all.

June 1877. There is enough poetry in what is left [in life], after all the false romance has been abstracted, to make a sweet pattern: e.g., the poem by H. Coleridge:

> 'She is not fair to outward view.'

So, then, if Nature's defects must be looked in the face and transcribed, whence arises the *art* in poetry and novel-writing? which must certainly show art, or it becomes mere mechanical reporting. I think the art lies in making these defects the basis of a hitherto unperceived beauty, by irradiating them with 'the light that never was' on their surface, but is seen to be latent in them by the spiritual eye.

28 Sept. 1877. An object or mark raised or made by man on a scene is worth ten times any such formed by unconscious Nature. Hence clouds, mists, and mountains are unimportant beside the wear on a threshold, or the print of a hand.

Jan. 1881. Style—Consider the Wordsworthian dictum (the more perfectly the natural object is reproduced, the more truly poetic the picture). This reproduction is achieved by seeing into the *heart of a thing* (as rain, wind, for instance), and is realism, in fact, though through being pursued by means of the imagination it is confounded with invention, which is pursued by the same means. It is, in short, reached by what M. Arnold calls 'the imaginative reason'.

3 June 1882. . . . As, in looking at a carpet, by following one colour a certain pattern is suggested, by following another colour, another; so in life the seer should watch that pattern among general things which his idiosyncrasy moves him to observe, and describe that alone. This is, quite accurately, a going to Nature; yet the result is no mere photograph, but purely the product of the writer's own mind.

17 Nov. 1883. Poem. We [human beings] have reached a degree of intelligence which Nature never contemplated when framing her laws, and for which she consequently has provided no adequate satisfactions.

19 April 1885. The business of the poet and novelist is to show the sorriness underlying the grandest things, and the grandeur underlying the sorriest things.

Jan. 1887. After looking at the landscape ascribed to Bonington in our drawing-room I feel that Nature is played out as a Beauty, but not as a Mystery. I don't want to see landscapes, i.e., scenic paintings of them, because I don't want to see the original realities—as optical effects, that is. I want to see the deeper reality underlying the scenic, the expression of what are sometimes called abstract imaginings.

The 'simply natural' is interesting no longer. The much decried, mad, late-Turner rendering is now necessary to create my interest. The exact truth as to material fact ceases to be of importance in art—it is a student's style—the style of a period when the mind is serene and unawakened to the tragical mysteries of life; when it does not bring anything to the object that coalesces with and translates the qualities that are already there,— half hidden, it may be—and the two united are depicted as the All.

5 Aug. 1888. To find beauty in ugliness is the province of the poet.

Oct. 1888. If you look beneath the surface of any farce you see a tragedy; and, on the contrary, if you blind yourself to the deeper issues of a tragedy you see a farce.

5 Aug. 1890. Reflections on Art. Art is a changing of the actual proportions and order of things, so as to bring out more forcibly than might otherwise be done that feature in them which appeals most strongly to the idiosyncrasy of the artist. The changing, or distortion, may be of two kinds: (1) The kind which increases the sense of vraisemblance: (2) That which diminishes it. (1) is high art: (2) is low art.

High art may choose to depict evil as well as good, without losing its quality. Its choice of evil, however, must be limited by the sense of worthiness.

Art is a disproportioning—(i.e., distorting, throwing out of proportion)—of realities, to show more clearly the features that matter in those realities, which, if merely copied or reported inventorially, might possibly be observed, but would more probably be overlooked. Hence 'realism' is not Art.

17 Oct. 1896. A novel, good, microscopic touch in Crabbe. He gives surface without outline, describing his church by telling *the colour of the lichens.*

Poetry. Perhaps I can express more fully in verse ideas and emotions which run counter to the inert crystallized opinion—hard as a rock—which the vast body of men have vested interests in supporting. To cry out in a passionate poem that (for instance) the Supreme Mover or Movers, the Prime Force or Forces, must be either limited in power, unknowing, or cruel—which is obvious enough, and has been for centuries—will cause them merely a shake of the head; but to put it in argumentative prose will make them sneer, or foam, and set all the literary contortionists jumping upon me, a harmless agnostic, as if I were a clamorous atheist, which in their crass illiteracy they seem to think is the same thing. . . . If Galileo had said in verse that the world moved, the Inquisition might have let him alone.

1899?. There is no new poetry; but the new poet—if he carry the flame on further (and if not he is no new poet)—comes with a new note. And that new note it is that troubles the critical waters.

Poetry is emotion put into measure. The emotion must come by nature, but the measure can be acquired by art.

Jan. 1899. No man's poetry can be truly judged till its last line is written. What is the last line? The death of the poet. And hence there is this quaint consolation to any writer of verse—that it may be imperishable for all that anybody can tell him to the contrary; and that if worthless he can never know it, unless he be a greater adept at self-criticism than poets usually are.

1900.

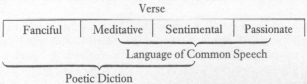

The confusion of thought to be observed in Wordsworth's teaching in his essay in the Appendix to *Lyrical Ballads* seems to arise chiefly out of his use of the word 'imagination'. He should have put the matter somewhat like this: In works of *passion and sentiment* (not 'imagination and sentiment') the language of verse is the language of prose. In works of *fancy* (or *imagination*), 'poetic diction' (of the real kind) is proper, and even necessary. The diagram illustrates my meaning.

March 1902. Poetry. There is a latent music in the sincere utterance of deep emotion, however expressed, which fills the place of the actual word-music in rhythmic phraseology on thinner emotive subjects, or on subjects with next to none at all. And supposing a total poetic effect to be represented by a unit, its component fractions may be either, say:

> Emotion three-quarters, plus Expression one quarter, or
> Emotion one quarter, plus Expression three-quarters.

This suggested conception seems to me to be the only one which explains all cases, including those instances of verse that apparently infringe all rules, and yet bring unreasoned convictions that they are poetry.

1904?. The old theologies may or may not have worked for good in their time. But they will not bear stretching further in epic or dramatic art. The Greeks used up theirs: the Jews used up theirs: the Christians have used up theirs. So that one must make an independent plunge, embodying the real, if only temporary, thought of the age. But I expect that I shall catch it hot and strong for attempting it!

1904. I suppose I have handicapped myself by expressing, both in this drama [*The Dynasts*] and previous verse, philosophies and feelings as yet not well established or formally adopted into the general teaching; and by thus over-stepping the standard boundary set up for the thought of the age by the proctors of opinion, I have thrown back my chance of acceptance in poetry by many years. The very fact of my having tried to spread over art the latest illumination of the time has darkened counsel in respect of me.

What the reviewers really assert is, not 'This is an untrue and inartistic view of life', but 'This is not the view of life that we people who thrive on conventions can permit to be painted'. If, instead of the machinery I adopted, I had constructed a theory of a world directed by fairies, nobody would have objected, and the critics would probably have said, 'What a charming fancy of Mr. Hardy's!' But having chosen a scheme which may or may not be a valid one, but is presumably much nearer reality than the fancy of a world ordered by fairies would be, they straightway lift their brows.

1906. I prefer late Wagner, as I prefer late Turner, to early (which I suppose is all wrong in taste), the idiosyncrasies of each master being more strongly shown in these strains. When a man not contented with the grounds of his success goes on and on, and tries to achieve the impossible, then he gets profoundly interesting to me. To-day it was early Wagner for the most part: fine music, but not so particularly his—no spectacle of the inside of a brain at work like the inside of a hive.

18 Aug. 1908. The Poet takes note of nothing that he cannot feel emotively.

If all hearts were open and all desires known—as they would be if people showed their souls—how many gapings, sighings, clenched fists, knotted brows, broad grins, and red eyes should we see in the market-place!

Oct. 1971. I hold that the mission of poetry is to record impressions, not convictions. Wordsworth in his later writings fell into the error of recording the latter. So also did Tennyson, and so do many other poets when they grow old. Absit omen!

I fear I have always been considered the Dark Horse of contemporary English literature.

I was quick to bloom; late to ripen.

I believe it would be said by people who knew me well that I have a faculty (possibly not uncommon) for burying an emotion in my heart or brain for forty years, and exhuming it at the end of that time as fresh as when interred. For instance, the poem entitled 'The Breaking of Nations' contains a feeling that moved me in 1870, during the Franco-Prussian war, when I chanced to be looking at such an agricultural incident in Cornwall. But I did not write the verses till during the war with Germany of 1914, and onwards. Query: where was that sentiment hiding itself during more than forty years?

Nov. 1917. I do not expect much notice will be taken of these poems [*Moments of Vision*]: they mortify the human sense of self-importance by showing, or suggesting, that human beings are of no matter or appreciable value in this nonchalant universe.

24 Jan. 1918. It is *the unwilling mind* that stultifies the contemporary criticism of poetry.

25 Jan. 1918. The reviewer so often supposes that where Art is not visible it is unknown to the poet under criticism. Why does he not think of the art of concealing art? There is a good reason why.

30 Jan. 1918. English writers who endeavour to appraise poets, and discriminate the sheep from the goats, are apt to consider that all true poets must be of one pattern in their lives and developments. But the glory of poetry lies in its largeness, admitting among its creators men of infinite variety. They must all be impractical in the conduct of their affairs; nay, they must almost, like Shelley or Marlowe, be drowned or done to death, or like Keats, die of consumption. They forget that in the ancient world no such necessity was recognized; that Homer sang as a blind old man, that Aeschylus wrote his best up to his death at nearly seventy, that the best of Sophocles appeared between his fifty-fifth and ninetieth years, that Euripides wrote up to seventy.

Among those who accomplished late, the poetic spark must always have been latent; but its outspringing may have been frozen and delayed for half a lifetime.

30 April 1918. By the will of God some men are born poetical. Of these some make themselves practical poets, others are made poets by lapse of time who were hardly recognized as such. Particularly has this been the case with the translators of the Bible. They translated into the language of their age; then the years began to corrupt that language as spoken, and to add grey lichen to the translation; until the moderns who use the corrupted tongue marvel at the poetry of the old words. When new they were not more than half so poetical. So that Coverdale, Tyndale, and the rest of them are as ghosts what they never were in the flesh.

May 1918. The poet is like one who enters and mounts a platform to give an address as announced. He opens his page, looks around, and finds the hall—*empty*.

My opinion is that a poet should express the emotion of all the ages and the thought of his own.

28 Nov. 1927. [from notes by Florence Hardy]. Speaking about ambition T. said to-day that he had done all that he meant to do, but he did not know whether it had been worth doing.

His only ambition, so far as he could remember, was to have some poem or poems in a good anthology like the *Golden Treasury*.

The model he had set before him was 'Drink to me only', by Ben Jonson.

PREFACE TO *SELECT POEMS OF*
WILLIAM BARNES

THIS volume of verse includes, to the best of my judgement, the greater part of that which is of the highest value in the poetry of William Barnes. I have been moved to undertake the selection by a thought that has overridden some immediate objections to such an attempt,—that I chance to be (I believe) one of the few living persons having a practical acquaintance with letters who knew familiarly the Dorset dialect when it was spoken as Barnes writes it, or, perhaps, who know it as it is spoken now. Since his death, education in the west of England as elsewhere has gone on with its silent and inevitable effacements, reducing the speech of this country to uniformity, and obliterating every year many a fine old local word. The process is always the same: the word is ridiculed by the newly taught; it gets into disgrace; it is heard in holes and corners only; it dies; and, worst of all, it leaves no synonym. In the villages that one recognizes to be the scenes of these pastorals the poet's nouns, adjectives, and idioms daily cease to be understood by the younger generation, the luxury of four demonstrative pronouns, of which he was so proud, vanishes by their compression into the two of common English, and the suffix to verbs which marks continuity of action is almost everywhere shorn away.

To cull from a dead writer's whole achievement in verse portions that shall exhibit him is a task of no small difficulty, and of some temerity. There is involved, first of all, the question of right. A selector may say: These are the pieces that please me best; but he may not be entitled to hold that they are the best in themselves and for everybody. This opens the problem of equating the personality—of adjusting the idiosyncrasy of the chooser to mean pitch. If it can be done in some degree—one may doubt it—there are to be borne in mind the continually changing taste of the times. But, assuming average critical capacity in the compiler, that he represents his own time, and that he finds it no great toil to come to a conclusion on which in his view are the highest levels and the lowest of a poet's execution, the complete field of the work examined almost always contains a large intermediate tract where the accomplishment is of nearly uniform merit throughout, selection from which must be by a process of sampling rather than of gleaning; many a poem, too, of indifferent achievement in its wholeness may contain some line, couplet, or stanza of great excellence; and contrariwise, a bad or irrelevant verse may mar the good remainder; in each case the choice is puzzled, and the balance struck by a single mind can hardly escape being questioned here and there.

A word may be said on the arrangement of the poems as 'lyrical and elegiac'; 'descriptive and meditative'; 'humorous'; a classification which has been adopted with this author in the present volume for the first time. It is an old story that such divisions may be open to grave objection, in respect, at least, of the verse of the majority of poets, who write in the accepted language. For one thing, many fine poems that have lyric moments are not entirely lyrical; many largely narrative poems are not entirely narrative; many personal reflections or meditations in verse hover across the frontiers of lyricism. To this general opinion I would add that the same lines may be lyrical to one temperament and meditative to another; nay, lyrical and not lyrical to the same reader at different times, according to his mood and circumstance. Gray's *Elegy* may be instanced as a poem that has almost made itself notorious by claiming to be a lyric in particular humours, situations, and weathers, and waiving the claim in others.

One might, to be sure, as a smart impromptu, narrow down the definition of lyric to the safe boundary of poetry that has all its nouns in the vocative case, and so settle the question by the simple touchstone of the grammar-book, adducing the *Benedicite* as a shining example. But this qualification would be disconcerting in its stringency, and cause a fluttering of the leaves of many an accepted anthology.

A story which was told the writer by Mr. Barnes himself may be apposite here. When a pupil of his was announced in the *Times* as having come out at the top in the Indian Service examination-list of those days, the schoolmaster was overwhelmed with letters from anxious parents requesting him at any price to make their sons come out at the top also. He replied that he willingly would, but that it took two to do it. It depends, in truth, upon the other person, the reader, whether certain numbers shall be raised to lyric pitch or not; and if he does not bring to the page of these potentially lyric productions a lyrical quality of mind, they must be classed, for him, as non-lyrical.

However, to pass the niceties of this question by. In the exceptional instance of a poet like Barnes who writes in a dialect only, a new condition arises to influence considerations of assortment. Lovers of poetry who are but imperfectly acquainted with his vocabulary and idiom may yet be desirous of learning something of his message; and the most elementary guidance is of help to such students, for they are liable to mistake their author on the very threshold. For some reason or none, many persons suppose that when anything is penned in the tongue of the country-side, the primary intent is burlesque or ridicule, and this especially if the speech be one in which the sibilant has the rough sound, and is expressed by Z. Indeed, scores of thriving story-tellers and dramatists seem to believe that by transmuting the flattest conversation into a dialect that never existed, and making the talkers say 'be' where they would really say 'is', a Falstaffian richness is at once imparted to its qualities.

But to a person to whom a dialect is native its sounds are as consonant with moods of sorrow as with moods of mirth: there is no grotesqueness in it as such. Nor was there to Barnes. To provide an alien reader with a rough clue to the taste of the kernel that may be expected under the shell of the spelling has seemed to be worth while, and to justify a division into heads that may in some cases appear arbitrary.

In respect of the other helps—the glosses and paraphrases given on each page—it may be assumed that they are but a sorry substitute for the full significance the original words bear to those who read them without translation, and know their delicate ability to express the doings, joys and jests, troubles, sorrows, needs and sicknesses of life in the rural world as elsewhere. The Dorset dialect being—or having been—a tongue, and not a corruption, it is the old question over again, that of the translation of poetry; which, to the full, is admittedly impossible. And further; gesture and facial expression figure so largely in the speech of husbandmen as to be speech itself; hence in the mind's eye of those who know it in its original setting each word of theirs is accompanied by the qualifying face-play which no construing can express.

It may appear strange to some, as it did to friends in his lifetime, that a man of insight who had the spirit of poesy in him should have persisted year after year in writing in a fast-perishing language, and on themes which in some not remote time would be familiar to nobody, leaving him pathetically like

> A ghostly cricket, creaking where a house was burned;

—a language with the added disadvantage by comparison with other dead tongues that no master or books would be readily available for the acquisition of its finer meanings. He himself simply said that he could not help it, no doubt feeling his idylls to be an extemporization, or impulse, without prevision or power of appraisement on his own part.

Yet it seems to the present writer that Barnes, despite this, really belonged to the literary school of such poets as Tennyson, Gray, and

Collins, rather than to that of the old unpremeditating singers in dialect. Primarily spontaneous, he was academic closely after; and we find him warbling his native wood-notes with a watchful eye on the predetermined score, a far remove from the popular impression of him as the naif and rude bard who sings only because he must, and who submits the uncouth lines of his page to us without knowing how they come there. Goethe never knew better of his; nor Milton; nor, in their rhymes, Poe; nor, in their whimsical alliterations here and there, Langland and the versifiers of the fourteenth and fifteenth centuries.

In his aim at closeness of phrase to his vision he strained at times the capacities of dialect, and went wilfully outside the dramatization of peasant talk. Such a lover of the art of expression was this penman of a dialect that had no literature, that on some occasions he would allow art to overpower spontaneity and to cripple inspiration; though, be it remembered, he never tampered with the dialect itself. His ingenious internal rhymes, his subtle juxtaposition of kindred lippings and vowel-sounds, show a fastidiousness in word-selection that is surprising in verse which professes to represent the habitual modes of language among the western peasantry. We do not find in the dialect balladists of the seventeenth century, or in Burns (with whom he has sometimes been measured), such careful finish, such verbal dexterities, such searchings for the most cunning syllables, such satisfaction with the best phrase. Had he not begun with dialect, and seen himself recognized as an adept in it before he had quite found himself as a poet, who knows that he might not have brought upon his muse the disaster that has befallen so many earnest versifiers of recent time, have become a slave to the passion for form, and have wasted all his substance in whittling at its shape.

From such, however, he was saved by the conditions of his scene, characters, and vocabulary. It may have been, indeed, that he saw this tendency in himself, and retained the dialect as a corrective to the tendency. Whether or no, by a felicitous instinct he does at times break into sudden irregularities in the midst of his subtle rhythms and measures, as if feeling rebelled against further drill. Then his self-consciousness ends, and his naturalness is saved.

But criticism is so easy, and art so hard: criticism so flimsy, and the life-seer's voice so lasting. When we consider what such appreciativeness as Arnold's could allow his prejudice to say about the highest-soaring among all our lyricists; what strange criticism Shelley himself could indulge in now and then; that the history of criticism is mainly the history of error, which has not even, as many errors have, quaintness enough to make it interesting, we may well doubt the utility of such writing on the sand. What is the use of saying, as has been said of Barnes, that compound epithets like 'the blue-hill'd worold', 'the wide-horn'd cow', 'the grey-topp'd heights of Paladore', are a high-handed enlargement of the ordinary ideas of the field-folk into whose mouths they are put? These things are justified by the art of every age when they can claim to be, as here, singularly precise and beautiful definitions of what is signified; which in these instances, too, apply with double force to the deeply tinged horizon, to the breed of kine, to the aspect of Shaftesbury Hill, characteristic of the Vale within which most of his revelations are enshrined.

Dialect, it may be added, offered another advantage to him as the writer, whatever difficulties it may have for strangers who try to follow it. Even if he often used the dramatic form of peasant speakers as a pretext for the expression of his own mind and experiences—which cannot be doubted—yet he did not always do this, and the assumed character of husbandman or hamleteer enabled him to elude in his verse those dreams and speculations that cannot leave alone the mystery of things,— possibly an unworthy mystery and disappointing if solved, though one that has a harrowing fascination for many poets,—and helped him to fall back on dramatic truth, by making his personages express the notions of life prevalent in their sphere.

As by the screen of dialect, so by the intense localization aforesaid, much is lost to the outsider who by looking into Barnes's pages only revives general recollections of country life. Yet many passages may shine into that reader's mind through the veil which partly hides them; and it is hoped and believed that, even in a superficial reading, something more of this poet's charm will be gathered from the present selection by persons to whom the Wessex R and Z are uncouth misfortunes, and the dying words those of an unlamented language that need leave behind it no grammar of its secrets and no key to its tomb.

T. H.
September 1908.

GENERAL PREFACE TO THE NOVELS
AND POEMS

In accepting a proposal for a definitive edition of these productions in prose and verse I have found an opportunity of classifying the novels under heads that show approximately the author's aim, if not his achievement, in each book of the series at the date of its composition. Sometimes the aim was lower than at other times; sometimes, where the intention was primarily high, force of circumstances (among which the chief were the necessities of magazine publication) compelled a modification, great or slight, of the original plan. Of a few, however, of the longer novels, and of many of the shorter tales, it may be assumed that they stand to-day much as they would have stood if no accidents had obstructed the channel between the writer and the public. That many of them, if any, stand as they would stand if written *now* is not to be supposed.

In the classification of these fictitious chronicles—for which the name of 'The Wessex Novels' was adopted, and is still retained—the first group is called 'Novels of Character and Environment', and contains those which approach most nearly to uninfluenced works; also one or two which, whatever their quality in some few of their episodes, may claim a verisimilitude in general treatment and detail.

The second group is distinguished as 'Romances and Fantasies', a sufficiently descriptive definition. The third class—'Novels of Ingenuity'—show a not infrequent disregard of the probable in the chain of events, and depend for their interest mainly on the incidents themselves. They might also be characterized as 'Experiments', and were written for the nonce simply; though despite the artificiality of their fable some of their scenes are not without fidelity to life.

It will not be supposed that these differences are distinctly perceptible in every page of every volume. It was inevitable that blendings and alternations should occur in all. Moreover, as it was not thought desirable in every instance to change the arrangement of the shorter stories to which readers have grown accustomed, certain of these may be found under headings to which an acute judgment might deny appropriateness.

It has sometimes been conceived of novels that evolve their action on a circumscribed scene—as do many (though not all) of these—that they cannot be so inclusive in their exhibition of human nature as novels wherein the scenes cover large extents of country, in which events figure amid towns and cities, even wander over the four quarters of the globe. I am not concerned to argue this point further than to suggest that the conception is an untrue one in respect of the elementary passions. But I would state that the geographical limits of the stage here trodden were not absolutely forced upon the writer by circumstances; he forced them upon himself from judgment. I considered that our magnificent heritage from the Greeks in dramatic literature found sufficient room for a large proportion of its action in an extent of their country not much larger than the half-dozen counties here reunited under the old name of Wessex, that the domestic emotions have throbbed in Wessex nooks with as much intensity as in the palaces of Europe, and that, anyhow, there was quite enough human nature in Wessex for one man's literary purpose. So far was I possessed by this idea that I kept within the frontiers when it would have been easier to overleap them and give more cosmopolitan features to the narrative.

Thus, though the people in most of the novels (and in much of the shorter verse) are dwellers in a province bounded on the north by the Thames, on the south by the English Channel, on the east by a line running from Hayling Island to Windsor Forest, and on the west by the Cornish coast, they were meant to be typically and essentially those of any and every place where

Thought's the slave of life, and life time's fool,

—beings in whose hearts and minds that which is apparently local should be really universal.

But whatever the success of this intention, and the value of these novels as delineations of humanity, they have at least a humble supplementary quality of which I may be justified in reminding the reader, though it is one that was quite unintentional and unforeseen. At the dates represented in the various narrations things were like that in Wessex: the inhabitants lived in certain ways, engaged in certain occupations, kept alive certain customs, just as they are shown doing in these pages. And in particularizing such I have often been reminded of Boswell's remarks on the trouble to which he was put and the pilgrimages he was obliged to make to authenticate some detail, though the labour was one which would bring him no praise. Unlike his achievement, however, on which an error would as he says have brought discredit, if these country customs and vocations, obsolete and obsolescent, had been detailed wrongly, nobody would have discovered such errors to the end of Time. Yet I have instituted inquiries to correct tricks of memory, and striven against temptations to exaggerate, in order to preserve for my own satisfaction a fairly true record of a vanishing life.

It is advisable also to state here, in response to inquiries from readers interested in landscape, prehistoric antiquities, and especially old English architecture, that the description of these backgrounds has been done from the real—that is to say, has something real for its basis, however illusively treated. Many features of the first two kinds have been given under their existing names; for instance, the Vale of Blackmoor or Blakemore, Hambledon Hill, Bulbarrow, Nettlecombe Tout, Dogbury Hill, High-Stoy, Bubb-Down Hill, The Devil's Kitchen, Cross-in-Hand, Long-Ash Lane, Benvill Lane, Giant's Hill, Crimmercrock Lane, and Stonehenge. The rivers Froom, or Frome, and Stour, are, of course, well known as such. And the further idea was that large towns and points tending to mark the outline of Wessex—such as Bath, Plymouth, The Start, Portland Bill, Southampton, etc.,—should be named clearly. The scheme was not greatly elaborated, but, whatever its value, the names remain still.

In respect of places described under fictitious or ancient names in the novels—for reasons that seemed good at the time of writing them—and kept up in the poems—discerning people have affirmed in print that they clearly recognize the originals: such as Shaftesbury in 'Shaston', Sturminster Newton in 'Stourcastle', Dorchester in 'Casterbridge', Salisbury Plain in 'The Great Plain', Cranborne Chase in 'The Chase', Beaminster in 'Emminster', Bere Regis in 'Kingsbere', Woodbury Hill in 'Greenhill', Wool Bridge in 'Wellbridge', Hartfoot or Harput Lane in 'Stagfoot Lane', Hazlebury in 'Nuttlebury', Bridport in 'Port Bredy', Maiden Newton in 'Chalk Newton', a farm near Nettlecombe Tout in 'Flintcomb Ash', Sherborne in 'Sherton Abbas', Milton Abbey in 'Middleton Abbey', Cerne Abbas in 'Abbot's Cernel', Evershot in 'Evershed', Taunton in 'Toneborough', Bournemouth in 'Sandbourne', Winchester in 'Wintoncester', Oxford in 'Christminster', Reading in 'Aldbrickham', Newbury in 'Kennetbridge', Wantage in 'Alfredston', Basingstoke in 'Stoke Barehills', and so on. Subject to the qualifications above given, that no detail is guaranteed,—that the portraiture of fictitiously named towns and villages was only suggested by certain real places, and wantonly wanders from inventorial descriptions of them—I do not contradict these keen hunters for the real; I am satisfied with their statements as at least an indication of their interest in the scenes.

Thus much for the novels. Turning now to the verse—to myself the more individual part of my literary fruitage—I would say that, unlike some of the fiction, nothing interfered with the writer's freedom in respect of its form or content. Several of the poems—indeed many—were produced before novel-writing had been thought of as a pursuit; but few saw the light till all the novels had been published. The limited stage to which the majority of the latter confine their exhibitions has not been adhered to here in the same proportion, the dramatic part especially having a very broad theatre of action. It may thus relieve the circumscribed areas treated in the prose, if such relief be needed. To be sure, one might argue that by surveying Europe from a celestial point of vision—as in *The Dynasts*—that continent becomes virtually a province—a Wessex, an Attica, even a mere garden—and hence is made conform to the principle of the novels, however far it outmeasures their region. But that may be as it will.

The few volumes filled by the verse cover a producing period of some eighteen years first and last, while the seventeen or more volumes of novels represent correspondingly about four-and-twenty years. One is reminded by this disproportion in time and result how much more concise and quintessential expression becomes when given in rhythmic form than when shaped in the language of prose.

One word on what has been called the present writer's philosophy of life, as exhibited more particularly in this metrical section of his compositions. Positive views on the Whence and the Wherefore of things have never been advanced by this pen as a consistent philosophy. Nor is it likely, indeed, that imaginative writings extending over more than forty years would exhibit a coherent scientific theory of the universe even if it had been attempted—of that universe concerning which Spencer owns to the 'paralyzing thought' that possibly there exists no comprehension of it anywhere. But such objectless consistency never has been attempted, and the sentiments in the following pages have been stated truly to be mere impressions of the moment, and not convictions or arguments.

That these impressions have been condemned as 'pessimistic'—as if that were a very wicked adjective—shows a curious muddle-mindedness. It must be obvious that there is a higher characteristic of philosophy than pessimism, or than meliorism, or even than the optimism of these critics—which is truth. Existence is either ordered in a certain way, or it is not so ordered, and conjectures which harmonize best with experience are removed above all comparison with other conjectures which do not so harmonize. So that to say one view is worse than other views without proving it erroneous implies the possibility of a false view being better or more expedient than a true view; and no pragmatic proppings can make that *idolum specus* stand on its feet, for it postulates a prescience denied to humanity.

And there is another consideration. Differing natures find their tongue in the presence of differing spectacles. Some natures become vocal at tragedy, some are made vocal by comedy, and it seems to me that to whichever of these aspects of life a writer's instinct for expression the more readily responds, to that he should allow it to respond. That before a contrasting side of things he remains undemonstrative need not be assumed to mean that he remains unperceiving.

It was my hope to add to these volumes of verse as many more as would make a fairly comprehensive cycle of the whole. I had wished that those in dramatic, ballad, and narrative form should include most of the cardinal situations which occur in social and public life, and those in lyric form a round of emotional experiences of some completeness. But

The petty done, the undone vast!

The more written the more seems to remain to be written; and the night cometh. I realize that these hopes and plans, except possibly to the extent of a volume or two, must remain unfulfilled.

T. H.
October 1911.

LETTERS TO ALFRED NOYES

On 9 December 1920 the London *Morning Post* reported a lecture by the poet Alfred Noyes, in which Noyes discussed the place that literature would take in the post-war world. For over a quarter of a century, Noyes said, the intellect of Europe had been almost entirely agnostic, and he cited Hardy as an example. 'He had the highest admiration for Mr. Thomas Hardy,' said the *Post* in its summary of the lecture, 'but what were they to make of a philosophy which told them that the Power behind the Universe was an imbecile jester?'

Hardy responded with a brief letter of protest.

Dorchester, 13*th December* 1920.

Dear Mr. Noyes,

Somebody has sent me an article from the *Morning Post* of December 9 entitled 'Poetry and Religion', which reports you as saying, in a lecture, that mine is 'a philosophy which told them (readers) that the Power behind the Universe was an imbecile jester'.

As I hold no such 'philosophy', and, to the best of my recollection, never could have done so, I should be glad if you would inform me whereabouts I have seriously asserted such to be my opinion.

Yours truly,
Th. Hardy

Noyes replied that his lecture had been abridged in the *Post* report, and that in fact he had praised Hardy as at the head of living writers; but he reasserted his disagreement with what he took to be Hardy's philosophy, which he thought led to the conclusion that the Power behind the Universe was malign, and he referred to poems by Hardy that he thought supported this view.

Hardy wrote again:

December 19*th*, 1920.

I am much obliged for your reply, which I really ought not to have troubled you to write. I may say for myself that I very seldom do give critics such trouble, usually letting things drift, though there have been many occasions when a writer who has been so much abused for his opinions as I have been would perhaps have done well not to hold his peace.

I do not know that there can be much use in my saying more than I did say. It seems strange that I should have to remind a man of letters of what, I should have supposed, he would have known as well as I—of the very elementary rule of criticism that a writer's works should be judged as a whole, and not from picked passages that contradict them as a whole—and this especially when they are scattered over a period of fifty years.

Also that I should have to remind him of the vast difference between the expression of fancy and the expression of belief. My imagination may have often run away with me; but all the same, my sober opinion—so far as I have any definite one—of the Cause of Things, has been defined in scores of places, and is that of a great many ordinary thinkers: that the said Cause is neither moral nor immoral, but *un*moral: 'loveless and hateless' I have called it, 'which neither good nor evil knows'—etc., etc.—(you will find plenty of these definitions in *The Dynasts* as well as in short poems, and I am surprised that you have not taken them in). This view is quite in keeping with what you call a Pessimistic philosophy (a mere nickname with no sense in it), which I am quite unable to see as 'leading logically to the conclusion that the Power behind the universe is malign'.

In my fancies, or poems of the imagination, I have of course called this Power all sorts of names—never supposing they would be taken for more than fancies. I have even in prefaces warned readers to take them as such—as mere impressions of the moment, exclamations in fact. But it has always been my misfortune to presuppose a too intelligent reading public, and no doubt people will go on thinking that I really believe the Prime Mover to be a malignant old gentleman, a sort of King of Dahomey—an idea which, so far from my holding it, is to me irresistibly comic. 'What a fool one must have been to write for such a public!' is the inevitable reflection at the end of one's life.

The lines you allude to, 'A Young Man's Epigram', dated 1866, I remember finding in a drawer, and printed them merely as an amusing instance of early cynicism. The words 'Time's Laughingstocks' are legitimate imagery all of a piece with such expressions as 'Life, Time's fool', and thousands in poetry and I am amazed that you should see any *belief* in them. The other verses you mention, 'New Year's Eve', 'His Education', are the same fanciful impressions of the moment. The poem called 'He abjures Love', ending with 'And then the curtain', is a love-poem, and lovers are chartered irresponsibles. A poem often quoted against me, and apparently in your mind in the lecture, is the one called 'Nature's Questioning', containing the words, 'some Vast Imbecility', etc.—as if these definitions were my creed. But they are merely enumerated in the poem as fanciful alternatives to several others, having nothing to do with my own opinion. As for 'The Unborn', to which you allude, though the form of it is imaginary, the sentiment is one which

I should think, especially since the war, is not uncommon or unreasonable.

This week I have had sent me a review which quotes a poem entitled 'To my Father's Violin', containing a Virgilian reminiscence of mine of Acheron and the Shades. The writer comments: 'Truly this pessimism is insupportable. . . . One marvels that Hardy is not in a madhouse.' Such is English criticism, and I repeat, why did I ever write a line! And perhaps if the young ladies to whom you lectured really knew that, so far from being the wicked personage they doubtless think me at present to be, I am a harmless old character much like their own grandfathers, they would consider me far less romantic and attractive.

In responding to this letter, Noyes wrote of his own philosophy that he had 'never been able to conceive a Cause of Things that could be less in any respect than the things caused'. Hardy replied:

Many thanks for your letter. The Scheme of Things is, indeed, incomprehensible; and there I suppose we must leave it—perhaps for the best. Knowledge might be terrible.

(Hardy's letters are quoted in *The Later Years of Thomas Hardy*, pp. 215–18.)

NOTES

In the explanatory notes that follow I have used the following abbreviations:

EL   Florence Emily Hardy, *The Early Life of Thomas Hardy* (London, 1928).
Letters III   Richard Little Purdy and Michael Millgate (eds.), *The Collected Letters of Thomas Hardy* (Oxford, 1982).
LY   Florence Emily Hardy, *The Later Years of Thomas Hardy* (London, 1930).
Orel   Harold Orel (ed.), *Thomas Hardy's Personal Writings* (London, 1967).
ORFW   Evelyn Hardy and F. B. Pinion (eds.), *One Rare Fair Woman: Thomas Hardy's Letters to Florence Henniker* (London, 1972).
Purdy   Richard Little Purdy, *Thomas Hardy: A Bibliographical Study* (Oxford, 1954; reissued 1978).
SCC   Viola Meynell (ed.), *Friends of a Lifetime: Letters to Sydney Carlyle Cockerell* (London, 1940).

Notes followed by (H) are Hardy's own notes, as they appear in printed texts of his work. All biblical quotations are from the Authorized Version.

WESSEX POEMS

In 1892, when Hardy seems first to have considered a book of poems, he wrote in his journal: 'Title:—"Songs of Five-and-Twenty Years".' (*LY*, p. 3). Five-and-twenty years would reach back to 1867, and a third of the fifty-one poems in *Wessex Poems* are dated in the late sixties. There are few from 1870–90, the first two decades of his novel-writing career, but in the nineties the flow of verse began again.

Wessex Poems was published 11 December 1898, but it must have been substantially prepared by February 1897, when Hardy wrote in his journal both his final choice of a title and his intention to include his own sketches as illustrations. He made thirty-two sketches in all—some of Wessex scenes, others of the settings of the Napoleonic narrative poems in the volume; thirty-one of these were printed in the first edition. Of the fifty-one poems in the book, only four had been previously published, two in periodicals and two in Hardy's own prose works.

   3 *Valenciennes*. Corporal Tullidge tells the story, briefly, in *The Trumpet-Major*, Ch. IV.

   5 *San Sebastian*. Hardy's principal source appears to have been W. F. P. Napier's *History of the War in the Peninsula*, Book XXII, Chapter 2, which provided not only details of the assault and military terminology, but also a hint of a rape.

   7 *The Stranger's Song*. 'Printed in "The Three Strangers", 1883'. (H)

16 *The Ivy-Wife.* Hardy's first wife, Emma, apparently took the poem personally. In a letter to a friend she wrote: 'Of recent poetry perhaps you admire "The Ivy Wife". Of course my wonder is great at any admiration for it . . .'

19 *Friends Beyond.* Some of the friends appear in other Hardy works: William Dewy in *Under the Greenwood Tree, Tess of the d'Urbervilles* (Ch. XVII), and 'The Dead Quire' (*Time's Laughingstocks*), Reuben Dewy in *Under the Greenwood Tree*, 'The Dead Quire', and 'The Fiddler of the Reels' (*Life's Little Ironies*), Farmer Ledlow in *Under the Greenwood Tree*, Lady Susan in 'The Noble Lady's Tale' (*Time's Laughingstocks*). Lady Susan's story is also related in both volumes of Florence Hardy's biography of her husband: see *EL*, pp. 11–12 and 213–14, and *LY*, pp. 12–13.

20 *Thoughts of Phena. EL*, p. 293, quotes the following from Hardy's diary for 5 March 1890: 'In the train on the way to London. Wrote the first four or six lines of "Not a line of her writing have I". It was a curious instance of sympathetic telepathy. The woman whom I was thinking of—a cousin—was dying at the time, and I quite in ignorance of it. She died six days later. The remainder of the piece was not written till after her death.' 'Phena' was Hardy's cousin, Tryphena Sparks, who lived at Puddletown, near Hardy's boyhood home at Higher Bockhampton. Her education and experience as a teacher may have provided Hardy with material for the career of Sue Bridehead in *Jude the Obscure*.

21 *Middle-Age Enthusiasms.* 'M. H.' is Hardy's sister Mary (1841–1915).

22 *In a Wood.* The poem is 'from *The Woodlanders*' only in the sense that novel and poem share an informing idea. The passage in the novel closest to the poem is the following, from Ch. VII:

> They went noiselessly over mats of starry moss, rustled through interspersed tracts of leaves, skirted trunks with spreading roots whose mossed rinds made them like hands wearing green gloves; elbowed old elms and ashes with great forks, in which stood pools of water that overflowed on rainy days and ran down their stems in green cascades. On older trees still than these huge lobes of fungi grew like lungs. Here, as everywhere, the Unfulfilled Intention, which makes life what it is, was as obvious as it could be among the depraved crowds of a city slum. The leaf was deformed, the curve was crippled, the taper was interrupted; the lichen ate the vigour of the stalk, and the ivy slowly strangled to death the promising sapling.

The first of the two dates attached to the poem, 1887, is the date of publication of *The Woodlanders*.

31 *'I look into my glass'.* In December 1892 Hardy wrote in his journal: 'I look in the glass. Am conscious of the humiliating sorriness of my earthly tabernacle, and of the sad fact that the best of parents could do no better for me . . . Why should a man's mind have been thrown into such close, sad, sensational, inexplicable relations with such a precarious object as his own body!' (*LY*, pp. 13–14).

POEMS OF THE PAST AND THE PRESENT

Hardy's second volume of poems was published 17 November 1901 (though it was dated 1902). It differs from his first in being made up almost entirely of recently written poems. Of the ninety-nine poems in the collection, only two are dated in the 1860s. Most of the other dated poems are occasional—from his European tours in 1887 and 1897, or related to historical events such as the Boer War and the death of Queen Victoria. Fourteen of the poems had previously appeared in periodicals.

34 *Drummer Hodge.* For Hardy's views on Hodge, the traditional name for a rustic character, see *Tess of the d'Urbervilles*, Ch. XVIII, and his essay, 'The Dorsetshire Labourer' (Orel, pp. 168–89).

39 POEMS OF PILGRIMAGE. Hardy and his first wife made journeys to Italy in March and April 1887 (see *EL*, pp. 244–58), and to Switzerland in June and July 1897 (see *LY*, pp. 66–70).

43 *Lausanne.* In the manuscript of *Poems of the Past and the Present* Hardy wrote and then cancelled the following footnote to line 16: 'Prose Works: "Doctrine and Discipline of Divorce".' In his own copy of the Wessex Edition he expanded the note to read:

'Truth is as impossible to be soiled by any outward touch as is the sunbeam; though this ill-hap wait on her nativity, that she never comes into the world, but like a bastard, to the ignominy of him that brought her forth.'—The Doctrine and Discipline of Divorce.

The quotation is from Milton's introductory address, 'To the Parliament of England'.

44 *The Mother Mourns.* *EL* quotes two relevant entries from Hardy's journal:

November 17 [1883]. Poem. We [human beings] have reached a degree of intelligence which Nature never contemplated when framing her laws, and for which she consequently has provided no adequate satisfaction. (*EL*, p. 213.)

April 7 [1889]. A woeful fact—that the human race is too extremely developed for its corporeal conditions, the nerves being evolved to an activity abnormal in such an environment. Even the higher animals are in excess in this respect. It may be questioned if Nature, or what we call Nature, so far back as when she crossed the line from invertebrates to vertebrates, did not exceed her mission. (*EL*, pp. 285–6.)

57 *To Lizbie Browne.* Lizbie Browne was the red-haired daughter of a Bockhampton gamekeeper, a year or two older than Hardy. See *EL*, pp. 33 and 270.

59 *The Well-Beloved.* Jordan Hill, near Weymouth, is the site of the ancient Roman station of Clavinium, of which remains still exist.

61 *A Broken Appointment.* Purdy (p. 113) associates the poem with Mrs Henniker, and identifies the setting as the British Museum.

69 *The Levelled Churchyard.* The churchyard is at Wimborne, where Hardy lived from 1881 to 1883.

73 *In Tenebris I.* The epigraph, in the Authorized Version (Psalm 102: 4), reads: 'My heart is smitten, and withered like grass.'

74 *In Tenebris II.* The epigraph, in the Authorized Version (Psalm 142: 4), reads: 'I looked on my right hand, and beheld, but there was no man that would know me: . . . no man cared for my soul.'

   l. 8. 1 Corinthians 15: 8: 'And last of all he was seen of me also, as of one born out of due time.'

75 *In Tenebris III.* The epigraph, in the Authorized Version (Psalm 120: 5–6), reads: 'Woe is me, that I sojourn in Mesech, that I dwell in the tents of Kedar! My soul hath long dwelt with him that hateth peace.'

TIME'S LAUGHINGSTOCKS

The poems of *Time's Laughingstocks* were written over nearly half a century. Of those given a date either in a manuscript or in some published edition, ten are from the 1860s, two from the seventies, one from the eighties, five from the nineties, and nineteen from the years 1901–9—the years since the publication of *Poems of the Past and the Present.* Of the ninety-four poems in the volume, twenty-nine had first appeared in periodicals. The book was published 3 December 1909.

79 *A Trampwoman's Tragedy.* When Hardy submitted the poem to the *Cornhill Magazine* it was rejected by the editor 'on the ground of not being a poem he could possibly print in a family periodical' (*LY*, p. 101). It was never published separately in England, though it appeared in America, and gained some notice there.

80 l. 27. *Windwhistle.* 'The highness and dryness of Windwhistle Inn was impressed upon the writer two or three years ago, when, after climbing on a hot afternoon to the beautiful spot near which it stands and entering the inn for tea, he was informed by the landlady that none could be had, unless he would fetch water from a valley half a mile off, the house containing not a drop, owing to its situation. However, a tantalizing row of full barrels behind her back testified to a wetness of a certain sort, which was not at that time desired.' (H)

81 l. 44. *Marshal's Elm* 'so picturesquely situated, is no longer an inn, though the house, or part of it, still remains. It used to exhibit a fine old swinging sign.' (H)

82 l. 79. *Blue Jimmy* 'was a notorious horse-stealer of Wessex in those days, who appropriated more than a hundred horses before he was caught, among others one belonging to a neighbour of the writer's grandfather. He was hanged at the now demolished Ivel-chester or Ilchester jail above mentioned—that building formerly of so many sinister associations in the minds of the local peasantry, and the continual haunt of fever, which at last led to its condemnation. Its site is now an innocent-looking green meadow.' (H)

83 *A Sunday Morning Tragedy*. Hardy submitted the poem to the *Fortnightly Review*, but it was rejected by the editor, who explained that his journal 'circulates among families'. Hardy described his subject as 'eminently proper and moral' in a letter published in *The Times* (13 August 1909).

91 *Autumn in King's Hintock Park*. The scene is Melbury Park, near Melbury Osmond, Dorset. Hardy wrote in a letter to his friend Edmund Gosse, 11 November 1906: 'though the scene as I witnessed it was a poem, it is quite another question if I have conveyed it to paper' (*Letters* III, p. 235).

92 *Shut Out That Moon*. l. 8. *Lady's Chair*. the constellation Cassiopeia.

93 *Reminiscences of a Dancing Man*. l. 14. Jullien, Louis Antoine (1812–60), composer of popular music, and conductor of concerts at which very large orchestras played popular and classical music.

95 *The Division*. Purdy associates the poem with Mrs Henniker (Purdy, p. 141).

106 *At Casterbridge Fair VI*. A WIFE WAITS. l. 3. *the Bow*. 'The old name for the curved corner by the cross-streets in the middle of Casterbridge.' (H)

At Casterbridge Fair VII. AFTER THE FAIR. l. 6. '"The Chimes" will be listened for in vain here at midnight now, having been abolished some years ago.' (H)

107 *The Dark-Eyed Gentleman*. l. 1. *leazings*. 'Bundle of gleaned corn.' (H)

108 *Julie-Jane*. 'It is, or was, a common custom in Wessex, and probably other country places, to prepare the mourning beside the death-bed, the dying person sometimes assisting, who also selects his or her bearers on such occasions.' (H)

l. 7. *Coats*. 'Old name for petticoats.' (H)

109 *A Church Romance*. The poem is quoted in *EL* (p. 17) as an account of Hardy's mother's first view of his father. The date is there given as '*circa* 1836'.

116 *After the Last Breath*. Hardy's mother, Jemima Hardy, died 3 April 1904.

119 *One We Knew*. M. H. is Mary Head Hardy, the poet's grandmother. See *LY*, p. 231.

121 *New Year's Eve*. ll. 11–12. 2 Corinthians 5: 4: 'For we that are in this tabernacle do groan, being burdened . . .'

122 *The Unborn*. See Hardy's letter to Noyes, above, pp. 502–3.

125 *George Meredith*. Meredith died on 18 May 1909. The poem was published in *The Times* on 22 May, the day of Meredith's funeral.

SATIRES OF CIRCUMSTANCE

Satires of Circumstance was published 17 November 1914. It consists almost entirely of recently written poems. Of those to which Hardy attached dates of composition, only two are from the nineties, and none is earlier; all of the others are from the years 1910–14, including the two principal groups, 'Satires of Circumstance' (dated 1910 in the manuscript) and 'Poems of 1912–13'. About a third of the poems had previously appeared in periodicals.

129 *Channel Firing.* In *LY* (p. 61) this poem is described as 'prophetic': it was published four months before the beginning of the First World War.

130 *The Convergence of the Twain.* The 'unsinkable' British ship the SS *Titanic* sank on her maiden transatlantic voyage on 15 April 1912, after a collision with an iceberg. Hardy's poem was first published in the souvenir programme of a charity performance in aid of the victims, given at the Royal Opera House, Covent Garden, on 14 May.

133 *After the Visit.* F. E. D. is Florence Emily Dugdale, whom Hardy married in 1914.

135 *'When I set out for Lyonnesse'.* Lyonnesse is the Romance name for the north Cornwall of Arthurian legend. Hardy first visited St Juliot, Cornwall, in 1870, and met his first wife there.

A *Thunderstorm in Town.* Purdy (p. 161) associates the poem with Mrs Henniker.

136 *Beyond the Last Lamp.* Hardy lived in Upper Tooting, south London, from 1878 to 1881.

139 *The Face at the Casement.* ll. 63–4. Song of Solomon 8: 6: 'jealousy is cruel as the grave.'

140 *Wessex Heights.* In a letter to a friend dated 6 December 1914 Florence Hardy wrote of this poem: 'It was written in '96, before I knew him—but the four people mentioned are actual women. One was dead and three living when it was written—now only one is living.'

l. 6. 1 Corinthians 13: 4: 'Charity suffereth long, and is kind . . .'

141 l. 19. The tall-spired town is Salisbury.

154 POEMS OF 1912–13. Hardy's first wife, Emma, died on 27 November 1912 (see *LY*, p. 154). In March 1913 Hardy revisited the scenes of their courtship in Cornwall. The two had been increasingly alienated from each other in the later years of their marriage, but her death revived Hardy's earlier feelings for her, and touched him with remorse, as many of his letters show (see *ORFW*, p. 163).

162 *The Voice.* Hardy recalls the reunion described in the second stanza in *EL*, p. 103.

167 *Beeny Cliff. EL*, p. 99, quotes from Hardy's diary of his first visit to St Juliot in March 1870: 'March 10. Went with E. L. G. to Beeny Cliff. She on horseback. . . . On the cliff. . . . "The tender grace of a day", etc. The run down to the edge. The coming home.' [The marks of elision are in the *EL* text.]

180 *The Moth-Signal.* Hardy used the same 'signal' in *The Return of the Native*, IV. 4.

183 *The Roman Gravemounds.* The cat was Hardy's own 'study cat'. See his letter to Mrs Henniker, 19 December 1910 (*ORFW*, p. 142).

188 *Exeunt Omnes.* 2 June 1913 was Hardy's seventy-third birthday, his first since the death of his wife.

189 SATIRES OF CIRCUMSTANCE. Hardy felt ill at ease with these poems. At the time of their periodical publication in the *Fortnightly* (1911) he wrote to Mrs Henniker: 'You will remember, I am sure, that being *satires* they are rather brutal. I express no feeling or opinion myself at all. They are from notes I made some twenty years ago, and then found were more fit for verse than prose' (*ORFW*, p. 146). When the bound volume appeared in November 1914 he wrote to friends regretting that the satires had been included, and in later editions he moved the 'Satires' from a position early in the book, preceding 'Poems of 1912–13', to the end.

MOMENTS OF VISION

Moments of Vision, published 30 November 1917, contains more poems than any other of Hardy's individual volumes. Almost all of them were recent: of those that carry a date of composition only two were written earlier than 1912 (both are from 1893). Ten of the poems are from 1912 or 1913, and continue the elegiac themes of the 'Poems of 1912–13' in *Satires of Circumstance*; others of later dates recall his courtship and the early years of his marriage.

Except for the 'Poems of War and Patriotism', very few of the poems had previously been published; all but three of the seventeen war poems appeared in newspapers or magazines, or in anthologies of war writing published for charitable causes.

199 *'We sat at the window'*. Hardy and his wife were in Bournemouth in July 1875, a year after their marriage (see *EL*, p. 141).

200 *Afternoon Service at Mellstock.* Hardy recalls his church-going as a child in *EL*, p. 23.

201 *Apostrophe to an Old Psalm Tune.* l. 12. William Henry Monk (1823–89) was musical editor of *Hymns Ancient and Modern* (first issued 1861).

202 *At the Word 'Farewell'.* Hardy described this poem as 'literally true' (*ORFW*, p. 179). His account of parting from Emma Gifford at the end of his first visit to Cornwall is in *EL*, p. 99.

204 *Heredity. EL*, p. 284, quotes the following journal entry for 19 February 1889: 'The story of a face which goes through three generations or more, would make a fine novel or poem of the passage of Time. The differences in personality to be ignored.' Hardy also used this idea in his novel, *The Well-Beloved.*

206 *Near Lanivet, 1872.* Hardy told several correspondents that the poem was based on an actual scene involving himself and his wife, before their marriage (see *ORFW*, p. 179).

210 *Quid Hic Agis?* The title is from the Vulgate text of 1 Kings 19: 9. In the Authorized Version it reads: 'What doest thou here?' The verses that follow, ending 'and after the fire a still small voice', were one of Hardy's favourite Biblical texts.

214 *The Blinded Bird.* Lines 15–20 paraphrase 1 Corinthians 13: 4–7.

220 *'In the seventies'.* The epigraph is from Job 12: 4 (Vulgate).

222 *The Wound.* A similar image occurs in *Tess*, Ch. XXI: 'The evening sun was now ugly to her, like a great inflamed wound in the sky.'

224 *The Oxen.* Hardy also used this folk-belief in *Tess*, Ch. XVII.

225 *The Pink Frock.* Hardy describes 'the lady of the "Pretty pink frock" poem' in *LY*, p. 31.

227 *The Last Signal.* William Barnes, the Dorset poet, was Hardy's teacher, friend, and neighbour. He died on 7 October 1886. As Hardy walked across the fields from Max Gate to the funeral the incident occurred that the poem describes (see *EL*, p. 240).

229 *The Chimes.* The chimes are those of St Peter's Church, Dorchester.

230 *The Figure in the Scene. EL*, p. 104, describes this poem as a memory of one of Hardy's visits to Cornwall during his courtship of Emma Gifford. Two sketches by Hardy corresponding to the description in the poem are in the Dorset County Museum.

231 *'Why did I sketch'.* See preceding note.

235 *Overlooking the River Stour.* Hardy and his first wife lived at Sturminster Newton, on the river Stour, from July 1876 to March 1878. He later called those years 'the Sturminster Newton idyll ... Our happiest time' (*EL*, p. 156).

238 *The Last Performance.* The pianist is Hardy's first wife, Emma. See *LY*, p. 153.

239 *The Interloper.* l. 31. The Fourth Figure is from Daniel 3: 25.

Logs on the Hearth. Hardy's sister Mary died on 24 November 1915.

241 *The Five Students.* Hardy identified one of the students as his friend Horace Moule, who committed suicide in 1873.

242 *The Wind's Prophecy.* l. 34. *Skrymer.* A sleeping giant in Norse mythology.

245 *Molly Gone.* Molly is Hardy's sister Mary, who died in 1915.

246 *Looking Across.* l. 5. 'Out there' is the graveyard at Stinsford Church: it contains the graves of Hardy's parents, his first wife, Emma, and his sister Mary.

251 *'It never looks like summer'.* The title is a remark of Emma Hardy's, which Hardy wrote on a drawing that he had made of her on Beeny Cliff, Cornwall, in 1870. The drawing is in the Dorset County Museum.

255 *He Revisits His First School.* The village school that Hardy attended is described in *EL*, p. 20.

256 *'I thought, my Heart'.* Hardy added a third verse to the manuscript of *Moments of Vision*, and also wrote it into his own copy of the Wessex Edition, but did not publish it in any of his books of verse. It was included, however, in Ruth

Head's *Pages from the Works of Thomas Hardy* (London, 1922), where it is described as 'unpublished third verse, specially communicated for this Selection'. The verse, which varies slightly in different versions, reads as follows in Hardy's Wessex Edition copy:

That kiss so strange, so stark, I'll take
When the world sleeps sound, and no noise will scare,
And a moon-touch whitens each stone and stake;
Yes; I will meet her there—
Just at the time she calls '*to-morrow*',
But I call '*after the shut of sorrow*'—
And with her dwell—
Inseparable
With cease of pain,
And frost and rain,
And life's inane.

Midnight on the Great Western. A similar scene occurs in *Jude the Obscure*, V. iii.

266 *In the Garden.* M. H. is Hardy's sister Mary, who died in 1915.

267 *Looking at a Picture on an Anniversary.* A date deleted on the manuscript—March 1913—suggests that the occasion of the poem was the forty-third anniversary of Hardy's first meeting with his first wife.

268 *The Choirmaster's Burial.* Hardy's grandfather, also Thomas, was the leader of the Stinsford Church choir from 1801 or 1802 until his death in 1837.

272 '*Men who march away*'. Hardy identified himself in a letter as the 'Friend with the musing eye'. The scene was the County Hall in Dorchester, in the first month of the 1914–18 war.

274 *In Time of 'the Breaking of Nations'.* 'Jer. li. 20.' (H) The Jeremiah text reads: 'Thou art my battle ax and weapons of war: for with thee will I break in pieces the nations, and with thee will I destroy kingdoms.'

The long gestation of the poem is mentioned in both *EL* and *LY*. *EL*, p. 104, describes the summer of 1870, when Hardy was in Cornwall, courting his first wife, while in Europe the Franco-Prussian War was in progress. 'On the day that the bloody battle of Gravelotte was fought they were reading Tennyson in the grounds of the rectory. It was at this time and spot that Hardy was struck by the incident of the old horse harrowing the arable field in the valley below, which, when in far later years it was recalled to him by a still bloodier war, he made into the little poem of three verses entitled "In Time of 'the Breaking of Nations'".' See also *LY*, p. 178.

Before Marching and After. F. W. G. was Frank William George, a distant cousin of Hardy. He was killed in the Gallipoli campaign in August 1915.

275 *A New Year's Eve in War Time.* One of Hardy's 'literally true' poems: he described the incident in a letter to Mrs Henniker (*ORFW*, p. 175).

LATE LYRICS AND EARLIER

Late Lyrics was published 23 May 1922. The dated poems show that for this book Hardy reached further back into the past than he had for his two previous volumes: there are poems from the 1860s, 1870s, 1890s, and 1900s, as well as several from the fertile poetic period that had followed the death of his first wife. Comparatively few of the poems had been previously published in periodicals.

279 *Apology.* This essay, Hardy's longest critical defence of his poems, caused him a good deal of doubt and anxiety: he feared that it was 'too cantankerous in respect of reviewers', and considered not publishing 'at all. See *SCC*, pp. 288–9.

280 *blank misgivings.* The quoted phrases are from Wordsworth's 'Ode: Intimations of Immortality', lines 142 and 145.

balancings of the clouds. Job 37: 16.

281 *. . . is not mine.* Harrison, commenting on the *Collected Poems*, had written: 'My philosophy of life is more cheerful and hopeful than that of these lyrics' ('Novissima Verba—II', *Fortnightly Review* (2 Feb. 1920), 183).

Romanist. This is Joseph Hone, who had written 'The Poetry of Mr Hardy' in the *London Mercury* (Feb. 1922).

familiar phrase. Matthew Arnold, 'The Study of Poetry'.

Mars Hill. See Acts 17: 16–31.

283 *Wordsworth again.* Preface to *Lyrical Ballads.*

all poetry. Coleridge, *Biographia Literaria*, Ch. XIV.

. . . shaken. Hebrews 12: 27.

284 *morality together.* 'However, one must not be too sanguine in reading signs, and since the above was written evidence that the Church will go far in the removal of "things that are shaken" has not been encouraging.' (H)

his ideas. Wordsworth, Preface to *Lyrical Ballads.*

Comte argued. Auguste Comte, *Social Dynamics, or The General Theory of Human Progress*, volume iii of *System of Positive Polity*, trans. Edward Spencer Beesly (London, 1876), p. 60.

mind and art. 'In Memoriam', LXXXVII. 21–2.

287 *Jezreel.* The advance of the British army under General Allenby across the Plain of Esdraelon in Palestine was announced in *The Times* on 23 September 1918.

288 *'According to the Mighty Working'.* The title is from the Order for the Burial of the Dead of the Church of England.

291 *At a House in Hampstead.* Hardy was a member of the National Committee for acquiring Wentworth Place, the house where Keats lived in Hampstead; his poem was written for a memorial volume published by the Committee in 1921, the centenary of Keats's death.

293 *'A man was drawing near to me'*. *EL*, p. 92, quotes Emma Hardy's recollections of the evening in March 1870 when Hardy first came to St Juliot, adding in a footnote: 'The verses entitled "A Man was drawing near to Me" obviously relate to this arrival.' The places named in the poem lie between St Juliot and the nearest railway station at Launceston.

298 *'Where three roads joined'*. The intersection is at Tresparrett Posts, near St Juliot.

'And there was a great calm'. The title appears twice in the New Testament: Matthew 8: 26, and Mark 4: 39. The poem was published in a special supplement to *The Times*, on the second anniversary of the armistice that ended the First World War.

304 *On Stinsford Hill at Midnight*. 'The girl was learnt to be one of the Salvation Army.' (H, manuscript). 'It was said that she belonged to a body of religious enthusiasts.' (H, Wessex Edition).

307 *At Lulworth Cove a Century Back*. 'In September 1820 Keats, on his way to Rome, landed one day on the Dorset coast, and composed the sonnet, "Bright star! would I were steadfast as thou art". The spot of his landing is judged to have been Lulworth Cove.' (H) Keats in fact did not write the sonnet there, but only made a fair copy of it.

314 *On the Tune Called the Old-Hundred-and-Fourth*. The tune is from Thomas Ravenscroft's *Whole Book of Psalms*, published in 1621 and for many years the common hymnal of the English Church.

315 *Voices from Things Growing in a Churchyard*. The church is Stinsford, the parish church of Hardy's childhood; the 'voices' are all actually buried there, as are members of Hardy's family.

319 *A Two-Years' Idyll*. Hardy and his first wife lived at Sturminster Newton from 1876 to 1878; Hardy later referred to those years as 'the Sturminster Newton idyll . . . Our happiest time' (see *EL*, p. 156).

331 *Vagg Hollow*. Hardy wrote in his journal for 20 April 1902: 'Vagg Hollow, on the way to Load Bridge (Somerset) is a place where "things" used to be seen—usually taking the form of a wool-pack in the middle of the road. Teams and other horses always stopped on the brow of the hollow, and could only be made to go on by whipping. A waggoner once cut at the pack with his whip: it opened in two, and smoke and a hoofed figure rose out of it' (*LY*, p. 96).

333 *The Country Wedding*. One of several narrative poems involving the 'Quire' of *Under the Greenwood Tree* (see also 'The Rash Bride', above).

344 *The Sun's Last Look on the Country Girl*. M. H. is Hardy's sister Mary, who died 24 November 1915.

348 *An Ancient to Ancients*. Hardy cites examples of artists and works of art popular in the England of his youth: 'The Bohemian Girl' (1843), an opera by Michael Balfe (1808–70); the painters William Etty (1787–1849), William Mulready (1786–1863), and Daniel Maclise (1806–70); novelists

Edward Bulwer-Lytton (1803–73), Walter Scott (1771–1832), Alexandre Dumas (1802–70), and George Sand (1804–76).

350 *Surview*. The epigraph, in the Authorized Version (Ps. 119: 59), reads: 'I thought on my ways'.

l. 18. 1 Corinthians 13: 13.

HUMAN SHOWS

In gathering together the poems of *Human Shows*, Hardy drew upon the recent and more distant past in much the same proportions as he had done in his previous volume, *Late Lyrics*: there are poems from the 1860s, 1890s, and 1900s, and five poems dated 1912 or 1913 that continue the sequence of elegies for his dead wife begun with the 'Poems of 1912–13' in *Satires of Circumstance*. The book was published on 20 November 1925.

As often before, some reviewers complained of Hardy's gloominess and pessimism. 'My sense of the oddity of this verdict', Hardy later wrote, 'may be imagined when, in selecting them, I had been, as I thought, rather too liberal in admitting flippant, not to say farcical, pieces into the collection.' (See 'Introductory Note' to *Winter Words*, above, p. 422.)

351 *Waiting Both*. ll. 7–8. Job 14: 14.

354 *Green Slates*. Hardy visited the Penpethy slate-quarries in Cornwall in 1870, while on his first visit to St Juliot, the home of his future wife, Emma.

361 *Sine Prole*. Purdy writes (p. 237) that 'this poem was suggested in form, by the sequences of Adam of S. Victor'. See *LY*, pp. 85–6, for Hardy's interest in medieval Latin hymns.

Ten Years Since. Hardy's first wife, Emma, had died 27 November 1912.

364 *'There seemed a strangeness'*. ll. 9–10. Isaiah 64: 4.

365 l. 14. 1 Corinthians 13: 12.

A Night of Questionings. l. 11. Joel 2: 25.

366 l. 44. Psalm 107: 23.

370 *A Light Snow-Fall after Frost*. Hardy and his wife lived in Surbiton briefly after their marriage in 1874.

371 *Winter Night in Woodland*. l. 23. These are the members of the Mellstock Quire (see *Under the Greenwood Tree*).

372 *Music in a Snowy Street*. Hardy's prose account of this incident, dated 26 April 1884, is in *EL*, p. 215. 'Curious scene,' he wrote. 'A fine poem in it.'

376 *Last Love-Word*. Purdy (p. 345) associates this poem with Mrs Henniker.

Nobody Comes. Compare *Jude the Obscure*, I. iv: 'Somebody might have come along that way who would have asked him his trouble, and might have cheered him . . . But nobody did come, because nobody does . . .'

382 *An Inquiry*. Epigraph: 'The sorrows of death compassed me' (Psalm 18: 4).

388 *Louie.* Hardy's youthful attachment to a farmer's daughter named Louisa is described in *EL*, pp. 33–4. She was buried in Stinsford churchyard, as was Hardy's first wife, Emma.

390 *Vagrant's Song.* l. 12. *back-brand.* 'the log which used to be laid at the back of a wood fire.' (H)

ll. 13 and 27. *Che-hane.* Meaning uncertain: perhaps a dialect phrase (from a children's game?) meaning 'I am safe'.

391 *Farmer Dunman's Funeral.* In his proof copy of *Human Shows* Hardy inserted the following stanza between stanzas two and three:

That no one should forget them
In boldest scrawls he inked
On the shelf where he had set them:
'Mind that this rum is drinked.'

392 *The Harvest Supper.* For Hardy's account of an actual harvest supper during his childhood see *EL*, pp. 24–6.

394 *On the Portrait of a Woman about to be Hanged.* The woman was Mrs Edith Thompson, hanged at Holloway Gaol, London, on 9 January 1923, for the murder of her husband.

396 *Once at Swanage.* A notebook entry of 1875 describes a similar scene in much the same images (*EL*, p. 142).

400 *Alike and Unlike.* Hardy visited Great Orme's Head with his wife on 18 May 1893: see *LY*, p. 18.

401 *Retty's Phases.* 'In many villages it was customary after the funeral of an unmarried young woman to ring a peal as for her wedding while the grave was being filled in, as if Death were not to be allowed to balk her of bridal honours. Young unmarried men were always her bearers.' (H) A draft of this poem—the earliest surviving poetic manuscript by Hardy—is in the Dorset County Museum; it is dated 22 June 1868.

402 *A Poor Man and a Lady.* 'The foregoing was intended to preserve an episode in the story of "The Poor Man and the Lady," written in 1868, and, like these lines, in the first person; but never printed, and ultimately destroyed.' (H)

407 *A Refusal.* On 14 July 1924 a group of political and literary men, including Hardy, wrote to *The Times* supporting Lord Rosebery's suggestion that a memorial to Lord Byron should be placed in Westminster Abbey in commemoration of the centenary of his death. The Dean of Westminster replied, rejecting the request on the grounds that 'a man who outraged the laws of our Divine Lord, and whose treatment of women violated the Christian principles of purity and honour, should not be commemorated in Westminster Abbey'.

419 *Before My Friend Arrived.* Purdy (p. 246) identifies the friend as Horace Moule. Hardy briefly mentions the suicide and funeral of Moule in *EL*, p. 126. See also 'Standing by the Mantelpiece', in *Winter Words*.

WINTER WORDS

Though Hardy prepared *Winter Words* when he was in his late eighties, it shows little diminution of his powers. The book is not made up, as one might expect, of poems left over from earlier days: in terms of dated poems it is similar to the earlier books, drawing a poem or two from each of the previous decades (except the 1870s), but depending for the bulk of its contents on poems written since the publication of the previous collection.

Hardy was understandably proud of his vigorous poetic old age, and planned to call attention to it by publishing *Winter Words* on his birthday—probably on 2 June 1928, when he would have been eighty-eight, though he left a blank space for the number in his draft of the preface, perhaps because he was not sure that he would have a completed manuscript ready so soon, or perhaps because he was tempted by the thought of publishing it at an even greater age.

Hardy died on 11 January 1928. His widow prepared the manuscript of his last book for publication, and it was published on 2 October 1928.

425 *To Louisa in the Lane.* For an account of Hardy's youthful attachment to Louisa Harding, see *EL*, pp. 33–4. See also 'Louie', in *Human Shows*.

426 *An Unkindly May.* For an account of the composition of this poem, in November 1927, see *LY*, p. 263.

435 *The War-Wife of Catknoll.* l. 37. *she must be crowned.* 'Old English for "there must be a coroner's inquest over her."'(H)

438 *Childhood among the Ferns.* An occasion similar to that in the poem is described in *EL*, pp. 19–20. See also *Jude the Obscure*, I. ii.

440 *'I watched a blackbird'.* A cancelled journal entry in a typescript of *LY* in the Dorset County Museum reads: 'April 15 [1900]. Easter Sunday. Watched a blackbird on a budding sycamore. Was near enough to see his tongue, and crocus-coloured bill parting and closing as he sang. He flew down: picked up a stem of hay, and flew up to where he was building.'

448 *Squire Hooper.* Hardy built his story on the life of Edward Hooper (d. 1795), as recounted in John Hutchins' *History and Antiquities of the County of Dorset*, vol. III (Westminster, 1868), pp. 384–5.

453 *Standing by the Mantelpiece.* H. M. M. was Hardy's friend and literary adviser, Horace Moule, the son of the Vicar of Fordington St George Church, Dorchester. Moule was eight years older than Hardy, and had studied at both Oxford and Cambridge: Hardy considered him a 'scholar and critic of perfect taste' (*EL*, p. 115), and took his advice on literary matters very seriously. Moule committed suicide on 24 September 1873. 'Before My Friend Arrived', in *Human Shows*, describes the day of his funeral in Dorchester.

469 *Dead 'Wessex' the Dog to the Household.* Hardy's dog, Wessex, died on 27 December 1926.

472 *Christmas in the Elgin Room.* Hardy wrote that he had begun the poem in 1905, but had not finished it until 1926. It was published in *The Times* on Christmas Day 1927—the last poem to be published during his lifetime.

473 *He Resolves to Say No More.* In a manuscript of the poem now in the Dorset County Museum Hardy annotated two lines:

l. 1. '(One line from Agathias, Greek epigrammatist.) ["O my heart, leave the rest unknown." Mackail's trans. 218]' (H)

l. 4. 'Rev. VI. 8' (H)

474 l. 18. Echoes John 8: 32: 'And ye shall know the truth, and the truth shall make you free.'

UNCOLLECTED POEMS

475 *Domicilium.* 'The following lines, entitled "Domicilium," are the earliest known poem by Mr. Thomas Hardy. It was written somewhere between the years 1857 and 1860, while he was still living with his parents at the charming cottage described in the verses, the birthplace of both himself and his father. The influence of Wordsworth, a favourite author of the youthful poet's, will be clearly perceived, also a strong feeling for the unique and desolate beauty of the adjoining heath.' [Headnote to the edition of the poem privately printed for Mrs Hardy in 1918.]

476 *On the Doorstep.* First published in the *Fortnightly Review* (April 1911) as the tenth of 'Satires of Circumstance in Twelve Scenes'. Hardy included the poem in the manuscript of *Satires of Circumstance* in 1914, but dropped it before the book was printed.

THE DYNASTS. The poems from *The Dynasts* are included here because Hardy considered them lyrics that were separable from their dramatic contexts. He included six of them in his *Selected Poems* in 1916, and added the seventh, 'Albuera', to the expanded selection that was published after his death as *Chosen Poems*. 'Two or three of them', he told an interviewer, '. . . are as good as anything in the *Collected Poems*.' (See Vere H. Collins, *Talks with Thomas Hardy at Max Gate 1920–22* (London, 1928), p. 30.)

The Night of Trafalgár. Dynasts, Part First, Act V, Scene vii. l. 2. 'In those days the hind-part of the harbour adjoining this scene was so named, and at high tides the waves dashed across the isthmus at a point called "The Narrows".' (H)

The setting is Weymouth, Dorset, the 'Budmouth' of the Wessex novels.

477 *Albuera. Dynasts*, Part Second, Act VI, Scene iv. The town of Albuera, in north-west Spain, was the scene of an important battle of the Peninsular Wars.

478 *Hussar's Song. Dynasts*, Part Third, Act II, Scene i.

479 l. 21. *sling-jacket.* 'Hussars, it may be remembered, used to wear a pelisse, dolman, or "sling-jacket" (as the men called it), which hung loosely over the shoulder. The writer is able to recall the picturesque effect of this uniform.' (H)

'*My Love's gone a-fighting*'. *Dynasts*, Part Third, Act V, Scene vi.

480 *The Eve of Waterloo. Dynasts*, Part Third, Act VI, Scene viii.

481 *Chorus of the Pities. Dynasts*, Part Third, Afterscene. l. 2. 'καθεῖλε ΔΥΝΑΣΤΑΣ ἀπὸ θρόνων.—Magnificat.' (H) The quoted text is Luke 1: 52: 'He hath put down the mighty from their seats.'

483 *Last Chorus. Dynasts*, Part Third, Afterscene. In a letter to his friend Edward Clodd, 20 February 1918, Hardy wrote: 'Yes: I left off on a note of hope. It was just as well that the Pities should have the last word, since, like *Paradise Lost*, *The Dynasts* proves nothing.' (LY, p. 275)

FURTHER READING

MAJOR EDITIONS

THE most readily available one-volume edition of Hardy's poetry is *Complete Poems*, ed. James Gibson (London, 1976). The Oxford English Text edition of *The Complete Poetical Works of Thomas Hardy*, ed. Samuel Hynes, is in process of publication: volume i (*Wessex Poems, Poems of the Past and the Present*, and *Time's Laughingstocks*) was published in 1982.

The Collected Letters of Thomas Hardy, eds. Richard Little Purdy and Michael Millgate (Oxford, 1978–) will be an edition of seven volumes. Of these, three have been published as of 1982: volume i: 1840–1892 (1978); volume ii: 1893–1901 (1980); volume iii: 1902–1908 (1982). Hardy's letters to Florence Henniker have been edited by Evelyn Hardy and F. B. Pinion under the title *One Rare Fair Woman* (London, 1972). His non-fictional prose writings have been collected by Harold Orel: *Thomas Hardy's Personal Writings* (London, 1967).

BIOGRAPHY

Robert Gittings, *Young Thomas Hardy* (London, 1975); *The Older Hardy* (London, 1978).

Florence Emily Hardy, *The Early Life of Thomas Hardy* (London, 1928) and *The Later Years of Thomas Hardy* (London, 1930). Ostensibly written by Hardy's second wife, but largely dictated by Hardy, these are invaluable for the passages from Hardy's unpublished journals (see extracts in 'Notes from Hardy's Journals' above, pp. 485–90).

Michael Millgate, *Thomas Hardy: A Biography* (Oxford, 1982). The most recent life, and now the standard one.

SCHOLARSHIP AND CRITICISM

J. O. Bailey, *The Poetry of Thomas Hardy* (Chapel Hill, 1970).

Patricia Clements and Juliet Grindle (eds.), *The Poetry of Thomas Hardy* (London, 1980). Essays by eleven Hardy critics.

Helmut E. Gerber and W. Eugene Davis, *Thomas Hardy: an annotated bibliography of writings about him* (De Kalb, Illinois, 1973).

James Gibson and Trevor Johnson, (eds.), *Thomas Hardy: Poems* (London, 1979). A collection of critical essays.

Samuel Hynes, *The Pattern of Hardy's Poetry* (Chapel Hill, 1961).

Kenneth Marsden, *The Poems of Thomas Hardy: A Critical Introduction* (London, 1969).

Norman Page (ed.), *Thomas Hardy: The Writer and his Background* (London, 1980). Essays by ten critics.

Tom Paulin, *Thomas Hardy: The Poetry of Perception* (London, 1975).

Richard Little Purdy, *Thomas Hardy: A Bibliographical Study* (Oxford, 1954; reprinted 1968).

James Richardson, *Thomas Hardy: The Poetry of Necessity* (Chicago, 1977).

The Southern Review, vol. vi (Summer, 1940). A Hardy number, now forty years old, but with important essays by W. H. Auden, R. P. Blackmur, John Crowe Ransom, Allen Tate, and others.

Dennis Taylor, *Hardy's Poetry, 1860–1928* (London, 1981).

Paul Zietlow, *Moments of Vision: The Poetry of Thomas Hardy* (Cambridge, Mass., 1974).

GLOSSARY

THIS list of dialectal, archaic, and obsolete words in Hardy's poems draws on Hardy's glossarial notes to his own works and to his edition of *Select Poems of Willam Barnes* (London, 1908), and on Barnes's works on the Dorset dialect: *Poems of Rural Life, in the Dorset Dialect: with a dissertation and glossary* (London, 1844), and *A Glossary of the Dorset Dialect, with a grammar* (Dorchester and London, 1886). Definitions taken from Hardy's own glosses are given verbatim, and are followed by (H). Those based on Barnes are marked (Barnes). All others follow the *Oxford English Dictionary*.

agone, ago
anigh, anight, near to (Barnes)
anywhen, at any time (Barnes)
a-topperèn, toppering; knocking on the head

back-brand, the log which used to be laid at the back of a wood fire (H)
bivering, with chattering teeth (H)
blooth, blossom (H); the blossom of fruit trees collectively (Barnes)
bride-ale, wedding-feast
brightsome, bright-looking
brimbles, brambles (Barnes)

caddle, quandary (H)
cark, to fret
causey, pavement
cheepings, shrill feeble sounds
chiel, female infant
chimley-tun, chimney-stack (H)
chore, chancel of a church; choir of singers
Christendie, Christendom
clam, to make clammy (H)
clinking off, running away
coats, old name for petticoats (H)
coll, to take one fondly round the neck (Barnes)
coney, rabbit
crooping, squatting down (H)
crowned, she must be, old English for 'there must be a coroner's inquest over her' (H)

darkle, to grow dark; to become cloudy or gloomy

darkling, occurring or being in the dark
daysman, arbitrator
dree, suffering
drongs, lanes (H)
drouth, dryness
drouthy, dry
drub, throb, beat
dumble, dumbledore, bumble-bee (Barnes)
durn, doorposts (H)

embowment, vaulting. Hardy glossed the dialect sense of 'bow' as 'arch'.
en, it (H)
enarch, to arch over, as with a rainbow
erst, at first; earlier

fall, autumn (H)
false, v., to be or make false
fane, temple
fay, faith
fulth, fullness
fust, to become mouldy or stale-smelling

gaingivings, misgivings
gallied, frightened (H)
garth, enclosed ground; the space within a cloister
grinterns, compartments in a granary (Barnes)

halterpath, bridle-path (H)
heft, weight (H)
ho, be anxious (H)
homealong, homeward (H)
honeysuck, honeysuckle
horned, sang loudly (H)

huddied, hidden (H)
husbird, rascal (H)

irk *n.,* tedium; annoyance
irked, vexed
knop, bud of a flower; a protuberance

leaze, *n.,* pasture (H); *v.,* to glean
leazings, bundle of gleaned corn (H)
leer, empty-stomached (H)
lew, shelter (H); screened from the wind; lee (Barnes)
lewth, shelter (H)
liefer, rather. 'Lief', as willingly, or soon (Barnes)
limber, limp (H); slender; yielding
linhay, lean-to building (H)
lumpered, stumbled (H)

mammet, a scarecrow (Barnes); a puppet
mere, marsh
mid, might (H)
mixens, manure-heaps (H)
moiling, toil, drudgery; confusion, uproar
moils, toils, turmoils, vexations

needle-thicks, pine-thickets
night-rail, dressing-gown
nipperkin, tot, dram of liquor

orts, remains (H)

passager, a migratory bird; the Peregrine falcon
patroon, patron; master
phasm, phantom, apparition
pipkin, small earthenware pot
plain, to emit a plaintive or mournful sound
popinjays, parrots
poppling, the bubbling of boiling liquid

quick, *v.,* to give or restore life to

rafted, roused (H)
roof-tree, home

sanct, sacred
scathed, hurt, injured

sengreen, houseleek, a pink-flowered plant that grows on walls and roofs
shrammed, numbed (H)
shroff, light fragments of wood-refuse (H)
skimmity-ride, satirical procession with effigies (H)
slats, slapping blows
slent, split, torn (Barnes)
slovening, being slothful or indolent
snocks, smart knocks (Barnes)
sock, *n.,* sob-like sound (H); *v.,* to sigh loudly
softling, of a soft nature
stillicide, dripping of water
subtrude, invade stealthily

tallet, loft (H)
tardle, entanglement (H)
teen, grief
therence, thence (Barnes)
thik, that (H)
thirtover, cross (H)
thrid them, thread their way
tidetimes, holidays (H)
totties, feet (H)
trant, trade as carrier (H); to carry goods, as a common carrier, in a waggon or cart (Barnes)
troth-plight, solemn promise of marriage
trow, believe, often expletively at the end of a sentence

unweeting, not knowing

vamp, *n.,* sole of a shoe (Barnes); *v.,* to tramp
vanned, winged
vlankers, fire-flakes, sparks (H)

wanzing, wasting away (H)
weeted, knew
whilom, at some past time
whiles, at, at times
wight, person (often implying contempt)
wist, knew
withinside, indoors, inside
withwind, bindweed (Barnes)
wold, old (H)

INDEX OF TITLES AND FIRST LINES